Scarecrow Author Bibliographies,
No. 44

Leo Tolstoy

an annotated
bibliography of
English-language
sources to 1978

David R. Egan
and
Melinda A. Egan

The Scarecrow Press, Inc.
Metuchen, N.J., & London
1979

A
012
T654e
1979

Library of Congress Cataloging in Publication Data

Egan, David R   1943-
    Leo Tolstoy, an annotated bibliography of English language
sources to 1978.

    (The Scarecrow author bibliographies ; no. 44)
    Includes indexes.
    1.   Tolstoĭ, Lev Nikolaevich, graf, 1828-1910--Bibliog-
raphy.   I.   Egan, Melinda A. , joint author.   II.   Title.
Z8883. 8. E37 [PG3385]   891. 8'3'3   79-16536
ISBN 0-8108-1232-0

TABLE OF CONTENTS

Table of Contents iv

INTRODUCTION

Purpose

The purpose of this bibliography is to provide a modern central listing of English language publications about Leo Tolstoy. Since serious research on Tolstoy must begin with the many Russian language critical studies of Tolstoy as well as with his own formal writings, diaries and correspondences, this bibliography is primarily directed at those who are unable to read Russian or who are interested in Tolstoy as he has been portrayed by Western analysts. For such individuals, this annotated, categorized, indexed and cross-referenced list should be of considerable value.

Scope

Included through 1977 are:

books: annotated
essays: annotated
chapters from general studies: annotated
periodical articles: annotated when obscured by title or
     when part of an anthology
introductions and prefaces to Tolstoy's works
reviews of Tolstoy's works and of monographs about him (a
     selection)
sermons and lectures
study guides to Tolstoy's major works
doctoral dissertations

Not included are:

newspaper articles (except for reviews)
letters to Tolstoy
works which mention Tolstoy but have no formal section on
     him (a few exceptions)
reviews of stagings of his dramas (a few exceptions)
masters theses

Annotations

The annotations are designed to establish the scope of a source

and its thesis where one exists or is clearly discernible. No attempt has been made to judge the validity of theses or the value of
particular sources, though sources which are widely acclaimed have
been so noted.

Format

Entries have been organized into as many categories as there
are major blocks of information on Tolstoy. Within categories, entries have been grouped alphabetically by type of publication (book,
essay, etc.). Because of the close interrelationship of Tolstoy's
life, works and philosophy, many sources touch upon several categories equally, thus making selection of a main listing (where an annotation and publication data would appear) somewhat of an arbitrary
decision. Consequently, considerable cross-referencing has been
necessary, and items so listed should be regarded as having poten-
tially as much value as main entries.

Reviews of studies devoted to Tolstoy appear beneath the entry
being critiqued. Reviews of Tolstoy's works are listed individually
in the appropriate category by either author or title, if no author
is given.

When an essay or article has appeared in another publication,
it has been noted beneath the entry to facilitate its location.

A Note on Accuracy

Because some 19th- and early 20th-century indexes give incom-
plete information on entries, sometimes re-word titles, and seem
to have difficulty with the spelling of Russian names, a significant
number of inaccuracies have worked their way into Tolstoy bibliographies, including the extensive ones of Weiner and Yassukovitch.
Approximately 125 items listed in early bibliographies and indexes
have been corrected, or deleted if not locatable where indicated.
Indexed items with spellings, titles or publication data different
from that of the original source are the most frequently corrected
mistakes. A particular source of confusion has been the spelling of
Tolstoy's name. The academic war over its spelling seems nearly
to predate Tolstoy and certainly has been an extensive and heated
dispute stopping just short of open hostilities. In the spirit of Tolstoyan pacifism, no attempt has been made in this bibliography to
standardize the spelling of his name in individual titles. However,
in the following cases only the 'oy' spelling has been employed:
publications by members of the Tolstoy family; indexed items using
abbreviations; sources not locatable to verify spelling; and in all
annotations. For a rationale for the use of this spelling, see Aylmer Maude, "How to Spell Tolstoy," Nation, 92 (16 March 1911),
265.

ABBREVIATIONS / PERIODICALS

Academy	Academy
Adam	Adam International Review
Addam J	Addam Journal
Adelphi	Adelphi
Alberta J Ed Res	Alberta Journal of Education Research
Am Admirer	American Admirer
Am Ben R	American Benedictine Review
Am Church M	American Church Monthly
Am Contribs	American Contributions to the International Conference of Slavists
Am Dialogue	American Dialogue
America	America
Am Hist R	American Historical Review
Am J Sociol	American Journal of Sociology
Am Law R	American Law Review
Am Lit	American Literature
Am Merc	American Mercury
Am R Sov Un	American Review on the Soviet Union
Am-Scand R	American-Scandinavian Review
Am Sociol	American Sociologist
Andover R	Andover Review
Ang-Sov J	Anglo-Soviet Journal
Ang Theo R	Anglican Theological Review
Annals Am Acad	Annals of the American Academy of Political and Social Science
ANQ	Andover Newton Quarterly
Architectural R	Architectural Review
Arena	Arena
Art and Ed	Art and Education

Art Exchange	Art Exchange
ASEER	American Slavic and East European Review
Asia	Asia
Asiatic R	Asiatic Review
Athenaeum	Athenaeum
Atlantic M	Atlantic Monthly
Avowals	Avowals
Balzac L	Balzac Library
Baptist Q R	Baptist Quarterly Review
Bellman	Bellman
Biblical W	Biblical World
Bib Sacra	Bibliotheca Sacra
Blackwood's M	Blackwood's Magazine
BNYPL	Bulletin of the New York Public Library
Bookbuyer	Bookbuyer
Bookman	Bookman
Book News	Book News
Books	Books (New York Herald Tribune)
Book-seller	Book-seller and Newsman
Book Week	Book Week (Chicago Sun)
Bos Trans	Boston Transcript
Br J Aesth	British Journal of Aesthetics
Bruno's R	Bruno's Review of Two Worlds
BSUF	Ball State University Forum
Bucknell R	Bucknell Review
Burl M	Burlington Magazine
Calcutta R	Calcutta Review
Calif Shavian	California Shavian
Calif Slavic S	California Slavic Studies
Calif U Chron	California University Chronicle
Cambr Q	Cambridge Quarterly
Canadian M	Canadian Magazine
Can Mus J	Canadian Music Journal
Can Slavic S	Canadian Slavic Studies
Can S P	Canadian Slavonic Papers

Catholic W	Catholic World
Cent M	Century Magazine
Century R	Century Review
Chamber's J	Chamber's Journal
Chaut	Chautauquan
Chicago R	Chicago Review
Chicago Sun Trib	Chicago Sunday Tribune
Choice	Choice
Christ C	Christian Century
Christ East	Christian East
Christian Sci M	Christian Science Monitor
Churchman	Churchman
Class J	Classical Journal
C Lit M	Central Literary Magazine
Col Engl	College English
Commonweal	Commonweal
Comp Lit	Comparative Literature
Comp Lit S	Comparative Literature Studies
Congreg R	Congregational Review
Conn R	Connecticut Review
Constructive Q	Constructive Quarterly
Contemp L	Contemporary Literature
Contemporary	Contemporary
Contemp R	Contemporary Review
Cornhill M	Cornhill Magazine
Coronet	Coronet
Cosmopolitan	Cosmopolitan
Country Life	Country Life
Craftsman	Craftsman
Criterion	Criterion
Critic	Critic
Critical Q	Critical Quarterly
Criticism	Criticism
Cur Hist	Current History
Cur Lit	Current Literature

Cur Op	Current Opinion
Daedalus	Daedalus
Dalhousie R	Dalhousie Review
Dial	Dial
Dissent	Dissent
Dome	Dome
Drama	Drama
Dublin M	Dublin Magazine
Eclectic M	Eclectic Magazine
Ecl Theatre J	Eclectic Theatre Journal
Economist	Economist
Edinbg R	Edinburgh Review
Ed Misc	Educational Miscellany
Ed R	Educational Review
Encounter	Encounter
Eng J	English Journal
English	English
Eng R	English Review
Es in Criticism	Essays in Criticism
ESQ	Emerson Society Quarterly
Ethical R	Ethical Record
Ethics	Ethics
Explicator	Explicator
Fact and Fiction	Fact and Fiction
FMLS	Forum for Modern Language Studies
Fortn R	Fortnightly Review
Forum	Forum
Fourth Int	Fourth International
Freeman	Freeman
Free R	Free Review
Freethought	Freethought
Gandhi M	Gandhi Marg
Genre	Genre
Golden Bks M	Golden Books Magazine
Good Words	Good Words
Great Thoughts	Great Thoughts

Grinnell R	Grinnell Review
Guardian	Guardian
Harper's B	Harper's Bazaar
Harper's M	Harper's Magazine
Harper's W	Harper's Weekly
Hartford St Lit	Hartford Studies in Literature
Hartf Sem R	Hartford Seminary Record
Harvard M	Harvard Magazine
Harvard Slavic S	Harvard Slavic Studies
Hibbert J	Hibbert Journal
Hispania	Hispania
Hispanic	Hispanic
Holiday	Holiday
Homiletic R	Homiletic Review
Horizon	Horizon
Hound and Horn	Hound and Horn
Hudson R	Hudson Review
Humane R	Humane Review
Humanitarian	Humanitarian
Hum Assoc B	Humanities Association Bulletin
Hum Assoc R	Humanities Association Review
IAAR	Institute of Asian and African Relations
IAC	Indo-Asian Culture
Iberomania	Iberomania
Ideal R	Ideal Review
Idler	Idler
Independent	Independent
Indian Lit	Indian Literature
Indian P B	Indian Publisher and Bookseller
International	International
Int J Ethics	International Journal of Ethics
Int J Psychoanl	International Journal of Psychoanalysis
Int Lit	International Literature
Int R Soc His	International Review of Social History
Int Studio	International Studio
Irrigation Age	Irrigation Age

J Aesth	Journal of Aesthetics
J Aesth Art Crit	Journal of Aesthetic Art and Criticism
J Aesth Ed	Journal of Aesthetic Education
J Ed	Journal of Education
J Gen Ed	Journal of General Education
J Hillside Hosp	Journal of Hillside Hospital
J Hist Ideas	Journal of History of Ideas
JJCL	Jadavpur Journal of Comparative Literature
JJQ	James Joyce Quarterly
J Philos	Journal of Philosophy
J Rus S	Journal of Russian Studies
J Sov Ed	Journal of Soviet Education
Judaism	Judaism
Kenyon R	Kenyon Review
KFLQ	Kentucky Foreign Language Quarterly
Labour M	Labour Magazine
Land and Freedom	Land and Freedom
Landfall	Landfall (New Zealand Quarterly)
Language Q	Language Quarterly
Leisure H	Leisure Hours
Lend a Hand	Lend a Hand
Leslie's M	Frank Leslie's Popular Monthly
Leslie's W	Leslie's Weekly
Life	Life
Lippincott's M	Lippincott's Magazine
Listener	Listener
Lit and Psych	Literature and Psychology
Lit D	Literary Digest
Literature	Literature
Lit H	Literary Heritage
Lit R	Literary Review
Lit W	Literary World
Living Age	Living Age
London M	London Magazine
London Q R	London Quarterly Review
Lon Merc	London Mercury

Lost Gen J	Lost Generation Journal
Lucifer	Lucifer
Mainstream	Mainstream
Manchester G	Manchester Guardian
Manchester Q	Manchester Quarterly
Manitoba Arts R	Manitoba Arts Review
Mass R	Massachusetts Review
Masses and Mainstream	Masses and Mainstream
McClure's	McClure's Magazine
Med Woman's J	Medical Woman's Journal
Mennonite Q R	Mennonite Quarterly Review
Mentor	Mentor
Message	Message
Metaphysical M	Metaphysical Magazine
Methodist R	Methodist Review
Midway	Midway
Mid W Q	Mid Western Quarterly
Modern Philol	Modern Philology
Modern R	Modern Review
Mod Fict St	Modern Fiction Studies
Mod Lang Notes	Modern Language Notes
Mod Lang R	Modern Language Review
Mod Rus Lit	Modern Russian Literature
Month	Month
Monthly R	Monthly Review
Mosaic	Mosaic
MSS	Melbourne Slavonic Studies
Munsey's	Munsey's Magazine
Museum J	Museum Journal
Music	Music
Musical T	Musical Times
Music and Letters	Music and Letters
N Amer R	North American Review
Nassau R	Nassau Review
Nat and Ath	Nation and Athenaeum

Nation	Nation
National M	National Magazine
National R	National Review
Neophil	Neophilogus
New Age	New Age
New Cent R	New Century Review
New Church R	New Church Review
New Direc	New Directions
New Eng M	New Englander Magazine
New Eng Q	New England Quarterly
New Eng Yale R	New Englander and Yale Review
New Leader	New Leader
New Order	New Order
New Pearson's	New Pearson's
New Republic	New Republic
New Review	New Review
New Russia	New Russia
New Sci R	New Science Review
New Society	New Society
New Sta	New Statesman
New St and Na	New Statesman and Nation
New Yorker	New Yorker
Nineteenth Cent	Nineteenth Century and After
Notes and Queries	Notes and Queries
Novel	Novel
Now	Now
NY Evening P	New York Evening Post
NY Herald Trib Bk R	New York Herald Tribune Book Review
NY Med J	New York Medical Journal
NY R Bks	New York Review of Books
NY Times	New York Times
NY Times M	New York Times Magazine
NZSJ	New Zealand Slavonic Journal
Occult R	Occult Review
Open Court	Open Court

Orbis Scriptus	Orbis Scriptus
Our Day	Our Day
Our Pulpit	Our Pulpit
Outing	Outing
Outlook	Outlook
Overland M	Overland Monthly
Oxford R	Oxford Review
Oxford S P	Oxford Slavonic Papers
Pan Am M	Pan American Magazine
Papers on Lang Lit	Papers on Language and Literature
Papyrus	Papyrus
Partisan R	Partisan Review
Personalist	Personalist
Phi Delta Kappan	Phi Delta Kappan
Philol Q	Philological Quarterly
Pilgrim	Pilgrim
PMLA	Publication of the Modern Language Association
Poet Lore	Poet Lore
Poetry	Poetry
Polemic	Polemic
Pop Science M	Popular Science Monthly
Positivist R	Positivist Review
PPNCFL	Proceedings of the Pacific Northwest Conference on Foreign Languages
Prairie S	Prairie Schooner
Pres Ref R	Presbyterian and Reformed Review
Prim Meth Q R	Primitive Methodist Quarterly Review
Proc Am Philol Asso	Proceedings from the American Philological Association
Proc Am Philos Soc	Proceedings from the American Philosophical Society
Proc Ang-Rus Lit Soc	Proceedings from the Anglo-Russian Literary Society
Pros Aust U Lang Lit Asso	Proceedings of the Australian University's Language and Literary Association
Proc Trans R S Can	Proceedings and Transactions of the Royal Society of Canada

Progres R	Progressive Review
Psy Today	Psychology Today
Public	Public
Pub Op	Public Opinion
Putnam M	Putnam Monthly
Quarterly R	Quarterly Review
Queen's Q	Queen's Quarterly
Reader's D	Reader's Digest
Reformed Ch R	Reformed Church Review
Rel in Life	Religion in Life
Reporter	Reporter
Resch St	Research Studies
Rev	Review
Ricerche Slav	Ricerche Slav
R Langues V	Revue des Langues Vivantes
RLT	Russian Literature Triquarterly
R Nat Lit	Review of National Literatures
Romanic R	Romanic Review
RRs	Review of Reviews
Rus Lit	Russian Literature
Rus R	Russian Review
Rus Stud	Russian Student
Sackbut	Sackbut
San Fran Chron	San Francisco Chronicle
Sat R	Saturday Review
Sat R Lit	Saturday Review of Literature
Sch and Soc	School and Society
School J	School Journal
Sci and Soc	Science and Society
Scientific M	Scientific Monthly
Scribner's M	Scribner's Magazine
Sc Sl	Scando-Slavica
Search Light	Search Light
SEEJ	Slavic and East European Journal
SEER	Slavonic and East European Review

SEES	Slavic and East European Studies (Études Slaves et Est-Européenes)
Sewanne R	Sewanee Review
Shaksp Asso B	Shakespeare Association Bulletin
Shenandoah	Shenandoah
Sight and Sound	Sight and Sound
Slavic Poetics	Slavic Poetics
Slavonic R	Slavonic Review
Slav R	Slavic R
SLRJ	Saint Louis University Research Journal of Arts and Sciences
So Atlantic B	South Atlantic Bulletin
So Atlan Q	South Atlantic Quarterly
Soc Cong	Socialist Congressman
Soc India	Socialist India
Sociol R	Sociological Review
So Hum R	Southern Humanities Review
Solidarity	Solidarity
So R	Southern Review
Soviet Ed	Soviet Education
Soviet Land	Soviet Land
Soviet Life	Soviet Life
Soviet R	Soviet Review
Sov Lit	Soviet Literature
Speaker	Speaker
Spectator	Spectator
Sprg Rep	Springfield Republican
Statesman	Statesman
St George	St George
St in Novel	Studies in the Novel, North Texas State
Story	Story
St Short Fic	Studies in Short Fiction
St Sov Un	Studies in the Soviet Union
Sunday M	Sunday Magazine
Survey	Survey
Survey G	Survey Graphic

SYB	Slavonic Yearbook
Symposium	Symposium
Theater	Theater
Theatre Arts M	Theatre Arts Monthly
Theatre W	Theatre Weekly
Theatre Workshop	Theatre Workshop
Theosoph P	Theosophical Path
Theosoph R	Theosophical Review
Theosoph Tract S	Theosophical Tract Series
Time M	Time Magazine
Times Ed Sup	Times Educational Sup
Times Lit Sup	Times Literary Supplement
Travel	Travel
Trivium	Trivium
Truth Seekers	Truth Seekers
TSLL	Texas Studies in Language and Literature
Two Worlds M	Two Worlds Monthly
UIS	Unity, Individual and Society
UKC R	University of Kansas City Review
UNESCO C	UNESCO Courier
Unitr R	Unitarian Review
Universal R	Universal Review
Universitas	Universitas
Unpopular R	Unpopular Review
USC Stud Comp Lit	University of Southern California Studies in Comparative Literature
Victorian M	Victorian Magazine
Virg Q R	Virginia Quarterly Review
Vogue	Vogue
VP	Victorian Poetry
Wascana R	Wascana Review
Western Hum R	Western Humanities Review
Western R	Western Review
Westm R	Westminister Review
Whim	Whim
W Home Com	Woman's Home Companion

Wilshire's M	Wilshire's Magazine
Wilson B	Wilson Library Bulletin
Wkly Bk R	Weekly Book Review (New York Herald Tribune)
W Lit	World Literature
W Meth M	Wesleyan Methodist Monthly
World R	World Review
World T	World Tomorrow
W Work	World's Work
Yale R	Yale Review
Young Man	Young Man

ABBREVIATIONS / ANTHOLOGIES

Because anthologies are not listed themselves by title but rather the sources within them have been extracted, annotated individually, and placed within the appropriate section, it is important that the following list of abbreviated titles be surveyed carefully.

AKMT   Gibian, George, ed. Anna Karenina, the Maude Translation: Backgrounds and Sources; Essays in Criticism. New York: Norton, 1970. An extensive collection of essays and excerpts from books, many translated expressly for this volume.

ASCEDM Dunlop, John B. et al. Aleksandr Solzhenitsyn: Critical Essays and Documentary Materials. Belmont, Mass.: Nordland, 1973. Contains a number of essays which discuss Tolstoy's influence on Solzhenitsyn or compare their fiction.

FV   Maude, Aylmer, ed. Family Views of Tolstoy. London: Allen & Unwin, 1926. A collection of seven essays on Tolstoy by family members and friends.

LLT   Lenin on Leo Tolstoy. Moscow: Novosti Press Agency Publishing House, 1972. A compilation of seven essays dealing with Tolstoy as a critic of the prevailing social-economic-political system.

LTCA   Gifford, Henry, ed. Leo Tolstoy: A Critical Anthology. Harmondsworth, England: Penguin, 1971. A collection of over 90 sources from biographers, literary critics, and contemporaries of Tolstoy, with useful background on the history of Tolstoy studies provided by the editor.

RLMEF   Davie, Donald, ed. Russian Literature and Modern English Fiction: A Collection of Critical Essays. Chicago: University of Chicago Press, 1965. A selection of ten essays analyzing Tolstoy's artistry and comparing him with others.

RLTC   Reminiscences of Lev Tolstoi by His Contemporaries. Moscow: Foreign Language Publishing House, 1961.

A series of 35 impressions of Tolstoy by relatives, friends, and acquaintances, many translated for this anthology.

TBPE   The Truxtun Beale Prize Essays on Tolstoy's "What Shall We Do Then?". Berkeley: University of California Press, 1912. A collection of five essays evaluating the basis and applicability of Tolstoy's social theories.

TCCE   Matlaw, Ralph, ed. Tolstoy: A Collection of Critical Essays. Englewood Cliffs, N. J.: Prentice-Hall, 1967. A compilation of 12 essays representing contemporary literary criticism, with a useful introduction to Tolstoy's fiction provided by the editor.

TCLA   Duffield, Holly Gene, and Manuel Bilsky, eds. Tolstoy and the Critics: Literature and Aesthetics. Chicago: Scott, Foresman, 1965. A discussion of artistic theory, examples of Tolstoy's views on art, and a collection of 22 essays dealing directly or indirectly with his philosophy of art.

TCRLC   Erlich, Victor, ed. Twentieth Century Russian Literary Criticism. New Haven, Conn.: Yale University Press, 1975. Includes three analyses of Tolstoy by Russian literary critics: Shklovsky, Eikhenbaum, and Aldanov.

TLFLR   Fülöp-Miller, Rene, ed. New Light on Tolstoy: Literary Fragments, Letters and Reminiscences Not Previously Published. London: Harrap, 1931. A collection of posthumous papers of Tolstoy along with essays by his wife and three friends.

TP   Maude, Aylmer. Tolstoy and His Problems. London: Richards, 1901. A compilation, by the biographer and friend of Tolstoy, of nine essays on Tolstoy's works and philosophy.

WPMT   Gibian, George, ed. War and Peace, the Maude Translation: Backgrounds and Sources; Essays in Criticism. New York: Norton, 1966. An extensive collection of essays and excerpts from books, many translated for this volume.

A FURTHER NOTE ON ANTHOLOGIES

In addition to the major anthologies noted in the previous section, the following works contain two or more titles on Tolstoy:

Baudouin, Charles. Contemporary Studies. Freeport, N.Y.: Books for Libraries Press, 1969; 288p.
    "Tolstoy's Diary," 9-18.
    "Tolstoy as an Educationalist," 19-23.
    "Tolstoy and the Realist Faith," 24-27.

Calder, Angus. Russia Discovered: Nineteenth Century Fiction from Pushkin to Chekhov. New York: Harper & Row, 1976; 302p.
    "Tolstoy to War and Peace: Man against History," 136-170.
    "Man, Woman and Male Woman: Tolstoy's Anna Karenina and after," 209-236.

Chesterton, Gilbert K., et al. Leo Tolstoy. New York: Pott, 1903; 40p.
    "Tolstoy," by Gilbert Chesterton.
    "Tolstoy as a Writer," by George Perris.
    "Tolstoy's Place in European Literature," by Edward Garnett.

Clutton-Brock, Arthur. More Essays on Books. London: Methuen, 1921; 174p.
    "Leo Tolstoy: The Novels," 149-159.
    "Tolstoy and Russia," 160-174.

Creelman, James. On the Great Highways. Boston: Lothrop, 1901; 418p.
    "The Avatar of Count Tolstoy," 120-140.
    "Tolstoy and His People," 141-156.

Farrell, James T. Literature and Morality. New York: Vanguard, 1946; 304p.
    "Tolstoy's War and Peace as a Moral Panorama of the Tsarist Feudal Nobility," 185-213.
    "History and War in Tolstoy's War and Peace," 214-230.
    "Tolstoy's Portrait of Napoleon," 231-245.
    "Leo Tolstoy and Napoleon Bonaparte," 246-266.
    "An Introduction to Anna Karenina," 296-304.

Gibbon, Monk, ed. The Living Torch, A. E. (George William Rus-
     sell). New York: Macmillan, 1938; 380p.
     "Tolstoi, " 305-309.
     "Tolstoi's Diary, " 309-310.
     "Tolstoi and George Sand, " 310-312.

Hapgood, Isabel F. Russian Rambles. Boston: Houghton, Mifflin,
     1895; 369p.
     "A Stroll in Moscow with Count Tolstoy, " 134-147.
     "Count Tolstoy at Home, " 148-202.

Hare, Richard. Portraits of Russian Personalities between Reform
     and Revolution. London: Oxford, 1959; 360p.
     "The Young Leo Tolstoy, " 150-195.
     "Tolstoy after War and Peace, " 196-244.

Hearn, Lafcadio. Life and Literature. Freeport, N. Y. : Books for
     Libraries Press, 1969; 393p.
     "Tolstoy's Theory on Art, " 288-299.
     "A Note upon Tolstoy's Resurrection, " 300-307.

Kronenberger, Louis, ed. Novelists on Novelists. Garden City,
     N. Y. : Doubleday, 1962; 387p.
     "Marcel Proust on Leo Tolstoi and Fyodor Dostoevski, " 161-
          163.
     "Thomas Mann on Leo Tolstoy, " 179-193.
     "Louis Auchincloss on Henry James and the Russian Novel-
          ists, " 215-225.

Lee, Vernon. Gospels of Anarchy. New York: Brentano's, 1909;
     372p.
     "Tolstoi as a Prophet: Notes on the Psychology of Asceti-
          cism, " 103-132.
     "Tolstoi on Art, " 133-158.

Lukacs, Georg. Studies in European Realism. New York: Grossett
     and Dunlap, 1974; 267p.
     "Tolstoy and the Development of Realism, " 126-205.
     "Leo Tolstoy and Western European Literature, " 242-264.

Mann, Thomas. Essays of Three Decades. New York: Knopf,
     1947; 472p.
     "Goethe and Tolstoy, " 93-175.
     "Anna Karenina, " 176-188.

Morgan, Charles. Reflections in a Mirror. New York: Macmillan,
     1945; 225p.
     "Tolstoy: War and Peace, " 192-200.
     "Tolstoy: The Second Epilogue, " 210-216.

Panin, Ivan. Lectures on Russian Literature. New York: Putnam,
     1889; 220p.
     "Tolstoy the Artist, " 154-189.
     "Tolstoy the Preacher, " 190-220.

Rahv, Philip. Image and Idea: Twenty Essays on Literary Themes. Norfolk, Conn.: New Directions, 1957; 241p.
"Tolstoy: The Green Twig and the Black Trunk, " 87-104.
"The Death of Ivan Ilyich and Joseph K., " 121-140.

Shestov, Lev. Dostoevsky, Tolstoy and Nietzsche. Athens, Ohio: Ohio University Press, 1969; 322p.
"The Good in the Teaching of Tolstoy and Nietzsche: Philosophy and Preaching, " 1-140.
"Dostoevsky and Nietzsche: The Philosophy of Tragedy, " 141-322. (includes an extensive discussion of Tolstoy).

Symons, Arthur. Studies in Prose and Verse. New York: Dutton, 1922; 291p.
"The Russian Soul: Gorki and Tolstoi, " 161-172.
"Tolstoi on Art, " 173-182.

Tsanoff, Radoslav A. The Problem of Life in the Russian Novel. Houston: Rice University Press, 1917; 272p.
"Count Tolstoy the Novelist, " 210-237.
"The Gospel of Tolstoy the Apostle, " 238-272.

Important collections of essays have also appeared in journals which have dedicated issues to Tolstoy:

Adam International Review, nos. 284-286 (1960).

Russian Review, 19 (April, 1960).

Russian Student, 5, no. 1 (Sept., 1928).

Slavonic Review, 7 (Jan., 1929).

REFERENCE SOURCES

ABSEES. Soviet and East European Abstract Series, 1971-. Glascow: University of Glascow. A bibliography drawing on 70 periodicals published in England. Replaces the Information Supplement to the journal Soviet Studies.

American Bibliography of Russian and East European Studies, 1956-1966. Bloomington: Indiana University, 1957-1967. Title has variations; see continuation, American Bibliography of Slavic and East European Studies, 1967-.

American Bibliography of Slavic and East European Studies, 1967-. Columbus: Ohio State University Press, 1972. See also American Bibliography of Russian and East European Studies, 1956-1966.

American Catalogue, 1876-1910. Reprinted, New York: Peter Smith, 1941.

American Library Association Index to General Literature, 2d ed. And Supplement. Chicago: American Library Association, 1901-1914. Main volume covers up to 1900; supplement covers 1900 to 1910. Forerunner of Essay and General Literature Index (q. v.).

Annual Library Index, 1905-1910. 6 vols. New York: Publisher's Weekly, 1906-1911.

Annual Literary Index, 1892-1904. New York: Publisher's Weekly, 1893-1905. 13 vols. Preceded by Cooperative Index to Periodicals, 1885-1892 and serves as a continuation of Poole's Index of Periodical Literature. American and English essays; includes chapters of books.

Annual Magazine Subject Index, 1907-1949. 43 vols. Boston: Faxon, 1908-1952. See Cumulated Magazine Subject Index.

Art Index, 1929-. New York: H. W. Wilson Co., 1929-.

Baldensperger, Fernand, and Werner P. Friederich. Bibliography of Comparative Literature. Chapel Hill: University of North Carolina Press, 1950; 701p. Covers literary influences.

Besterman, T. A World Bibliography of Bibliographies, 4th ed.   5
    vols. Lausanne: Societas Bibliographica, 1966.

Bibliographic Index; A Cumulative Bibliography of Bibliographies,
    1937-. New York: H. W. Wilson Co., 1938-.

Bibliography of Russian Literature in English Translation to 1945.
    Totowa, N. J.: Rowman & Littlefield, 1972; 74p., 96p. A com-
    bination of Maurice B. Line's Bibliography of Russian Literature
    in English Translation to 1900 (q. v.) and Amrei Ettlinger and
    Joan M. Gladstone's Russian Literature, Theatre and Art, a
    Bibliography, 1900-1945 (q. v.).

Biography Index; A Cumulative Index to Biography Material in Books
    and Magazines. New York: H. W. Wilson Co., 1947-. Cover-
    age begins Jan. 1, 1946.

Birkos, Alexander S., and Lewis A. Tamb. Academic Writer's
    Guide to Periodicals. Vol. II: East European and Slavic Studies.
    Kent, Ohio: Kent State University Press, 1973; 572p.

Book Review Digest, 1905-. New York: H. W. Wilson Co., 1905-.

Book Review Index, 1965-. Detroit: Gale Research Co., 1965-.

Breed, P. F., and F. M. Sniderman. Dramatic Criticism Index.
    Detroit: Gale Research Co., 1972; 1022p.

Brenni, Vito J. William Dean Howells: A Bibliography. Metuchen,
    N. J.: Scarecrow Press, 1973; 212p.

British Books in Print; the Reference Catalogue of Current Litera-
    ture, 1874-. London: Whitaker, 1874-.

British Education Index, 1954-. London: Library Association,
    1961-.

British Humanities Index, 1962-. London: Library Association,
    1963-. A continuation in part of the Subject Index to Periodicals
    (q. v.).

British Museum. Department of Printed Books. General Catalogue
    of Printed Books. 263 vols. London: Trustees of the British
    Museum, 1959-1966. Coverage through 1955. Ten-year supple-
    ment (1956-1966) issued in 1968, 50 vols; five-year supplement
    (1966-1970) issued in 1971-1972, 26 vols.

British National Bibliography, 1950-. London: Council of British
    National Bibliography, 1950-. Cumulated Subject Catalogue,
    1951/1954-, published 1958-; Cumulated Index, 1950/1954-, pub-
    lished 1955-.

Canadian Catalogue of Books ... with Imprint 1921-1949. 2 vols.

Toronto: Toronto Public Libraries, 1959. Superseded by
Canadiana (q. v.).

Canadian Essay and General Literature Index, 1973-. Toronto: University of Toronto Press, 1973-.

Canadian Index to Periodicals and Documentary Films, 1948-1959.
Ottawa: Canadian Library Association, 1962; 1180p. Superseded by Canadian Periodical Index [1960-] (q. v.).

Canadian Periodical Index, 1928-1947. Toronto: Public Libraries
Branch, Ontario Department of Education, 1928-1947.

Canadian Periodical Index [1960-]. Ottawa: Canadian Library Association, 1964-. A continuation of the Canadian Index... (q. v.).

Canadiana, 1950-. Ottawa: National Library of Canada, 1951-.
Succeeds Canadian Catalogue of Books (q. v.).

Catholic Periodical Index, 1930-1966. New York: Catholic Library
Association, 1939-1967. Superseded by Catholic Periodical and
Literature Index (q. v.).

Catholic Periodical and Literature Index, 1967/1968-. Haverford,
Pa. : Catholic Library Association, 1968-. A continuation of
Catholic Periodical Index (q. v.).

Comprehensive Dissertation Index, 1861-1972. 37 vols. Ann Arbor,
Mich. : University Microfilms, 1973-. With annual supplements.

Cooperative Index to Periodicals, 1885-1892. New York: Office
of Publishers' Weekly, 1886-1893.

Cumulated Dramatic Index, 1909-1949. 2 vols. Boston: G. K.
Hall, 1965. A cumulation of the F. W. Faxon Co. 's 41-vol.
Dramatic Index, 1909-1949.

Cumulated Magazine Subject Index, 1907-1949. Boston: G. K.
Hall, 1964. A cumulation of the F. W. Faxon Co. 's Annual
Magazine Subject Index into one sequence.

Cumulative Book Index [CBI]; A World List of Books in the English
Language, 1928/1932-. New York: H. W. Wilson Co. , 1933-.
Published 1898-1928 under the title United States Catalog (q. v.),
with Cumulative Book Index as title for supplements.

Cumulative Index to Periodical Literature, 1959-1970. Princeton:
National Library Service Corp. , 1959-1970.

Cumulative Index to Periodicals, 1896-1902. Cleveland: Hellman,
Taylor Co. , 1896-1902.

Current Index to Journals in Education, 1969-. New York: CCM Information Co. , 1969-.

Dossick, Jesse J. Doctoral Research on Russia and the Soviet
   Union. New York: New York University Press, 1960; 248p.
   Supplement appears in December issues of the Slavic Review.

Education Index, 1929-. New York: H. W. Wilson Co. , 1932-.

English Catalogue of Books ... Issued ... in Great Britain and Ireland, 1801-1965. London: S. Low, 1864-1901; Publishers Cir-
   cular Ltd. , 1906-1966.

           . Index to the English Catalogue of Books, 1837-1889.
   London: S. Low, 1858-1893. A subject catalog for The English Catalogue; after 1889 the subject catalog is included in the
   annual volumes.

Essay and General Literature Index, 1900-1933. With Supplements
   to the Present. New York: H. W. Wilson Co. , 1934-. Indexes collections of essays and miscellaneous works.

Ettlinger, Amrei, and Joan M. Gladstone. Russian Literature,
   Theater and Art: A Bibliography of Works in English Published
   from 1900-1945. Port Washington; N. Y. : Kennikat Press, 1971.
   Now combined into Bibliography of Russian Literature in English
   Translation to 1945 (q. v.).

Fisher, Harold H. , ed. American Research on Russia. Bloomington: Indiana University Press, 1959; 240p.

Gray, Richard A. A Guide to Book Review Citations; A Bibliography of Sources. Columbus: Ohio State University Press, 1969;
   221p.

           , and Dorothy Villmow. Serial Bibliographies in the Hu-
   manities and Social Sciences. Ann Arbor, Mich. : Pierian
   Press, 1969; 345p.

Grierson, Philip. Books on Soviet Russia, 1917-1942. London:
   Metheun, 1943; 354p.

Guide to Social Science and Religion in Periodical Literature. Flint,
   Mich. : National Periodical Library, 1965-.

Harvard University. Library. Slavic History and Literatures. 4
   vols. Cambridge, dist. by Harvard University Press, 1971.

Horecky, Paul L. Russia and the Soviet Union: A Bibliographic
   Guide to Western-Language Publications. Chicago: University
   of Chicago Press, 1965; 473p.

Humanities Index, 1974-. New York: H. W. Wilson Co. , 1974-.
   Succeeds in part Social Sciences and Humanities Index (q. v.).

Index India, 1967-. Jaipur: Rajasthan University Library, 1967-.

Index to American Little Magazines, 1920-1947. 3 vols. Denver:
    Swallow Press, 1965-1969. See first Sader, Marion. See also
    Index to Little Magazines.

Index to American Little Magazines [from 1900], comp. Stephen H.
    Goode. Troy, N.Y.: Whitson Publishing Co., 1969-1974. A
    retrospective vol.; see Sader, Marion, and also Index to Little
    Magazines.

Index to Commonwealth Little Magazines, 1964/1965-. New York:
    Johnson Reprint Co., 1966-.

Index to Little Magazines 1940-1942, comp. Stephen H. Goode. New
    York: Johnson Reprint Corp., 1967. See Sader, Marion.

Index to Little Magazines, 1948-. Denver: Swallow Press, 1949-.
    Coverage of 1920-1947 is found in Index to American Little
    Magazines (q.v.). See first Sader, Marion.

Index to Psychoanalytic Writings. New York: International Uni-
    versities Press Inc., 1956-1969.

Index to Religious Periodical Literature, 1949/1952-. Berkeley:
    American Theological Library Assoc., 1953-. Includes author
    index to book reviews.

Indian National Bibliography, 1958-. Calcutta: Central Reference
    Library, 1958-.

International Bibliography of Political Science, 1953-. London:
    Tavistock, 1953-.

International Index to Periodicals, 1907-1965. Name changed to
    Social Sciences and Humanities Index (q.v.) in 1965.

Kearney, Elizabeth I., and Louise S. Fitzgerald. The Continental
    Novel: A Checklist of Criticism in English, 1900-1966. Me-
    tuchen, N.J.: Scarecrow Press, 1968; 460p.

Kerner, Robert J. Slavic Europe: A Select Bibliography in the
    Western European Languages. Cambridge, Mass.: Harvard
    University Press, 1918.

Kiell, Norman. Psychiatry and Psychology in the Visual Arts and
    Aesthetics; A Bibliography. Madison: University of Wisconsin
    Press, 1965; 250p.

_____. Psychoanalysis, Psychology and Literature: A Bibliogra-
    phy. Madison: University of Wisconsin Press, 1963; 225p.

Leo Tolstoy: A Selected List of Books Now in Print, Compiled by
    the Tolstoy Society. National Book Council, 1933. Only books
    in English are included.

Lewanski, Richard Casimir. The Slavic Literatures [to 1960]. New
York: New York Public Library and Ungar, 1967; 630p. (Ungar's Literatures of the World in English Translation series,
vol. 2.)

Line, Maurice B. A Bibliography of Russian Literature in English
Translation to 1900. London: London Library Assoc. , 1963;
74p. Now combined into Bibliography of Russian Literature in
English Translation to 1945 (q. v.).

London Bibliography of the Social Sciences [1929-]. London: Man-
sell, 1934-1975. 31- vols. Publisher, coverage, indexing, supplement details all vary. Volumes 1-5 published by London
School of Economics.

Lowe, John A. "Tolstoi, " in Modern Drama and Opera; Reading
Lists on the Works of Various Authors. Boston, 1915; vol. 2,
137-142.

Maichel, Karol. Guide to Russian Reference Books. 6 vols. Stanford, Calif. : Hoover Institution, 1962-1967.

Martianoff, Nikolai Nikolaevich. Books Available in English by
Russians and on Russia Published in the United States, 4th ed.
New York: Martianoff, 1942; 48p.

Matlaw, R. "Russian Literature, " in Modern Language, vol. 2,
Italian, Spanish, German, Russian and Oriental Literature. ed.
Victor Lange. Englewood Cliffs, N. J. : Prentice-Hall, 1968;
p. 185-222.

Methodist Periodical Index, 1961-. Nashville: The Methodist Publishing House Library, 1963-.

Mihailovich, Vasa D. Modern Slavic Literatures: A Library of Literary Criticism. New York: Ungar, 1972. In progress; vol.
1, Russian Literature, 424p.

Modern Language Association of America. MLA International Bibliography of Books and Articles on the Modern Languages and
Literatures, 1921-1954/1955, annuals reprinted by MLA in 1958.
1956-1968 volumes reprinted New York: Kraus, 1968. (Title
for years 1921-1955 MLA American Bibliography.)

Music Index: The Key to Current Music Periodical Literature.
Detroit: Information Service, 1950-.

Nadel, George. Bibliography of Works in the Philosophy of History,
1945-1968. Middletown, Conn. : Wesleyan University Press,
1968.

National Bibliography of Indian Literature, 1901-1953. New Delhi:
Sahitya Akademi, 1962-1970. To be in 4 vols.

National Library Service Cumulative Book Review Index, 1905-1974.
    Princeton: NLS Co., 1975.

National Union Catalog..., 1953-1957; 1958-1962; 1963-1967; 1952-
    1955; also a cumulative vol., 1956 through 1967.   Ann Arbor,
    Mich.: Edwards, 1958, 1961, 1969; New York: Rowman & Lit-
    tlefield, 1963, 1970-1972 (cum. vol.).   Continues U.S. Library
    of Congress Catalog... (q. v.).

Neiswender, Rosemary. Guide to Russian Reference and Language
    Aids. New York: Special Libraries Assoc., 1962; 92p.

New York. Public Library. Research Libraries. Dictionary Cata-
    log of the Research Libraries ... since January 1, 1971. New
    York: New York Public Library, 1972-. Supplement, 1977.

    _____. Slavonic Division. Dictionary Catalog of the
    Slavonic Collection. 26 vols. Boston: G. K. Hall, 1959.

New York Times Book Review (1896-1976). 136 vols. (including 5
    vols. of Index). New York: Arno, 1970.

Nineteenth Century Readers' Guide to Periodical Literature, 1890-
    1899, with Supplementary Indexing 1900-1922. 2 vols. New
    York: H. W. Wilson Co., 1944.

Olgin, J. O. A Guide to Russian Literature 1820-1917. New York:
    Harcourt, Brace and Howe, 1920.

Palmer, Helen H., and Anne J. Dyson. European Drama Criticism
    [1900-1966]. Hamden, Conn.: Shoe String, 1968; 460p. Sup-
    plement (1967-1969), 1970; 243p.

Philosopher's Index; An International Index to Philosophical Period-
    icals, 1967-. Bowling Green, Ohio: Bowling Green University,
    1967-.

Poole's Index to Periodical Literature, 1802-1881 (rev. ed.).   2
    vols. Boston: Houghton, 1891 (1882). Supplements covering
    1882-1906 issued 1887-1908.

Psychological Abstracts. Cumulated Subject Index, 1927-1960.
    Boston: G. K. Hall, 1966. Supplements (covering 1961-1965
    and 1966-1968) issued 1968-1971.

Publications of Canadian Slavists: A Bibliography. Daniel Dorotich,
    ed. Vancouver: University of British Columbia, 1967; 53p.

Readers' Guide to Periodical Literature, 1900-. New York: H. W.
    Wilson, 1905-.

Religious and Theological Abstracts, 1958-. Youngstown, Ohio:
    Theological Publications, Inc., 1958-.

Review of Reviews: Index to the Periodicals of 1890-1902. 13 vols.
London: Review of Reviews, 1891-1903. (Title varies first 4
vols.: Annual Index of Periodicals and Photographs and Index
to the Periodical Literature of the World.)

Richardson, Ernest C. An Alphabetical Subject Index and Index En-
cyclopaedia to Periodical Articles on Religion 1890-1899. 2
vols. New York: Scribner's, 1907-1911.

Sader, Marion. Comprehensive Index to English Language Little
Magazines 1890-1970. 8 vols. Millwood: Kraus-Thompson,
1976.

Schultheiss, Thomas. Russian Studies 1941-1958. Ann Arbor,
Mich.: Pierian Press, 1972; 395p. A cumulation of the Annual Bibliographies from the Russian Review.

Sheehy, Eugene P. Guide to Reference Books, 9th ed. Chicago:
American Library Association, 1976; 1015p.

Simmons, John S. G. Russian Bibliography, Libraries and Archives.
London: Oxford University Press, 1973; 76p.

Social Sciences and Humanities Index, 1907/1915-1974. New York:
H. W. Wilson Co., 1916-1974. Former name, International Index to Periodicals; succeeded in part by Social Sciences Index
(q. v.) and in part by Humanities Index (q. v.), both in mid-1974.

Social Sciences Index, 1974-. New York: H. W. Wilson, 1974-.
Succeeds in part Social Sciences and Humanities Index (q. v.).

Spector, S. D. Checklist of Paperbound Books on Russia. Albany:
Univ. of the State of New York, State Ed. Dept., 1964.

Stanford University. Hoover Institution on War, Revolution and
Peace. Library Catalogs of.... 63 vols. Boston: G. K.
Hall, 1969. 5-vol. supplement, 1972.

Subject Index to Periodicals, 1915-1961. London: Library Assoc.,
1919-1962. Years 1915-1918 titled Athenaeum Subject Index.
In 1963 (beginning 1962 coverage) divided into British Humanities Index (q. v.) and other special subjects.

Thurston, Jarvis A., et al. Short Fiction Criticism: A Checklist
of Interpretations since 1925 of Stories and Novelettes, 1800-
1958. Chicago: Swallow Press, 1960.

Tod, Dorothea D., and Audrey Cordingley. A Check List of Canadian Imprints, 1900-1925. Ottawa: Canadian Bibliographic Cen-
tre, 1950; 370p.

Ulrich's International Periodicals Directory. New York: Bowker,
1932- (biennial).

United States Catalog; Books in Print [1899-1928]. New York: H. W. Wilson Co., 1899-1928. There have been 4 editions: 1899, 1902, 1912, 1928. Title changes to Cumulative Book Index (q. v.) after 1928.

United States. Library of Congress. Catalog of Books Represented by Library of Congress Cards Issued to July 31, 1942. Ann Arbor, Mich.: Edwards, 1942-1946. And supplements, covering 1942-1947. Continued by National Union Catalog (q. v.).

_____. _____. Cyrillic Union Catalog. New York: Readex Microprint Corp., 1963. (Microform.)

_____. _____. List of Recent Writings on Tolstoi. Washington, D. C., 1906.

_____. _____. National Union Catalog see under National....

Vir, Dharna. Gandhi Bibliography. Delhi: Udyog Shala Press, 1967; 575p.

Walker, Warren S. Twentieth-Century Short Story Explication; Interpretations, 1900-1966 of Short Fiction since 1800. Hamden, Conn.: Shoe String Press, 1967. Supplements, 1967-1969 and 1970-1972.

Wellesley Index to Victorian Periodicals, 1824-1900. London: Routledge and Paul, 1966-. (In progress.)

Whitaker's Cumulative Book List...; A Classified List of Publications, 1924-. London: Whitaker, 1924-.

Woodworth, David. Guide to Current British Journals, 2d ed. 2 vols. London: Library Assoc., 1973.

Wright, E. T. A Classified List of Books Relating to Russia and Russian Affairs. London, 1917; 23p.

Yassukovich, A. "Tolstoy in English, 1878-1929: A List of Works by and about Tolstoy Available in the New York Public Library. " Bulletin of the New York Public Library, vol. 33, no. 7 (July, 1929).

Yearbook of Comparative and General Literature. Bloomington: Indiana University, 1952-. Designed as a supplement to Baldensperger (q. v.).

Year's Work in Modern Language Studies, 1929/1930-. London: Oxford University Press, 1931-.

Zenkovsky, Serge A., and David L. Armbruster. Guide to the Bibliographies of Russian Literature. Nashville, Tenn.: Vanderbilt University Press, 1970; 62p.

Section I

BIOGRAPHICAL INFORMATION FROM
FAMILY, FRIENDS, ACQUAINTANCES, AND VISITORS

BOOKS

1 Behrs, Stepan A.   Recollections of Count Leo Tolstoy Together
with a Letter to the Women of France on "The Kreutzer
Sonata."   Trans. by Charles Turner.   London: Heinemann,
1896; 235p.   A brief biography of Tolstoy precedes an account, by his brother-in-law, of family life up to the date of
Tolstoy's spiritual awakening.   His philosophy is restated
with attention given to how it radically affected his personality and, consequently, his family relations.   The continued
devotion of the family to him is noted, though some of its
members, particularly his wife, disagreed with much of his
philosophy.

2 Biriukov, Paul.   Leo Tolstoy; His Life and Work.   New York:
Scribner's, 1906; 370p., illus.   As volume 1 of the four-
volume Russian-language biography of Tolstoy, by a close
friend, his life is discussed only up to the date of his mar-
riage.   Based on much primary information, including the
personal cooperation of Tolstoy, the study presents a thor-
oughly documented, very positive account of the principal
events and individuals that shaped his life, philosophy, and
work.   Reviewed in:
Academy, 70 (26 May 1906), 498.
Athenaeum, 2 (18 Aug. 1906), 178.
Critic, 49 (Aug. 1906), 188.
Dial, 41 (1 Aug. 1906), 59, by Annie R. Marble.
Forum, 38 (July 1906), 97, by William T. Brewster.
Independent, 61 (15 Nov. 1906), 1163.
Lit D, 33 (15 Sept. 1906), 357.
Nation, 83 (19 July 1906), 60.
N Y Times, 11 (9 June 1906), 368.
N Y Times, 11 (1 Dec. 1906), 800.
Putnam's M, 1 (Oct. 1906), 110.
RRs, 34 (July 1906), 124.

3 Biriukov, Paul.   The Life of Tolstoy.   London: Cassell, 1911;
xii, 168p., illus.   A condensation of the four-volume Russian
language biography by Tolstoy's close friend.   Tolstoy's life

is surveyed with emphasis placed upon his intellectual development, spiritual crisis, and consequent creation of a
unique brand of Christianity. Throughout, the sincerity of
Tolstoy in fiction and philosophy as well as in his personal
life and activities is stressed. His increasingly difficult
family situation is chronicled carefully, and the contradiction
between his philosophy and the life which surrounded him at
Yasnaya Polyana is identified as the source of the discontent
which drove him to flee from his family in 1910. In all, a
very favorable account providing considerable firsthand information. Reviewed in:
Athenaeum, 2 (28 Oct. 1911), 518.
Nation, 94 (7 March 1912), 237-238.
N Y Times, 17 (11 Feb. 1911), 71.

4 Biriukov, Paul.   Tolstoy's Love Letters; With a Study on the
Autobiographical Elements in Tolstoy's Work. Trans. by S.
Koteliansky and V. Woolf. London: Hogarth, 1923; xiv,
134p. Following a discussion of the author's relationship
with Tolstoy and the reproduction of the letters of Tolstoy
and his fiancée, true-life sources of characters and episodes
in his fiction are examined. With autobiographical elements
being defined as "facts which bear upon Tolstoy's own personality and upon people ... intimately connected with him," the
following works are examined for their utilization of true-
life characters and incidents: Childhood, Boyhood, Youth,
Sevastopol, Country Squire's Morning, Albert, Anna Karenina,
War and Peace, Resurrection, Living Corpse, Father Sergius,
and The Devil. In the course of the survey, much insight is
gained into the truly realistic nature of Tolstoy's fiction.

5 Bulgakov, Valentin F.   The Last Year of Leo Tolstoy. Trans.
by Ann Dunnigan, intro. by George Steiner. New York:
Dial, 1971; xxv, 235p. The intrigues, struggles, and crises
which plagued Tolstoy in his last year are presented by way
of the diary of his personal secretary for the year 1910.
Much additional information is provided as Bulgakov relates
Tolstoy's thoughts on a wide range of problems, events, and
individuals in 1910 Russia. Background for the diary's en-
tries is provided by an introduction which traces the develop-
ment of Tolstoy's philosophy and its negative effect on his
marital relationship. Reviewed in:
Am His R, 77 (April 1972), 549, by A. P. Mendel.
Encounter, 38 (Feb. 1972), 83, by E. B. Greenwood.
Harper's M, 242 (March 1971), 105-106, by Edwin Yoder,
   Jr.
Listener, 86 (25 Nov. 1971), 725, by John Bayley.
Nation, 213 (27 Sept. 1971), 276, by Hugh McLean.
New Republic, 164 (20 Feb. 1971), 31.
N Y R Bks, 17 (30 Dec. 1971), 24, by John Bayley.
N Y Times, (9 May 1971), 34.
Times Lit Sup, (8 Oct., 1971), 1217.

6   Chertkov, Vladimir G.   The Last Days of Tolstoy.   Trans. by
      Nathalie Duddington.   Millwood, N.Y.:   Kraus, 1973 (reprint
      of the 1922 publication); xxvi, 151p.   A survey of Tolstoy's
      later life, written by his principal disciple, designed to clear
      up the many misunderstandings surrounding the last years and
      days of Tolstoy.   Two circumstances are isolated as deserv-
      ing special attention in studying his later life: a terribly
      painful homelife and his remarkable fortitude amidst this try-
      ing situation.   Exposed is the nearly constant strife between
      Tolstoy and his wife, which intensified in the weeks before
      his flight from home, that sapped his spiritual strength and
      drove him to despair.   Also discussed are the details sur-
      rounding his will and last few days of life away from home.

7   Goldenweizer, A. B.   Talks with Tolstoy.   Trans. by S. Kotelian-
      sky, intro. by Henry Finch.   New York: Horizon, 1969.
      Volume 1 of the diary of the Russian musician and friend of
      Tolstoy in which a chronological account of Goldenweizer's
      many conversations with Tolstoy is presented with "no attempt
      to select what would be interesting from a special point of
      view, or to supply any connection between one entry and an-
      other." Insight is provided into a wide range of subjects re-
      lated to Tolstoy including his homelife, personality, philosophy,
      and prejudices.   Reviewed in:
        Christian Sci M, (9 April 1970), 11.

8   Kenworthy, John.   A Pilgrimage to Tolstoy.   London, Brother-
      hood, 1896; 45p.   A compilation of letters written from Rus-
      sia by Kenworthy in which is described his impression of
      Tolstoy and those around him, especially Chertkov.   Recol-
      lected are conversations with Tolstoy on the meaning of life,
      the peasants, religion, and the evil of Russian censorship, as
      well as shorter comments on a host of lesser subjects.

9   Kenworthy, John.   Tolstoy: His Life and Works.   New York:
      Haskell, 1971 (reprint of 1902 publication); x, 225p., illus.
      A favorable account of Tolstoy's life and writings based on
      the author's "intimate relation of principle and of personal
      friendship and correspondence with Tolstoy." Most attention
      is given to Tolstoy's intellectual development and philosophy,
      the author's conversations with him being the prime source
      of information.   Also included is a survey of Tolstoy's in-
      fluence in England, a complete account of which can be found
      in Kenworthy's Tolstoy's Teaching and Influence in England.
      Reviewed in:
        Athenaeum, (6 Sept. 1902), 309.

10   Kuzminskaya, Tatyana A.   Tolstoy as I Knew Him; My Life at
      Home and at Yasnaya Polyana.   Trans. by Nora Sigersit et
      al., intro. by Ernest J. Simmons.   New York: Macmillan,
      1948; ix, 437p., illus.   Memoirs of the sister-in-law and
      close friend of Tolstoy in which a variety of biographical in-
      formation is given but with particular depth surrounding the

writing of War and Peace. The autobiographical nature of
the novel is illustrated by reference to events and individuals from Tolstoy's life that were transferred to it, including Kuzminskaya's being the model for the character
"Natasha. " Additionally, much detail is presented on in-
numerable aspects of the personal life of Tolstoy, with the
consequence that the account is deemed, in the introduction
by Simmons, "a veritable treasure-trove of biographical
material. " Reviewed in:
  ASEER, 9, no. 2 (1950), 145-147, by Leonid Strakhovsky.
  Atlantic M, 182 (Sept. 1948), 105, by C. J. Rolo.
  Christian Sci M, (29 July 1948), 11.
  Nation, 167 (28 Aug. 1948), 236, by Margaret Marshall.
  New Yorker, 34 (28 Aug 1948), 63, by Edmund Wilson.
  N Y Times, (15 Aug. 1948), 4, by Alfred Kazin.
  Rus R, 8 (Oct. 1949), 353-355, by Helen Muchnic.
  Sat R Lit, 31 (14 Aug. 1948), 21, by William Soskin.
  Wkly Bk R, (25 July 1948), by Joshua Kunitz.

11 Maude, Aylmer, ed. Family Views of Tolstoy. Trans. by
    Louise and Aylmer Maude. London: Allen and Unwin,
    1926; 220p. A brief introduction, by the English friend of
    Tolstoy, precedes a collection of seven essays by members
    and friends of the Tolstoy family. The essays (which are
    annotated individually in the next section) are by Tatiana,
    his eldest daughter; his niece, Vera Nagorny; his youngest
    daughter, Alexandra; Nikolay Apostolov, a disciple; Sofia
    Stakhovich, a family friend; and two are by Tolstoy's eldest
    son, Sergius.

12 Maude, Aylmer. The Life of Tolstoy. Volume I: The First
    Fifty Years, xv, 490p. ; volume II: The Later Years, xvi,
    570p. London: Oxford, 1930 (revision of 1908-1912 publi-
    cation). Based on close contact with Tolstoy, the Russian
    language biographies of Gusev and Biriukov, and on the as-
    sistance of Tolstoy's wife, the study presents a comprehen-
    sive, favorable discussion of life, works, and beliefs. In
    the first volume, Tolstoy's life is traced up to 1878, with
    his works of fiction receiving special attention, although de-
    tail is also provided on those influences which shaped his
    complex personality. The second volume concentrates on
    his polemical works. Most concern is shown for his social
    views, particularly on non-resistance, and the opposition
    which they incurred from the tsarist government. Also
    closely examined are the circumstances associated with his
    flight from home and eventual death. An interesting analy-
    sis of Countess Tolstoy's Later Diary appears in Appendix
    II. Reviewed in:
      Bookman, 32 (Dec. 1910), 422, by George Sampson.
      Cur Lit, 50 (Jan. 1911), 62-64.
      N Y Times, (10 Dec. 1910), 695.
      RRs, 42 (Dec. 1910), 758.
      Sackbut, 10 (June 1930), 311-313, by H. Ould.

Sat R, 110 (29 Oct. 1910), 552.
Times Lit Sup, (26 Sept. 1918), 445-446.
Other biographical studies of Tolstoy by Maude that are
either condensations or brief precursors of his two-volume
biography are: Leo Tolstoy (New York: Dodd, Mead, 1918;
ix, 331p.), Leo Tolstoy and His Works (New York: Haskell, 1974 [a reprint of the 1918 condensation]); Leo Tolstoy: A Short Biography (London: Richards, 1902; 24p.),
Leo Tolstoy (Manchester, England: Broadbent, 1900; 32p.
[also in TP, 1-31]).

13   Micek, Eduard. The Real Tolstoy. Austin, Texas: Czech
Literary Society, 1958; iv, 61p. Conversations with and
impressions of Tolstoy, as recorded by a variety of his
contemporaries, are presented along with the author's opin-
ion of him. Considered are his relationships with Turgenev,
Fet, Bunin, Chekhov, Gorky, Makovitsky, Strakhov, Masaryk, and others. A general biographical sketch of Tolstoy,
his novels Anna Karenina and War and Peace, his dramas,
and religious beliefs, is also included.

14   Micek, Eduard. Tolstoy, the Artist and Humanist: Impressions and Evaluations. Austin, Texas: Czech Literary
Society, 1961; iii, 99p. The author's impressions of Tolstoy and Yasnaya Polyana, based on a 1909 visit, are
mixed with the impressions of a number of Tolstoy's contemporaries. Discussed are Chertkov, Repin, Gandhi,
Tolstoy's wife, and others. Tolstoy's later works, The
Kreutzer Sonata and Resurrection, are examined, and a
favorable account of his philosophy and world impact is
given.

15   Newton, William Wilberforce. A Run through Russia: The
Story of a Visit to Count Tolstoi. Hartford, Conn.: Student Publishing Co., 1894; 211p. A discussion of the life
and works of Tolstoy on the basis of scholarship and the
author's personal contact with Tolstoy. His spiritual growth
is traced to his conversion, with his skepticism seen as
the force driving him to find some meaning to life: "he
was in search of faith and could not rest until he found it."
His literary talents and creations are extolled, and his
powers of observation and profound capacity for introspection identified as the source of his remarkable realism.
Examples from his works are presented to demonstrate his
command of realism, followed by a restatement of his views
on war, religion, and immortality as expressed by Tolstoy
in conversations with Newton.

16   Polner, Tikhon. Tolstoy and His Wife. Trans. by Nicholas
Wreden. New York: Norton, 1945; 222p. An examination,
by a family friend, of Tolstoy's courtship and marriage,
his initially happy years with his wife, and the difficulties
that their marriage encountered, later in life, as a conse-

quence of his philosophy. In addition to providing much de-
tail on family relations, the effect on his work of events
and developments in his personal life is illustrated. Re-
viewed in:
Atlantic M, 176 (Oct. 1945), 152, by Ernest J. Sim-
    mons.
Christian Sci M, (12 Aug. 1945), 12, by Edmond Stev-
    ens.
Nation, 161 (28 July 1945), 89, by Philip Rahv.
New Republic, 113 (3 Sept. 1945), 290, by James T.
    Farrell.
New Yorker, 21 (7 July 1945), 66.
N Y Times, (1 July 1945), 1, by S. Toksvig.
Rus R, 5 (Augumn 1945), 125-126, by Alexander Naza-
    roff.
Sat R Lit, 28 (30 June 1945), 10, by M. Gordon.
Wkly Bk R, (8 July 1945), 1, by Joseph W. Krutch.
Yale R, 35 (Autumn 1945), 156, by Ernest J. Simmons.

17   Sergyeenko, P. A.   How Count L. N. Tolstoy Lives and Works.
     Trans. by Isabel F. Hapgood. New York: Crowell, 1899;
     100p. , illus. The home environment and life style of Tol-
     stoy are discussed and an account given of numerous con-
     versations between Tolstoy and Sergyeenko, a close friend.
     Tolstoy's routine and family relations are noted, and his
     opinions on scores of individuals and subjects are recol-
     lected sympathetically and with little analysis by Sergyeen-
     ko. Reviewed in:
     Critic, 34 (May 1899), 417-423.

18   Steiner, Edward A.   Tolstoy, the Man. London: 1904.

19   Steiner, Edward A.   Tolstoy, the Man and His Message. New
     York: Revell, 1908; xxi, 310p. , illus. A mixture of
     biography and literary-philosophical analysis based on the
     author's personal contact with Tolstoy and his disciples.
     His lifestyle, beliefs, and works are all presented positively
     as is the impact which Tolstoy has had on the modern
     world. He is upheld to all as an admirable model because
     of his keen insight and sensitive conscience in relentless
     pursuit of truth in both his life and his creations. Reviewed
     in:
     Annals Am Acad, 34 (July 1909), 216, by Scott Nearing.
     Independent, 67 (14 Oct. 1909), 883.
     Lit D, 39 (18 Sept. 1909), 446.
     N Y Times, (2 Oct. 1909), 582, by Christian Gauss.

20   Stockham, Alice B.   Tolstoi: A Man of Peace. Chicago:
     Stockham, 1900. Descriptions of Yasnaya Polyana, Tol-
     stoy's wife, and his living and working habits are given on
     the basis of Stockham's turn of the century visit to Tolstoy.
     With no analysis provided, his views on warfare, nonre-
     sistance, and the doctrine of brotherly love are restated

along with an account of his mid-life spiritual awakening.
Also in Ellis, Havelock, The New Spirit (Washington, D. C.:
National Home Library, 1935), p. 87-140.

21   Tolstoy, Alexandra.   The Real Tolstoy; A Critique and Commentary on the Book "Tolstoy" by Henri Troyat.   Morris-
town, N. J. : Henry S. Evans, 1968; 11p.   An attack, by Tolstoy's daughter, on Troyat's biography on the grounds that he
"uses his imagination and invents situations, thoughts and
events that add up to a distorted picture of the life and
character of Tolstoy and his family. " Troyat is also criticized for over-reliance on the diary of Tolstoy's wife,
which is labeled as a biased source, and for scores of inaccuracies due to his projecting what Tolstoy might have
said or felt in a particular situation.

22   Tolstoy, Alexandra.   Tolstoy: A Life of My Father.   Trans.
by E. R. Hapgood.   New York: Harper, 1953; 543p. , illus.   A detailed account, by Tolstoy's daughter, of his life
on the basis of diaries and personal memories.   Family affairs and relations are most frequently discussed, with
much reference to specific individuals and episodes that in-
fluenced him.   His personality, work, and beliefs are all
presented in a sympathetic light.   Reviewed in:
   Christian Sci M, (17 Sept. 1953), 11, by Kathleen Can-
      nell.
   New Yorker, 29 (19 Sept. 1953), 121.
   N Y Herald Trib Bk R, (13 Sept. 1953), 5, G. Pauld-
      ing.
   N Y Times, (13 Sept. 1953), 6, Rene Fülöp-Miller.
   Rus R, 13 (April 1954), 156-157, by Helen Iswolsky.
   Sat R Lit, 36 (3 Oct. 1953), 35, by Gleb Struve.
   Time M, 62 (28 Sept. 1953), 90.
   Times Lit Sup, (16 July 1954), 449-450.

23   Tolstoy, Alexandra.   The Tragedy of Tolstoy.   Trans. by Elena
Varneck.   New Haven, Conn. : Yale University Press, 1933;
294p. , illus.   Particulars of family life are given, by Tolstoy's daughter, on the basis of reminiscences of events
and conversations in an attempt to counter-balance the nega-
tive effect on his reputation caused by the publication of the
diary of his wife.   His sincerity and convictions as well as
the nobility of his thought are all upheld.   Reviewed in:
   Bos Trans, (22 April 1933), 1, by Nathan H. Dole.
   Christian Sci M, (15 April 1933), 6, by V. S. Pritchett.
   Commonweal, 17 (26 April 1933), 725, by C. Radziwill.
   Nation, 136 (12 April 1933), 413, by D. Brewster.
   New Republic, 74 (12 April 1933), 250, by A. B. Gold-
      enweizer.
   N Y Times, (26 March 1933), 1, by Alexander Nazaroff.
   Sat R Lit, 9 (25 March 1933), 502; (8 Apr. 1933), 528
      by M. Gordon.
   Spectator, 151 (25 Aug. 1933), 259, by S. Spender.

Survey G, 22 (June 1933), 328, by O. Tead.
Times Lit Sup, (13 July 1933), 473.
World T, 16 (July 1933), 452, by P. Jones.
Yale R, 22 (Spring 1933), 599, by John Cournos.

24 Tolstoy, Ilya. Reminiscences of Tolstoy by His Son Count Ilya
Tolstoy. Trans. by George Calderon. London: Chapman
and Hall, 1914; viii, 310p., illus. A remembrance of daily
life at Yasnaya Polyana including descriptions of the estate,
the many visitors to Tolstoy, recreational activities, and
numerous family affairs. Little information is given on
Tolstoy's literary activities but much detail is presented
on virtually every aspect of his relationship with his family,
although no judgment is passed on his behavior including
its role in the deterioration of his marriage. Many illustrations are contained in the work. Reviewed in:
Athenaeum, 1 (9 Jan. 1915), 26.
Dial, 57 (16 Nov. 1914), 387, by O. Wanamaker.
Lit D, 49 (21 Nov. 1914), 1017.
Nation, 99 (19 Nov. 1914), 698.
N Amer R, 200 (Dec. 1914), 945-946.
Sat R, 118 (14 Nov. 1914) Sup. 3.

25 Tolstoy, Ilya. Tolstoy, My Father. Trans. by Ann Dunnigan.
Chicago: Cowles, 1971; 322p., illus. A revised version
of the 1914 work (item 24) with a few additional memoirs
added just prior to the author's 1933 death. Excerpts in
RLTC, 121-137. Reviewed in:
Atlantic M, 228 (Dec. 1971), 135, by Phoebe Adams.
Economist, 234 (17 June 1972), 63.
N Y R Bks, 17 (30 Dec. 1971), 24, by John Bayley.
New Yorker, 48 (6 May 1972), 146.
N Y Times, (28 Nov. 1971), 38, by F. D. Reeve.
Rus R, 31 (April 1972), 204, by Elisabeth Stenbock-
    Fermor.
Sat R Lit, 54 (20 Nov. 1971), 47, by Maurice Fried-
    berg.
Times Lit Sup, (23 June 1972), 704.
Virg Q R, 48 (Spring 1972), 62-63.

26 Tolstoy, Leo L. The Truth about My Father. London: Murray, 1924; xiii, 229p. An attempt to present an accurate
account of Tolstoy's home life to counter the allegedly in-
accurate accounts given by biographers who have over-em-
phasized the Tolstoys' diaries as sources. Tolstoy's family
life is portrayed as an unusually happy one, and it is maintained that the diaries sometimes give a different image
than this only because entries were frequently made in
haste and under the influence of strained emotions. Additionally recollected are views on such subjects as religion,
violence, and marriage as expressed by Tolstoy in conversations with the many visitors to Yasnaya Polyana. Reviewed in:

Nat and Ath, 35 (17 May 1924), 207, by Edward Gar-
nett.
Lit D, (July 1924), 593, by Alexander Nazaroff.
Lit R, (21 June 1924), 846, by Walter Yust.
New Sta, 23 (17 May 1924), 168.
N Y Times, (11 May 1924), 4, by Simeon Strunsky.
Sat R, 137 (26 Apr. 1924), 442.
Times Lit Sup, (17 Apr. 1924), 233.

27 Tolstoy, Sergei. Tolstoy Remembered by His Son Sergei Tolstoy. Trans. by Maura Budberg. New York: Atheneum,
1962; viii, 234p. A survey of Tolstoy's family life, in the
1862-1881 period, precedes a series of recollections on
such subjects as hunting, farming, traveling, Tolstoy's
reading tastes, and his work with the Doukhobors. Special
attention is given to the last days of Tolstoy, his will,
flight, and death. The work concludes with an account of
his relationship with ten individuals who were close to him
including Turgenev, Repin, and Chertkov. An epilogue is
appended on his views on music. Reviewed in:
Chi Sun Trib, (15 April 1962), 5, by Thomas Riha.
Christian Sci M, (16 April 1962), 13, by Roderick
Nordell.
Guardian, (24 Nov. 1961), 13, by Emanuel Litvinoff.
New Sta, 62 (24 Nov. 1961), 800, by A. Alvarez.
New Yorker, 38 (14 April 1962), 185-186.
Sat R Lit, 45 (31 March 1962), 17, by Ernest J. Sim-
mons.
Spectator, (1 Dec. 1961), 829, by Francis Hope.
Time and Tide, (25 Jan. 1962), 32, by Olivia Manning.
Times Lit Sup, (3 Nov. 1961), 782.
A more complete account of Sergei Tolstoy's discussion
of his father's feelings toward music is in FV, 131-168.
Excerpts from his reminiscences appear in RLTC, 106-120.

28 Tolstoy, Sofia. The Autobiography of Countess Sophie Tolstoi.
Trans. by S. Koteliansky and L. Woolf. London: Hogarth,
1922; 126p. Written three years after Tolstoy's death, the
autobiography of his wife presents information on family,
friends, and visitors as well as on his literary works.
Also recounted is her trying relationship with Tolstoy after
his turn to religion and prophecy, especially because of his
views on property and other material wealth and to the
crowd of "strangers" that came to surround him at Yasnaya
Polyana, a group whose values and presence she could not
tolerate. Reviewed in:
Nation, 116 (7 Feb. 1923), 155, by Nathan Asch.
N Y Times, (12 Nov. 1922), 3, by Austin Hay.
N Y Trib Bk R, (5 Nov. 1922), 9, by Burton Rascoe.
Spectator, 129 (12 Aug. 1922), 214.
Times Lit Sup, (13 July 1922), 456.

29 Tolstoy, Sofia. The Countess Tolstoy's Later Diary, 1891-1897.
Trans. and intro. by Alexander Werth. Freeport, N. Y. :

Books for Libraries Press, 1971 (reprint of 1929 publication); 267p. An irregularly-kept diary by Tolstoy's wife in which her increasing dissatisfaction with her marriage becomes apparent. Although some glimpses of happy family life are visible, most frequently chronicled are the disputes between her and Tolstoy who is criticized for being "vain, hypocritical, and a poor father." Reviewed in:
Sat R Lit, 6 (28 June 1930), 1155.
Spectator, 143 (12 Oct. 1929), 500.
Times Lit Sup, (17 Oct. 1929), 815.
Also see Appendix II of Aylmer Maude's Life of Tolstoy vol. II, The Later Years.

30 Tolstoy, Sofia. The Diary of Tolstoy's Wife, 1860-1891. Trans. by Alexander Werth. London: Gollancz, 1928; 272p. Although there are only 233 entries for a span of 28 years, the early diary of Tolstoy's wife provides much information and insight into his personality, work, friends, and philosophy as well as into their marital relationship. Many of the later entries relating to their marriage illustrate her growing dissatisfaction with Tolstoy's views on the value of a simple, nonmaterial style of life and her consequent frustration over no longer being able to share in his life as she had done in the early years of their relationship. Reviewed in:
Bos Trans, (9 March 1929), 3, by Nathan H. Dole.
Nation, 129 (3 July 1929), 19, by Dorothy Brewster.
Nat and Ath, 44 (24 Nov. 1928), 294, by Leonard Woolf.
New Republic, 54 (27 Feb. 1929), 49, by Rose Strunsky.
N Y Evening P, (16 March 1929), 11, by Clifton Fadiman.
N Y Times, (28 Oct. 1928), 1, Avrahm Yarmolinsky.
Outlook, 151, (9 Jan. 1929), 73, by Ernest Boyd.
Sat R Lit, 5 (9 March 1929), 749, by Manya Gordon.
Spectator, 141 (24 Nov., 1928), 791.
Times Lit Sup, (20 Dec. 1928), 998.

31 Tolstoy, Sofia. The Final Struggle, Being Countess Tolstoy's Diary for 1910. Intros. by Aylmer Maude and Sergei Tolstoy. New York: Oxford, 1936; 399p. Two lengthy introductions provide historical background and analysis of the diary of Tolstoy's wife in the last year of his life. Interspersed with the Countess' entries are parallel entries from Tolstoy's diary thereby allowing comparison of their respective reflections on conversations and episodes from their daily lives. Most obvious are Tolstoy's pangs of conscience over having to be part of the worldly affairs that so concerned his wife, and his wife's negative reaction to his philosophy as well as her concern for the poor state of their relationship. Excerpts in RLTC, 37-40, 46-93. Reviewed in:

Bos Trans, (30 Jan. 1937), 2, by G. Richards.
Christian Sci M, (30 Dec. 1936), 10, by V. S. Pritch-
    ett.
Commonweal, 25 (12 Feb. 1937), 447, by C. Radziwill.
Forum, 97 (March 1937), 160, by M. Calum.
Nation, 144 (6 March 1937), 272, by A. Marburg.
New Republic, 90 (3 March 1937), 116, by D. Dudley.
New St and Na, 12 (14 Nov. 1936), 774, by D. Garnett.
N Y Times, (31 Jan. 1937), 8, by Alexander Nazaroff.
Sat R Lit, 15 (30 Jan. 1937), 12, by M. Gordon.
Times Lit Sup, (14 Nov. 1936), 923.

32 Tolstoy, Tatiana [married name, Sukhotin]. The Tolstoy Home.
    Trans. by Alec Brown. New York: AMS, 1966 (reprint
    of 1906 publication); 325p. Daily life and routine at Yasnaya
    Polyana are described, by Tolstoy's eldest daughter, as
    noted in her diary. Impressions of the many visitors to
    Tolstoy are given, with particular attention to his disciples.
    In addition to the large amount of information presented on
    family affairs and relations, the philosophy and work of
    Tolstoy is the focus of numerous entries. Reviewed in:
    ASEER, 10, no. 4 (1951), 312, by Peter Rudy.
    Commonweal, 54 (27 April 1951), 66, by John Cournos.
    Nation, 172 (7 April 1951), 327, by A. Marburg.
    N Y Herald Trib Bk R, (27 May 1951), 10, Joshua
        Kunitz.
    N Y Times, (25 March 1951), 5, by E. J. Simmons.
    Sat R Lit, 34 (13 June 1951), 13, by Janko Lavrin.
    Time, 57 (9 April 1951), 114.
    Times Lit Sup, (1 Dec. 1950), 760.

ESSAYS AND CHAPTERS from general works

33 Alexeyev, V. I. "Talks with Tolstoy" in TLFLR, 298-304. An
    account, by the tutor (1877-1881) of Tolstoy's children, of
    how Tolstoy came to him for help because he was "falling
    to temptation" in reference to the servants' cook, Domna.
    Also discussed is the unrelated subject of Tolstoy's sense
    of humor.

34 Bernstein, Herman. "Leo Tolstoy" in Celebrities of Our Time.
    Freeport, N. Y.: Books for Libraries Press, 1968 (reprint
    of 1924 publication); 3-16. Based on conversations that
    took place at Yasnaya Polyana, impressions of Tolstoy and
    his various philosophic beliefs are presented. Included is
    a letter to Bernstein from Chertkov who criticized the au-
    thor's first analysis of Tolstoy's personality and doctrine.
    Also in With Master Minds: Interviews. New York: Uni-
    versal Series Co. , 1913; 7-25.

35 Beveridge, Albert J. "Three Russians of World Fame" in The
    Russian Advance. New York: Harper and Brothers, 1904;

426-462. On the basis of a visit to Yasnaya Polyana, Tolstoy's personality is described and his words on religion
and contemporary Russian statesman repeated. Tolstoy is
regarded as being unpopular with Russian liberals and con-
servatives alike because of his fanatical devotion to impractical political and religious beliefs. His influence,
nevertheless, is considered to be widespread as is the es-
teem with which he is held in Russia as an artist and a
man, if not a philosopher.

36 Biancolli, Louis L. "Leo Tolstoy: An American Reformer
Stoutly Resists the Doctrine of Non-resistance in the Country Place of a Great Pacifist" in The Book of Great Conversations: Edited from Historical Sources in Dramatic
Form and with Biographical Sketches (New York: Simon &
Schuster, 1948; 419-427). A reproduction of an 1886 conversation between Tolstoy and George Kennan on the issue
of non-resistance to evil. Preceding the account of the
conversation, Tolstoy's pacifist beliefs are summarized and
the means by which Kennan came to meet with him at Yasnaya Polyana are described. Recounted, essentially, is
Kennan's contention that violent intervention is necessary in
certain circumstances (a case of abuse in a Siberian prison
is cited) if the world is ever to advance to a more humane
level; and Tolstoy's response that protests must be made
against all varieties of inhumanity but violence must be
avoided.

37 Bunin, Ivan A. "Leo Tolstoy" in Memoirs and Portraits. Garden City, N. Y.: Doubleday, 1951; 17-30. Bunin's early
infatuation with all that Tolstoy stood for, and his consequent
attempts at becoming a "Tolstoyan" are noted before his
pilgrimage to Yasnaya Polyana is recollected. The impression which Tolstoy made on him then and on several other
occasions is sketchily discussed. Anecdote oriented, there
is no consideration of the substance of Tolstoy's philosophy
or works.

38 Chaikovsky, P. I. "Extracts from a Diary" in RLTC, 289-290.
Presented is the entry for July 1, 1886, in the diary of
Tchaikovsky, the Russian composer, in which is described
his initial meeting with Tolstoy. The powerful impression
made on him by Tolstoy is noted, but the focus of the entry
is Tolstoy's positive and highly emotional reaction to the
music of Tchaikovsky.

39 Chekhov, Anton. "Letters to Alexei Suvorin" in LTCA, 96-100.
In a series of four letters, written between 1888 and 1894,
Chekhov discusses Tolstoy's philosophy and several of his
works of fiction. Generally indicated is his declining respect for Tolstoy because of disenchantment with his views
on women, medicine, and the progress of civilization.

40 Chekhov, Anton. "Letter to Mikhail Menshikov" in LCTA, 100-
    101. In a 1900 letter, Chekhov briefly touches upon the
    general importance of Tolstoy to him and all of Russian
    literature: "without him the literary world would be a flock
    without a shepherd. " However, when Chekhov turns to
    Tolstoy's most recent creation, he criticizes Resurrection
    for its narrow approach to criminology and theology.

41 Cockerell, Sydney. "Count Leo Tolstoy" in Friends of a Life-
    time, ed. by Viola Meynell. London: Cape, 1940; 78-86.
    On the basis of a July 12, 1903, visit to Yasnaya Polyana,
    Tolstoy's work with the persecuted religious sect "the
    Doukhobors" and with common folk of his district is dis-
    cussed as is the opposition that his activities have aroused
    from both church and state. Tolstoy's personality and
    tastes are also noted and his opinion of Dickens and Ruskin
    is recollected.

42 Creelman, James. "The Avatar of Count Tolstoy" in On the
    Great Highway. Boston: Lothrop, 1901; 120-140. A brief
    account of the evolution of Tolstoy's philosophy precedes a
    reproduction of a conversation on the purpose of The Kreut-
    zer Sonata in which Tolstoy stated his intent was to launch
    a "protest against animality and make an appeal for the
    Christianity of Christ. "

43 Creelman, James. "Tolstoy and His People" in On the Great
    Highway, 141-156. Recounted is Tolstoy's work with local
    peasants as an example of his pursuit of a life consistent
    with his philosophical views. Also noted is his portrayal
    of the peasant in his works of fiction. As an afterthought,
    a protest is made against his excommunication from the
    Orthodox Church, claiming that Tolstoy is a classic exam-
    ple of a true Christian.

44 Davydov, Vladimir. "From the Reminiscences of an Actor" in
    RLTC, 324-326. An account of the Russian actor's meeting
    with Tolstoy to ask permission to give a public reading of
    his drama The Power of Darkness. Davydov's reading of
    several of the play's scenes and Tolstoy's tearful reaction
    are presented as is Tolstoy's own reading of a scene.

45 Davydov, Nikolai V. "Lev Nikolayevich Tolstoi" in RLTC, 172-
    178. A discussion, by the lawyer and friend of Tolstoy,
    of Tolstoy's thorough research of the Russian legal system
    in preparation for his writing of Resurrection. Also pre-
    sented is how Davydov influenced him in writing three of
    his plays: The Power of Darkness, The Fruits of the En-
    lightenment, and The Living Corpse.

46 Fet, Afanasy A. "Reminiscences" in RLTC, 141-143. A de-
    scription, by the Russian poet and friend of Tolstoy, of a
    hunting episode in which Tolstoy was mauled by a bear.

47 Fülöp-Miller, Rene. New Light on Tolstoy: Literary Frag-
    ments, Letters, and Reminiscences Not Previously Pub-
    lished. New York: Harrap, 1931; 330p, illus. A collec-
    tion of Tolstoy's posthumous papers, whose publication was
    personally authorized by Sofia Tolstoy, precedes four es-
    says by friends and relatives. The essays are annotated
    individually in this section.

48 Ganz, Hugo. "A Visit to Count Tolstoi" in The Downfall of
    Russia: Under the Surface in the Land of Riddles. London:
    Hodder and Stoughton, 1905; 274-320. An account of the
    highly favorable impression made on Ganz by Tolstoy's ap-
    pearance and manner during his visit to Yasnaya Polyana
    precedes a restating of Tolstoy's words to him on a variety
    of subjects including war, peasants, Doukhobors, and Tol-
    stoy's opinions of Kant, Goethe, Heine, Schiller, Nietzsche,
    and Shakespeare. This essay also appeared in Ganz's The
    Land of Riddles, Russia of Today, 285-331.

49 Gilyarovsky, V. A. "Men of Starogladoskaya" in RLTC, 152-
    160. A description of Tolstoy's stay in the Caucasus as
    told to Gilyarovsky, a Russian writer, by a man who lived
    in the cossack village of Starogladoskaya at the same time
    as Tolstoy. Some insight is provided into Tolstoy's writing
    of The Cossacks.

50 Gintsburg, Ilya Y. "Memories of the Past" in RLTC, 327-338.
    An account of Gintsburg's visit to Yasnaya Polyana to sculp-
    ture a bust of Tolstoy, and Tolstoy's reaction to the condi-
    tions associated with posing for him and for Repin who was
    working on a painting of Tolstoy. His views on art, espe-
    cially sculptoring, and on Shakespeare are noted as is his
    discussion of his work on Resurrection Hadji Murat.

51 Gorki, Maxim. "Lev Tolstoi" in Literary Portraits. Moscow:
    Foreign Language Publishing House, 1958; 9-102. Pre-
    sented are fragmentary notes written by Gorky while in the
    Crimea at the same time as Tolstoy who was recovering
    from a serious illness. The subjects related include Tol-
    stoy's views on religion, science, women, romanticism,
    nature, and a variety of individuals all of which reveal much
    about him. Also included is an unfinished letter written by
    Gorky under the influence of Tolstoy's 1910 flight and death
    in which Gorky reacts negatively to Tolstoy's flight as a
    plea for martyrdom but eulogizes him when his flight leads
    to death.
        Gorky's widely acclaimed notes of Tolstoy have also
    been published under the following titles: On Literature
    (Seattle: University of Washington Press, 1973), 292-348;
    Reminiscences of Tolstoy, Chekhov and Andreyev (London:
    Hogarth, 1968 [reprint of 1934 publication]), 13-84; His
    Nameless Love (Moscow: Progress Publishers, 1974); and
    in RLTC, 371-432.

52 Gusev, Nikolai N. "Lev Tolstoi's Daily Regime" in RLTC, 230-234. Discussed by Tolstoy's private secretary are the details of a typical day in the 1907-1910 period of his life. The normal pattern is seen as: morning walk, mail reading, coffee, work in study until lunch, reception of visitors, afternoon walk or ride, nap, dinner, light work in study, chess, and to bed by 11:00.

53 Hapgood, Isabel F. "Count Tolstoy at Home" in Russian Rambles, 148-202. A detailed account of a trip to Yasnaya Polyana dealing with Tolstoy's personality, family life and philosophy. Numerous small anecdotes involving Tolstoy are also related.

54 Hapgood, Isabel F. "A Stroll in Moscow with Count Tolstoy" in Russian Rambles. New York: Arno Press, 1970 (reprint of 1895 publication); 134-147. Conversations and activities with Tolstoy while visiting him in Moscow are recollected. Particularly noted is the attention that his peasant dress attracted as well as his views on philanthropy. Tolstoy's general philosophy is defended ("he is not crazy") and he is presented as an earnest and provocative thinker.

55 Koni, Anatoly F. "Lev Nikolayevich Tolstoi" in RLTC, 179-189. A recollection, by the Russian lawyer, of an 1887 visit to Yasnaya Polyana during which Tolstoy presented his views on such subjects as peasants, family happiness, and literary critics. Most detail is provided on their discussion of a legal case which eventually served as the source for Tolstoy's novel Resurrection.

56 Korolenko, Vladimir G. "The Great Pilgrim: Three Encounters with L. N. Tolstoi" in RLTC, 278-288. Reminiscences, by the Russian writer, of meetings with Tolstoy in 1886, 1902 and 1910, and how Tolstoy appeared to him as three different though related individuals. Following this generalization, information is only presented on the first meeting (the manuscript was never completed) in which the question of Tolstoy contributing an article to Russkaya Misl was discussed.

57 Kramskoi, Ivan N. "Letter to P. M. Tretyakov" in RLTC, 275-77. An 1873 account, by the Russian artist, of a conversation with Tolstoy concerning Kramskoi's seeking permission to paint Tolstoy. The conditions imposed by Tolstoy are noted, especially his asserting his right to destroy the painting if he did not like it.

58 Kurpin, Alexander I. "My Meeting with Tolstoi on the Steamboat 'St. Nicholas'" in RLTC, 357-361. A recollection, by the Russian novelist, of his first meeting of Tolstoy in which is described Tolstoy's effect on various passengers (crew, common people, foreigners) on the steamboat St. Nicholas.

59 Lopatin, Vladimir M.   "Stage Reminiscences" in RLTC, 399-
     404.   A discussion of the Russian lawyer and actor's visit
     to Yasnaya Polyana, in 1889, to take part in an amateur
     production of Fruits of Enlightenment.   Tolstoy's highly
     positive reaction to Lopatin's performance is recounted as
     are Tolstoy's views on art, especially his negative assess-
     ment of Shakespeare.

60 Makovitsky, Dusan P. et al.   "The Last Illness and Death of
     Lev Nikolayevich Tolstoi" in RLTC, 258-261.   An account,
     by three attending physicians, of the details of Tolstoy's
     deterioration in health in the week preceding his death.   In
     addition to the symptoms of his ailment, Tolstoy's last
     words and actions are noted.

61 Makovistsky, Dusan P.   "Lev Nikolayevich's Departure from
     Yasnaya Polyana" in RLTC, 253-258.   A description, by
     Tolstoy's private physician, of the details surrounding Tol-
     stoy's 1910 flight from home.   The arrangements for trans-
     portation, his frame of mind on the day of departure, and
     his relief after departure are all discussed.

62 Makovitsky, Dusan P.   "Tolstoy and the Revolution of 1905" in
     TLFLR, 308-330.   Extracts from the diary of Tolstoy's
     physician in which Tolstoy's negative reaction to the violence
     of the 1905 revolution in Russia and his blaming "liberal
     and revolutionary speeches" for inciting simple folk to rebel
     are recounted.   His views on the need for a simple, peace-
     ful society with minimal government are also recollected.

63 Maude, Aylmer.   "Leo Tolstoy" in TP, 1-31.   A survey, by
     Tolstoy's friend and biographer, of the highlights of his life
     with emphasis on his spiritual awakening and the value of
     that which he came to preach.   Also published in pamphlet
     form under the same title by Albert Broadbent of Manchester
     in July, 1900.

64 Maude, Aylmer.   "Talks with Tolstoy" in TP, 32-65.   An ac-
     count of a conversation with Tolstoy that developed over
     Maude's questioning him on the contradiction between his
     ideas and lifestyle.   Also included is a disconnected series
     of Tolstoy's views on various authors and books.

65 Mechnikov, Ilya I.   "A Day with Tolstoi in Yasnaya Polyana" in
     RLTC, 235-239.   A recollection, by the Russian bacteri-
     ologist, of a 1909 visit to Tolstoy in which Tolstoy pre-
     sented his views on science, religion, pacificism and
     Goethe.

66 Morozov, Vaily S.   "Recollections of a Pupil of the Yasnaya
     Polyana School" in RLTC, 144-151.   A description, by his
     favorite student, of Tolstoy as a teacher.   Tolstoy's en-
     thusiasm for education is established, and his inspiring of

students with tales of war and hunting as well as by his
obvious love for them as individuals is related.

67   Nagorny, Vera.   "The Original of Natasha in War and Peace"
     in FV, 25-70.   A discussion by Tolstoy's niece, of his
     writing of War and Peace in general and the source for the
     character Natasha in particular.   Also provided is insight
     into Tolstoy's home situation at the time of his writing the
     novel.

68   Nemirovich-Danchenko, V. I.   "Reminiscences of Tolstoi" in
     RLTC, 351-356.   An account, by the Russian playwright
     and director, of a conversation in which Tolstoy presented
     his opinion of Ibsen, whose talent he questioned, and
     Chekhov, whose works he commended.   Also noted is the
     author's staging of The Power of Darkness, and Tolstoy's
     reaction to the production.

69   Norman, Henry.   "Count Tolstoi at Home and Abroad" in All
     the Russias: Travels and Studies in Contemporary European
     Russia, Finland, Siberia, the Caucasus, and Central Asia.
     New York: Scribner's, 1904; 47-63.   Based on a 1901
     visit to Yasnaya Polyana, Tolstoy's estate and work habits
     are described before a discussion of his religious views is
     presented including his excommunication from the Russian
     Orthodox Church.   Tolstoy's general philosophy is sum-
     marized and labeled "nihilistic" but no threat to the system
     since he is considered to be a mere dreamer.

70   Repin, Ilya.   "Count Lev Nikolayevich Tolstoi: Personal Im-
     pressions and Reminiscences" in RLTC, 290-301.   An ac-
     count, by the Russian painter, of Tolstoy's daily routine
     and passion for physical labor precedes numerous anecdotes
     illustrating the flavor, depth and sincerity of Tolstoy's
     thinking.   Additionally discussed are his contacts with
     peasants.

71   Repin, Ilya.   "Tolstoy and the Peasants" in TLFLR, 291-293.
     Presented is a short description of several unpleasant ex-
     periences that Tolstoy had with peasants including one in
     which Tolstoy was urged by a peasant "to die" and was
     called a "bloodsucker. "

72   Repin, Ilya.   "Tolstoy as I Knew Him" in RLTC, 302-323.   A
     discussion of conversations with Tolstoy from 1880 to 1907
     dealing with the circumstances and events of his life rather
     than his philosophy.   Depicted is Tolstoy's simple life style,
     work in the fields, his homes in Moscow and at Yasnaya
     Polyana, work in the famine in the early 1890's, and his
     horsemanship as an example of his youthful vigor.

73   Rusanov, Gavriil A.   "Visit to Yasnay Polyana" in RLTC, 161-
     171.   The views of Tolstoy on various authors are dis-

cussed as presented in an 1883 conversation with Rusanov.
Noted are Shchedrin (especially praised), Shakespeare,
Dostoevsky, Goncharov, Lermontov, and Gogol.

74 Schuyler, Eugene. "Count Leo Tolstoy Twenty Years Ago" in
Selected Essays. New York: Scribner's, 1901; 205-300.
Based on a 1868 visit to Yasnaya Polyana and subsequent
conversations, Tolstoy's views on War and Peace, which
he was then writing, are recollected, with most attention
given to the sources for his characters. Also noted is his
attitude toward peasants as well as his pedagogical views.
Also in Scribner's M, 5 (1889), 537-552; 6 (1889), 732-747.

75 Stakhovich, Sofya. "Some Sayings of Tolstoy" in FV, 123-130.
A short list of Tolstoy's phrases on a variety of subjects
is presented with no analysis by the author.

76 Stanislavsky, Konstantin S. "I Make the Acquaintance of Tolstoi" in RLTC, 345-350. An account of the famous stage
director's 1893 meeting of Tolstoy at Davydov's home.
Tolstoy's impressive personal appearance is noted and his
interest in an Ostrovsky play is discussed. Also recollected are his words about his own play, The Power of
Darkness, as well as his anti-war views. Also in his My
Life in Art. Boston: Little, Brown, 1924; 217-225.

77 Stead, William T. "Count Tolstoi and His Gospel" in Truth
About Russia. London: Cassell, 1888; 393-457. On the
basis of a one-week stay at Yasnaya Polyana, Stead describes Tolstoy's routine, estate, and family, particularly
his relationship with his wife. Also discussed, in a favorable light, is Tolstoy's philosophy of non-resistance as well
as his religious beliefs in general with a lengthy discussion
of his interpretation of Christ and his teachings. Additional
information is given on his views on celibacy, peasants,
temperance, property, and the need for social reform in
Russia.

78 Stevens, Thomas. "With Count Tolstoi" in Through Russia on
a Mustang. London: Cassell, 1891 (reprinted in 1970 by
Arno); 92-115. Recollections of an 1890 conversation with
Tolstoy in which was discussed such subjects as religion,
non-resistance, property, peasants, education, and the nature of American government. Also recounted are the many
"pilgrims" who visited Yasnaya Polyana.

79 Tolstoy, Alexandra. "Tolstoy's Home Leaving and Death" in
FV, 169-218. A detailed account of the daily life of Tol-
stoy from the time he left home until his death at Astapovo.
No information of substance is given as to the reasons for
Tolstoy's flight from his family, but rather his thoughts and
actions in his last days are presented.

80 Tolstoy, Sergius. "Music in Tolstoy's Life" in FV, 131-161.
Tolstoy's intense feeling for music is discussed by his son
as is how music influenced Tolstoy's life and how he, in
turn, analyzed music as an art form.

81 Tolstoy, Sergius. "Tolstoy's Humor" in FV, 109-122. In spite
of his "well-developed sense of humor," it is claimed that
Tolstoy refrained from use of humor in his works for fear
of seeming to have a frivolous attitude toward his subject.
Several examples of his humor displayed in conversations
are recollected.

82 Tolstoy, Sofya. "Tolstoy at Work" in TLFLR, 294-97. An account is given, by Tolstoy's wife, of his passion for labor
and of how she assisted him by copying his notes for some
of his works of fiction. Tolstoy's moods of depression
when not engrossed in a project of some type are also
noted.

83 Tolstoy, Tatiana [married name, Sukhotin]. "How My Father
and I Dealt with the Land Question" in FV, 87-108. A description, by Tolstoy's daughter, of how her father deplored
the excessive property taxes levied by the government on
the peasants. Her disposal of the estate which she inherited
is also discussed.

84 Velichkina, Vera. "With Lev Nikolayevich during the Famine"
in RLTC, 190-218. A recollection, by a Russian physician
who worked with Tolstoy in the 1892 famine, of Tolstoy's
work with the peasants during this national crisis. His
philosophy of aid to the peasants is discussed as are the
circumstances associated with the famine.

85 Veresayev, V. V. "Lev Tolstoi" in RLTC, 362-370. An account, by the Russian author and critic, of a first meeting
with Tolstoy and subsequent conversations. Illustrated are
Tolstoy's views on the importance of striving toward self-
perfection and on the happiness which love brings. Also
related is his response to Veresayev's interpretation of the
epigraph of Anna Karenina.

86 White, Andrew D. "Walks and Talks with Tolstoi" in Discovery
of Europe: The Story of an American Experience in the
Old World, ed. P. Rahv. Boston: Houghton Mifflin, 1947;
359-383. A recollection of conversations with Tolstoy on
such subjects as the condition of the Russian peasants,
women, Quakers, property, Old Believers, and religion.
Tolstoy is criticized for the extremity of his views which,
in turn, is linked to the negative effect of the "Russian environment. "

87 Yelpatyevsky, Sergei Y. "Reminiscences of Lev Nikolayevich
Tolstoi" in RLTC, 219-229. A discussion, by the Russian

physician, of his contact with Tolstoy during the serious illness of the latter while at Gaspara. The nature of his illness is discussed and conversations recollected on Tolstoy's dislike for modern medicine and his ravenous desire for physical labor. Also noted are his views on Chekhov and his love for the writings of Dickens.

PERIODICAL ARTICLES

88 Addams, Jane. "A Visit to Tolstoy," McClure's, 36 (Jan. 1911), 295-302. Also in Munsey's, no. 4 (May 1915).

89 Baeza, Richard. "Talks with Tolstoi," Living Age, 319 (1923), 70-75, 127-132.

90 Bentzon, T. "A Recent Interview with Tolstoy," Critic, 41 (Dec. 1902), 570-74. Also in RRs, 26 (1902), 481-82.

91 Bobrinskoy, Alexis. "Tolstoy Seen through the Eyes of a Child: Personal Reminiscences," Listener, 65 (5 Jan. 1961), 32-33, illus.

92 Bulgakov, Valentin F. "New Tolstoyana," Living Age, 312 (31 Oct. 1922), 92-97, 155-161. Conversations between Bulgakov and Tolstoy concerning personal information, habits, and family life. Translated from a two-part article in Rassegna Italiana, Part I (14 Jan. 1922), Part II (21 Jan. 1922).

93 Bulgakov, Valentin F. "Tolstoy in the Last Year of His Life," Harper's B, 104 (Jan. 1971), 58-61. Excerpt from his The Last Year of Leo Tolstoy.

94 Bunin, Ivan A. "My Meetings with Tolstoy," Contemp R, 145 (May 1934), 591-599.

95 Bunin, Ivan A. "My Reminiscences of Tolstoy," Dial, 83 (Oct. 1927), 271-282.

96 Butler, E. M. "Rilke and Tolstoy: Three Versions of the Russian Visit," Mod Lang R, 35 (Oct. 1940), 494-505.

97 Calderon, George L. "A Call on Tolstoi," Lit W, 28 (1897), 160-161.

98 "Chat about Tolstoy," Critic, 34 (Jan. 1899), 10-11. Tolstoy's ideas and views are presented by way of quotes from Halperin-Kaminsky.

99 Cockerell, Sir Sydney; Sir Shane Leslie, Leo Rabeneck, and Alexandra Tolstoy. "Living Memoirs of Tolstoy: Symposium on the Russian Novelist," Listener, (Dec. 1915), 1099-1011, illus.

100   "Count Tolstoi Interviewed," W Lit, 1 (Apr. 1892), 10.

101   Creelman, James.   "Tolstoy's Conversation with an American, "
      Bruno's R, 1, no. 1 (Nov. 1920), 8-10.

102   Creelman, James.   "Visit to Tolstoy, " Harper's W, 36 (16
      Apr. 1892), 380.

103   Crosby, Ernest H. "A Conversation with Ernest H. Crosby
      Embodying Personal Impressions of Count Tolstoy as Phi-
      losopher, Prophet and Man, " Arena, 25 (1901), 429-439.

104   Crosby, Ernest H.   "Count Tolstoy at Home, " Leslie's W, 87
      (1898), 374.

105   Crosby, Ernest H.   "Tolstoy's Answer to the Riddle of Life:
      An American Admirer of Tolstoy, " Open Court, 17 (Dec.
      1903), 708-712.

106   Crosby, Ernest H.   "Two Days with Count Tolstoy, " Progres
      R, 2 (Aug. 1897), 407-422.

107   Evans, E. E.   "A Nearer View of Count L. Tolstoi, " Open
      Court, 16 (July 1902), 396-414.   A discussion of Anna
      Seuron's (Governess at Yasnaya Polyana) insights into the
      daily life of Tolstoy.   For a response see A. Maude,
      "Misinterpretation of Tolstoy, " Open Court, 16 (1902),
      590-601.

108   Everling, S. N.   "Three Evenings with Count Leo Tolstoy, "
      Nineteenth Cent, 93, no. 555 (May 1923), 786-792 and 93,
      no. 556 (June 1923), 841-849.   Recollections of meetings
      with Tolstoy and a few close friends.   The many visitors
      and pilgrims wanting to see Tolstoy are discussed along
      with comments on several foreign writers.

109   George, Henry, Jr.   "Tolstoy in the Twilight, " W Work, 18
      (Oct. 1909), 12144-12154.   Henry George, Jr. , comments
      on his visit to Yasnaya Polyana where Tolstoy expressed
      support of Henry George Sr. 's views.   The Tolstoy family
      and their love of music is mentioned.

110   George, Henry, Jr.   "A Visit to Tolstoy, " W Work, 15 (Feb.
      1910), 251-261.

111   Gilder, Jeanette Leonard.   "Tolstoi.   How the Russian Novelist
      Lives and Works, " Critic, 34 (1899), 417-423.

112   Gorki, Maxim.   "Notes on Tolstoi and Other Recollections, "
      Dial, 78 (1925), 96-106.   Translated from the Russian by
      William A. Drake and Max Stetsky.

113   Gorki, Maxim.   "Reminiscences of Tolstoi.   A Letter, " Lon
      Merc, 2 (1920), 304-315.   Translated by S. Koteliansky

and L. Woolf. For annotation see Gorki, Maxim, "Lev Tolstoi" in Literary Portraits, Section I, essays.

114 Gorky, Maxim. "Tolstoy's Wife," Listener, 53 (May 1955), 839-840. A previously unpublished fragment by Gorky on Tolstoy's wife.

115 "Gorky on Tolstoy," Two Worlds M, 2, no. 2 (Jan. 1927), 170.

116 Helbig, Nadine. "Tolstoy at Sixty," Bookman, 32, no. 5 (Jan. 1911), 467-473. A visit to Tolstoy in 1888 prompts a discussion of his appearance, his wife, and love of music.

117 Ilyin, E. K. "Under a Haystack: A Meeting with Tolstoi," Lon Merc, 3, no. 12 (1956), 20-25.

118 "Interview with Tolstoi," Outlook, 66 (Dec. 1900), 828-835. A general discussion of Tolstoy of his religious and philosophical ideas.

119 Islavin, L. V. "Tolstoy's Letters to His Cousin," Lon Merc, 15, no. 86 (Dec. 1926), 148-156.

120 Kennan, George. "A Visit to Count Tolstoi," Cent M, n. s. 12 (June 1887), 252-265. The main theme of the discussion is on Tolstoy's views on social conditions; the possibility of his arrest because of these ideas is mentioned. Also in Living Age, 194 (23 July 1892), 210-217.

121 Kenworthy, John C. "Thoughts on a Recent Visit to Tolstoy," St George, 3 (1900), 191-193.

122 Kenworthy, John C. "A Visit to Count Tolstoy," Humane R, 1 (Oct. 1900), 262-267.

123 Kuskova, Yekaterina D. "The Tolstoy Life Drama: A Daughter's Story," Living Age, 325 (6 June 1925), 506-510. During an interview with Alexandra Tolstoy family affairs are discussed--in particular, Tolstoy's rift with his wife and his flight from Yasnaya Polyana.

124 Lodian, L. "Irrigation in Russia: A Professional Visit to the Tolstoi Domain near Tula," Irrigation Age, 13 (1899), 239-243.

125 Lodian, L. "The Russian Victor Hugo Seen among His Books," Book-seller, 16 (1899), 12-14.

126 MacQueen, Peter. "Russia's Gray Giant Talks for the National," National M, 14 (1901), 579-584.

127 MacQueen, Peter. "Tolstoy on America," Leslie's M, 52, no. 610 (Oct. 1901), 610-614, illus.

128   Maude, Aylmer. "Leo Tolstoy," Contemp R, 134 (Sept. 1928),
      321-328. A discussion of Tolstoy's personality and a
      criticism of his political views, especially on non-resist-
      ance.

129   Maude, Aylmer. "Leo Tolstoy," Rus R, 1, No. 1 (1912), 27-
      31.

130   Maude, Aylmer. "The Many-Sided Tolstoy," Listener, (4 Jan.
      1933), 2-4, 20, illus.

131   Maude, Aylmer. "Misinterpretation of Tolstoy," Open Court,
      16 (1902), 590-601. An attack on E. Evans' positive re-
      view of Seuron's writings on Tolstoy on the grounds that
      her testimony has been discredited by the entire Tolstoy
      family. See Evans, E. E. "A Nearer View of Count Leo
      Tolstoi," Open Court, 16 (July 1902), 396-414.

132   Maude, Aylmer. "My Last Visit to Tolstoy," Bookman, 24
      (Oct. 1906), 108-114.

133   Maude, Aylmer. "Recollections of Tolstoy," Slavonic R, 7
      (Jan. 1929), 475-481. A general discussion of Tolstoy's
      ideas on art, religion, and literature. Maude's relation-
      ship with Tolstoy is also mentioned.

134   Maude, Aylmer. "A Talk with Miss Jane Addams and Leo
      Tolstoy," Humane R, 3 (Oct. 1902), 203-218.

135   Maude, Aylmer. "Talks with Tolstoy," New Cent R, 7 (May
      1900), 404-418. Tolstoy's views on books and writers
      are discussed based on conversations with Tolstoy.
      Kropotkin and Henry George are among the writers men-
      tioned.

136   Maude, Aylmer. "Tolstoy's Character," Queens Q, 40 (Nov.
      1933), 530-540.

137   Maude, Louise. "Tolstoy in 1906," Bookman, 24 (Oct. 1906),
      104-107. A description of family life and the Tolstoy
      children along with a discussion of Tolstoy's views on so-
      cial reform.

138   Nagoroff, A. "New Tolstoy Diary," Sat R Lit, 3 (4 Dec.
      1926), 386.

139   Narodny, Ivan. "Tolstoy: Another View," Outlook, 92 (12
      June 1909), 380-382.

140   Narodny, Ivan. "Tolstoy: by Ivan Narodny," Craftsman, 19,
      no. 4 (Jan. 1911), 323-329. A positive assessment of
      Tolstoy based on personal contact with the novelist.

141   Nicchia, A.   "My Last Memory of Tolstoy," Craftsman, 4
      (Apr. 1903), 45-48.

142   Norman, H.   "Tolstoy at Home," Scrib M, 28 (1900), 299-302.

143   Pasternak, Leonid.   "My Meeting with Tolstoy," Rus R, 19
      (Apr. 1960), 122-131.

144   Pasternak, Leonid.   "Working with Tolstoy," Adam, no.'s
      284-6 (1960), 23-31.

145   Rice, R.   "Profiles: From Yasnaya Polyana to Valley Cot-
      tage," New Yorker, 28 (15 Mar. 1952), 34-47 and 28 (22
      Mar. 1952), 36-59.   A discussion of the life of Alexandra
      Tolstoy and her relationship with her father.

146   Robinson, G. W.   "A Meeting with Tolstoy," Good Words, 45
      (1904), 281-283.

147   Schuyler, E.   "Count Tolstoi Twenty Years Ago, Scrib M, 5
      (May 1889), 537-552 and 6 (June 1889), 732-747.   Also in
      his Selected Essays, 207-299.

148   Steiner, Edward.   "Interview with Tolstoi," Outlook, 66 (1 Dec.
      1900), 828-835.

149   Steiner, Edward.   "A Pilgrimage to the Home of the Tolstoys,"
      W Home Com, 31 (Aug. 1904), 12-13.

150   Steiner, Edward.   "Questions I Asked Tolstoi," Christ C, 41
      (13 Nov. 1924), 1469-1471.

151   Steiner, Edward.   "Tolstoy Today," Outlook, 75 (5 Sept. 1903),
      35-42.

152   Steiner, Edward.   "Tolstoy's Marriage and Family Life,"
      Outlook, 75 (3 Oct. 1903), 267-276.

153   Steiner, Edward.   "Visit to Tolstoy's Home," Chaut, 36 (Mar.
      1903), 581-591.

154   Stevens, William B.   "Personal Recollections of Count Tolstoy
      in 1891 and 1892," Proc Ang-Rus Lit Soc, 80 (1917), 32-
      55.

155   Stevens, William B.   "Visit to Count Tolstoy," Cornhill, n. s.
      18 (June 1892), 597-610.   Also in Living Age, 194 (July
      1892), 210-217 with excerpts in RRs, 5 (July 1892), 739-
      740.

156   "Talk about Tolstoy: Interview with Mr. Tchertkoff," Young
      Man, 13 (1899), 80.

157 Tchaikovsky. "Diaries of Tchaikovsky, " Sat R Lit, 28 (13
     Oct. 1945), 17. Tchaikovsky's feelings for Tolstoy are
     discussed.

158 Thompson, Grace A. "A New Englander's Visit to the Tolstoy
     Estate, " New Eng M, n. s. 43 (Feb. 1911), 587-591.

159 Tolstoy, Alexandra. "Memories of My Father, " Yale R, 22
     (Winter 1933), 264-287.

160 Tolstoy, Alexandra. "My Father's Legacy of Wisdom, "
     Coronet, 49 (Nov. 1960), 33-38.

161 Tolstoy, Alexandra. "Tolstoy and Music, " Rus R, 17 (Oct.
     1958), 258-262.

162 Tolstoy, Ilya A. "Memories of My Grandfather, " Rus Stud,
     5, no. 1 (Sept. 1928), 2-5. Also in Mentor, 15 (Oct.
     1927), 36-40.

163 Tolstoy, Ilya L. "Reminiscences of Tolstoy by His Son Count
     Ilya Tolstoy, " Fortn R, n. s. 5 (June 1914), 951-963; n. s.
     6 (Sept. 1914), 497-517. Translated by George Calderon.
     Also in Cent M, n. s. 66 (June 1914), 187-196; n. s. 66
     (July 1914), 418-428; n. s. 66 (Aug. 1914), 561-573.

164 Tolstoy, Sophia A. "Countess Tolstoy's Version of Her Mari-
     tal Woes, " Cur Op, 74 (Jan. 1923), 82-84.

165 Tolstoy, Sophia A. "Tolstoy in the U. S. R. R. , " Ang-Sov J, 7,
     no. 1 (Spring 1946), 33-35, illus. Tolstoy's granddaughter
     discusses his stature in the Soviet Union.

166 Tolstoy, Tatiana [married name, Sukhotin]. "At My Father's
     Side: From the Diary, " Sov Lit, 10 (1975), 112-127.

167 "Tolstoy Manuscripts, " Living Age, 320 (March 1924), 525.
     An account of the content of papers presented to the
     Prague National Museum by D. P. Makovitsky, Tolstoy's
     personal physician.

168 "Tolstoy's Wife in her Diary, " Lit D, 99 (10 Nov. 1928), 28.
     An examination of Tolstoy's wife's jealousy and her dislike
     of his disciples.

169 Van Ness, T. "A Morning with Tolstoi, " Lit W, 20, no. 4
     16 (Feb. 1889), 50. A survey of Tolstoy's views on
     Henry George, Charles Dickens, and Matthew Arnold as
     well as a description of Tolstoy at Yasnaya Polyana.

170 Veresayev, V. "A Day with Tolstoy, " Horizon, 6 (August
     1942), 82-91. A discussion of Tolstoy's fiction based on
     a visit to him by a doctor who was asked to be his per-
     sonal physician.

171   Von Hoffenberg, T.   "A Vacation with Tolstoy, " Living Age,
      319 (17 Nov. 1926), 311-316 and 319 (1 Dec. 1926), 359-
      361.   On the basis of a visit to Yasnaya Polyana, Tol-
      stoy's routine, including his love for physical labor,
      views on music and association with Repin and Strakhov
      are examined.   Translated from Deutsche Allgemeine
      Zeitung (21 Sept. 1926), 9, 16, 23.

172   White, Andrew D.   "Walks and Talks with Tolstoy, " McClure's
      16 (April 1901), 507-518.   Also in Idler, 19 (July 1901),
      479-486; and Philip Rahv, Discovery of Europe, 359-383.

      See also   217, 259, 261, 277, 343, 494, 776, 1216, 1300,
      1302, 1304, 1779, 1790, 1802, 1925.

ADDITIONAL BIOGRAPHICAL INFORMATION

BOOKS

173 Abraham, Gerald. Tolstoy. London: Duckworth, 1935; 144p.,
     bib. 142-144. Designed as an introduction to Tolstoy as
     part of the "Great Lives Series," a general account is
     given of the leading events in his life with only passing
     notice given to his literary work.

174 Asquith, Cynthia. Married to Tolstoy. Boston: Houghton
     Mifflin, 1961; 188p., illus. The relationship between Tol-
     stoy and his wife is analyzed with emphasis on its loving
     nature despite great differences in character, ideas, and
     values. The difficulties that confronted Countess Tolstoy,
     especially those associated with being the wife of a living
     legend, are discussed as are those she encountered as
     supervisor of family and estate alike. Sympathetically
     considered is the crisis she went through at the time of
     Tolstoy's flight from home, and subsequent death, in 1910.
     Reviewed in:
          Christian Sci M, (10 August 1961), 7, by Harold Hob-
               son.
          Guardian, (16 Sept. 1960), 6, by Isabel Qigly.
          N Y Herald Trib Bk R, (13 August 1961), 8, by Vir-
               gillia Peterson.
          New Yorker, 37 (7 Oct. 1961), 211.
          N Y Times, (13 August 1961), 4, by David Magar-
               shack.
          Sat R Lit, 44 (19 August 1961), 14-16, by Ivar Spector
               and Alexandra Tolstoy.
          Spectator, (23 Sept. 1960), 456, by Gilbert Phelps.
          Times Lit Sup, (23 Sept. 1960), 612.

175 Carroll, Sara N. The Search: A Biography of Leo Tolstoy.
     New York: Harper and Row, 1973, 170p., bib. 150-153,
     illus. Designed for beginning readers of Tolstoy, only
     a general survey of Tolstoy's personal life is presented
     with little concern for his literary activities. Events and
     people which influenced his life are discussed as are his
     relations with family, his religious beliefs, and philosophy
     of life, all in a sympathetic vein.

176 Chebotarevskaya, Y. , et al. Tolstoi's Moscow Home. Mos-
       cow: Foreign Language Publishing House, 1957; 88p. ,
       illus. An account, published in conjunction with the Tol-
       stoy Museum, of Tolstoy's experiences and work in Mos-
       cow along with a description of each of the home's parts,
       with most attention being given to his study. Also in-
       cluded is a lengthy list of main dates in his life and work
       while in Moscow.

177 Collis, John S. Marriage and Genius: Strindberg and Tol-
       stoy, Studies in Tragi-Comedy. London: Cassell, 1963;
       ix, 310p. , bib. 295-298, illus. Tolstoy's courtship and
       decision to marry are discussed, and his initial marital
       happiness surveyed before a detailed account is given of
       the deterioration of his relationship with his wife to the
       point of nearly constant friction. The role played in the
       collapse of their marriage by his philosophy and disciples,
       most notably Chertkov, is stressed. Reviewed in:
           Contemp R, (July 1963), 51.
           Listener, (20 June 1963), 1045, by T. G. Rosenthal.
           Spectator, (24 May 1963), 672, by B. S. Johnson.
           Times Lit Sup, (7 June 1963), 410.

178 Crankshaw, Edward. Tolstoy: The Making of a Novelist.
       New York: Viking, 1974; 276p. , bib. 272-273, illus. It
       is contended that an understanding of Tolstoy's personal
       life is the best means of gaining insight into the meaning
       of his literary creations. Consequently, episodes and
       events from his life are discussed and linked to the gene-
       sis and substance of his fiction. It is concluded that his
       failure to live his ideals actually enriched his works but
       makes it impossible to accept him as a teacher: "A man
       is as good as his actions, and Tolstoy's actions were too
       often simply bad. " Additionally, scores of photographs
       and illustrations are included. Reviewed in:
           America, 131 (28 Sept. 1974), 156.
           Christian Sci M, (24 April 1974), 5, by Robert Nye.
           Economist, 251 (29 June 1974), 128.
           New Sta, 88 (16 August 1974), 224, by V. S. Pritch-
             ett.
           New Yorker, 50, (29 April 1974), 135-136.
           Rus R, 34 (Jan. 1975), 108-109, by Kathyrn Feuer.

179 Dole, Nathan H. The Life of Lyof N. Tolstoi. Intro. by Ilya
       Tolstoy. New York: Scribner's, 1923; 467p. , ix, illus.
       A broad biography of Tolstoy, stressing his personal life
       rather than detailed analysis of his writings. The standard
       highlights of his life are treated along with a host of lesser
       topics such as his interest in music (a subject which re-
       ceives more attention than War and Peace), his pilgrim-
       ages, and interest in foreign lands. A detailed chronology
       of his life as well as comments on Tolstoyan colonies and
       on characterizations of Tolstoy by his contemporaries ap-

pears in a series of appendices. Reviewed in:
Nation, 94 (7 March 1912), 237-238.
Outlook, 100 (13 April 1912), 837.
RRs, 45 (Jan. 1912), 114.

180 Fausset, Hugh I'Anson. Tolstoy: The Inner Drama. New
York: Russell and Russell, 1968 (reprint of the 1927
publication); 320p., illus. An examination of the role
played by Tolstoy's personality in his writings and personal life based on the contention that he was an individual
characterized by an inner struggle between instinct and
consciousness, and therefore it is in light of "this violent
temperamental conflict ... that his life, his art, and his
ideas may be most fruitfully examined. " The positive
and negative aspects of this struggle are discussed, with
the struggle itself being identified as the driving force behind his creativity. His philosophic views are critically
surveyed and the conclusion reached that he "served humanity more notably as an indicter of false civilizations
than as a prophet of a true one. " Reviewed in:
Nat and Ath, 42 (12 Nov. 1927), 254.
SEER, 6 (Dec. 1927), 478, by Monica Gardner.
Times Lit Sup, (22 Dec. 1927), 974.

181 Forbes, Neville. Tolstoi. London, 1911.

182 Garnett, Edward. Tolstoy, His Life and Writings. New
York: Haskell, 1974 (reprint of the 1914 publication);
107p., bib. 99-101. A general survey of the standard
landmarks of Tolstoy's life and literary career is pre-
sented with no attempt at interpretation. Designed to be
an introduction to Tolstoy as part of the Modern Biography
Series. Reviewed in:
Bos Trans, (9 May 1914), 8, Nathan H. Dole.
Independent, 80 (5 Oct. 1914), 80.
RRs, 49 (June 1914), 758.

183 Gibelli, Vincenzo. The Life and Times of Tolstoy. Feltham,
England: Hamlyn, 1970; 75p.

184 Green, K. R. Leo Tolstoy. London: Commercial Press,
1935.

185 Gudzii, N. K. Leo Tolstoy, 1828-1910. N. p., n. p., 1953;
19p. A brief Soviet critique of Tolstoy's life and philosophy on the 125th anniversary of his birth. Tolstoy is
commended for his protest against the evils associated
with capitalism and the tsarist state, and for sincere concern for human welfare, but is criticized for adherence
to non-violence in the face of the need for radical change
in Russian political, social, and economic conditions.

186 Hoffman, Modest, and Andre Pierre. By Deeds of Truth:
      The Life of Leo Tolstoy. Trans. by Ruth Fermaud. New
      York: Orion, 1958; vii, 268p. , illus. A study of the life
      of Tolstoy drawing heavily on his works for biographical
      information but not analyzing his writings from a literary
      perspective. The leading events in his life are traced,
      with frequent quotations presented from the diaries of
      friends and family. His early life, religious beliefs, and
      social concerns receive most attention amidst a generally
      favorable account of his personality and beliefs. Re-
      viewed in:
          Chi Sun Trib, (30 March 1958), 8, by Richard Sulli-
              van.
          Sat R Lit, 41 (19 April 1958), 19, Alexandra Tol-
              stoy.

187 Lavrin, Janko. Tolstoy: A Psycho-Critical Study. London:
      Collins, 1924; ix, 223p. An investigation of the psycho-
      logical forces that influenced the development of Tolstoy's
      personality and literature with emphasis placed on the
      process by which he reached his philosophy rather than
      the philosophy itself: "Tolstoy the sufferer is nearer and
      dearer to us than Tolstoy the teacher. " His attempt to
      resolve the conflict between the physical and spiritual
      needs within him is isolated as the source of much that
      appears contradictory about his life and works, and is also
      seen as the directing force behind his intellectual develop-
      ment: "His instinct for self-preservation urged him
      towards those views and ideas which would most probably
      help him to endure the pain of his inner conflict. " His
      struggle is sympathetically viewed, and it is asserted that
      any philosophy that evolves out of such suffering is much
      more valuable than "hundreds of truths which have only
      been thought. "

188 Leon, Derrick. Tolstoy: His Life and Work. London: Rout-
      ledge, 1944; xiv, 372p. , bib. 360-367. A balance of bio-
      graphical and literary analysis is presented as the major
      landmarks in Tolstoy's life are discussed. Although parts
      of his philosophy and some polemical works are consid-
      ered, emphasis is placed on the "personal" Tolstoy.
      Special concern is shown for the events of his later
      life, especially those associated with his death. Numerous
      illustrations and photographs are included. Reviewed
      in:
          New St and Na, 27 (29 April 1944), 291, by Leonard
              Woolf.

189 Merezhkovski, Dmitri S. Tolstoi as Man and Artist, with an
      Essay on Dostoevski. Westport, Conn. : Greenwood,
      1970 (reprint of the 1902 publication); 310p. The works

of Tolstoy the artist are regarded as being incomprehensible without first understanding Tolstoy the man because his life and personality were the foundation of his writing. The autobiographical elements in his early writings and his Confession are analyzed as a means of determining the basis of his personality and philosophy. His life and work are both then discussed in light of the intensely personal and highly religious philosophy that he developed. Reviewed in:

Bookman, 17 (August 1903), 645-647.
Independent, 55 (15 Jan. 1903), 153-154.
For a discussion of Merezhkovski's analysis of Tolstoy as an artist, see item 454.
For lengthy discussions of Merezhkovski's book, see William Courtney, The Development of Maurice Maeterlinck and Other Sketches of Foreign Writers, 119-128; and James Huneker, Ivory Apes and Peacocks, pp. 81-88.

190 Mishcheriko, A. I. Yasnaya Polyana. Trans. by A. Weise. Tula, Soviet Union, 1966; 40p. , illus.

191 Nazaroff, Alexander I. Tolstoy, the Inconstant Genius: A Biography. New York: Stokes, 1929; 332p. , bib. 321-324, illus. An account of the personal development of Tolstoy with emphasis on those influences (family, Rousseau, university life, military experiences) which shaped his character. His increasingly dogmatic and contradictory nature is the focus of the second half of the study with his views being generally criticized, especially those dealing with art, nihilism, and the peasantry, for narrowmindedness and extremism. Reviewed in:

Bos Trans, (24 Dec. 1929), 2.
N Y Herald Trib Bk R, (15 Dec. 1929), 1, by Dorothy Brewster.
N Y Times, (15 Dec. 1929), 5, by Herbert Gorman.
Outlook, 153 (11 Dec. 1929), 589, by W. R. Brooks.

192 Obituary Notices and Accounts of the Funeral of Count Tolstoy. New York, 1910, 31p.

193 Perris, George H. Leo Tolstoy, the Grand Mujik: A Study in Personal Evolution. Intro. by F. Volkhovsky. London: Unwin, 1898; ix, 236p. A general survey of Tolstoy's life, works, and ideas along with numerous digressions on the nature of the Russia in which he matured. The effect of family life and personal influences, such as Rousseau and Turgenev, on his development is examined as are those historical events, especially the Crimean War and the reforms of Alexander II, that affected him in the middle span of his life. Separate from his personal evolution, Tolstoy's philosophy of the simple life and his

contact with the peasantry is discussed. Reviewed in:
Academy, 54 (13 August 1898), 139-140.
Athenaeum, 2 (17 Sept. 1898), 382-383.
Critic, 33 (Sept. 1898), 184-189, by J. L. G.

194 Philipson, Morris. The Count Who Wished He Were a Peas-
ant. New York: Random House, 1967; 170p. , bib. 167-
170, illus. A standard survey, designed for beginning
readers of Tolstoy, of the personal side of Tolstoy's life
with minor discussion of his literary work and philosophy.
Reviewed in:
Commonweal, 86 (26 May 1967), 298, by E. M.
Graves.
N Y Times, (7 May 1967), 26, by Guy Daniels.
Sat R Lit, 50 (13 May 1967), 58, by Zena Sutherland.
Slav R, 28, no. 2 (1969), 351-352, by Richard Gustaf-
son.

195 Puzin, N. , ed. Yasnaya Polyana: The Lev Tolstoi Estate
Museum. Moscow: Progress Publishers, n. d. , 115p. ,
illus. A history of Yasnaya Polyana from Tolstoy's early
years through its restoration after World War II precedes
a description of each of the estate's structures and rooms.
Events from Tolstoy's life that occurred in each room are
described, and numerous photographs and illustrations are
presented.

196 Rappoport, A. S. Tolstoi: His Life, Works, and Doctrine.
London, 1908.

197 Rolland, Romain. Tolstoy. Trans. by Bernard Miall. Port
Washington, N. Y. : Kennikat, 1972 (reprint of the 1911
publication); 256p. On the basis of personal contact and
early sympathy with Tolstoy's beliefs as well as on thor-
ough scholarship, a comprehensive account is presented
of Tolstoy's life, work and philosophy. The intertwining
nature of his personal experiences and artistic creations
is stressed as an analysis of his principal beliefs unfolds.
The severity and contradictions associated with many of
his beliefs, particularly on art, are noted but his extremism is defended as the "privilege of genius. " Beneath
the inconsistencies in his beliefs and actions a uniformity
is seen in the power of his lifelong struggle to find truth.
In all, the magnitude of his thought and creations is regarded as dwarfing the disputes of critics and biographers
who attempt to analyze him. Reviewed in:
Athenaeum, 2 (16 Dec. 1911), 768.
Nation, 94 (7 March 1912), 237-238.
No Amer R, 195 (Jan. 1912), 135.
N Y Times, (3 Dec. 1911), 797; (10 Dec. 1911), 817.

198 Rothkopf, Carol Z. Leo Tolstoy. New York: Franklin Watts,
1968; 146p. Designed to stimulate further inquiry by

youthful readers, Tolstoy's life, personality, and inner struggles are surveyed in a general and non-critical fashion.

199 Sarolea, Charles. <u>Count Leo Tolstoy: Life and Work.</u> London, 1912.

200 Simmons, Ernest J. <u>Leo Tolstoy.</u> Boston: Little, Brown 1946; 2 vols. (852p.), bib. 815-836 (which appears only in a special edition), illus. A widely acclaimed, detailed analysis of Tolstoy's life and work based on much primary information. A balance of biographical information, literary criticism, and philosophic analysis is presented with an objective tone maintained throughout. The connection between his early life and later works and beliefs is illustrated, and the autobiographical nature of his fiction is identified as one of the leading sources of his command of realism. The basic principles of his philosophy are established, with their origins, substance, and impact on his life receiving more attention than critical analysis. Tolstoy's concern with the evils of modern civilization, and his consequent support of a simple, Christian existence is discussed and linked to his increasingly difficult relationship with his wife. In all, a comprehensive and sympathetic treatment. Reviewed in:
<u>ASEER,</u> 6 (May 1947), 214-216, by George Bobrinskoy.
<u>Book Week</u> (Chicago Sun), (1 Dec. 1946), 51, by Marie Seton.
<u>Christian Sci M,</u> (11 Jan. 1947), 12.
<u>Nation,</u> 164 (25 Jan. 1947), 103, by R. P. Blackmur.
<u>New Republic,</u> 116 (27 Jan. 1947), 37, by Fred Wertham.
<u>New Yorker,</u> 22 (23 Nov. 1946), 119, by H. Basso.
<u>N Y Herald Trib Bk R,</u> (15 Dec. 1946), 1, by Joseph Barnes.
<u>N Y Times,</u> (1 Dec. 1946), 8, Philip Rahv.
<u>San Fran Chron,</u> (24 Nov. 1946), 10, by George Snell.
<u>Sat R Lit,</u> 30 (18 Jan. 1947), 17, by E. C. Ross.
<u>SEER,</u> 25, no. 65 (1946), 455-477, Waclaw Lednicki.

201 Simmons, Ernest J. <u>Tolstoy.</u> Boston: Routledge and Kegan Paul, 1972; 259p., xi, bib. 249-253. A condensation and revision of a variety of Simmons' writings on Tolstoy designed to serve as a general, though somewhat sophisticated, introduction for the non-specialist. The historical context within which Tolstoy developed, and the close relationship between his life, art, and beliefs are stressed. Reviewed in:
<u>Economist,</u> 246, (17 Feb. 1973), 108.
<u>Rus R,</u> 6 (Spring 1947), by Alexander Nazaroff.
<u>Times Lit Sup,</u> (11 May 1973), 532.
<u>Western Hum R,</u> 27 (Fall 1973), 41, by D. H. Stewart.

202 Tolstoi: A Loan Exhibit from Soviet Museums Presented by
     the British Library, 3 June-30 August, 1976. London:
     British Museum, 1976; 16p. A collection of photographs,
     sketches, and illustrations dealing with Tolstoy's life and
     work accompanied by a brief text for each exhibit. Exhi-
     bits are grouped under the following headings: Early
     Years; War and Peace; Anna Karenina; Resurrection; Later
     Years; Heritage in the USSR; and Impact on England.

203 Townsend, R. S.   Tolstoi for the Young. London: Paul,
     1916; 200p. A general survey of Tolstoy's life and liter-
     ature designed as an introduction to him for non-adult
     readers.

204 Troyat, Henri.   Tolstoy.   Trans. by Nancy Amphoux.   New
     York: Doubleday, 1969; 924p., bib. 882-889, illus. A
     detailed analysis of Tolstoy's personal life, activities, and
     writings presented in a chronological as opposed to the-
     matic fashion. Special concern is shown for the relation-
     ship between his personality and philosophical-ethical be-
     liefs, for the contradictions in his philosophy, and for the
     inconsistencies between his beliefs and lifestyle. Analysis
     of his writings is presented as an extension of the discus-
     sion of his personal development, which is the study's
     focus. Carefully noted is the deterioration of his marriage
     due mostly to his philosophy and trying personality. Re-
     viewed in:
         Atlantic M, 220 (Dec. 1967), 142-143, by Oscar Hand-
             lin.
         Christian Sci M, (7 Dec. 1967), 22.
         Comp Lit S, (Dec. 1968), 502, by N. Rzhevsky.
         Harper's M, 235 (Dec. 1967), 108-110, by Justin
             Kaplan.
         New Sta, 75 (15 March 1968), 335-336, by V. S.
             Pritchett.
         N Y R Bks, (25 Feb. 1971), 6, by Edmund Wilson.
         N Y Times, (17 Dec. 1967), 1, by James Lord.
         Reporter, 38 (8 Feb. 1968), 41.
         Rus R, 28 (April 1969), 217-220, by Kathryn Feuer.
         Sat R Lit, 51 (20 Jan. 1968), 25.
         Slav R, 28, no. 2 (June 1969), 351-352, by Richard
             Gustafson.
         Times Lit Sup, (23 May 1968), 527.
         Virg Q R, (Summer 1968), 120.
         For a lengthy critical review of Troyat's biography,
     see item 21.

205 Turberville, A. C.   Leo Tolstoy.   London, 1908, 312p.

206 Waleffe, Pierre.   Leo Tolstoy.   Trans. by Adel Negro, intro.
     by M. R. Hofmann.   Geneva: Minerva, 1969; 110p., il-
     lus.   A brief survey of the leading episodes in Tolstoy's
     life, with little concern for his literary activities, pre-

cedes a lengthy collection of annotated photographs and
sketches dealing with his acquaintances, family, and sur-
roundings.

207 Walsh, Walter. Tolstoy's Emblems, Collected by Walter Walsh.
London: Daniel, 1909; 122p.

208 Winstanley, Lilian. Tolstoy. London: Jack, 1914; 15p. A
short, general account of Tolstoy's life, works, and world
significance.

ESSAYS AND CHAPTERS from general works

209 Acker, Helen. "Leo Nikolayevich Tolstoy" in Three Boys of
Old Russia. New York: Nelson, 1944; 11-122. A fanciful account of Tolstoy's life presented by way of sketches
written as tales. Subjects treated are his home life,
work with the schools, and his contact with the peasants
of his region. Designed for juvenile readers.

210 Aldanov, Mark. "The Enigma of Tolstoy" in TCRLC, 201-
211. A discussion of the contradictions and enigmas in
Tolstoy's life with suggestions given on their possible
sources. Prince Andrei, of War and Peace, is examined
as the character created by Tolstoy who provides most insight into Tolstoy's life because he closely paralleled the
stages of Tolstoy's own development. It is concluded,
however, that Tolstoy remains a riddle: "Who has fath-
omed the secret unity of his primary thrust? Who can
say that he has understood Lev Tolstoy?"

211 Baudouin, Charles. "Tolstoy's Diary" in Contemporary
Studies. Freeport, N.Y.: Books for Libraries Press,
1969 (reprint of the 1924 publication); 9-18. A commentary on the value of Tolstoy's later diary claiming
that it is not as useful as his earlier diaries because his
spiritual crises had passed and, therefore, the inward
conflicts that were the focus of his early journals were
no longer there to reveal. The later diary is regarded
as illustrating the fact that Tolstoy remained highly critical of himself, and that he was a sincere and dynamic
"seeker of the truth" until the very end of his life.

212 Blok, Aleksandr. "The Sun over Russia" in LTCA, 126-127.
A brief and positive assessment of Tolstoy's impact on
Russia. It is asserted that all Russians, no matter what
faith, profession, or philosophy they follow, "have drawn
in with their mother's milk at least some small part of
Tolstoy's great vital power." Excerpt translated from
Zolotoe runo, nos. 7-9 (1908).

213 Booth, Edward T. "While the Earth Remaineth: Yasnaya
Polyana, 1826-1876" in God Made the Country. Freeport,

N. Y. : Books for Libraries Press, 1971 (reprint of the
1946 publication); 246-266.   A study of the "happy and
productive years" of Tolstoy with the Yasnaya Polyana
estate depicted as the symbol of this admirable phase in
his life.   Tolstoy, the severe and moralizing prophet, is
sharply contrasted with the Tolstoy of the pre-conversion
years.   His early carefree life, his creative work at Yasnaya Polyana in the 1862-1876 period, and the happiness
that pervaded his environment are all warmly and positively discussed, with much reference to his letters to his
cousin Alexandra as a source of information.

214   Crosby, Ernest H.   "Seventieth Birthday of the Grand Old Man
      of Russia" in Social Gospel.   Commonwealth (Georgia),
      1898.

215   Eastman, Fred.   "Leo Tolstoy" in Men of Power.   Freeport,
      N. Y. : Books for Libraries Press, 1970 (reprint of the
      1939 publication); 81-135.   Tolstoy's life is seen as being
      the story of "an intense struggle between two natures: a
      lower and a higher, " a struggle which he saw not only in
      himself but in human beings in general.   It is maintained
      that Tolstoy was at first content to portray this conflict
      only in his fiction, but later was moved to remodel his
      entire life in an attempt to resolve this conflict, and,
      lastly, turned to preaching to the world as a means of
      elevating all men's spirituality.   Although his life is re-
      garded as having been a failure in many respects, Tolstoy
      is commended for "lifting the spiritual horizons of the
      whole race" by his struggle.

216   Fausset, Hugh I'Anson.   "Leo Nikolayevitch Tolstoy" in The
      New Spirit.   London: Dobson, 1946; 18-31.   In order to
      understand any of Tolstoy's writings, it is maintained that
      one must be fully aware of "the forces and ideas which
      possessed him and which he struggled to reconcile in
      himself. " This struggle between the physical and spiritual
      sides of Tolstoy is seen as exceptionally intense and re-
      sponsible for many themes in his fiction as well as for
      his spiritual conversion and consequent polemical works.

217   Gosse, Edmund W.   "The Unveiling of Tolstoi" in Books on
      the Table.   New York: Scribner's, 1921; 77-82.   A dis-
      cussion of the reminiscences of Tolstoy presented by
      Maxim Gorky as being a possible source for misinter-
      pretation by those who would focus only on his unflattering
      remarks and disregard his obvious and continuing respect
      for Tolstoy.

218   Graham, Stephan.   "Tolstoy's Flight from Home" in The Way
      of Martha and the Way of Mary.   New York: Macmillan,
      1915; 131-136.   Tolstoy's 1910 flight from home is con-
      sidered to be the most interesting aspect of his entire life

because he at last sought to sever his ties with the material world and live true to his beliefs. The tragic circumstances associated with his death at Astapovo are seen as only heightening the "beautiful and pathetic" nature of his pilgrimage.

219 Hackett, Francis. "He Knew the Tolstoys" in On Judging Books in General and in Particular. New York: Day, 1947; 140-143. A discussion of Tolstoy's harried marital relations, with much reference to Polner's book Tolstoy and His Wife (item 16). Sofia Tolstoy is presented as a possessive matriarch willing to serve her husband but unwilling to accept his peasant ways and disciples.

220 Hare, Richard. "The Young Leo Tolstoy" in Portraits of Russian Personalities between Reform and Revolution. London: Oxford, 1959; 150-195. A survey of the sources of confusion that have hampered solid understanding of Tolstoy's complex personality precedes a discussion of his youth as a source of insight into the character of the mature Tolstoy. Episodes examined are his military service, contact with intellectual circles of the capital tour of Europe, educational work, and his marriage.

221 Hind, C. Lewis. "Tolstoy" in Authors and I. Freeport, N.Y.: Books for Libraries Press (reprint of 1921 publication); 280-83. An impressionistic general survey of Tolstoy's later life and activities sparked by the author's having heard a man state that he planned to write a play about Tolstoy. Tolstoy's life is praised and the conclusion reached: "is he not too great, too elusive, too spiritual for a play?"

222 Hingley, Ronald. Russian Writers and Society, 1825-1904. New York: McGraw-Hill, 1967; 257p., bib. 248-51, illus. Although no separate chapter is dedicated to Tolstoy, a wide range of biographical information is presented by way of Tolstoy's being discussed in relation to the following aspects of Russian society: church, state, peasants, bureaucracy, army, education, censorship, legal system, and the revolutionary movement.

223 Lavrin, Janko. "Tolstoy" in Russian Literature. London: Benn, 1928; 43-46. A list of the various elements composing Tolstoy's personality is presented as is an account of the principal events in his life before an analysis is given of the complexity of his character. He is seen as having two major strands in his personality, one simple and primitive, the other skeptical and egotistical. It is argued that Tolstoy sought refuge from his inquisitive self-consciousness in the "harmony of a patriarchal group soul." A more detailed discussion by Lavrin of this thesis, along with much information on Tolstoy's philosophy appears in his Tolstoy: A Psycho-Critical Study.

224   Littlejohn, David. "Troyat's Tolstoy" in Interruptions. New
      York: Grossman, 1970; 153-59. A favorable discussion
      of Troyat's biography which is praised for its insight into
      the divergent drives of Tolstoy's personality and their re-
      lationship to his art, philosophy, and family life.

225   Lynd, Robert. "Tolstoy's Double Life" in Books and Writers.
      Freeport, N. Y.: Books for Libraries Press, 1970 (re-
      print of the 1952 publication); 95-99. It is argued that
      Tolstoy struggled consistently and fervently in youth and
      maturity alike in trying to live a "good life, " a struggle
      often overlooked by biographers, with a notable exception
      being Simmons.

226   Maude, Aylmer. "Leo Tolstoy" in TP, 1-31. A survey of
      the principal events in Tolstoy's life with emphasis placed
      on those episodes and individuals that led him to his
      spiritual awakening, all of which are presented positively.

227   Pasternak, Boris. "An Essay in Autobiography" in LTCA,
      393-394. An account, by the Russian author, of Tolstoy's
      coffin being placed on the train at Astapovo Station pre-
      cedes a brief description of Tolstoy's leading characteristic
      as a novelist--his penetrating vision, which produces a
      unique brand of creative contemplation.

228   Poggioli, Renato. "Lev Tolstoy as Man and Artist" in TCCE,
      14-27. Tolstoy's life is regarded as having consisted of
      a number of paradoxes: a born aristocrat who embraced
      the cause of the common man but who could never sever
      himself from his breeding; a conservative by temper but
      by reason and faith a radical; and a personality which
      combined self-hatred and self-love, humility and pride.
      In all, Tolstoy's life is presented as a perpetual conflict
      between reason and sentiment, intellect and conscience.
      His unity is seen as resting in the consistent interplay of
      these contrasting factors producing an extraordinary per-
      sonality. Also in Oxford S P, 10 (1962), 25-37; and The
      Spirit of the Letter (Cambridge, Mass.: Harvard Univer-
      sity Press, 1956).

229   Ponsonby, Arthur, and Dorothea Ponsonby. "Tolstoy" in
      Rebels and Reformers. New York: Holt, 1919; 269-310.
      Designed for young readers or those without time to read
      lengthy biographies, a general survey of Tolstoy's life,
      writings, and beliefs is presented without critical com-
      mentary except for a conclusion stating that although Tol-
      stoy was an extremist he has presented to the world a
      "higher, more spiritual ideal which by degrees we may be
      able to approach. "

230   Rilke, Rainer Maria. "Letter to Clara Rilke" in LTCA, 127.
      Tolstoy's death is sadly noted and is seen as being the

tragic fulfillment of that inner struggle which drove him through life and literature.

231   Rilke, Rainer Maria. "Letter to L. H. " in <u>LCTA</u>, 151-152. A 1915 letter, by the German poet, discussing Tolstoy's views on death and his preoccupation with it as stemming from his fear of dying.

232   Russell, George W. "Tolstoi" in <u>The Living Torch</u>. Freeport, N. Y. : Books for Libraries Press, 1970 (reprint of the 1937 publication); 305-309. Tolstoy's personality is scanned and seen to be excessively serious: "I feel that there is something fundamentally wrong because of that grim face which glowers at me all the time. " Tolstoy's power of concentration is considered to be associated with this seriousness, and is deemed "abnormal and shortsighted" and responsible for his extremist philosophy, the worst example of which is his work <u>What Is to Be Done?</u>

233   Russell, George W. "Tolstoi's Diary" in <u>The Living Torch</u>, 309-310. Tolstoy's youthful diary is criticized for having few profundities and for revealing only the life of a most ordinary young man. Since no insight is provided by his early diary into the qualities that led him to greatness in his later years, it is contended that the only reason it was ever published was because it <u>was</u> Tolstoy's diary.

234   Saunders, Beatrice. "Count Leo Tolstoy" in <u>Portraits of Genius</u>. London: Murray, 1959; 187-199. Emphasis is placed on the effect that Tolstoy's early childhood had upon his life. His skepticism, thirst for knowledge, affection for Rousseau, and his obsession for plans on which to base his life are all regarded as youthful characteristics that deeply influenced his adult life. His spiritual awakening is discussed in light of this contention, and the effect of this awakening on his family is also examined. Lastly noted is the serious loss suffered by the literary world because of his casting aside fiction writing for moralizing.

235   Schnittkind, Henry T. , and Dana A. Schnittkind. "Tolstoy" in <u>Living Biographies of Famous Novelists</u>. New York: Garden City Pub. Co. , 1943; 229-242. Tolstoy's life and works are surveyed with the conclusion reached that he is unique as an example of one of those "rare men who instead of rising from the ranks to superior ambition, voluntarily descended to the ranks because of superior compassion. " His later life is critically assessed, especially his philosophic views, and it is stated that "it was the tragedy of Tolstoy to outlive his own greatness. " Also in <u>Fifty Great Modern Lives</u>, 238-245.

REVIEWS OF TOLSTOY'S DIARIES AND LETTERS

236 The Diaries of Leo Tolstoy. Youth, 1847-1852. Trans. by
        C. J. Hogarth and A. Sirnis, pref. by C. T. Wright.
        New York: Dutton, 1918. Reviewed in:
        Athenaeum, (Nov. 1917), 598.
        Bos Trans, (19 Jan. 1918), 8, by Nathan H. Dole.
        N Y Times, (11 Nov. 1917), 461.
        RRs, 57 (Feb. 1918), 221.
        Sat R, 124 (20 Oct. 1917), 311.
        Spectator, 119 (3 Nov. 1917), 471.
        Times Lit Sup, (21 June 1917), 289; (4 Oct. 1917),
            470.
        Yale R, 8 (Oct. 1918), 197-199, by William L.
            Phelps.

237 The Journal of Leo Tolstoy; First Volume, 1895-1899. Trans.
        by Rose Strunsky. New York: Knopf, 1917; 288p. Re-
        viewed in:
        Independent, 92 (6 Oct. 1917), 67.
        Lit D, 55 (17 Nov. 1917), 40.
        N Y Times, (5 August 1917), 288.
        N Amer R, 206 (17 Nov. 1917), 793.
        RRs, 56 (17 Oct. 1917), 439.
        Sprg Rep, (7 Sept. 1917), 6.

238 The Last Diaries of Leo Tolstoy. Trans. by Lydia Weston-
        Kesich, intro. by Leon Stilman. New York: Putnam,
        1960; 285p. Reviewed in:
        N Y Herald Trib Bk R, (28 May 1961), 26.
        Sat R Lit, 43 (20 August 1960), 26.

239 The Letters of Tolstoy and His Cousin, Countess Alexandra
        Tolstoy (1857-1903). Trans. by Leo Islavin. New York:
        Dutton, 1929; 232p. Reviewed in:
        Bookman, 69 (August 1929), 664, by Norah Meade.
        Bos Trans, (26 June 1929), 2.
        New Sta, 33 (8 June 1929), 272.
        N Y Evening P, (13 July 1929), 7, by Edwin Seaver.
        N Y Herald Trib Bk R, (14 July 1929), by Babette
            Deutsch.
        N Y Times, (16 June 1929), 4, by Alexander Nazaroff.
        Outlook, 152 (10 July 1929), 433.
        RRs, 80 (Sept. 1929), 14, by W. B. Shaw.
        Sat R, 147 (20 April 1929), 546.
        Spectator, 142 (23 March 1929), 482.
        Times Lit Sup, (14 March 1929), 202.

240 Tolstoy; Literary Fragments, Letters and Reminiscences Not
        Previously Published. Ed. by Rene Fülöp-Miller, trans.
        by Paul England. London: Harrap, 1931; 330p. (In-
        cludes four essays about Tolstoy which are annotated else-
        where in this bibliography.) Reviewed in:

N Y Herald Trib Bk R, (17 May 1931), 6, by Avrahm
    Yarmolinsky.
Bos Trans, (18 July 1931), 1.
N Y Times, (26 April 1931), 9, by Alexander Nazar-
    off.
Outlook, 158 (24 June 1931), 248, by F. Robbins.
Sat R, 151 (23 May 1931), 762, by A. Nicholson.
Sat R Lit, 7, (27 June 1931), 925, by Alexander Kaun.
Spectator, 146 (20 June 1931), 977, by E. H. Carr.
Times Lit Sup, (21 May 1931), 404.
Yale R, 21 (Autumn 1931), 213, by John Cournos.

241 The Private Diary of Leo Tolstoy, 1853-1857. Trans. by
     Louise Maude and Aylmer Maude. New York: Doubleday,
     Page, 1927; 256p. Reviewed in:
     Nation, 125 (19 Oct. 1927), 430, by Leonard Woolf.
     Nat and Ath, 41 (1 Oct. 1927), 840, by Leonard Woolf.
     New Sta, 29 (8 Oct. 1927), Sup 14, by R. E. Roberts.
     N Y Evening P, (22 Oct. 1927), 15, by A. Nikolaieff.
     N Y Times, (29 August 1927), 1, by Alexander Nazar-
        off.
     Times Lit Sup, (15 Sept. 1927), 621.

PERIODICAL ARTICLES

242 Abbott, Lyman. "Tolstoy: An Estimate," Outlook, 92 (15
     May 1909), 105-108.

243 "About Tolstoy," Independent, 55 (8 Oct. 1903), 2419-2420.

244 Aldanov, Mark A. "New Light on Tolstoy," Slavonic R, 6
     (June 1927), 162-167. A discussion of new Russian lan-
     guage publications on Tolstoy, and a commentary on the
     many preparations associated with those publications which
     will be issued in honor of the centenary of his birth.
     Most attention is given to Gusev's Life of Lev N. Tolstoy.

245 Aldanov, Mark A. "Some Observations on Tolstoy," Slavonic
     R, 5, no. 14 (1926), 305-314. An examination of the
     numerous cases of misinterpretation and misquoting of
     Tolstoy by those visitors to Yasnaya Polyana who took
     notes on their conversations with him.

246 Aldanov, Mark A. "Some Reflections on Tolstoy and Tolstoy-
     ism," Slavonic R, 7 (Jan. 1929), 482-492.

247 Arkhangelskaya, T. "In the Yasnaya Polyana Library," Sov
     Lit, 10 (1975), 127-130.

248 Arthaud, C. "Tolstoy and the House That Haunted Him, Yas-
     naya Polyana: Excerpts from Homes of the Great,"
     Vogue, 152 (1 Nov. 1968), 174-175.

249   Beaux, C.   "On a Portrait of the Young Tolstoy, " Cent M, 67
       (March 1904), 780.

250   Birkett, G. A.   "Official Plans for Tolstoy's Funeral Made in
       1902, " SEER, 30, no. 74 (Dec. 1951), 2-6.

251   Blavatsky, Mdme.   "On Diagnosis and Palliatives, " Lucifer, 6
       (July 1890), 353.

252   Brussel, Clara.   "Tolstoy: d. Astapovo Railroad Station, "
       Poetry, 70, no. 2 (May 1974), 76-77.

253   Bushman, I. N.   "The Tolstoy Jubilee in the U. S. S. R. , " St
       Sov Un, 1, no. 1, 125-135.

254   Calderon, George L.   "The Wrong Tolstoi, " Monthly R, 3, no.
       8, (1901), 129-141.   A discussion of the "right" and the
       "wrong" Tolstoy in reference to those aspects of Tolstoy's
       thought followed most closely by his disciples.   Particular
       concern is shown for his religious and moral views (the
       "wrong Tolstoy") and their interpretation by his followers.
       Also in Living Age 229 (29 June 1901), 819-827.

255   "Celebration of Tolstoy's Seventieth Birthday, " Bookman, 8,
       no. 2 (Oct. 1898); 106-107.   A speech given by Israel
       Zangwill, at a September 1, 1898, celebration of Tolstoy's
       birth, is the focus of the article.   Also included is a let-
       ter from William Dean Howells praising Tolstoy as a man
       but criticizing his views on art.

256   "Centenary of Tolstoy, " RRs, 78 (Oct. 1928), 438-439.   A
       survey of the opinions of a number of individuals who were
       close to or have written about Tolstoy, most notably Gorky
       and Galsworthy.

257   Chambers, Kellett.   "Tolstoy and the Movies, " Harper's W,
       61 (10 July 1915), 39.

258   Chapiro, J.   "Conversations with Gerhart Hauptmann, " Living
       Age, 336 (July 1929), 336-340.   Recollections from an in-
       terview with Hauptmann in which he discussed Tolstoy's
       views on religion, morality, and ethics as well as his
       flight from Yasnaya Polyana.

259   Christesen, N.   "Victor Lebrun as a Living Witness to Tol-
       stoy in the years 1900-1910, " Proc Aust U Lang and Lit
       Assoc, (1971), 434-443.

260   Colbron, G. I.   "Essays, Letters and Miscellanies, " Bookman,
       13 (April 1909), 182p.   Tolstoy is viewed positively for
       his work with the famine and for the immense quantity of
       quality work he produced.

261 "Correspondence between Tolstoy and N. N. Strachov," Nation, 96 (6 March 1913), 236.

262 "Count and Countess Tolstoi," Pub Op, 12, no. 1 (23 Jan. 1892), 405. Their work with the Russian famine is surveyed.

263 "Count Leo Tolstoi," Fortn R, 48 (Dec. 1887), 783-784.

264 "Count Leo Tolstoi," Pub Op, 10, no. 18 (7 Feb. 1891), from Revue des Revues, Paris, Feb. 1891. A discussion of M. Nazarief's article concerning Tolstoy's University days.

265 "Count Tolstoi: Interesting Reminiscences of His Youth," RRs, 2 (Dec. 1890), 698-690. Excerpts from an article originally published in Historical Messenger concerning Nazarief's early contact with Tolstoy at the University. His early impression was unfavorable.

266 "Count Tolstoi's Life and Works," Westm R, 130 (Sept. 1888), 278-293. Excerpts reprinted in Pub Op, 6 (1888), 171.

267 "Count Tolstoy," Outlook, 96 (3 Dec. 1910), 761-762. Praise of Tolstoy's life and work with special attention given to his fiction as a means of describing Russia to the world and Russia alike.

268 "Count Tolstoy and the Dorpat University," Outlook, 75 (7 Nov. 1903), 525-526. On Tolstoy's being named an honorary member of the Dorpat University despite opposition by some bishops on the Board of Directors.

269 Davis, Paxton. "Tolstoy," Shenandoah, 14, no. 2, (Winter 1963), 11. A poem.

270 Davis, Robert G. "Art and Anxiety," Partisan R, 12 (1945), 310-321.

271 Dawson, W. J. "Tolstoy: The Young Man and His Message," Young Man, 9 (Dec. 1895), 397.

272 "Death of Tolstoy," Independent, 69 (24 Nov. 1910), 1122-1124. Brief description of Tolstoy's flight from Yasnaya Polyana and his death.

273 Demidov, Aleksei A. "Iasnaia Polana," Living Age, 315 (1922), 759-760. Translated from Nakanune, 12 Nov. 1922.

274 "The Destruction of the Tolstoy Museum," Museum J, 41 (March 1942), 298 and 42 (May 1942), 43.

275 "Dinner in Honor of Tolstoy's Seventieth Birthday," Critic, 33 (1898), 276.

276 Dole, Nathan H. "How to Spell Tolstoy," Bookbuyer, 17
     (1898), 89-95. Also in Nation, 92 (16 Feb. 1911), 165.

277 Dovidoff, L. T. "Count Leon Tolstoi," Cosmopolitan, 12
     (April 1891), 719-724. Survey of Tolstoy's life and be-
     liefs based on her acquaintance with several people who
     visited him.

278 Durland, Kellogg. "Tolstoy at Home," Independent, 69 (1 Dec.
     1910), 1191-1195.

279 "Eulogy," Independent, 69 (24 Nov. 1910), 1162-1163.

280 Farrell, J. T. "Tolstoy: Husband and Writer," New Republic,
     113 (3 Sept. 1945), 290-292.

281 Flynt, Josiah. "Tolstoy at Home," Pub Op, 38 (1905), 651-
     654.

282 Fovitsky, Aleksei L. "Behind the Scenes with a Genius,"
     New Pearson's, 49 (July 1923), 27-30.

283 Freeman, John. "Wives of the Russians," Lon Merc, (Dec.
     1928), 181-183. Review of the diary of Tolstoy's wife.

284 Funke, L. B. "Yasnaya Polyana, a Modern Shrine," Travel,
     66 (April 1936), 32-33.

285 Gandhi, Mahatma. "Letter to Tolstoy," Adam, nos. 284-286
     (1960), 167-169.

286 Garnett, D. "Tolstoy's Last Day," Living Age, 351 (Jan.
     1937), 457-460.

287 "General Gossip of Authors and Writers," Cur Lit, 30 (June
     1901), 665-666. An examination of Tolstoy's method of
     work.

288 Gillett, J. "The Last Days of Tolstoy," Sight and Sound, 41,
     no. 3 (Summer 1972), 141. On a BBC program of the
     same title.

289 Gleboff, Sophie. "A Trip to Iasnaia Poliana," Living Age,
     317, (1923), 590-594. Translated from Le Figaro 21,
     April, 1923.

290 "The Good End," Nation, 8 (1910), 326-327. Concerning the
     circumstances of Tolstoy's death. Also in Living Age,
     267 (10 Dec. 1910); 692-694.

291 Gordon, M. "Tolstoy at War with Himself," Sat R Lit, 28
     (30 June 1945), 10.

292   Gosse, Sir Edmund W.   "Count Lyof Tolstoi, " Contemp R, 94
     (Sept. 1908), 270-285.   Reprinted in Living Age, 259 (Oct.
     1908), 11-23.

293   Graham, Stephan.   "Tolstoy's Flight, " Bookman, 42 (1916),
     639-641.

294   "The Grand Moujik, " Chamber's J, Sixth series, 12, no. 601
     (July 1909), 437-440.   Short biography of Tolstoy and
     praise for his work with the peasants.

295   "The Great Countryman and His Views of Rural Life, " W
     Work, 16 (Sept. 1910), 367-379.

296   "Greater Love Hath No Man Than This, That a Man Lay Down
     His Life for His Friends, " Craftsman, 19, no. 4 (Jan.
     1911), 413-415.   Notes by the editor on the occasion of
     Tolstoy's death praising his life and his views.

297   Gribble, Francis.   "Count Tolstoy, " Literature, 9, no. 9 (31
     August 1901), 195-197, illus.   Discussion of the impres-
     sions of pilgrims who have visited Tolstoy.

298   Gusev, N. N.   "Tolstoy the Man, " Adam, nos. 284-286 (1960),
     142-147.

299   Hale, E. E.   "Leo Tolstoi, " Cosmopolitan, 7 (1889), 415-417.

300   Handley, Frances.   "Leo Tolstoi;   A Character Sketch, " Our
     Day, 15 (August 1895), 71-76.

301   Hapgood, Isabel F.   "Count Tolstoy at Home, " Atlantic M, 68
     (Nov. 1891), 659-699.

302   Hapgood, Isabel F.   "Tolstoi's Christian Name, " Nation, 46
     (22 March 1888), 237-238.   On the spelling of Tolstoy's
     first name.

303   Hapgood, Isabel F.   "Tolstoy as He Is, " Munsey's, 15 (August
     1896), 555-563.   A discussion of Tolstoy's social theories
     and how life at Yasnaya Polyana is inconsistent with them.

304   Hapgood, Isabel F.   "Tolstoy at Home, " Atlantic M, 68 (Nov.
     1891), 596-620.   A survey of family life and Tolstoy's
     habits.

305   Haspels, G. F.   "Tolstoy: His Personality and Writings, "
     Constructive Q, 3 (Dec. 1915), 865-883.

306   Heath, Richard.   "Count Lev Tolstoi: His Life and Writings, "
     Leisure H, 38 (1889), 158-167.

307   Hewlett, M.   "Tolstoy, " Fortn R, 94 (Dec. 1910), 1127.   A
     poem.   Also in Living Age, 267 (31 Dec. 1910), 865.

308   "Home Life of Tolstoi, " Cur Lit, 29 (August 1900), 149.

309   "Horror of War, " Independent, (16 April 1903), 889-893.   Article in which Tolstoy's recollections of his war days are interspersed with comments by Maude.

310   "How Tolstoy Died, " Living Age, 336 (August 1929), 447.

311   Howells, William D.   "In Honor of Tolstoy, " Critic, n. s. 30 (Oct. 1898), 288.   Written on the occasion of Tolstoy's seventieth birthday celebration.   Also in Bookman, 8 (Oct. 1898), 107.

312   Howells, William D.   "Lyof N. Tolstoy, " N Amer R, 188 (Dec. 1908), 842-859.   Article in response to Tolstoy's eightieth birthday.   A positive survey of his fiction and work in religion, ethics and aesthetics.   Reprinted under "Reasons for Tolstoy's Fame, " N Amer R, 192 (Dec. 1910), 729-745.

313   Howells, William D.   "Lyof Tolstoi, " Harper's W, 31 (23 April 1887), 299-300.

314   Howells, William D.   "My Favorite Novelist and His Best Book, " Munsey's, 17 (April 1897), 18-25.

315   Hubbard, Elbert.   "Leo Tolstoy: An Interpretation Done in Little, " Cosmopolitan, 34 (1903), 442-450.   A discussion of Tolstoy's personal life and a survey of his philosophy.

316   Hyde, G. M.   "In Honor of Tolstoy; A Dinner in Celebration of the Seventieth Birthday of the Russian Novelist and Reformer, " Critic, 33 (1898), 276-291.   Speeches by Israel Zangwill, Ernest H. Crosby, Abraham Cohan, James Jefferson, Stewart Woodford and R. W. Gilder honoring Tolstoy with letters from other notables who could not attend.

317   Johnston, C.   "Tolstoy at Home, " Arena, 20 (Oct. 1898), 480-490.

318   Kanzer, Mark.   "Writers and the Early Loss of Parents, " J Hillside Hosp, 2 (1953), 148-151.   A psycho-analytic study.

319   Katz, Gershon.   "The Last of the Masters, " Westm R, 181 (Jan. 1914), 93-100.   A survey of Tolstoy's life and work following the three stages Tolstoy used to describe his life: lustful, service to man, and service to God.

320   Kaun, Alexander.   "The Last Days of Leo Tolstoy with Translations from His Diary and Letters, " Atlantic M, 129 (March 1922), 299-306.

321   Kaun, Alexander.   "Tolstoy, 1828-1928, " Dial, 85 (Sept. 1928), 231-233.

322   Kemp, Harry. "Tolstoy, " Independent, 69 (1 Dec. 1910), 1190.
      A poem.

323   Lednicki, W. "Tolstoy between War and Peace, " Calif Slavic
      S, 4 (1967), 73-91.

324   "Leo Tolstoi, " Booknews, 22, no. 253 (Sept. 1903), 2. A re-
      view of London Bookman's new feature: "Biographies, "
      with a discussion on the March 1901 article concerning
      Tolstoy and Chesterton's biography of Tolstoy.

325   "Leo Tolstoi, " National M, 14: 579.

326   "Leo Tolstoi, 1828-1928, " Nation, 127 (5 Sept. 1928), 213. A
      survey of Tolstoy's literary greatness as well as the para-
      doxes in his life that drove him to his 1910 flight.

327   Leyda, Jay. "Tolstoy on Film, " Sight and Sound, 24, no. 1
      (July-Sept. 1954), 18-20, 52, illus. Based on photos of
      Tolstoy from 1908 to 1910 by Russian producer Alexander
      Drankov.

328   London, Mona. "Tolstoy: Man and Master, " Overland M, n.
      s. 86 (April 1928), 105-118.

329   L'vov, Nikolai N. "How Tolstoy Died, " Living Age, 321 (24
      May 1924), 979-986. Translated from La Revue Mondiale,
      15 April 1924.

330   Lynch, Hannah. "Lyof Nikolayevich Tolstoy, " Edinbg R, 214
      (July 1911), 218-251. A discussion of ten studies about
      Tolstoy in German, French, Russian and English including
      Maude's Life of Tolstoy. Other authors are: Seuron,
      Bienstock, Biriukov, Bitout, Turgenev, Lowenfeld, Uspen-
      sky and Arbuzova.

331   Macovicki, D. "Living Voices of Lev Tolstoy; Extracts from
      Yasnaya Polyana Notes, " Sov Lit, 10 (1975), 101-111.
      Trans. by V. Talmy.

332   Marble, Annie R. 'Early Life of Leo Tolstoy, " Dial, 41
      (August 1906), 59-60. Discussion of Tolstoy's youth with
      frequent references to Biriukov's Leo Tolstoy, His Life
      and Works.

333   Marble, Annie R. "The Personality and Teachings of Tolstoy, "
      Dial, 37 (1904), 8-10.

334   Maude, Aylmer. "The Centenary of Tolstoy's Birth, " Homi-
      letic R, 96, no. 4 (Oct. 1928), 261-266. An examination
      of Tolstoy's views on art, religion, non-resistance and
      war.

335 Maude, Aylmer. "Concerning Tolstoy: reply to M. Gordon, "
Sat R Lit, 7 (13 Sept. 1930), 128.   A letter to the editor
by Maude correcting misleading and incorrect statements
made by Gordon in his review of Diary of Tolstoy's Wife
in Sat R Lit, 28 June 1930.

336 Maude, Aylmer. "How to Spell Tolstoy, " Nation, 92 (16
March 1911), 265.

337 Maurois, Andre. "The Greatest, " Adam, nos. 284-286 (1960),
14.

338 McDougall, E. M. "On L. Tolstoy, " Sunday M, 21 (Oct.
1892), 706.

339 Meader, C. L. "Leo Tolstoi, " Rus Stud, 5, no. 1 (Sept.
1928), 6-7, illus.   Concerning the diversity of Tolstoy's
interests.

340 "Men and Women of the Outdoor World; Count Tolstoi, " Outing,
43, no. 6 (1904), 725-727.   An account of Tolstoy's activities, at the age of 75, stressing his daily routine.

341 Merritt, Theodore E. "Tolstoy at the Piano, " Dalhousie R,
36, no. 1 (Spring 1956), 28-35.   A discussion of Tolstoy's
love for music.   Excerpts from family diaries and publications are included.

342 Mirsky, D. S. "Some Remarks on Tolstoy, " Lon Merc, 20,
no. 116 (June 1929), 167-175.   Mirsky defends Tolstoy's
moral views and personality.   An attempt to be objective
in discussing the differences between Tolstoy and his wife.

343 Modell, David. "Tolstoy's Letters to His Wife, " N Amer R,
200, no. 10 (Oct. 1914), 592-602.

344 Morand, K. "Fiftieth Anniversary of the Deaths of Tolstoy
and L. Delisle at the Bibliotheque Nationale, " Burl M,
103 (Feb. 1961), 78.

345 Nazaroff, Alexander. "Tolstoy Comes to St. Petersburg, "
Bookman, 68, no. 1 (Sept. 1928), 28-35.   An account of
Tolstoy's initiation to literary society at an 1885 dinner
given by Nekrasov after the success of Tolstoy's Sebastopol
Stories.   Tolstoy's rudeness at the dinner is noted and his
subsequent quarrels with literary figures, especially Turgenev, are discussed.

346 Nolin, Bertil, and Bengt A. Lundenberg. "A Letter from Lev
Tolstoj to P. E. Hansen Plus Some Remarks on the Text
of the Jubilee Edition of Tolstoj's Collected Works, " Sc
Sl, 13 (1968), 59-65.

347 Novak, D. "An Unpublished Essay on Leo Tolstoy by Peter
     Kropotkin, " Can S P, 3 (1958), 7-26. Novak introduces
     Kropotkin's essay indicating why the work remained un-
     published for so long. He suggests that the purpose of
     the essay is to "present a more unified and integrated
     picture of Tolstoy as an artist. "

348 Noyes, George R. "My Glimpse of Tolstoy, " VP, 14, no. 4
     (1960), 31-34.

349 Noyes, George R. "Tolstoy, " Calif U Chron, 30 (Oct. 1928),
     452-455. On the 100th anniversary of Tolstoy's birth,
     Tolstoy's fiction is praised as the source of his enduring
     fame while his philosophy is criticized.

350 Oliver, S. "The Beginnings of Tolstoy, " Living Age, 245 (10
     June 1905), 698-701.

351 "On Tolstoy, " RRs, 11 (April 1895), 565.

352 Ould, Herman. "Tragedy of the Later Tolstoy, " Sackbut, 10,
     no. 11 (June 1930), 311-313. A discussion of Tolstoy's
     later life with much reference to Maude's views.

353 Pasternak, Leonid. "Chromo-lithographic Portrait of Tolstoy
     by Pasternak, " Int Studio, 36 (Feb. 1909), 332-333.

354 Peattie, D. C. "Wars and Peace of Leo Tolstoy, " Reader's
     D, 70 (April 1957), 156-160. A survey of the struggles
     within Tolstoy that led to his philosophy of life.

355 Perris, George H. "Tolstoy's Russia, " Forum, 29 (August
     1900), 751-760. A discussion of elements that are Rus-
     sian in characteristic in Tolstoy's life and works.

356 Peterson, E. D. "Leo Tolstoy: A Remembrance, " Am Merc,
     91 (Dec. 1960), 41-47.

357 Phillips, S. "Tolstoy, " Living Age, 268 (4 Feb. 1911), 316-
     317. A poem.

358 Poggioli, Renato. "Lev Tolstoy as Man and Artist, " Oxford
     S P, 10 (1962), 25-37. A discussion of Tolstoy's life
     consisting of a series of paradoxes. Conflict is noted be-
     tween his reason and sentiment, intellect and reason and
     as writer and moralist. A brief analysis of Tolstoy's
     works is made to support this contention. Also in TCEE,
     14-27; and Poggioli, Renato, Spirit of the Letter (Cam-
     bridge, Mass. : Harvard University Press, 1965).

359 Pritchett, V. S. "Tolstoy, " New St and Na, 10 (28 Dec.
     1935), 1013-1014.

360 Ragg, A. E. "To Count Tolstoy: A Poem, " Canadian M, 17
     (May 1901), 44.

361 Rahv, Philip. "Concerning Tolstoy, " Partisan R, 13:420-432.
     Annotated under his Image and Idea. Twenty Essays on
     Literary Themes. "Concerning Tolstoy, " appears as an
     introduction to Rahv's The Short Novels of Tolstoy (Chi-
     cago: Dial Press, 1946), which is also in The New Parti-
     san Reader, 1945-1953 (New York: Harcourt, Brace,
     1953). The same article appears under a new title:
     "Tolstoy: The Green Twig and the Black Trunk" in
     Rahv's Image and Idea. Twenty Essays on Literary
     Themes (Norfolk, Conn. : New Directions Books, 1957);
     and in his Literature and the Sixth Sense (Boston: Hough-
     ton Mifflin, 1969).

362 "Renunciation of Tolstoy, " Harper's W, 54 (26 Nov. 1910), 6.
     Discussion of Tolstoy's flight from home and subsequent
     death.

363 "The Reverse of Tolstoy, " Lon Merc, 19, no. 111 (Jan. 1929),
     225-227. A survey which praises Tolstoy's fiction but
     criticizes him as a teacher.

364 Roberts, Ellis R. "Leo Tolstoy: 1828-1928, " Bookman (L),
     74 (August 1928), 239-243.

365 Rogers, James F. "The Physical Tolstoy, " Scientific M, 7
     (Dec. 1918), 555-562. A discussion of Tolstoy's love of
     physical labor, his powerful physique, and the influence
     of the physical on his philosophy.

366 Ross, Michael P. "What Tolstoi Means to Me, " Rus Stud, 5,
     no. 1 (Sept. 1928), 1.

367 Rudy, P. "Leo Tolstoy's Enigmatic 'A History M. D. ', "
     Philol Q, 39, no. 1 (June 1960), 126-129. An examination
     of the possible meaning of the abbreviation "M. D. " in
     Tolstoy's diary.

368 Ruhl, A. "Tolstoy's Home and the Russian Revolution, " Out-
     look, 137 (11 June 1924), 230-231.

369 Sackville-West, V. "Tolstoy, " Nation (L), 43 (8 Sept. 1928),
     729-730.

370 Sarolea, Charles. "The Unity of Tolstoy's Life and Work, "
     Contemp R, 99 (Jan. 1911), 34-41.

371 Sedgwick, H. D. "Tolstoy's Life and Work, " W Work, 3
     (April 1902), 1953-1960.

372 Shifman, A. "Fifty Thousand Letters Attest to the Idealism
     of Leo Tolstoy, " UNESCO C, 14 (Jan. 1961), 23-26.

51   Additional Biographical

Letters received by Tolstoy during his lifetime.

373   Simmons, Ernest J.   "L. N. Tolstoi: A Cadet in the Cauca-
      sus, " SEER, 20 (1941); 13-27.

374   Simmons, Ernest J.   "Leo Tolstoi, the Later Years, " Atlantic
      M, 177 (June 1946), 177-200; 178 (July 1946), 157-180;
      178 (August 1946), 157-180; 178 (Sept. 1946), 161-184.
      A serialization of segments from Simmons' biography of
      Tolstoy, Vol. II.

375   Simmons, Ernest J.   "Recent Publications on L. N. Tolstoi, "
      SYB, (1941), 338-346.

376   Simmons, Ernest J.   "Soviet Scholarship and Tolstoy, " Am R
      Sov Un, 4, no. 2 (June 1941), 52-61.

377   Simmons, Ernest J.   "Tolstoy Gets Married, " Rus R, 1 (Nov.
      1941), 40-55.

378   Simmons, Ernest J.   "Tolstoy's Childhood, " Rus R, 3, no. 2
      (Spring 1944), 44-64.

379   Simmons, Ernest J.   "Tolstoy's University Years, " SEER, 59,
      no. 22 (1944), 16-36.

380   Simmons, Ernest J.   "Young Tolstoy, " Atlantic M, 176 (Sept.
      1945), 97-106; 176 (Oct. 1945), 97-106; 176 (Nov. 1945),
      97-106; 176 (Dec. 1945), 97-106.   A serialization of Sim-
      mons' biography of Tolstoy, Vol. I.

381   "Sketch of Tolstoy, " Harper's W, 45 (1901), 696.   A discussion
      of a possible trip to England by Tolstoy and of how he is
      viewed in England.

382   Smaltz, A. G.   "Modernism at the Home of Tolstoy, " Drama,
      19 (Oct. 1928), 4-7.

383   Sokolosky, Anatol.   "Leo N. Tolstoy: On the Occasion of the
      140th Anniversary of His Birth, " Lang Q, 7, nos. 3-4
      (1969), 2-4.

384   Stanislavski, K.   "Lev Nikolaevich Tolstoi, " Forum, 71 (1924),
      442-447.

385   Stanton, T.   "Notes on Count Tolstoy, " Open Court, 25 (Feb.
      1911), 123-127.

386   Stead, William T.   "Problem of the Tolstoy Household, " Cos-
      mopolitan, 40 (Jan. 1906), 291-296.

387   Steiner, E. A.   "Tolstoy the Man, " Dial, 37 (1 July 1904), 8-
      9.

388   Stewart, H. L.   "Tolstoy as a Problem in Psychoanalysis,"
      Proc Trans R S Can, 17 (1923), 29-39.

389   Strunsky, Rose.   "Tolstoy and Young Russia," Atlantic M, 107
      (April 1911), 490-497.   A discussion of Tolstoy's life in
      relation to political, social and economic developments in
      Russia.

390 Strunsky, Simeon.   "All the World Honors Tolstoy," N Y
      Times M, (9 Sept. 1928), 1-2, 18.

391   Strunsky, Simeon.   "Tolstoy the Reformer at Eighty," Nation,
      87 (August 1908), 179-182.

392   Tasker, J. G.   "Tolstoy's Farewell Message," Contemp R,
      100 (1911), 44-48.

393   Telford, John.   "Count L. Tolstoi," Lon Q R, 115 (1911), 123-
      128.

394   Thompson, Maurice.   "Studies of Prominent Novelists," Book
      News, 6 (1887), 9-11.

395   Thompson, Maurice.   "Tolstoi," Lit W, 18, no. 17 (20 August
      1887), 265-266.   A negative survey of Tolstoy's philos-
      ophy, character, and actions.

396   "Tolstoi," Book News, 7, no. 81 (May 1888), 268-270.   A
      brief biography and outline of Tolstoy's works and philos-
      ophy.

397   "Tolstoi," Harper's W, 54 (3 Dec. 1910), 6.   A survey of
      Tolstoy's life, particularly his conversion and religious
      views.   Family life is also discussed.

398   "Tolstoy," Chaut, 40 (Jan. 1905), 469.   A brief biography and
      survey of works.

399   "Tolstoy," Independent, 69 (24 Nov. 1910), 1162-1163.   Editor-
      ial on the occasion of Tolstoy's death; a tribute.

400   "Tolstoy," Nation, 91 (24 Nov. 1910), 490-492.   A survey of
      Tolstoy's life and works.

401   "Tolstoy," Calif U Chron, 30 (Oct. 1928), 452-455.

402   "Tolstoy among Revolutionists," Living Age, 335 (Dec. 1928),
      293.   On the celebration, in Russia, of the Tolstoy cen-
      tenary.

403   "Tolstoy and Greek," Class J, 32, no. 8 (May 1937), 491-492.
      Discussion of Tolstoy's learning the Greek language.

404   "Tolstoy and His Family Estate," RRs, 19 (April 1899), 490, illus. Chertkov is used as the source of a discussion concerning money and the Tolstoy estate.

405   "Tolstoy and Russia," Times Lit Sup, 17 (26 Sept. 1918), 445-446. Excerpts and discussion of Maude's Leo Tolstoy, along with a survey of Tolstoy's views on war and morality.

406   "Tolstoy and the Children," Lit D, 104 (22 March 1930), 22. Concerning Tolstoy's attitude toward his children during their youth.

407   "Tolstoy and the Superstitions of Science," Arena, 20 (July 1898), 52-60.

408   "Tolstoy at Eighty," RRs, 38 (Oct. 1908), 443-448.

409   "Tolstoy at Eighty," Outlook, 90 (19 Sept. 1908), 98-99. A protest against the Russian government's banning of celebrations honoring Tolstoy's 80th birthday and a description of the celebrations that took place despite the ban.

410   "The Tolstoy Celebration," Spectator, 101 (12 Sept. 1908), 354-355. In honor of Tolstoy on his 80th birthday. A brief description of his life, his works and his philosophy.

411   "Tolstoy in Flight," Cur Lit, 49 (Dec. 1910), 597-598.

412   "Tolstoy Letters," Living Age, 309 (18 June 1921), 688-690. Translated from L'Humanité of 3 April 1921. A discussion of Tolstoy's letters to Chekhov.

413   "Tolstoy Miscellany," Pub Op, 29, no. 19 (Nov. 1900), 600.

414   "Tolstoy Postcards," Bookman, 34 (Sept. 1911), 114, illus. Illustrations of postcards sold throughout Russia in memory of Tolstoy.

415   "Tolstoy the World Figure," Cur Lit, 45 (Nov. 1908), 520-525.

416   "Tolstoy through French Eyes," RRs, 26 (Oct. 1902), 481-482. A review of T. Benzon's article on Tolstoy which appeared in Revue des Deux Mondes.

417   "Tolstoy's Attitude toward Copyright; a summary," RRs, 10 (Nov. 1890), 558.

418   "Tolstoy's Christian Name," Lit W, 19, no. 8 (14 April 1888), 120-121. A survey of the spelling and misspelling of Tolstoy's first name.

419   "Tolstoy's Daily Life," Critic, n. s. 39 (August 1901), 105-106.

420 "Tolstoy's Death, " Outlook, 96 (3 Dec. 1910), 754-755.

421 "Tolstoy's Domestic Relations, " Lit D, 18 (10 June 1899), 664-
        665. A discussion of the discrepancy between Tolstoy's
        philosophy and his life style at Yasnaya Polyana, and an
        examination of his wife's thoughts on his radical views.

422 "Tolstoy's Eightieth Birthday, " Living Age, 257 (16 May 1908),
        433-434. A survey of Tolstoy's accomplishments.

423 "Tolstoy's Funeral, " Independent, 69 (1 Dec. 1910), 1181.

424 "Tolstoy's Home Life, " Cur Lit, 26 (Oct. 1899), 308-309.

425 "Tolstoy's Illness, " Critic, n. s. 40 (April 1902), 290-292.

426 "Tolstoy's Jubilee, " Independent, 64 (11 June 1908), 1320-1321.
        Article in commemoration of Tolstoy's 80th birthday ap-
        pearing in "Survey of the World" sections; discusses his
        life and his major novels.

427 "Tolstoy's Little Joke, " Harper's W, 47 (1903), 985. An ac-
        count of a "joke" played by Tolstoy on some American
        tourists to Yasnaya Polyana which illustrates Tolstoy's
        dislike for casual visitors.

428 "Tolstoy's Prevision, " Lit D, 49 (22 August 1914), 306-307.
        A discussion of Tolstoy's prediction in 1910 of the begin-
        ning of a war in 1914.

429 "Tolstoy's Seventy-fifth Birthday, " W Work, 7, no. 1 (Nov.
        1903), 4061-4062. A brief survey of Tolstoy's philosophy.

430 "Tolstoy's Struggle with His Lower Nature, " Cur Lit, 41 (Oct.
        1906); 434-435.

431 "The Tragedy of Count L. Tolstoy, " McClure's, n. s. 1 no.
        4 (August 1925), 538-559. A discussion of the problems
        between Tolstoy and his wife, using Bulgakov's account
        as a reference.

432 "Twixt Life and Death, " Spectator, 105 (19 Nov. 1910), 849.
        An examination of the reasons why Tolstoy left his home,
        with a general discussion of his views.

433 Van der Veer, C. "Tolstoy and His Wife. The Tragedy of
        Yasnaya Polyana, " RRs (L), 71 no. 424 (May to June
        1925), 421-424. An attempt to give an objective account
        of the relationship between Tolstoy and his wife.

434 "Varied Views of Tolstoy, " RRs, 43 (Jan. 1911), 97-99, illus.
        Portraits of Tolstoy at different ages.

435 Vengerova, Zinaida. "Tolstoy's Last Days, " Fortn R, 95
     (Feb. 1911), 289-299. Reprinted in Living Age, 268
     (March 1911), 707-714.

436 Weatherby, W. J. "Fragment of Undiscovered Tolstoy, "
     Guardian, 8 (15 Sept. 1930), 1.

437 Weisenthal, Morris. "Tolstoy at Arazmas, " Furioso, 5 no. 3
     (Summer 1950), 67. A poem.

438 "What Count Tolstoy Might Have Been, " Outlook, 98 (1 July
     1911), 470-471. A discussion of insights into Tolstoy's
     life provided by the publication of 281 of his letters; es-
     pecially noted is Tolstoy's near emigration to England in
     1872.

439 "Why Tolstoy Left His Home, " RRs, 43 (Feb. 1911), 245-246.

440 Williams, William C. "Tolstoy, " New Direc, 11 (1949), 358-
     359. A poem.

441 Witte, Sophie. "The Tragedy of Tolstoy, " Independent, 62 (20
     June 1907), 1439-1447. Trans. by Herman Bernstein. A
     biographical account of Tolstoy's life to 1907, and a sym-
     pathetic discussion of his major works.

442 Woolf, Leonard. "Tolstoy's Diary, " Nation, 125 (19 Oct.
     1927), 430. A discussion of Tolstoy's diary from 1853-
     1857 as translated by Maude.

443 Yarmolinsky, Avraham. "The Tolstoy Memorial Exhibit, "
     NYPLB, 32 (1928), 653-654.

444 Yarmolinsky, Avraham. "Tolstoy: September 9, 1928, "
     Wilson B, 3 no. 16 (1928), 396-399.

445 "The Young Tolstoy, " Times Lit Sup, 16 (21 June 1917), 289-
     290.

446 Zirkoff, Boris de. "The Youth of Count Tolstoy, " Theosoph P,
     30, no. 4 (April 1926), 334-346. Tolstoy's youtful activ-
     ities are discussed in light of his conversion.

447 Zweig, Stefan. "A Day from Tolstoy's Life, " Living Age, 334
     (1 Jan. 1928), 56-62.

     See also: 2, 3, 21, 96, 99, 104, 107, 116, 449, 452, 453,
        455, 456, 460, 465, 469, 470, 472, 475, 476, 477, 485,
        486, 488, 491, 492, 493, 499, 503, 508, 510, 521, 532,
        539, 552, 568, 654, 839, 947, 1216, 1217, 1219, 1220,
        1222, 1223, 1225, 1226, 1227, 1229, 1233, 1247, 1249,
        1255, 1259, 1260, 1264, 1271, 1272, 1273, 1274, 1277,
        1283, 1284, 1291, 1293, 1307, 1335, 1753, 2036, 2037,
        2042, 2045.

Section III

FICTION--GENERAL

BOOKS

448 Bayley, John. Tolstoy and the Novel. London: Chatto and
Windus, 1966; 316p. An analysis of Tolstoy's leading
works of fiction. Tolstoy is placed within the development
of 19th-century Russian literature, with comparisons made
to Pushkin and Dostoevsky. In examining his novels,
War and Peace receives far more attention than other
works (roughly one-half of the study), with special concern
for his ideas on warfare, nature, and the family as well
as the novel's major characters, its form and style. Anna
Karenina and Resurrection are then surveyed, followed by
a concluding section on Tolstoy's influence on Pasternak's
Dr. Zhivago. Reviewed in:
   Es in Criticism, (April 1967), 221, by T. Binyon.
   Hudson R, (Summer 1967), 335, by M. Murdick.
   New Sta, 72 (28 Oct. 1966), 663-664, by Christopher
      Ricks.
   N Y R Bks, 9 (14 Sept. 1967), 3.
   Rus R, 26 (July 1967), 308, by R. L. Strong.
   Slav R, 26, no. 3 (Sept. 1967), 510-511, by Ralph
      Matlaw.
   SEEJ, 12 (Summer 1968), 253-254, by Temira Pach-
      muss.
   Times Lit Sup, (8 Dec. 1966), 437.
   Virg Q R, (Summer 1967), 116.
   Yale R, 57 (Oct. 1967), 131, by William Frohock.

449 Benson, Ruth C. Women in Tolstoy. The Ideal and the Erotic.
Chicago: University of Illinois Press, 1973; 141p., bib. 139-
41. An examination of Tolstoy's views on women, romantic
love, marriage, and sexuality as presented in Family Hap-
piness, War and Peace, Anna Karenina, The Cossacks,
The Kreutzer Sonata, The Devil, and Father Sergius.
The conflict between his instincts and conscience is dis-
cussed as revealed in his fiction and life. Reviewed in:
   Choice, 11 (Sept. 1974), 953.
   Psy Today, 8 (Nov. 1974), 155.
   Rus R, 33 (July 1974), 338-339, by Mollie S. Rosen-
      han.

Slav R, 33, no. 4 (1973), 833, by Joan D. Grossman.
SEEJ, 18 (1974), 79-80, by Edwina Blumberg.

450   Cain, Thomas G. S. Tolstoy. New York: Harper & Row,
       1977; xiii, 210p., bib. 205-208. A study of Tolstoy from
       a literary perspective. Individual works of fiction are
       analyzed with the strand uniting them identified as being
       "Tolstoy's introspective quest for a stable concept of truth
       and moral order." The autobiographical character of his
       literary creations is stressed, hence special attention is
       given to his Confession as a spiritual autobiography. The
       study concludes with an examination of Hadji Murat as
       Tolstoy's last major piece of fiction, excluding drama
       which is not part of the author's focus. Reviewed in:
            Contemp R, 230 (June 1977), 335.
            Economist, 262, (5 Feb. 1977), 120.
            SEER, 55 (Oct. 1977), 534-535, by R. F. Christian.
            Times Lit Sup, (20 May 1977), 627, by E. B. Green-
               wood.

451   Christian, R. F. Tolstoy: A Critical Introduction. Cam-
       bridge, England: Cambridge University Press, 1969; vii,
       291p., bib. 279-284. A discussion of Tolstoy's leading
       works of fiction "treating them in their own right as works
       of literature, not as biographical evidence or contributions
       to a philosophical system." Tolstoy's style, language,
       method, characterizations, and intent are systematically
       analyzed, with the great majority of attention given to
       War and Peace and Anna Karenina. The continuity in his
       writings is emphasized, the last part of Anna Karenina
       being viewed as leading logically to his Confession which,
       in turn, is interpreted as a prelude to his religious writ-
       ings and their artistic embodiment in Resurrection. Re-
       viewed in:
            AUMLA, (Nov. 1970), 360, by J. D. Goodlife.
            Cambr Q, 5 (Autumn 1970), 115-123, by John Bayley.
            FMLS, 7, no. 1 (1971), 28-35, by Forsyth.
            Rus R, 29 (Oct. 1970), 472-473, by Ralph Matlaw.
            SEEJ, 15 (1971), 69-71, by Sigrid McLaughlin.
            Slav R, 29, no. 4 (Dec. 1970), 751, by Ernest J.
               Simmons.
            Times Lit Sup, (18 Dec. 1969), 1447.

452   Eikhenbaum, Boris. The Young Tolstoi. Trans. by Boucher
       et al. Ann Arbor, Mich.: Ardis, 1972; 152p. The gen-
       eral theory of "Formalism" is presented before an analy-
       sis is given of Tolstoy's early (1855-1862) literary activ-
       ity. The focus is the stylistic and compositional devices
       employed in Childhood, Caucasian Sketches, The Cossacks,
       and Sevastopol Sketches. It is concluded that by the end
       of the time period being studied, Tolstoy's basic literary
       path had been determined, since he had completed his
       search for a new literary form.

453 Hayman, Ronald. Tolstoy. London: Routledge and Kegan
    Paul, 1970; x, 116p., bib. 110-116. An introduction to
    Tolstoy's artistic ability by way of examples grouped un-
    der these headings: characterization, inner and outer
    landscape, group scenes, irony and satire, inner mono-
    logue, and dialogue. His narrative method is discussed
    and then illustrated by examples from his works in which
    he describes such subjects as cossack women, Polish
    soldiers, historical theory, children, and bird hunting.
    Reviewed in:
       Rus R, 30 (April 1971), 204-205, by Lauren Leighton.

454 Merezhkovski, Dmitri S. Tolstoi as Man and Artist, with an
    Essay on Dostoevski. Westport, Conn.: Greenwood, 1970;
    310p. An interpretive discussion of Tolstoy's literary
    style precedes an examination of his use of detail in War
    and Peace and Anna Karenina. His descriptions of the
    human body are discussed as is his mastery at presenting
    "bodily sensations": "Tolstoy is the greatest depictor of
    the physico-spiritual region in natural man: that side of
    the flesh which approaches the spirit." His minute physi-
    cal descriptions of characters are seen as blending into
    one unique and living picture that stirs the imagination of
    the reader and makes his characters seem real. The
    study concludes with an examination of the relation between
    art and religion in the thought of Dostoevsky and Tolstoy.
    Excerpts in LTCA, 113-122; RLMEF, 75-98; and TCCE,
    56-64. The first part of this study is annotated in Section
    II (item 189). For reviews, see list at entry 189.

455 Noyes, George R. Tolstoy. New York: Dover, 1968 (reprint
    of 1918 publication); xiv, 395p., bib. 367-371. An analy-
    sis of Tolstoy's major literary works arguing that their
    unique strengths and weaknesses both stem from the "in-
    tensely personal character of the observation of life on
    which they are based." The intimate connection between
    his life and works is consistently pointed out and identified
    as the key to his mastery of realism: "No author was
    more loath to depart from the material of life than was
    Tolstoy, no one was more absolutely a realist in the most
    literal sense of the term." Following a survey of his fic-
    tion, his ideas and activities in education, religion, and
    art are discussed, with Rousseau seen as having provided
    much of the philosophical-ethical basis for his beliefs.
    Reviewed in:
       Catholic W, 107 (June 1918), 404.
       Outlook, 119 (15 May 1918), 122-123.
       RRs, 58 (August 1918), 219.
       Yale R, 8 (Oct. 1918), 197-198, by William L. Phelps.

456 Redpath, Theodore. Tolstoy. New York: Hillary House, 1960;
    128p., bib. 116-128. Designed as an introduction to Tol-
    stoy's fiction and philosophy as a means of stimulating

further inquiry. Discussed is the close relation between
Tolstoy's personality and his fiction, hence the disparate
nature of much of his early work and the more linear and
economic character of his later writings, since his spiritual crisis had passed. In all, his psychological insight,
critical powers of observation, and consequent astonishingly
vivid realism are commended, and, when linked with his
penchant for raising the most disturbing of questions, is
seen as the root of his enduring fame. Reviewed in:
    AUMLA, (Nov. 1960), 110, by A. D. Hope.
    London M, (March 1960), 75, by J. M. S. Tompkins.
    Notes and Queries, (June 1960), 233, by Clifford
        Leech.

457 Simmons, Ernest J. Introduction to Tolstoy's Writings. Chi-
        cago: University of Chicago Press, 1969; viii, 219p.,
        bib. 212-214. A general discussion of Tolstoy's fiction
        and non-fiction based on the author's many introductions
        to Tolstoy's works, his essays about him, and his lengthy
        biography Leo Tolstoy. Short sketches, with a balance of
        summary and critical commentary, are presented on War
        and Peace, Anna Karenina, and Resurrection as well as
        on his lesser writings, which are grouped under broad
        headings. The study concludes with an assessment of
        Tolstoy's status in the contemporary world. Reviewed in:
        Can Slavic S, 4, no. 2 (Summer 1970), 346-347, by
            Alexander Zweers.
        Rus R, 28 (April 1969), 222, by Kathryn Feuer.
        SEEJ, 13 (Fall 1969), 394-395, by Elisabeth Trahan.
        Slav R, 28, no. 2 (1969), 351-352, by Richard Gustaf-
            son.
        Virg Q R, 44 (Summer 1968), 116.

ESSAYS AND CHAPTERS from general works

458 Auchincloss, Louis. "James and the Russian Novelists," in
        Reflections of a Jacobite. Boston: Houghton Mifflin,
        1961; 157-171. James' celebrated critical comments on
        the lack of composition and economy in Tolstoy's works
        of fiction are themselves criticized for being contradictory
        and often meaningless. Tolstoy's War and Peace, the
        focus of much of James' criticism, is praised for its
        composition, unity, and craftsmanship, with no signs of
        "flopping looseness" being seen. Similar support is given
        to Tolstoy in his Anna Karenina, except in the instance of
        Levin's "boring" discourses on agricultural theory. Ex-
        cerpts from this essay appear in Kronenberger, Louis,
        ed., Novelists on Novelists (Garden City, N. Y. : Double-
        day, 1962), 215-225.

459 Berry, Thomas E. "Tolstoi," in Plots and Characters in
        Major Russian Fiction. Hamden, Conn. : Shoe String

Press, 1977. Designed to encourage and facilitate the
reading of Russian literature, the work presents a summary of the plot of Tolstoy's major works of fiction, followed by an alphabetical list and short description of all
characters.

460 Brandes, George. "Tolstoi, " in Impressions of Russia. New
York: Crowell, 1966; 264-276. Tolstoy's fiction is applauded for its "fidelity to reality" and its "quality of
divination" both of which are seen as being products of the
intensely autobiographical nature of his works. War and
Peace is discussed as the leading example of his mastery
of realism before turning to a critical assessment of his
later works.

461 Brewster, Dorothy. East-West Passage: A Study in Literary
Relationships. London: Allen & Unwin, 1954; 328p. No
separate chapter appears on Tolstoy, but the spread of
his works, and Russian literature in general, throughout
Europe and America is discussed. Surveyed is the critical reception of Tolstoy in various Western literary col-
umns and writings; the reviews of Arnold, de Vogue,
Howells, Hapgood, Gosse, Galsworthy, and Lawrence are
presented.

462 Bruckner, Alexander. "Tolstoy, " in A Literary History of
Russia. London: T. Fisher Unwin, 1908; 364-389. An
interpretive survey of Tolstoy's basic works of fiction
against the background of the development of his philosophy. An argument is presented against the "often spoken
of change in Tolstoy, " claiming that in his literature and
life Tolstoy may have turned down various paths in his
search for truth, but always remained true to himself and
a sincere realist with penetrating vision.

463 Calder, Angus. "Literature and Morality: Leskov, Chekhov,
and the Late Tolstoy" in Russia Discovered: Nineteenth
Century Fiction from Pushkin to Chekhov. New York:
Harper and Row, 1976; 237-280. Tolstoy's later works
are discussed and seen to represent the conclusion of an
era in Russian literature. His death is not only considered to mark the end of the golden age of Russian prose
but also the beginning of the triumph of that which he opposed most fervently: radicalism and materialism.

464 Calder, Angus. "Tolstoy to War and Peace: Man against History" in Russia Discovered, 136-170. Tolstoy is considered, in his early works, to be stylistically an artist of
the 18th century and totally resistant to trends in the literature and direction of the Russia of his age, most notably progress, individualism, capitalism, and revolutionary socialism. His fiction is discussed as a reaction to
these trends and as a means for him to present his own
world view.

465 Civevskij, Dmitrij. "Tolstoj" in History of Nineteenth Century
     Russian Literature. Nashville: Vanderbilt University
     Press, 1974; 170-198. A brief sketch of Tolstoy's life
     precedes a general, though somewhat interpretive, survey
     of his fiction, especially his three major novels. Addi-
     tionally examined are his artistic views and general phi-
     losophy.

466 Clutton-Brock, Arthur. "Leo Tolstoy: The Novels" in More
     Essays on Books. London: Metheun, 1921; 149-159.
     The literature of Tolstoy is seen as ranking with the real-
     ist masterpieces of all time. War and Peace and Anna
     Karenina are discussed as proof of this contention as well
     as of the subtlety of his artistry. It is concluded that
     his fiction "does not overawe us with its greatness, but
     gently persuades of it; he does not make us impatient of
     reality, but reconciles us to it. "

467 Davie, Donald. "Tolstoy, Lermontov and Others" in RLMEF,
     164-199. Following a critique of The Kreutzer Sonata,
     Tolstoy's fiction in general is examined and criticized for
     being limited because he was the product of an age which
     saw "rights of will" overriding "rights of intelligence. "
     As such a product, Tolstoy is not considered to be an in-
     novator. He is then compared to other authors, with Ler-
     montov receiving most praise as an innovator, unlike Tol-
     stoy, in advance of his age.

468 Edel, Leon. "Dialectic of the Mind: Tolstoy" in The Modern
     Psychological Novel. Gloucester: Smith, 1972; 147-153.
     Tolstoy's psychological expertise is presented in a positive
     light, and it is stated that he "may yet come to be judged
     as the most significant precursor of the modern psycho-
     logical novel and stream of consciousness. " Passages
     from Anna Karenina and War and Peace are discussed as
     proof of Tolstoy's skill as a subjective novelist.

469 Eikhenbaum, Boris M. "Leo Tolstoy: Book One, The Fifties, "
     in LTCA, 194-96. Tolstoy's life and unique artistic abil-
     ities are seen as a consequence of two processes at work
     within him: observation and reflection. Translated from
     his Lev Tolstoy: Kniga pervaya 50-e gody.

470 Eikhenbaum, Boris M. "On Tolstoy's Crises, " in TCRLC, 97-
     101. Tolstoy's personal crises are judged to be a re-
     sponse to his search for new artistic forms and their ra-
     tionale. His works are seen as representing a "crisis"
     in Russian artistic prose by his having introduced primi-
     tivism and a "non-poetic art. " See his Young Tolstoi,
     from which this interpretation in taken, for a more com-
     plete annotation of his views on the relationship of Tol-
     stoy's art and personal life.

471   Field, Andrew.   "Viktor Shklovsky on Leo Tolstoy, " in The
      Complection of Russian Literature.   New York: Athene-
      um, 1971; 125-130.   Tolstoy's development of the tech-
      nique of "interior monologue" and the collision of various
      stages of self-awareness as a means of presenting the
      evolution of a character's thought is discussed, with the
      focus being Tolstoy's uncompleted work The Story of Yes-
      terday (1851).   A brief examination of his characterization
      of Anna of Anna Karenina is also presented.

472   Freeborn, Richard, et al.   "Tolstoy" in Russian Literary Atti-
      tudes from Pushkin to Solzhenitsyn.   London: Macmillan,
      1976; 60-78.   Tolstoy's literary genius is viewed as rest-
      ing in his ability to "mirror life so accurately" that we ac-
      cept his fiction as life.   His "infectious sincerity" in all
      of his literature, and "the sheer truthfulness of his vi-
      sion" are seen as dwarfing the negative impression made
      by the contradictions between his philosophy and life style.
      Several Russian literary critics are cited to support this
      interpretation.

473   Gide, Andre.   Journals.   Vol. III, 1928-1939.   New York:
      Knopf, 1948; 243p.   Tolstoy's self-imposed retreat from
      fiction writing in his later years is interpreted, by the
      French novelist and critic, as being due to "the decline
      of his creative faculties. "   Also in LTCA, 197-98.

474   Gosse, Edmund.   "Count Lyof Tolstoi, " in Critical Kit-Kats,
      New York: Dodd, Mead, 1896; 113-131.   Tolstoy's fiction,
      especially Anna Karenina and War and Peace, is praised
      for its realistic qualities and for propagating a belief "in
      the beauty and nobility of the human race. "   His abandon-
      ment of fiction writing for the sake of preaching his newly
      formed religious views is deplored, and a plea is made
      for him to return to "the literature of Anna Karenina. "
      Also in his Collected Essays (London, 1913), Vol. III,
      113-131; and LTCA, 100-01 (excerpts).

475   Griswold, Hattie Tyng.   "Lyeff Tolstoi, " in Personal Sketches
      of Recent Authors.   Chicago: McClurg, 1898; 251-265.
      Tolstoy's literary efforts prior to his spiritual awakening
      are positively assessed before his later philosophical be-
      liefs are criticized as the source of the decline of his
      artistic creations.   His post-conversion works are labeled
      "irrelevant and almost childish, " and therefore "no longer
      hold the attention of the world. "

476   Hamburger, Kate.   "Tolstoy's Art, " in TCCE, 65-77.   A
      study of the style and method in each of Tolstoy's major
      works of fiction based on the contention that "the autobio-
      graphical impetus is related to the inner principle of form
      in the Tolstoyan epic, " a relation of which Tolstoy was
      unaware.   Childhood, Boyhood, Youth, War and Peace,

and <u>Anna Karenina</u> are discussed in light of this interpretation.

477 Henley, William E. "Tolstoi: The Man and the Artist, " in
     <u>Views and Reviews: Essays in Appreciation</u>, Vol. I. New
     York: AMS, 1970 (reprint of 1908 publication); 266-272.
     Tolstoy is discussed as being two men, one a mystic, and
     the other a realist. This division within him is seen as
     having played a crucial role in determining the nature of
     his novels. Tolstoy's epics, it is argued, deal with the
     eternal issues of life, with the artistic and mystic meeting
     and taking hands sometimes to profit, more often to harm.
     A brief discussion of <u>War and Peace</u> and <u>Ivan Ilyich</u> fol-
     lows this contention.

478 Kropotkin, Petern. "Turgeneff; Tolstoy" in <u>Russian Literature</u>.
     New York: Blom, 1967 (reprint of 1905 publication); 109-
     148. A survey, by the Russian anarchist and critic, of
     Tolstoy's works with special concern for their historical
     context, most notably the development of the revolutionary
     movement and the impact of the reforms of Alexander II.
     Tolstoy's fiction as well as his views on education, reli-
     gion, ethics, and art are all discussed sympathetically,
     with the claim made that "no man since the time of Rous-
     seau has so profoundly stirred the human conscience. "
     Also in <u>Ideals and Realities in Russian Literature</u> (New
     York: Knopf, 1915), 110-150.

479 Kunitz, Joshua. "From the Eighties to the Revolution of 1917, "
     in <u>Russian Literature and the Jew: A Sociological Inquiry
     into the Nature and Origin of Literary Patterns</u>. New
     York: Columbia University Press, 1929; 95-165. Tol-
     stoy's infrequent mention in his works of Jews is linked
     to his inability to present a complimentary image of the
     Jew, which is due to the effects of the anti-Semitism prev-
     alent in the Russia of his era. It is argued that since
     his talents stemmed from the sincerity with which he ap-
     proached his subjects, he could not, as a product of his
     age, artistically depict the tragedy of Russian Jews.

480 Lavrin, Janko. "Tolstoy, " in <u>An Introduction to the Russian
     Novel</u>. London: Methuen, 1947; 113-125. A discussion
     of the distinctions between Dostoevsky and Tolstoy is pre-
     sented before a general survey is made of Tolstoy's basic
     works. His fictional and philosophical writings are seen
     as sharing a common "rootedness in the soil" and a mutual
     opposition to modern civilization. In all, his artistic cre-
     ations are much more positively presented than his moral
     and philosophic views.

481 Leontiev, Konstantin. "The Novels of Count L. N. Tolstoy:
     Analysis, Style, and Atmosphere, " in <u>Essays in Russian</u>

Literature, The Conservative View: Leontiev, Rozanov, Shestov. Athens: Ohio University Press, 1968; 225-356. An early landmark (the original was published in 1890) in formal analytical criticism of Tolstoy's work, the study presents an assessment of his fiction in general with detailed analysis being reserved for Anna Karenina and War and Peace. War and Peace is praised as a "healthy tragedy" which captures the atmosphere of a great time in Russian history, but is criticized for inauthenticity in characters and their reactions to events: "the basic design is true, the colors are too rich and bright." Suggested changes are simplification of language, less introspection, elimination of "flowery" turns of speech, and less slavophilic idolization of simple folk. Anna Karenina is judged to be superior to War and Peace because its characters are more true to their time and represent a more accurate view of life. Excerpt appears in LTCA, 80-96.

482   Lindstrom, Thais. "The Great Truth Tellers," in A Concise History of Russian History, Vol. I From the Beginnings to Chekhov, 166-180. A brief comparison of Tolstoy and Dostoevsky precedes an analysis of Tolstoy's fiction, with only single paragraphs on writings other than Anna Karenina and War and Peace. A very general and sympathetic treatment.

483   Lukacs, Georg. "Leo Tolstoy and Western European Literature," in Studies in European Realism, 242-264. The "false" interpretations of Tolstoy from reactionary and conservative quarters are criticized, and Tolstoy is presented as a progressive in the Chernyshevsky tradition in that he sought to regenerate the spirit of freedom within the Russian people. His works are praised as an effective means of disseminating that which he tried to attain in his own life, "a clear vision of truth via a love embracing all mankind." Excerpts in WPMT, 1423-29.

484   Lukacs, Georg. "Tolstoy and the Development of Realism," in Studies in European Realism. New York: Grosset & Dunlap, 1974 (reprint of 1964 publication); 126-205. Tolstoy is seen, by the Marxist literary critic, as being remarkable for developing the traditions of the great realists at a time when realism was degenerating in world literature into naturalism and formalism: "He saved the idea that great art is rooted in the people and must perish if it is torn from its native soil." With much reference to Lenin's analysis of Tolstoy, it is concluded that at a time when Russia was on the eve of its bourgeois revolution, Tolstoy was the master of bourgeois realism. Excerpts in TCCE, 78-94.

485   Mais, Stuart P. "Tolstoy," in Why We Should Read. Freeport, N.Y.: Books for Libraries Press, 1967 (reprint

of 1921 publication); 284-291. Tolstoy's fiction is favorably analyzed from the perspective of his use of gestures,
physical traits, and small characteristics in painting personalities, but he is criticized for his lack of "spiritual
liberty" as argued by Turgenev. Additionally his life is
surveyed, especially his spiritual conversion and its negative effects on his marriage.

486 Mann, Thomas. "Tolstoi: On the 100th Anniversary of His
     Birth, " in Past Masters and Other Papers.   Freeport,
     N. Y. : Books for Libraries Press, 1968 (reprint of 1933
     publication); 157-166. The epic and timeless character of
     Tolstoy's fiction is discussed against the background of
     his tragic struggle to give meaning to his life. His works
     of fiction are praised, but his philosophy is not accepted
     as being practical.

487 Mathewson, Rufus W.   The Positive Hero in Russian Litera-
     ture.   Stanford, Calif. : Stanford University Press, 1975.
     No separate chapter on Tolstoy. It is stated that Tol-
     stoy's heroes were unacceptable to radical critics of 19th-
     century Russia because they lacked "combative spirit" or
     "proper social orientation, " and because his heroes' dis-
     covery of truth was too tentative. Nonetheless, it is sug-
     gested that his later artistic views can be linked in spirit
     with those of the Soviet regime. Also discussed is his
     influence on Solzhenitsyn's August, 1914.

488 Merezhkovsky, Dmitri S.   "Tolstoy as Artist, " in RLMEF,
     123-138.   Excerpt from his book. See item 454 for an
     annotation of his thesis, which is similar to that of this
     excerpt.

489 Merezhkovsky, Dmitri S.   "Tolstoy, Seer of the Flesh, " in
     TCCE, 56-64.   Excerpt from his book. See item 454 for
     an annotation of his thesis, which is similar to that of this
     excerpt.

490 Merezhkovsky, Dmitri S.   "Tolstoy's Physical Descriptions, "
     in AKMT, 802-810.   Excerpt from his book. See item
     454 for an annotation of his thesis, which is similar to
     that of this excerpt.

491 Mirsky, D. S.   "Tolstoy after 1880, " in A History of Russian
     Literature from Its Beginnings to 1900, 305-325.   Tol-
     stoy's major works after his spiritual conversion are dis-
     cussed in light of his desire to propagate his religious
     and moral views as well as his anti-materialist philos-
     ophy.   His radical views on the nature of "good art" are
     examined, as is his consistent contempt for accepted
     norms in literary form.   Contains his History of Russian
     Literature from Earliest Times to the Death of Dostoev-
     sky, and the first two chapters of his Contemporary Rus-
     sian Literature, 1881-1925.

492 Mirsky, D. S. "Tolstoy before 1880, " in A History of Rus-
     sian Literature from Its Beginnings to 1900. New York:
     Random House, 1958; 256-275. Tolstoy's place in Russian
     literature as the most important author from a moral
     perspective is established before a justification is pre-
     sented for dividing the analysis of his work into halves
     because of the "profound change in his artistic views" that
     accompanied his religious conversion. To 1880, his work
     is discussed as being representative of the "realistic
     school" of Russian literature, especially through his use
     of "superfluous detail. " Consistent in all of his work, it
     is argued, is his contempt for modern civilization, his
     search for life's meaning, and rejection of accepted liter-
     ary "good form. "

493 Muchnic, Helen. "Lev Nikolayevich Tolstoy, " in An Introduc-
     tion to Russian Literature. New York: Doubleday, 1947;
     181-222. A positive assessment of Tolstoy's lifelong pur-
     suit for truth precedes a survey of his fiction with heavy
     emphasis on War and Peace. Designed as an introduction,
     the standard topics and works are discussed.

494 Nekrasov, N. A. "Notes on Journals for December, 1855 and
     January, 1856, " in LTCA, 29-30. Tolstoy is praised by
     Nekrasov, the Russian poet and editor of The Contempo-
     rary, as an unusually talented realist although his works
     are seen as suffering from a lack of unity and therefore
     seem to leave the reader with an impression of incom-
     pleteness. Tolstoy's work, Sevastopol in August, 1855,
     is used as an example to prove this contention, with its
     merits seen as far out-weighing its deficiencies. Trans-
     lated from Sovremennik, no. 2, 1856.

495 O'Connor, Frank. "Tolstoy and the Surrender of the Will, "
     in The Mirror in the Roadway: A Study of the Modern
     Novel. New York: Knopf, 1956; 148-164. Tolstoy's lit-
     erary genius is regarded as stemming from his ability
     "to see and describe with absolute fidelity what his char-
     acters are doing and thinking. " This talent, coupled with
     his powerful expression of his personal vision of life, it
     is claimed, makes him "among the most original writers
     who ever lived. " Anna Karenina and, especially, War and
     Peace are presented as proof of this claim.

496 Olgin, Moissaye J. "L. N. Tolstoi" in A Guide to Russian
     Literature. New York: Russell and Russell, 1971 (re-
     print of 1920 publication); 114-119. A brief survey of
     Tolstoy's three major novels is given along with a short
     analysis of War and Peace by critics P. Kogan and R.
     Ivanov-Razumnik, all in a favorable light.

497 Priestley, John B. "The Novelists" in Literature and Western
     Man. New York: Harper and Brothers, 1960; 250-256.

Tolstoy's War and Peace and Anna Karenina are commended as being unquestionably great works of fiction,
whereas his early works concerning military life and autobiography are regarded as "preparation for the writing of
his two masterpieces," and his later works are considered to exhibit only flashes of greatness because he had
"lost the spark" responsible for the majesty of his two
major novels. The contradictions in his life are then
discussed before a positive assessment is given of War
and Peace and Anna Karenina.

498   Proust, Marcel. "Tolstoi" in On Art and Literature. London:
        Chatto & Windus, 1957; 378-380. It is argued that Tol-
        stoy's literary work is that of a genius, a creator who
        could take a few simple themes and shape them into
        masterpieces. Scenes from War and Peace and Anna
        Karenina are briefly presented as evidence for the con-
        tention that Tolstoy repeated himself simply yet creatively
        in his works. Also in Kronenberger, 161-163.

499   Rascoe, Burton. "Tolstoi: The Painter" in Titans of Litera-
        ture from Homer to the Present. Freeport, N.Y.: Books
        for Libraries Press, 1970 (reprint of 1932 publication);
        411-420. The source of Tolstoy's literary genius is
        identified as his acute social and moral conscience com-
        bined with his boundless energy. His excessive energy is,
        in turn, seen as being rooted in the "severe conscience"
        which forced him to attempt to harmonize his beliefs and
        actions. His life and works are traced in light of this
        contention, with emphasis placed on his failure to find
        peace of mind.

500   Roberts, Morris. Henry James' Criticism. New York: Octa-
        gon Books, 1970; 87, 94, 97, 131 (no separate chapter on
        Tolstoy). Tolstoy's artistic talents are critically assessed
        by James with Tolstoy's works judged to be characterized
        by "hopelessly bemuddled waste" and a "general absence
        of art." Deplored is the fact that many young authors
        study Tolstoy instead of Turgenev who is considered to
        be superior to him as a writer. James' dislike of all
        "looseness" in literary style is then discussed, especially
        his much quoted "loose baggy monster" criticism of War
        and Peace.

501   Salaman, Esther P. "Tolstoy" in The Great Confession from
        Aksakov and DeQuincey to Tolstoy and Proust. London:
        Penguin, 1973; 67-195. A lengthy analysis of the auto-
        biographical elements in Tolstoy's fiction with much use
        of draft versions and notes as a means of gaining insight
        into the process followed by Tolstoy in creating his works
        as well as into the complex nature of his personality.
        Tolstoy's drafts are seen to be different from most draft
        versions of fiction in that his were due not to the need to

cut, coordinate or polish his work but rather were in response to the "waves of inspiration" which went through
his mind as he continued to develop his ideas. It is concluded that few writers' works in all history are as intensely autobiographical as his: "Tolstoy is everywhere
in his works. "

502 Schulz, Robert K. "Lev Nikolayevich Tolstoj" in The Portrayal
of the German in Russian Novels: Goncharov, Turgenev,
Dostoevskij, Tolstoj. Munich: Sagner, 1969; 155-182.
Tolstoy's observations on Germans are discussed before
an analysis is presented of his description of Germans in
his fiction. It is maintained that his Germans are "limited, narrow, heartless, and egotistical, " and lack funda-
mental humane traits. " He is linked with Dostoevsky as
being part of that group of Russians who were severely
critical of German elements in Russia, and then unfairly
generalized their criticism to apply to all Germans.

503 Scott, William T. "The Paradoxes in the Life and Writings
of Tolstoi" in Chesterton and Other Essays. New York:
Eaton and Mains, 1912; 123-144. It is contended that "in
attempting to make an estimate of Tolstoy, we find ourselves dealing with paradoxes at almost every turn. " The
only point not considered to be in doubt is his literary
greatness. The leading qualities of this greatness are
identified as being his superior style, sincerity and imagination. Tolstoy the moralizer is criticized for engaging
in the "baldest of idealism, " a stark paradox in comparison to his literary realism.

504 Shaw, George Bernard. "Tolstoy: Tragedian or Comedian, "
in Pen Portraits and Reviews. London: Constable, 1932;
260-266. Tolstoy's very subtle yet highly effective use of
humor in his fiction is discussed with the contention advanced that he "could slay a soul with a corkscrew without
letting you know either that he was a humorist or that you
are laughing. " Also examined is his social doctrine, which
is judged to be exceptionally negative, and its destructive
effect on those who follow his teachings. Excerpts in
LTCA, 172-174. Originally in Lon Merc, 4 (May 1921),
31-34.

505 Shklovsky, Victor. "Art as Technique" in Russian Formalist
Criticism: Four Essays, ed. L. T. Lemon and Marion
J. Reis. Lincoln: University of Nebraska Press, 1965;
3-24. An analysis of Tolstoy's technique of "defamiliari-
zation, " by which is meant his description of objects that
are familiar as if they were being seen for the very first
time and thereby necessitate a complete examination. It
is maintained that several hundred passages could be cited
as examples of his use of this technique in his fiction and
non-fiction alike.

506 Shklovsky, Victor. "Parallels in Tolstoy, " in TCRLC, 81-85.
    An examination of Tolstoy's use of parallels to emphasize
    his points as made in Three Deaths, A Story of a Horse,
    War and Peace, and Anna Karenina. Tolstoy is consid-
    ered to have used a "staircase-like construction" of people
    and events which collectively represent the "unfolding of
    a single type. " Examples of this technique abound in his
    works, it is claimed, with War and Peace and Anna Kar-
    enina judged to be the best illustrations of his parallelism.

507 Simmons, Ernest J. "Tolstoy: My Hero Is Truth" in Intro-
    duction to Russian Realism. Bloomington: Indiana Uni-
    versity Press, 1965; 135-180. The nature of Tolstoy's
    realism is explored within the context of the development
    of Russian literature in the 19th century, with frequent
    parallels drawn with Pushkin, Gogol, and Dostoevsky.
    Tolstoy is particularly commended for his skill in present-
    ing ideas in a complex, intimate autobiographical fashion,
    which results in a ranking of his realism "among the
    most convincing in world literature. " A detailed analysis
    of War and Peace is presented as substantiation for this
    claim.

508 Sisk, Jean. "Leo Tolstoy" in Three Masters of Russian Fic-
    tion. Lessons in Critical Reading and Writing. New
    York: Harcourt Brace Jovanovich, 1970; 85-176. The
    nature of Tolstoy's art is illustrated by way of a collec-
    tion of opinions on his personality and works as well as
    by way of excerpts from his major writings. Mirsky and
    Gorky provide the introduction to Tolstoy, while the author
    surveys his literary technique and characterizations. In-
    terspersed are groups of questions designed to stimulate
    the reader's thought.

509 Slonim, Marc. "Tolstoy" in The Epic of Russian Literature
    from Its Origins through Tolstoy. New York: Oxford,
    1964; 309-346. Tolstoy's fiction is examined with the key
    to understanding it viewed as being an awareness of his
    background, especially his social class, family, and per-
    sonal experiences. The uniformly high quality of his real-
    ism in describing peasant and aristocratic life is regarded
    as being a product of his being an aristocrat by birth but
    having immense feeling for the peasant and his way of life.
    Examples of his portrayal of peasant and aristocratic life
    are given, with most reference to War and Peace. For a
    shorter survey of Tolstoy by Slonim see his "Tolstoy" in
    An Outline of Russian Literature (New York: Oxford Uni-
    versity Press, 1958), 145-157.

510 Spector, Ivar. "Lev Nikolayevitch Tolstoy, " in The Golden
    Age of Russian Literature. Seattle: University of Wash-
    ington Press, 1938; 96-126. A brief summary of the
    major events in Tolstoy's life precedes a plot summary

of The Cossacks, War and Peace, Anna Karenina, and
Resurrection. Tolstoy and Dostoevsky are then contrasted,
with major differences seen in their physical constitutions,
style of living, social background, relation to the government, and, most importantly, their views on religion,
man, and life. The philosophical content of each of his
leading works is discussed, with reference to similarity
to Eastern philosophy, and it is concluded that the greatness of his creations made him "an institution in the
Golden Age of Russian Literature. " For a condensed version of this account, see his "Lyov N. Tolstoy, " in An
Introduction to Russian History and Culture (Princeton,
N. J. : D. Van Nostrand, 1969), 196-209.

511   Steuart, John A.   "To Count Lyof N. Tolstoi, " in Letters to
      Living Authors.   New York: United States Book Co. ,
      1890; 70-84.   A letter to Tolstoy in support of Matthew
      Arnold's contention that Tolstoy's work was the major
      reason for Europe's becoming aware of Russian literature.
      His ideas on religion and property are praised but seen
      as inapplicable to Western Europe.   The manner in which
      Tolstoy is viewed in the West is also discussed.

512   Trainor, Edward A.   "Tolstoy: Novelist and Moralist, " in
      Six Novelists: Stendhal, Dostoevsky, Tolstoy, Hardy,
      Dreiser, and Proust, ed. William Schutte et al.   Pitts-
      burgh: Carnegie University Press, 1959; 29-40.
      Tolstoy is judged to be one of the world's finest novelists,
      but his philosophy and activities are criticized.   In spite
      of the weaknesses of his philosophy, the qualities that led
      him to become a moral teacher are seen as the source of
      his greatness as a novelist, these qualities being "sensi-
      tive perception of the material world, " an "ability to know
      man truly, " and the "ability to recreate truth through
      words. "   Examples are taken from War and Peace and
      Anna Karenina to prove this contention.

513   Tsanoff, Radoslav A.   "Count Tolstoy the Novelist" in The
      Problem of Life in the Russian Novel.   Houston: Rice
      University Institute Pamphlet, 1917; 210-237.   The sever-
      ity and earnestness of Tolstoy's judgments, even though
      they represent a rejection of the basic principles of mod-
      ern civilization, are considered the very source of the
      universal attention which he commands.   His fiction is
      discussed in line with this contention, and it is concluded
      that in spite of his quest and fame he failed to "find his
      soul. "   Nonetheless, his search is regarded as "one of
      the most powerful spiritual documents of modern times. "

514   Uspensky, Boris.   A Poetics of Composition.   Trans. by V.
      Zavarin and S. Wittig.   Berkeley: University of California
      Press, 1974.   Not available for annotation, but listed as
      a discussion of the variety of categories for describing the

fictional point of view, such as ideological, psychological, compositional, logical, and spatial. Major examples come from the works of Dostoevsky and Tolstoy, especially War and Peace.

515 Waliszewski, K.   "The Preachers" in A History of Russian Literature. Port Washington, N. Y.: Kennikat, 1969 (reprint of 1927 publication); 360-400. A brief biographical survey and general comments on Tolstoy's place in world literature precede a discussion of the central theme of his works as being that "no individual is capable of attaining anything at all by his own strength." Tolstoy's distrust of individualism, which is criticized for being overly fatalistic, is illustrated by examples from his fiction, especially War and Peace and Anna Karenina.

516 Wilkinson, William C.   "Tolstoy" in Some New Literary Valuations. New York: Funk and Wagnalls, 1909; 349-395. Tolstoy is commended for his literary achievements, but criticized for lack of "final soundness and justness of judgment." His fiction is analyzed for those qualities that have made it great while reference is continually made to the lack of balance in his thought, especially as exhibited in The Kreutzer Sonata. It is concluded, however, that in spite of the deficiencies in his thinking, Tolstoy is an inspiration for all the world because of the power of his thought.

517 Williams, H. W.   "Literature" in Russia of the Russians. New York: Scribner's, 1914; 178-227. An analysis of Russian literature in the later years of Tolstoy centered around the question of why Tolstoy and Dostoevsky had no immediate successors of ability equal to theirs. The growth of concern for political, social and economic issues is considered to be responsible for lessening the influence and appeal that literature previously had. Although the quality of literature at the end of the century is regarded as being lower than in the great age of Russian prose, and although Tolstoy himself did not like the direction that Russian literature was heading, similarities between the two eras are seen in their concern for the great questions of life as well as in their mutual "childlike" disregard for the consequences of their pursuits.

518 Wilson, Edmund.   "Notes on Tolstoy" in A Window on Russia. New York: Farrar, Straus & Giroux, 1972; 160-183. Favorable comments on Troyat's biography, especially agreeing with Troyat's assessment of Tolstoy's inconsistencies, precede a random selection of opinions on Tolstoy, his works and their value for Western readers. There follows a discussion of the decline in the quality of his art after his religious conversions due largely to his later works' being "deformed by his moralistic bias."

519 Wolkonsky, Serge M. "Leo Tolstoi" in Pictures of Russian
     History and Russian Literature. Boston: Lamson, Wolffe,
     1897; 237-270. The artistic creations of Tolstoy are dis-
     cussed and commended for their epic panorama and excep-
     tional realism. His stature as a thinker, however, is
     considered to be minimal and actually at war with his
     artistic stature. In fact, the most striking feature of his
     intellect is identified as the "contrast between the uniting
     power of his literature and the disintegration preached
     by his philosophy. " His philosophy is praised only in that
     it represents a campaign against insincerity.

520 Woolf, Virginia. "The Russian Point of View" in The Common
     Reader. New York: Harcourt, Brace, 1925; 243-256.
     The Russian perspective is defined as being an odd and
     alien one defying accurate translation, with Tolstoy's works
     considered to be a prime example. Since English-language
     translations of Tolstoy's fiction cannot do justice to this
     "Russian point of view, " it is considered to be remarkable
     that his realism is still powerfully penetrating in the eyes
     of the English reader. So unique are Tolstoy's introspec-
     tive qualities that they exert a disquieting influence on the
     reader, so that of all the Russian writers he is judged to
     be the one who "most enthralls us and most repels. " Ex-
     cerpt in LTCA, 188-190.

521 Zweig, Stefan. "Tolstoy" in Adepts in Self-Portraiture: Casa-
     nova, Stendhal, Tolstoy. London: Cassell, 1952 (reprint
     of 1930 publication); 199-336. Tolstoy is presented as
     "the supreme example of spiritual self-contemplation of
     self-portraiture" in that he made everything in the real
     world turn back into his own personality. His fiction is
     thus interpreted as being a microcosm of his own ego.
     Numerous examples are raised to support this contention,
     with much insight provided into the spiritually autobio-
     graphical nature of his artistic creations. Also in his
     Master Builders: A Typology of the Spirit (New York:
     Viking, 1939; 757-903).

PERIODICAL ARTICLES

522 Adams, A. E. "Pobedonostev's Thought Control, " Rus R, 11,
     no. 4 (Oct. 1952), 241-246. Concerning Pobedonostev as
     official censor, and his power to encourage writers with
     views similar to his own. Tolstoy is seen as his victim.

523 Adams, R. J. "Tolstoy and Children's Art: Sincerity and
     Expression, " Art and Ed, 26 (March 1973), 4-5.

524 Anzulovic, Branimir. "Tolstoi and the Novel, " Genre, 3, no.
     2 (March 1970). The form of the novel and Tolstoy's at-
     titude toward it are examined by way of War and Peace and
     Anna Karenina.

525 Arabazhin, K. "Leo Tolstoy and His Significance, " Country
     Life, (14 Oct. 1916), 470-471, illus.

526 Baring, Maurice. "Tolstoy and Tourgeniev, " Quarterly R, 211
     (July 1909), 180-202. Also in Landmarks in Russian Lit-
     erature, 50-73.

527 Berthold, A. "Translators, Translations and Tolstoy, " Wilson
     B, (May 1933), 546-548.

528 Burton, R. G. "An Appreciation of Russian Fictional Litera-
     ture, " Westm R, 144 (Nov. 1895), 539.

529 Cecil, Lord David. "The Novelist's Problem, " Adam, nos.
     284-286 (1960), 9-13. A discussion of Tolstoy's realism,
     the "problem" being making fiction seem real.

530 Cecil, Lord David. "Some Reflection on the Art of Leo Tol-
     stoy, " Oxford S P, 11 (1964), 60-68.

531 "Count Leo Tolstoy's Novels, " Nineteenth Cent, 5 (April 1879),
     651.

532 "Count Tolstoi's Novels, " Sat R, 63 (1 Jan. 1887), 22-23. A
     discussion of the duality of Tolstoy in his novels: The
     Cossacks, War and Peace and Anna Karenina.

533 "Count Tolstoy, " Dial, 25, no. 293 (1 Sept. 1898), 121-123.
     An account praising Tolstoy's fiction but rejecting his
     philosophical views.

534 Curtis, J. M. "Notes on Spatial Form in Tolstoy, " Sewanee
     R, 78, no. 3 (Summer 1970), 517-530.

535 Decker, Clarence. "Victorian Comment on Russian Realism, "
     PMLA, 52 (June 1937), 542-549. Concerning Tolstoy's
     literary reputation in England, with a discussion compar-
     ing his brand of realism to French realism. Tolstoy's
     realism is praised as are the four journals which are
     considered to be responsible for establishing his reputation
     in England: Contemporary Review, Fortnightly Review,
     Spectator, and Saturday Review.

536 Dos Passos, John. "On Re-reading Tolstoy, " Adam, nos. 284-
     286 (1960), 17-18.

537 Edwards, G. C. "Tolstoy, " Sewanee R, 9 (1901), 452-472.
     A general survey of Tolstoy's fiction and non-fiction.

538 Eikhenbaum, Boris. "How Tolstoy Worked, " Story, 8, no. 43
     (Feb. 1936), 2, 4-5, 101. Trans. by Charles Malamuth.
     Discusses the enormity of the task of publishing Tolstoy's
     complete works.

539   Eikhenbaum, Boris.   "On Lev Tolstoy, " RLT, 10 (Fall 1974),
      198-200.   Trans. by R. Parrott and P. Frantz.   A dis-
      cussion of Tolstoy and realism as well as an examination
      of the theory of a dual nature in Tolstoy.   Using On Art
      as an example, the change from Tolstoy as writer to
      Tolstoy as teacher is analyzed.

540   Ellis, H.   "The Supreme Russian, " New St, 9 (22 Sept. 1971),
      590-591.

541   Eppens, E. H.   "Tolstoy and the Heroic Element in Men, "
      Homiletic R, 64 (July 1912), 813.

542   "An Estimate of Tolstoy, " Bookman, 28 (Oct. 1908), 110-111.
      An overview of British criticism of Tolstoy, in particular,
      S. Strunsky, G. K. Chesterton and R. Strong.

543   Fedin, K.   "The Genius of Tolstoy, " Atlantic M, 205 (June
      1960), 85-86.   Trans. by E. Zarudnaya.

544   Finch, C. E.   "Tolstoy as a Student of the Classics, " Classi-
      cal J, 47 (March 1952), 205-210.

545   Galsworthy, John.   "Tolstoy as a Novelist, " Nation, 127 (5
      Sept. 1928), 218-219.

546   Garnett, E.   "Tolstoy's Place in European Literature, " Book-
      man, 19 (March 1901), 184-187.

547   Gill, Charles W.   "Tolstoy the Novelist, " Chaut, 69 (Feb.
      1913), 312-319.

548   Goldenweiser, A.   "Tolstoy Saga, " New Republic, 74 (12 April
      1933), 250-251.

549   Gorlin, Mikhail.   "The Interrelation of Painting and Literature
      in Russia, " SEER, 25, no. 64 (1946), 134-148.   Trans.
      by N. Brodiansky.

550   Gosse, E.   "Count Leo Tolstoy, " Contemp R, 94 (Sept. 1908),
      272.

551   Greenwood, E. B.   "Eikhenbaum, Fomalism and Tolstoy, "
      Es in Criticism, 23 (Oct. 1973), 372-387.

552   Grindea, Miron.   "The Slav Homer, " Adam, nos. 284-286
      (1960), viii-xvi.   Introduction to the issue dedicated to
      Tolstoy on the 50th anniversary of his death.

553   Hichens, R.   "Tolstoy the Novelist, " Eng R, 47 (Sept. 1928),
      306-313.   A discussion of Tolstoy's literary greatness
      using The Two Hussars as an example.   Also an introduc-
      tion to The Two Hussars for the Centenary Edition of

Tolstoy's works, Oxford University Press, trans. by Louise Maude and Aylmer Maude.

554 Hillman, A. M. "Tolstoy and Translations, " Sat R Lit, 28 (13 Oct. 1945), 25. A letter to the editor correcting a statement made previously that Garnett never translated Tolstoy.

555 Jameson, Storm. "A Sense of Proportion, " Adam, nos. 284-286 (1960), 169-170.

556 Johnston, C. "How Count Tolstoy Works, " Arena, 21 (1899), 269-272.

557 Kinloch, Alexander. "Translating Tolstoy, " Sat R, 99 (21 Jan. 1905), 81. On the impossibility of an adequate translation of Power of Darkness with reference to the Maude, Shaw, Beerbohm feud over this issue.

558 Lavrin, Janko. "Tolstoy: A Peculiar Blend. A Classic Revalued, " Sat R Lit, 33 (16 Dec. 1950), 19, 39. A discussion, in honor of the 40th anniversary of Tolstoy's death, of the blend of artistic and ethical elements in his work.

559 Losskii, N. O. "Tolstoy as Seer of Both Flesh and Spirit, " Ang Theo R, 43 (Oct. 1961), 394-397.

560 Lovett, Robert M. "Tolstoy: The Lesson of the Artist, " New Republic, 56 (5 Sept. 1928), 63-66.

561 "Lyoff Tolstoi, Artist and Preacher, " Lippincott's M, 90 (Dec. 1912), 747-754. An introduction to Tolstoy's short story A Long Exile, also titled God Sees the Truth but Bides His Time.

562 Mabie, H. W. "Tolstoy as Author, " Outlook, 88 (28 March 1908), 743-746.

563 Maude, Aylmer. "Leo Tolstoy, " Spectator, 141 (1 Sept. 1928), 259-260. A discussion of the lack of good translations of Tolstoy's works. The centenary edition is seen as a resolution to this problem.

564 Maude, Aylmer. "Translations of Tolstoy, " Sat R, 99 (28 Jan. 1905), 110-111. An examination of the difficulties encountered when translating Tolstoy with relation to the Weiner translations and to Shaw's comments made in a previous issue.

565 Moore, George. "Avowals. A Series of Confessions of a Young Man, " Lippincott's M, 72 (Nov. 1903), 608-616 and 72 (Dec. 1903), 697-703. Also in his Avowals (London: Riverside Press, 1919), pp. 137-164.

566   Morawski, S.   "Lenin as a Literary Theorist, " Sci and Soc,
        29 (Winter 1965), 2-25.

567   Murdoch, Iris.   "Negative Capability, " Adam, nos. 284-286
        (1960), 172-173.

568   Norman, Sir Henry B.   "Russia of Today, " Scrib M, 28 (1900),
        387-406.

569   Noyes, G. R.   "Tolstoy as a Man of Letters, " Calif U Chron,
        13 (April 1911), 146-163.   An analysis of Tolstoy's fiction
        in terms of its sincerity, technique, style, and insight into
        human nature, and a discussion of his views on art.

570   "Of Count Lyof N. Tolstoi.   Donovitch's Confession (Shockingly
        Translated), " Cornhill M, 62 (Oct. 1890), 376-378.   A
        satire on Tolstoy's art and philosophy.   Also in Living
        Age, 187 (15 Nov. 1890), 412-413.

571   Oliver, D. E.   "Russian Literature.   Leo Tolstoy, " Manchest-
        er Q, 37, no. 148 (Oct. 1918), 239-259.   A discussion of
        Tolstoy's works and his ability to bring out the meaning
        of life.

572   Orel, Harold.   "English Critics and the Russian Novel, "
        SEER, 33, no. 81 (June 1955), 457-469.

573   Pachmuss, Temira.   "Tolstoi, Lev Nikolayevich, " W Lit,
        5888: 415-416.

574   Perloff, Marjorie G.   "Realism and the Confessional Mode of
        Robert Lowell, " Contemp L, 11 (1970), 470-487.   Illus-
        trates the use of metonymy by instances from Tolstoy
        whose work Lowell admired for its ability to contain hu-
        man richness in simple descriptive language.

575   Perris, G. H.   "Leo Tolstoy as Writer, " Bookman, 19 (March
        1901), 180-184.   Also in Chesterton, Perris and Garnett,
        Leo Tolstoy.

576   Phelps, William L.   "Tolstoy as a Man of Letters, " Independ-
        ent, 69 (1 Dec. 1910), 1188-1190.

577   Prescott, D.   "Our Tolstoi Club, " Century M, n. s. 21 (March
        1892), 761-772.   A general discussion of Russian realism
        with reference to Tolstoy.

578   Raleigh, John H.   "Tolstoy and Sight: The Dual Nature of
        Reality, " Es in Criticism, 21 (April 1971), 170-179.

579   Remizov, Alexey.   "The Miraculous in Tolstoy, " Slavonic R,
        7 (1929), 473-475.   An examination of Tolstoy's creativity
        as a result of his faith in man.

580 Richards, D. J. "Wit and Worship--Two Impulses in Modern
     Russian Literature, " RLT, 14 (Winter 1976), 7-19.

581 "A Russian Novelist, " Spectator, 59 (10 July 1886), 938.

582 "A Russian Novelist and English, " Nation, 100 (25 Feb. 1914),
     214.

583 Saintsbury, George. "The Literary Prophets of the Later
     Nineteenth Century, " Independent, 54 (18 Dec. 1902), 3023-
     3026.

584 Sampson, George. "Some Russian Novelists, " Bookman, 53
     (Oct. 1917), 8-14, illus. A discussion of Gogol, Dostoev-
     sky, Turgenev, Chekhov and Tolstoy.

585 "The Secret Press in England, " Bookman, 15, no. 4 (1927),
     217. On the publication of Tolstoy's works printed by a
     secret press in England.

586 Shaw, George B. "Bernard Shaw's Criticism of Tolstoy, "
     Cur Lit, 51 (July 1911), 71-72.

587 Shaw, George B. "Tolstoy: Tragedian or Comedian, " Lon
     Merc, 4, no. 19 (May 1921), 31-34. A restatement of a
     speech given at a dinner commemorating Tolstoy. Dis-
     cusses Tolstoy's technique and humor.

588 Shaw, George B. "Translating Tolstoy, " Sat R, 99 (1905), 48.
     A discussion of the difficulties associated with translating
     Tolstoy and a defense of the Maude translations criticized
     in an earlier issue of the Saturday Review.

589 Slonim, Marc. "Four Western Writers on Tolstoy, " Rus R,
     19, no. 2 (Spring 1960), 187-204. A survey of Chester-
     ton, Shaw, Rolland and Mann in relation to their works
     on and views of Tolstoy.

590 Struve, Gleb. "Monologue Intérieur: The Origins of the
     Formula, " PMLA, 69, no. 5 (Dec. 1954), 1101-1111.

591 Struve, Gleb. "Tolstoy in Soviet Criticism, " Rus R, 19 (April
     1960), 171-180.

592 Sydney, Oliver. "Beginnings of Tolstoy, " Speaker, n. s. 12
     (1905), 144-146. A discussion of the difficulties associ-
     ated with translating Tolstoy and a positive assessment of
     War and Peace in response to the Dent publication. Also
     in Living Age, 245 (10 June 1905), 698-701.

593 "Tolstoi, a Hundred Years, a Hundred Volumes, " Living Age,
     335 (Sept. 1928), 64. On the Russian preparations for the
     centennial of Tolstoy's birth.

594   "Tolstoy and Korolenko, " Nation, 46 (8 March 1888), 203-204.

595   "Tolstoy and the Russian Censor, " Outlook, 69 (16 Nov. 1901), 694-695. Examples of works by Tolstoy censored by the Tsarist government.

596   "Tolstoy on Trial, " Outlook, 137 (August 1924), 530. An attack on the Bolshevik government's labeling of Tolstoy's works as "bourgeois. "

597   "Tolstoy's Place in World Literature, " Cur Lit, 50 (Jan. 1911), 87-90. An examination of Tolstoy's influence on world literature as described by W. Howells and H. Ellis.

598   "Tolstoy's Writings, " Lit W, 18, no. 20 (Oct. 1887), 321. A list of Tolstoy's writings from 1852-1856.

599   "Two Opinions of Tolstoy, " Lit W, 18, no. 15 (1887), 233-234. An analysis of the opposing views of Maurice Thompson and William Howells with regard to their interpretations of Tolstoy's literary and philosophical standing.

600   Urban, Wilbur M.   "Tolstoy and the Russian Sphinx, " Int J Ethics, 28 (Jan. 1939), 220-239. A study of the Russian atmosphere in Tolstoy's works.

601   Weiner, Leo.   "Tolstoy as a Novelist, " Hound and Horn, 2, no. 2 (Jan. -March 1921), 132-139.

602   Weiner, Leo.   "The Translating of Tolstoy, " Sat R, 99 (4 March 1905), 274-275. A response to Maude's critique of Weiner's translation of War and Peace.

603   Wells, C. W.   "Tolstoy as Literary Artist, " Calif U Chron, 11 (Oct. 1909), 315-324.

604   Willcocks, Mary P.   "Tolstoi, " Eng R, 34 (June 1922), 513-529.   Tolstoy's literature and philosophy discussed with regard to Eastern and Western standards.

DISSERTATIONS

605   Benson, Ruth C.   "The Ideal and the Erotic: Tolstoy's Heroines in Love and Marriage, " Yale University, 1969.

606   Freeborn, R. H.   "Trends of Development in the Russian Nineteenth Century Realistic Novel (1830-1880), " Oxford University, 1958.

607   Gregory, Paul.   "The Theme of Moscow in Russian Literature of the Nineteenth Century, " Vanderbilt University, 1973.

608 Karapinka, Orysia. "The Idea of the City in Russian Letters
     from Pushkin to Tolstoy, " University of California at
     Berkeley, 1972.

609 Schulz, Robert K. "The Changing Portrayal of the German as
     a Character in the Prose Works of I. A. Goncharov, I.
     S. Turgenev, F. M. Dostoevsky and L. N. Tolstoy, "
     Florida State University, 1970.

610 Sorokin, Boris. "Lev Tolstoy in Pre-revolutionary Russian
     Criticism, " University of Chicago, 1974.

See also: 2,   3,   4,   7,   9,   12,   13,   14,   16,   17,   18,   24,   26,
           27,   28,   29,   30,   32,   51,   170,   173,   178,   180,   181,   182,
           183,   184,   185,   186,   187,   188,   189,   191,   193,   194,   196,
           197,   198,   199,   200,   201,   203,   204,   205,   208,   210,   215,
           216,   223,   226,   228,   229,   243,   266,   267,   270,   280,   292,
           299,   305,   312,   319,   323,   326,   328,   330,   347,   355,   358,
           361,   370,   371,   375,   376,   380,   384,   394,   455,   637,   925,
           942,   976,   1217,   1220,   1222,   1223,   1225,   1226,   1227,
           1229,   1230,   1237,   1238,   1239,   1247,   1248,   1254,   1255,
           1257,   1258,   1259,   1260,   1271,   1273,   1274,   1275,   1283,
           1294,   1313,   1317,   1326,   1352,   1384,   1389,   1405,   1458,
           1526,   1527,   1616,   1661,   1665,   1729,   1804,   1805,   1808,
           1815,   1816,   1821,   1827,   1833,   1849,   1850,   1854,   1865,
           1929,   1951,   1961,   1977,   1990,   2037,   2046.

..

Section III continued

FICTION--ANNA KARENINA

BOOKS

611   Coming, Andrew G.   Tolstoy's "Anna Karenina":   The Problem
      of Form.   Athens: Ohio University Press, 1973; 13p.

612   Freedman, Elaine H.   Anna Karenina: Chapter Notes and
      Criticism.   New York: American R. D. M. Corp. , 1965.

613   Gibian, George, ed.   Anna Karenina, the Maude Translation:
      Backgrounds and Sources; Essays in Criticism.   New
      York: Norton, 1970; viii, 920p.   The Maude translation
      of Anna Karenina precedes a collection of materials de-
      signed to provide background information on and insight
      into the novel.   Included are writings from Tolstoy in
      which he discusses various aspects of his work on Anna
      Karenina, a biographical sketch by Mirsky (from his A
      History of Russian Literature), and a wide range of criti-
      cal opinions on the novel.   See the "Essays" section for
      annotations of these critical studies.

614   Gunn, Elizabeth.   A Daring Coiffeur: Reflections on War and
      Peace and Anna Karenina.   Totowa, N. J. :   Rowman &
      Littlefield, 1971; 146p.   Anna Karenina is labeled "an
      adult tragedy" about "interlocking human isolation, " rather
      than a novel about adultery and marriage and is analyzed
      in light of this contention.   Rising above the tragedy and
      isolation in the characters' lives, it is argued, is Tol-
      stoy's contention that one must not judge others, a con-
      tention seen as odd in view of his moralizing in both Anna
      Karenina and War and Peace.   Reviewed in:
         Contemp R, 220 (May 1972), 227.
         Encounter, 38 (Feb. 1972), 82.
         Listener, 86 (25 Nov. 1971), 725, by John Bayley.
         New Statesman, 82 (24 Sept. 1971), 402, by V. S.
            Pritchett.
         Slav R, 32 (June 1973), 425, by Kathryn Feuer.
         St in Novel, (Spring 1972), 86, by E. Wasiolek.
         Times Lit Sup, (3 Sept. 1971), 1056.

615 Mooney, Harry. Tolstoy's Epic Vision: A Study of War and
     Peace and Anna Karenina. Tulsa: University of Tulsa
     Press, 1968; 88p. An analysis of War and Peace and
     Anna Karenina as epics rather than novels on the grounds
     that such an approach yields an increased awareness of
     the works' unique qualities. Both novels are seen as
     epics because of their characters' Homeric "profound com-
     mittment to land and nature, family and society, " and
     Tolstoy's uniting "man and nature at a level of almost
     mystical communication. " These thematic epic qualities
     of Tolstoy's art, along with the epic quality of his imagi-
     nation, are illustrated by numerous references to scenes
     and characters from both novels. Reviewed in:
          Rus R, 28, (April 1969), 222, by Kathryn Feuer.
          SEEJ, 13 (Summer 1969), 244-45, by C. Nicholas Lee.
          Slav R, 29, no. 4 (1970), by Willis Konick.

616 Reaske, Herbert E. Leo Tolstoy's Anna Karenina. New York:
     Simon & Schuster, 1965. A study guide to Anna Karenina
     designed to provide plot summary as well as an analysis
     of themes, techniques, style, and characters. Also in-
     cluded is a short survey of literary criticism of the novel.

617 Stenbock-Fermor, Elisabeth. The Architecture of Anna Karen-
     ina: A History of Its Writing, Structure, and Message. Lisse,
     Neth. : Ridder, 1975; 127p. , bib. 125-27. An account of
     Tolstoy's writing of Anna Karenina (by reference to drafts),
     publication details, and reaction to the novel upon its re-
     lease, precedes a detailed structural analysis. The
     "architecture" of Anna Karenina is analyzed in terms of
     identifying the "invisible pillars" that support the "arches"
     on both sides of "the vault" as a means of isolating the
     "keystone" of the novel. It is concluded that Tolstoy in-
     tentionally concealed his keystone, but it can be identified
     as centered about "the family idea" and love, with asso-
     ciated pitfalls. Reviewed in:
          SEEJ, 20 (Winter 1976), 475-76, by E. J. Blumberg.
          SEER, 54 (July 1976), 456-57, R. F. Christian.

618 Sturman, Marianne. Anna Karenina: Notes. Lincoln, Neb. :
     Cliff's Notes, 1965; 77p. A study guide providing chapter
     summaries, character sketches, and critical notes along
     with analysis of plot, structure, and technique.

ESSAYS AND CHAPTERS from general works

619 Arnold, Matthew. "Anna Karenina as Life, Not Literature, "
     in AKMT, 798-801. Tolstoy's "extraordinary fineness of
     perception" and "sincere fidelity to it" are seen as being
     responsible for his achieving absolute reality in all as-
     pects of Anna Karenina, thereby making the novel seem
     more like a piece of life than fiction. Excerpt from his

"Count Leo Tolstoi" (annotated in Section IV) in Essays in Criticism, pp. 253-299. Originally in Fortn R 48 (Dec. 1887); 783-799. Also in LTCA, 60-80.

620   Bayley, John. "The Worlds of Love" in The Characters of Love: A Study in the Literature of Personality. New York: Basic Books, 1960; 22-26. The character Stiva from Anna Karenina is discussed as a sterile individual who tells us nothing about the art which produces him and who is certainly not "a man of our time." Stiva is also judged not to be Tolstoy's type of man since he represented a hindrance to the achievement of Tolstoy's ideal society.

621   Beach, Joseph Warren. "Dramatic Present: Thackeray, Tolstoy" in The Twentieth Century Novel: Studies in Technique. New York: Century, 1932; 164-176. A comparison of Anna Karenina to Thackeray's Vanity Fair in terms of their sectioning, dispersal of material, and use of time. Tolstoy is seen as having fewer sections by theme, a greater concentration of emphasis, and a more intense use of time than Thackeray.

622   Blackmur, Richard P. "The Dialectic of Incarnation: Tolstoi's Anna Karenina" in Eleven Essays in the European Novel. New York: Harcourt, Brace, and World, 1964; 3-26. Tolstoy's novels, especially Anna Karenina, are viewed as characterized by the interrelationship of dialectical opposites, of "contrasted human spirits." Discussed in line with this contention is the illicit affair of Anna and Vronsky, and the lawful relationship of Kitty and Levin, with special concern for their interaction with society. Parallels are also made between Anna and Levin, who in "separate and opposed ways" sought to transcend society by way of a "full incarnation." Also in Kenyon R, 12 (Summer 1950), 433-456; TCCE, 127-145; and AKMT, 899-917.

623   Boyd, Alexander F. "An Anatomy of Marriage: Leo Tolstoy and Anna Karenina" in Aspects of the Russian Novel. London: Chatto and Windus, 1972; 87-108. The analysis of marriage is considered to be a "prominent feature of the middle period of Tolstoy's creative activity" during which time he vacillated between the idealized marriage presented in Family Happiness and the bitter denunciation of marriage in The Kreutzer Sonata. Anna Karenina is discussed at length as a work falling in the center of this period and containing elements common to both extremes but "more complex and artistically superior" to both works.

624   Bychkov, S. O. "The Social Bases of Anna Karenina" in AKMT, 822-835. An analysis of the leading characters of Anna Karenina as they relate to the changing nature of

post-Emancipation Russian society. Levin is regarded as
representing those who were tormented by the influx into
Russia of "bourgeois foreign civilization"; Vronsky and
Karenin are considered to be typical examples of a social
milieu pervaded by the evils of capitalist civilization; and
Anna is seen as being the "accuser of bourgeois-aristo-
cratic society" by way of her tragic death.   Excerpt translated from L. N. Tolstoy v shkole, ed. by V. Golubkov.
Moscow, 1960; 159-177.

625 Calder, Angus.   "Man, Woman and Male Woman: Tolstoy's
     'Anna Karenina' and After" in Russia Discovered: Nine-
     teenth Century Fiction from Pushkin to Chekhov.   New
     York: Harper and Row, 1976; 209-236.   A discussion
     of Anna as a woman and of her symbolizing, along with
     the milieu in which she functioned, the values of the new
     Russia which followed the reforms of the early 1860's, in
     contrast to the character Levin, who is regarded as repre-
     senting the old Russia.

626 Cary, J.   Art and Reality: Ways of the Creative Process.
     New York: Harper, 1958.   Not available for annotation
     but listed as having a section on Anna Karenina, 161-166.

627 Clayre, Alasdair.   "Levin in the Fields" in Work and Play:
     Ideas and Experiences of Work and Leisure.   New York:
     Harper and Row, 1974; 147-150.   The scene in Anna
     Karenina in which Levin works with peasants in the hay-
     fields is labeled as "one of the finest descriptions of
     satisfying physical work in any novel."   Levin's state of
     "self-loss in work," and the consequent relaxed rhythm
     of his actions, is contrasted with the state of mind that
     he has when thinking abstractly about peasant labor and
     agricultural reforms.   Tolstoy is seen as not having
     wanted to focus further "these two distinct visions" asso-
     ciated with Levin and labor.

628 Dostoevsky, Fydor M.   The Diary of a Writer.   New York:
     Scribner's, 1949; 783-795.   Anna Karenina is portrayed
     as a uniquely Russian novel with which no work in con-
     temporary European literature can compare.   In partic-
     ular, Tolstoy's psychological and soulful presentation of
     the guilt felt by Anna is contrasted with the sterile, legal-
     istic European conception of guilt.   More broadly, Tol-
     stoy's insight into the spiritual side of man is commended
     for making clear that no rational Western philosophy can
     regenerate man, but rather only faith can be his salvation.
     Excerpts in AKMT, 789-794; and LTCA, 49-54.

629 Eikhenbaum, Boris M.   "Anna Karenina and the Literary Tradi-
     tion" in AKMT, 810-811.   Anna Karenina is discussed as
     a novel which "does not follow European traditions as
     much as it brings them to a head and goes beyond them. "

More than just a model of the European family novel and the French adultery novel, Anna Karenina is regarded as a work that reflects Tolstoy's personal evolution because of the dialectical nature of its unity. Translated from Lev Tolstoy: Semidesyatye gody (Leningrad, 1960), 151-152.

630 Eikhenbaum, Boris M. "The Composition of Anna Karenina: Its Russian and Western Antecedents" in AKMT, 812-815. Tolstoy's art is compared to that of Pushkin, with the contention that, in Anna Karenina, he made use of themes and plot that Pushkin conceived but never brought to full fruition. Both men are considered to be similar in their concern for "a strict artistic system based on the principle of high realism." Excerpt translated from Lev Tolstoy: Semidesyatye gody, 177-189.

631 Eikhenbaum, Boris M. "The Puzzle of the Epigraph, N. Schopenhauer" in AKMT, 815-821. The relationship between Anna Karenina's epigraph and meaning is analyzed with the conclusion reached that both assert that the consequence of bad actions is not "vengeance by the people but one's own sufferings." Additionally, the source of the epigraph is interpreted as being Schopenhauer's The World as Will and Idea, and not the Gospel, because its wording is most similar to that of the former writing. Excerpt translated from Lev Tolstoy: Semidesyatye gody, 195-204.

632 Eisenstein, Sergei. Film Form. Essays in Film Theory. New York: Harcourt, Brace, 1949; 153-157 (no separate chapter on Tolstoy). Tolstoy's remarkable realism, particularly in Anna Karenina and The Kreutzer Sonata, is discussed as being not the result of the feelings and actions of the novels' characters, but rather the consequence of his being able to make characters and episodes correspond exactly "with the relation of the author to phenomenon being described," an association which has, in turn, positively effected his method of composition. Also in LTCA, 204-207.

633 Farrell, James T. "An Introduction to Anna Karenina" in Literature and Morality. New York: Vanguard, 1946; 296-304. Originally the introduction to the Living Library edition of Anna Karenina, a brief discussion of the novel's leading characters is presented against the background of Tolstoy's intent in writing this work.

634 Furbank, Phillip N. "Anna Karenina," in The Nineteenth Century Novel and Its Legacy. London: Open University Press, 1973.

635 Gifford, Henry. "Anna, Lawrence and the Law" in RLMEF, 148-152. A discussion of D. H. Lawrence's criticism

of Tolstoy, in Anna Karenina, for infidelity to realism for
the sake of "a mere theory of right and wrong. " Favorably presented is Lawrence's contention that the relationship of Anna and Vronsky represents true and natural love
but that Tolstoy refused to accept this because he was
more concerned with philosophizing. Tolstoy is condemned
for this: "when a novelist puts his thumb on the scale to
pull down the balance to his own predilections, that is immorality. " Also in AKMT, pp. 843-46. Originally in
Critical Q, 1, no. 3 (Autumn 1959), 203-06. Also in
LTCA, pp. 299-303.

636 Gifford, Henry. "Further Notes on Anna Karenina" in RLMEF,
     160-63. In response to criticism by Raymond Williams
     (see item 665) of his support for Lawrence's attack on
     Tolstoy, Gifford presents further information on the sub-
     ject of Tolstoy's having been unfaithful to Anna for the
     sake of didactic message. Draft versions of the novel
     are quoted to demonstrate that Tolstoy clearly intended to
     make Anna evil and unrepentent but that she eventually
     was presented in a much more sympathetic light, though
     she still suffered the terrible death of the original "evil
     Anna. " This unfair treatment of Anna is seen as support-
     ing Lawrence's contention that Tolstoy "tampered with the
     scales" for the sake of philosophy. Also in AKMT, 853-
     56; and LTCA, 311-14. Originally in Critical Q, 2, no.
     2 (Summer 1960), 158-160.

637 Gifford, Henry. "Tolstoy: Art and Conscience" in The Novel
     in Russia from Pushkin to Pasternak. London: Hutchin-
     son, 1964; 85-96. The genesis, development, and leading
     characters of Anna Karenina are discussed as a means of
     illustrating Tolstoy's artistic genius. Central to the high
     quality of his artistry, it is claimed, is the element of
     "rejuvenescence" in his works: "there is always a way
     back to innocence. " Anna is presented as a leading ex-
     ample of this even to the point of her death where she
     flashes back to her childhood joys.

638 Gromeka, M. S. "The Epigraph and the Meaning of the Nov-
     el" in AKMT, 801. The basic message of Anna Karenina
     is interpreted as being that happiness cannot come if funda-
     mental moral laws are violated, hence Anna's misery is
     seen as a consequence of her disregard for the family
     unit and society's dictates. The epigraph, "mine is the
     vengeance, and I shall repay, " is the judgment awaiting
     transgressors of morality. Translated from Russkaia
     Mysl, no. 2 (1883).

639 Hardy, Barbara. "Form and Freedom: Tolstoy's Anna Karen-
     ina" in The Appropriate Form: An Essay on the Novel.
     London: Athlone, 1964; 174-211. The vivid realism of
     Anna Karenina is seen as a consequence of the novel's

being free "from the simplifications of stereotype" and
lacking any contrivance. By never allowing technical devices to "distort characters and action, " and by his subtle
yet effective presentation of moral judgments, Tolstoy is
unique, it is claimed, among the world's great artists.
In addition, in spite of the "largeness and looseness" of
Anna Karenina, the novel is regarded as cohesive because
it is centered about two stories "inconspicuously divided. "
Excerpts in AKMT, 877-899.

640 Hardy, Barbara. "A Note on Certain Revisions in Anna Karenina" in The Appropriate Form, 212-16. An appendix in
which is noted revisions in Anna Karenina dealing with
Anna's death, her relationship with Vronsky, and the use
of light in the novel.

641 Hare, Richard. "Tolstoy after War and Peace" in Portraits
of Russian Personalities between Reform and Revolution.
London: Oxford University Press, 1959; 196-244. A description of Tolstoy's writing of Anna Karenina, and some
comparisons to War and Peace precede a detailed examination of the characters Anna and Levin. In particular,
Levin's haunting doubts about life's meaning, his thoughts
of suicide, and his craving for emotional union with the
peasantry, are all interpreted as being "significant pre-
ludes to that desperate state of mind" that led Tolstoy to
his spiritual crisis and his Confession. Tolstoy's later
life and works are surveyed, with What Is Art receiving
special attention as the work that represents the culmina-
tion of a lengthy phase in his life.

642 Jackson, Robert L. "Chance and Design in Anna Karenina"
in The Discipline of Criticism: Essays in Literary Theory, Interpretation, and History. New Haven, Conn. :
Yale University Press, 1968; 315-330. Chapter 18 of
Anna Karenina is discussed as evidence that the real art
of Tolstoy rests in his ability to blend chance events into
a coherent design. It is argued that the "elements in
Anna which are her fate" are presented, in this chapter,
against the background of elements of chance which become a meaningful design and lead to her death at the
very station and by the same means as the death of the
guard depicted in the chapter.

643 Jones, Peter. "Action and Passion in Anna Karenina" in
Philosophy and the Novel: Philosophical Aspects of Mid-
dlemarch, Anna Karenina, The Brothers Karamazov, A la
recherche du temps perdu, and of the Methods of Criticism. Oxford, England: Clarendon, 1975; 70-111. A
discussion of the novel's characters' active and passive
responses to two questions, What is to be done? and
What is the meaning of the situation in which I find my-
self? It is concluded that most of the characters, "finding

no acceptable answer to the question in their particular
context, do nothing, and allow themselves to be passive
precisely when action is called for. " An analysis of the
various reasons for the passivity of Anna Karenina's
characters is also included.

644 Leavis, Frank. "Anna Karenina: Thought and Significance in
a Great Creative Work" in Anna Karenina and Other Essays. London: Chatto and Windus, 1967; 9-32. Anna
Karenina is considered an example of the highest type of
literary creativity because it so powerfully represents
Tolstoy's concern for significance in his art as well as
in his life. Those who criticize the novel for its "lack
of composition" are, it is argued, overlooking the broader
importance of the work for the sake of lesser considera-
tions. Its leading characters are discussed as examples
of Tolstoy's creative genius, and the conclusion is reached
that it is "the great European novel. " Excerpts in LTCA,
372-375.

645 Littell, Philip. "Anna Revisited" in Books and Things. Freeport, N. Y. : Books for Libraries Press, 1969 (reprint of
1919 publication); 160-166. The very positive effect on
the author in his youth exerted by the beauty and grace
of Anna against the background of her terrible death is
discussed before an "adult impression, " based on a re-
reading, of the novel is presented. Although no longer
having as powerful an impact on the author, the novel is
still seen as being a masterpiece because it is so realistic
and comprehensive in its description of life.

646 Lovett, Robert M. "Anna Karenina" in Preface to Fiction:
A Discussion of Great Modern Novels. Freeport, N. Y. :
Books for Libraries Press, 1968; 26-40. Anna Karenina
is discussed as an important novel because it was the
first Russian novel to win popularity in the West, and
therefore initiated Russian literary influence in Europe.
It is also judged to be an impressive piece of fiction because it meets the two criteria of greatness: "truth to
the life of selected individuals, " and "truth to the funda-
mental meaning of life. "

647 Lubbock, Percy. The Craft of Fiction. New York: Viking,
1957; 236-250 (no separate chapter on Tolstoy). Tolstoy
is criticized in Anna Karenina for too strict an adherence
to a simple chronology of the characters' lives without
sufficient background or a "shift of point of view away
from the immediate scene to a more commanding height. "
In particular, the character Anna is not considered to be
developed fully enough before her crisis with Vronsky, and
Vronsky is especially shallow because of lack of background on him before he becomes involved with Anna:
"Tolstoy should have created Vronsky with a more certain

touch before he allowed him to cause such a disaster. "
Also in AKMT, 835-842 under the title "The Defects of
Anna Karenina. "

648 Lukacs, Georg. "The Social Background of the Parallel Plots
in Anna Karenina" in AKMT, 821-822. It is stated that
the parallel plots that exist in the novel "stress that the
heroine's fate, while typical and necessary, is yet an ex-
tremely individual one, " and is in response to "very
specific social and individual conditions. " From his The
Historical Novel, 142; see full annotation under entry 877.

649 Mann, Thomas. "Anna Karenina" in Essays of Three Decades.
New York: Knopf, 1947; 176-188. Originally the introduction to the 1939 Random House edition of Anna Karenina, this essay discusses the novel in light of Tolstoy's
later views on art, and the contention is made that his
conversion and later philosophy were evident in Anna
Karenina and earlier works. Also examined is how Tolstoy wrote the novel, and how the character Levin is a
near duplicate of Tolstoy. Also in Kronenberger, 179-
193.

650 Merezhkovsky, Dmitri S. "Tolstoy's Physical Descriptions"
in AKMT, 802-810. Tolstoy's minute physical descriptions
of characters, especially Anna, are seen as blending into
one, unique and living picture that stirs the imagination of
the reader and makes his characters seem real. Tolstoy's narratives about characters, as opposed to the
words of the characters themselves, are viewed as his
typical means of portraying their personalities, a means
which is effective but excessive in some instances.
Translated from L. Tolstoy i Dostoevsky: Zhizn', Tvor-
chestvo, i Religiia (St. Petersburg-Moscow, 1912).
See the annotation of his Tolstoi as Man and Artist with
an Essay on Dostoevski (entries 189 and 454) for additional
information on Tolstoy's characterizations as described
by Merezhkovsky.

651 Mihajlov, Mihajlo. "A New Approach to Anna Karenina" in
Underground Notes. Mission, Kan. : Sheed Andrews and
McNeed, 1976; 153-168. An attack on the sociological
explanations of Anna's death on the grounds that Anna,
not society, was to blame for her own death. Anna's actions are discussed as being understandable and "normal, "
given the circumstances in which she placed herself. It
is maintained that, even in a society more progressive
than her own, Anna would feel just as guilty and act the
same way, if not more so, since "with the humanization
social relations and the liberation of man, the individual's
responsibility increases. "

652 Muchnic, Helen. "The Steeplechase in Anna Karenina" in Russian Writers: Notes and Essays. New York: Random

House, 1971; 126-138. The steeplechase scene is discussed as a microcosm of the design of Anna Karenina.
Each of the novel's major strands is evident in this
scene, it is claimed, with the fate of Vronsky and Anna
particularly highlighted by the tragic death of the horse
"Frou-Frou. " Also included in this volume are reviews
by the author of Bayley's Tolstoy and the Novel, and
Kuzminskaya's Tolstoy as I Knew Him: My Life at Home
and at Yasnaya Polyana.

653 Peck, Harry T. "Tolstoi's Anna Karenina" in Studies in Several Literatures.   Freeport, N. Y. : Books for Libraries
Press, 1968 (reprint of 1909 publication); 227-237. Anna
Karenina is seen as a great work of art, not in the usual
sense, but as an odd example of great fiction writing because it is loosely constructed about two unrelated themes:
the illicit love of Anna and Vronsky, and the spiritual
development of Levin. Adding to the novel's uniqueness,
it is contended, is its powerful and highly developed realism, due largely to the autobiographical nature of Tolstoy's
art. The result is labeled a masterpiece of realistic literature: "breathing life itself. "

654 Reeve, F. D. "Anna Karenina" in The Russian Novel. London: Mullen, 1967; 236-273. Tolstoy is seen as having
been tormented during his life by a moral anguish due to
the conflict "between the accomplishments he believed
himself capable of and the experiences he underwent. "
This conflict, along with his continuous examination of his
own morality, is judged to be central in determining the
personality of many of his works' characters, but especially Levin of Anna Karenina. Additionally, the style and
method used by Tolstoy in the novel is discussed, as are
the social conventions which he sought to expose.

655 Speirs, Logan. "Anna Karenina: A Study in Structure" in
LTCA, 334-37. Anna Karenina, for all its bulk, is,
nonetheless, viewed as being structured along distinctly
clear lines because all characters and incidents impinge
"in some way on the lives of the two chief characters,
Levin and Anna. " Tolstoy presented such detail, it is
maintained, so that his characters would be seen function-
ing in as many different settings as possible thereby giving
the reader a complete picture of their personalities. As
a result, the novel leaves the reader with a complex but
distinct recollection of two characters pursuing different
paths and having opposite fates. Also in Neophilologus,
50 (1966), 3-28.

656 Steiner, George. "The Beginning of Anna Karenina" in AKMT,
865-875. The very beginning of the novel from the epigraph through the introduction of the major characters is
discussed as an example of Tolstoy's mastery of interwoven

themes and structure: "The novels of Tolstoy grow out
of some inward principle of order whereas those of lesser
novelists are stitched together. " From Tolstoy or Dostoevsky: An Essay in the Old Criticism, 58-71; see under
entry 1805 for a broader annotation.

657   Steiner, George. "The Ending of Anna Karenina" in AKMT,
      875-77. The vitality of Tolstoy's novels is regarded as
      resting not only in their densely interwoven plots, but
      also in their disregard for traditional, neat conclusions.
      A draft version of a conclusion to Anna Karenina is dis-
      cussed as proof of this contention. Tolstoy's characters,
      it is argued, have such vitality that they are capable of
      adapting to virtually any conclusion that he wished to im-
      pose on them. From Tolstoy or Dostoevsky: An Essay
      in the Old Criticism, 102-05. See under entry 1805 for a
      broader annotation.

658   Stern, J. P. "Effi Briest; Madame Bovary; Anna Karenina" in
      AKMT, 281-87. A comparison of Anna Karenina to two
      other adultresses, with the conclusion reached that she is
      more honest and open with husband and society alike about
      her affair than are her two counterparts. Moreover, as
      a character with spiritual depth, Anna responds much
      more to her conscience as she judged herself to have
      violated moral law, whereas, it is argued, her counter-
      parts responded to social and family conventions. From
      Mod Lang R, 52 (1957), 363-375.

659   Stern, J. P. "The Social Code and the Moral Problem" in
      AKMT, 856-865. It is maintained that "Anna's violation
      of the social code is a trivial matter in comparison with
      the moral problem which she cannot solve, " and that Tol-
      stoy intended to present this moral-spiritual law as the
      most absolute dictate of all. It is suggested that Tolstoy
      became more sympathetic to Anna as a character as she
      began to realize and accept the moral implications of her
      adultery, and thereby yield to higher law. From his
      Reinterpretations (New York: Basic Books, 1964), 323-29.

660   Strakhov, Nikolai N. "Levin and Social Chaos" in AKMT, 794-
      98. Anna Karenina is discussed as a novel having two
      connected layers centered about, on the one hand, the
      sensual relationship of Anna and Vronsky, and, on the
      other, the spiritual struggle of Levin. The relationship
      of Anna and Vronsky is described as one of the most
      classic, realistic portrayals of the development and de-
      mise of the elusive spiritual phenomenon known as "love. "
      The struggle of Levin is examined, with the conclusion
      reached that he found salvation, whereas Anna did not,
      because Tolstoy felt that the educated part of Russia was
      morally sterile and mired in spiritual chaos, and that
      peasant Russia, which Levin accepted, was at peace with

itself. Excerpt translated from Kriticheskie Stati ob I. S.
Turgeneve i L. N. Tolstom (St. Petersburg, 1895), 447-
451.

661 Trilling, Lionel. "Anna Karenina" in The Opposing Self. Nine
Essays in Criticism. London: Secker & Warburg, 1955;
66-75. Anna Karenina is discussed as a classic, not because of its realism (since Tolstoy did not originate or
have a monopoly on realism), but because it, and his fiction in general, is accepted as the norm by which others
are judged. The unique quality of his realism is regarded as being its subjective nature: it is Tolstoy's
moral vision of the world which, by his skill in presenting characters and scenes in Anna Karenina, the reader
happily accepts as reality. Excerpt in LTCA, 273-276.
Originally the introduction to Anna Karenina (Cambridge,
England: Limited Editions Club, 1951).

662 Turgenev, Ivan. "Letter to Ya. P. Polonsky" in LTCA, 47.
A brief critical description of Anna Karenina as being
"sour, with an odour of Moscow, incense, spinsterhood,
and the Slavophil thing. "

663 Van Kaam, Adrian, and Katherine Healy. "Anna in Tolstoy's
Anna Karenina" in The Demon and the Dove: Personality
Growth through Literature. Pittsburgh: Duquesne University Press, 1967; 169-196. Anna is considered to be
Tolstoy's most superb character, and is interpreted as
being a "masterful embodiment of existential struggle
culminating in personal disaster. " Examined is the development of her character "throughout her existential
psychological struggle" with five crises of increasing intensity leading to the disintegration of her personality and,
eventually, to suicide.

664 Weitz, Morris. "Anna Karenina: Philosophy and the Word"
in Philosophy in Literature: Shakespeare, Voltaire, Tolstoy, Proust. Detroit: Wayne State University Press,
1963; 24-39. Anna Karenina is discussed as support for
the contention that "philosophy and literature can be combined to their mutual enrichment. " Tolstoy's philosophical themes are seen as being that "much of human life
... is good" and that "transgression of moral principles
is to be punished by God not man whose duty is to understand and forgive. " Because of his artistry, Tolstoy's
message is not considered to have in any way impeded
the development of the novel.

665 Williams, Raymond. "Lawrence and Tolstoy" in RLMEF, 152-
160. Lawrence's critique of Anna Karenina is attacked for
failure to recognize that Tolstoy functioned apart from
what Lawrence implied was an accepted general purpose
scale to measure true or real actions of characters. The

development of Anna's life is discussed as proof of the soundness of Tolstoy's characterization and the limited vision of Lawrence as a critic. From Critical Q, 2, no. 1 (Spring 1960), 33-39.

666 Yarmolinsky, Avrahm. "Tolstoy's War and Peace and Anna Karenina" in Russian Literature. Chicago: American Library Association, 1931; 31-38. A brief introduction to both novels. War and Peace, in spite of its lengthy and possibly erroneous statements on philosophy, is labeled a work of genius because of its characterizations. Additionally, the novel is valuable as a source of insight into Tolstoy's character, it is argued, because it reveals "the ethical strain" that was to emerge so forcefully later in his life. Anna Karenina is discussed in a similar manner for its autobiographical elements, and is praised, as a work of fiction, for its representing a fine blend of the physical and ethical aspects of life.

INTRODUCTIONS TO EDITIONS of Anna Karenina

667 Andreyev, Nikolay. Anna Karenina. Trans. by Rochelle S. Townsend. New York: Dutton, 1958; 427p.

668 Edmonds, Rosemary. Anna Karenina. Trans. by Rosemary Edmonds. Harmondsworth: Penguin, 1977; 852p.

669 Farrell, James T. Anna Karenina. Trans. by Constance Garnett. New York: World Publishers, 1946; 912p.

670 Galsworthy, John. Anna Karenina. Trans. by Louise Maude and Aylmer Maude. London: Oxford, 1937 (centenary edition).

671 Gibian, George. Anna Karenina. New York: Harper, 1959; 1090p.

672 Gibian, George, ed. Anna Karenina, the Maude Translation: Backgrounds and Sources; Essays in Criticism. New York: Norton, 1970.

673 Kent, Leonard J. , and Nina Berberova. Anna Karenina. Trans. by Constance Garnett. New York: Modern Library, 1965; 855p.

674 Long, E. Hudson. Anna Karenina. New York: Dodd, Mead, 1966; 897p.

675 Lunacharsky, Anatole. Anna Karenina. Trans. by Constance Garnett. Moscow: State Publishing House, 1933.

676 Mann, Thomas. Anna Karenina. Trans. by Constance Garnett. New York: Random House, 1939; 2 vols (520/523p.).

677 Magarshack, David. Anna Karenina. Trans. by David Magar-
      shack. New York: New American Library, 1961; 807p.

678 Maude, Aylmer. Anna Karenina. Trans. by Louise Aylmer
      and Aylmer Maude, with a foreword by George Gibian.
      New York: W. W. Norton, 1968; 742p.

679 Maude, Aylmer. Anna Karenina. Trans. by Louise Aylmer
      and Aylmer Maude. London: Oxford, 1939; 2 vols.
      (520p. , 464p.).

680 Simmons, Ernest J. Anna Karenina. New York: Franklin
      Watts, 1976; 1323p.

681 Townsend, Rochelle S. Anna Karenina. Trans. by Rochelle
      S. Townsend. New York: Dutton, 1913; 2 vols.

682 Trilling, Lionel. Anna Karenina. Cambridge, England: Lim-
      ited Editions Club, 1951.

683 Troyat, Andre. Anna Karenina. Trans. by Constance Garnett.
      New York: Modern Library, 1950; 950p.

PERIODICAL ARTICLES

684 "Anna and Emma, " Queens' Q, 81 (Autumn 1974), 487-489.

685 "Anna Karenina, " Athenaeum, 2 (28 Dec. 1901), 871.

686 "Anna Karenina, " Blackwood's M, 170 (Nov. 1901), 713-715.

687 "Anna Karenina, " Bookman (L), 39 (Jan. 1911), 197.

688 "Anna Karenina, " Dial, 7 (1886), 13-14.

689 "Anna Karenina, " Independent, 55 (1903), 744-746.

690 "Anna Karenina, " Lit W, 17, no. 3 (17 April 1886), 127-128.

691 "Anna Karenina, " Nation, 73 (21 Nov. 1901), 404-405.

692 "Anna Karenina, " Westm R, 146 (July 1896), 108.

693 Arnold, Matthew. "Count Leo Tolstoy: Anna Karenina and
      Certain Religious-Philosophical Writings of Tolstoy, "
      Fortn R, 48 (1887), 183-199. Also in his Essays in
      Criticism, 253-299; reprinted in Living Age, 176 (1888),
      82-92.

694 Baumgarten, Murray. "Irtenev, Olenin, Levin: Three Char-
      acters in Search of Nature, " Century R, 14 (1970), 188-
      200.

695   Berenson, B.   "The Writings of Tolstoy, " Harvard M, 3, no.
      4 (Jan. 1887), 138-149. A discussion of Anna Karenina,
      My Religion and Childhood, Boyhood, Youth.

696   Blackmur, R. P.   "Anna Karenina: The Dialectic of Incarna-
      tion, " Kenyon R, 12 (Summer 1950), 433-456. Also in
      Blackmur, R. P., Eleven Essays in the European Novel,
      3-26.

697   Call, Paul.   "Anna Karenina's Crime and Punishment: The
      Impact of Historical Theory Upon the Russian Novel, "
      Mosaic, 1 (1967), 94-102.

698   Castro, Dominador C.   "Constantine Dimitrich Levin: A Con-
      temporary Christian Agnostic Poor in Spirit, " SLRJ, 6
      (1975), 306-324.

699   Christian, R. F.   "The Passage of Time in Anna Karenina, "
      SEER, 44, no. 104 (Jan. 1967), 207-210.

700   Dole, N. H.   "Tolstoy's Astronomy, " Athenaeum, 1, no. 3884
      (5 April 1902), 436. A defense of Tolstoy's astronomy,
      in reference to a scene involving Levin in Anna Karenina,
      against White's attack in a previous issue of Athenaeum,
      on the grounds that White misinterpreted the scene in
      question.

701   Ducusin, Dionisio S.   "The Experience of Nothingness in Anna
      Karenina: A Study of the Essential Differences of Anna
      and Alexandrovitch, " SLRJ, 6 (1975), 293-305.

702   Flint, Martha M.   "The Epigraph of Anna Karenina, " PMLA,
      80 (Sept. 1965), 461-462.

703   Friedman, Simon.   "Detail and Accident in Anna Karenina, "
      PPNCFL, 26 (1975), 164-166.

704   Galsworthy, J.   "Anna Karenina, " Bookman (L), 74 (August
      1928), 218-219.

705   Gibian, George.   "Two Kinds of Human Understanding and the
      Narrator's Voice in Anna Karenina, " Orbis Scriptus, 92
      (1966), 315-322.

706   Gifford, Henry.   "Anna, Lawrence and 'The Law', " Critical
      Q, 1, no. 3 (Autumn, 1959), 203-206. Also in AKMT,
      843-846 and LTCA, 299-303.

707   Gifford, Henry.   "Further Notes on Anna Karenina, " Critical
      Q, 2, no. 2 (Summer 1960).

708   Giraud, E.   "Countess Anna Karenina: A Supreme Achieve-
      ment, " Living Age, 321 (10 May 1924), 919-920.

95   Fiction--Anna Karenina

709 Gorin, Bernard. "Feminine Types in Tolstoy's Works, "
     Sewanee R, 16, no. 4 (Oct. 1908), 442-451. An exami-
     nation of the female characters in War and Peace, Resur-
     rection, Family Happiness and Anna Karenina.

710 Gorodetzky, Nadezhda. "Anna Karenina, " SEER, 24, no. 63
     (Jan. 1946), 121-126.

711 Greenwood, E. B. "The Unity of Anna Karenina, " Landfall,
     15, no. 2 (June 1961), 124-133.

712 Grossman, J. D. "Tolstoy's Portrait of Anna: Keystone in
     the Arch, " Criticism, 18 (Winter 1976), 1-14.

713 "Interpreting Tolstoy, " Times Lit Sup, 53 (16 July 1954), 449-
     450. A discussion of a new translation of Anna Karenina
     by Rosemary Edmonds with references to Alexandra
     Tolstoy's A Life of My Father.

714 Jones, Peter. "Action and Passion in Anna Karenina, " FMLS,
     7 (1971), 1-27.

715 Jones, W. G. "George Eliot's Adam Bede and Tolstoy's Con-
     ception of Anna Karenina, " Mod Lang R, 61 (3 July 1966),
     473-481.

716 Klimenko, Michael. "Anna Karenina as an Expression of
     Schopehauer's Wille zum Leben, " PPNCFL, 21 (April
     1970), 271-278.

717 Laugel, Auguste. "Anna Karenina and War and Peace, " Na-
     tion, 40 (1885), 70-71.

718 Laugel, Auguste. "Tolstoi's New Novel, " Nation, 41 (1885),
     112-113.

719 Leavis, F. R. "Anna Karenina: Thought and Significance in
     a Great Creative Work, " Cambridge Q, 1 (Winter 1965-
     1966), 5-27. Also in Anna Karenina and Other Essays,
     9-32.

720 Low, Frances H. "Anna Karenina, An Appreciation, " Fortn
     R, 96 (Oct. 1911), 728-744.

721 Lvov-Anokhin, B. "A Ballet Version of Anna Karenina, "
     Soviet Life, 199, no. 4 (April 1973), 51-53.

722 Manning, C. A. "Tolstoy and Anna Karenina, " PMLA, 42
     (June 1927), 505-521.

723 Nemurovitch-Danchenko, V. I. "Anna Karenina: The Staging
     of a Novel, " Theatre Workshop, 1 (Oct. 1937), 7-13.

724   Portnoff, George.   "The Influence of Tolstoy's Anna Karenina
      on Galdos' Realidad, " Hispania, 15 (May 1932), 208-214.

725   Pursglove, Michael.   "The Smiles of Anna Karenina, " SEEJ,
      17, no. 1 (1973), 42-48.

726   Ralston, W.   "Novels of Count L. Tolstoy, " Nineteenth Cent,
      5 (April 1879), 650-669.   A discussion of War and Peace
      and Anna Karenina.   Also in Living Age, 141 (1879), 409-
      429.

727   Schevitch, S. E.   "Russian Novels and Novelists of the Day, "
      N Amer R, 128 (March 1879), 326-334.   A discussion of
      Tolstoy's Anna Karenina, War and Peace and Childhood,
      Boyhood, Youth with a comparison to Turgenev.

728   Schultze, Sydney P.   "The Chapter in Anna Karenina, " RLT,
      10 (1974), 351-359.   Traces Tolstoy's use of simple yet
      elegant form in refining his concept of the "chapter. "

729   Schultze, Sydney P.   "Notes on Imagery and Motifs in Anna
      Karenina, " RLT, 1 (Fall, 1971), 366-374.

730   Shaw, Michael.   "Anna Karenina: A Double Dactyl, " RLT,
      8 (1974), 571.

731   Siegel, George.   The Fallen Woman in Nineteenth Century
      Russian Literature, " Harvard Slavic S, 5 (1970), 81-107.

732   Simpson, Lucie.   "Tolstoy's Heroines, " Fortn R, n. s. 124
      (Oct. 1928), 474-483.   A discussion of Anna in Anna
      Karenina and Natasha in War and Peace.

733   Sinaiko, H. L.   "The Value of the Very Large Novel in a
      General Education Course: A Case for Anna Karenina, "
      J Gen Ed, 12 (Oct. 1959), 209-221.

734   Slade, Tony.   "Anna Karenina and the Family Ideal, " So R,
      1 (1963), 85-90.

735   Sorokin, Boris.   "Dostoevsky on Tolstoy: The Immoral Mes-
      sage of Anna Karenina, " Conn R, 6 (1973), 25-33.

736   Speirs, Logan.   "Anna Karenina: A Study in Structure, " Neo-
      phil, 50 (1966), 3-28.

737   Stern, J. P.   "Effi Briest, Madame Bovary and Anna Karen-
      ina, " Mod Lang R, 52 (1957), 363-375.   An analysis of
      the three heroines in relation to their social setting.
      Also in AKMT, 281-287.

738   Stevens, Martin.   "A Source for Frou-Frou in Anna Karenina, "
      Comp Lit, 34 (1972), 63-71.

739 Stewart, D. H. "Anna Karenina: The Dialectic of Prophecy, "
PMLA, 79 (June 1964), 266-282.

740 Symons, A. "Anna Karenina, " Sat R, 95 (1903), 227-228.

741 Tyler, Morris F. "Tolstoy's Novels, " New Eng Yale R, 46
(1887), 193-205. A discussion of Anna Karenina and
War and Peace.

742 White, W. H. "Tolstoy's Astronomy, " Athenaeum, 2, no.
3870 (28 Dec. 1901), 879. Claims Tolstoy made an error
in the position of Venus in the snipe shooting scene in
Anna Karenina.

743 Wierzbicka, Anna. "The Semantic Structure of Words for
Emotions, " Slavic Poetics, Item 2862 (1973), 499-505.

744 Williams, R. "Lawrence and Tolstoy, " Critical Q, 2, no. 1
(Spring 1960), 33-39. Also in RLMEF, 152-160.

745 Williams, R. "Tolstoy, Lawrence and Tragedy, " Kenyon R,
25 (Autumn 1963), 633-650.

746 "Writing Anna Karenina, " Bookman, 40 (Oct. 1914), 133-134.
A discussion of Tolstoy's writing of Anna Karenina with
information supplied by Ilya Tolstoy from his book Remem-
brances of Tolstoy by His Son.

747 Yousovsky, Josef. "Anna Karenina, " Theatre Arts M, 21
(Nov. 1937), 853-860.

748 Zweers, A. F. "Is there Only One Anna Karenina?, " Can
S P, 11, no. 2 (1969), 272-281.

DISSERTATIONS

749 Chan, Lois M. "Figures in the Carpet: A Study of Leading
Metaphors of Six Realistic Novels, " University of Ken-
tucky, 1971.

750 Low, Frederick E. "The Troubled Heroine: Flaubert's Emma,
Tolstoy's Anna, Goethe's Gretchen and the Condition of
Feminine Fulfillment, " City University of New York, 1972.

751 Schultze, Sydney P. "Anna Karenina: A Structural Analysis, "
University of Indiana, 1974.

See also: 4, 39, 85, 450, 451, 454, 458, 459, 466, 468, 471,
474, 477, 481, 489, 495, 497, 498, 506, 507, 512, 515,
524, 532, 853, 1230, 1236, 1256, 1260, 1261, 1263, 1264,
1280, 1290, 1320, 1333, 1811, 1824, 1835, 1836, 1845,
1936, 2038.

Section III continued

FICTION--KREUTZER SONATA

BOOKS

752 Comstock, A. The Kreutzer Sonata. New York: Broadway
Publishing Co. , 1904.

753 Couplan, W. C. Tolstoi's 'Kreutzer Sonata. ' A Discourse
by W. C. Coupland. London: South Place Ethical Society, 1890.

754 Gregor, J. Whose to Blame? A Woman's Version of The
Kreutzer Sonata. London: Sonnenschein, 1894; 174p.

755 Ingersoll, Robert G. Love the Redeemer. London: Progressive Publishing Co. , 1890; 15p. See under entry 757 for
annotation.

756 Kenyon, Margrave. Madansena, Slave of Love. Re Tolstoi,
A Counter Song to Anti-Marriage. London: Hall and
Lovitt, 1890; 68p.

ESSAYS AND CHAPTERS from general works

757 Ingersoll, Robert G. "Tolstoi and The Kreutzer Sonata" in
Essays in Criticism. New York: Farrell, 1897; 64-77.
Tolstoy's philosophy of life is summarized and then labeled
as "a kind of insanity; nature soured or withered; deformed so that celibacy is mistaken for virtue. " Tolstoy's venemous beliefs are regarded as being best represented by The Kreutzer Sonata where he sought to justify
his view of man as "a vile and base creature" but failed,
nonetheless, because the reader's sympathy falls to the
wife and not the husband in the end. Tolstoy's views on
love, marriage, and women are discussed and severely
criticized for being inhuman and warped. Also in N
Amer R, 151 (Sept. 1890), 289-299; and excerpt in Truth
Seekers, 17 (1890), 580-581. Reprinted as a pamphlet
titled Love the Redeemer (London: Progressive Publishing
Co. , 1890), 15p.

758 Maurois, Andre. "Tolstoy and Married Life" in The Art of
     Writing. New York: Dutton, 1960; 212-223. A discus-
     sion of the views on conjugal love presented by Tolstoy in
     The Kreutzer Sonata and Family Happiness against the
     background of Tolstoy's own married life. Although the
     two works appeared at different stages of his life they
     are regarded as being similar in that both reveal his
     passionate yet moral nature, his disgust with contempo-
     rary sexual values, and the flavor of his relationship with
     his wife.

INTRODUCTIONS TO EDITIONS of The Kreutzer Sonata

759 Ervine, John. The Devil and Cognate Tales. Trans. by
     Louise Maude and Aylmer Maude. London: Oxford,
     1934 (Centenary Edition); vol. 16, 375p.

760 Maude, Aylmer. The Kreutzer Sonata and Other Stories.
     Trans. by Louise Maude and Aylmer Maude. London:
     Oxford, 1924; 358p.

761 Maude, Aylmer. The Kreutzer Sonata, Devil and Other Tales.
     Trans. by Louise Maude and Aylmer Maude. London:
     Oxford, 1940; 375p.

PERIODICAL ARTICLES

762 Bartol, C. A. "Tolstoy and The Kreutzer Sonata, " Forum,
     10 (Nov. 1890), 264-269.

763 Baylen, Joseph. "A Letter on Tolstoy, W. T. Snead and
     The Kreutzer Sonata, " ASEER, 16, no. 1 (1957), 79-81.

764 Bird, Frederic M. "The Lapse of Tolstoi, " Lippincott's M,
     46 (1890), 273-275. A criticism of The Kreutzer Sonata
     as a novel, making Tolstoy's views unacceptable.

765 Black, Alex. "The Truth about Women: The Unrevealed
     Views of Tolstoy, " Harper's M, 143 (Nov. 1921), 753-757.

766 Boguslawsky, Amalie K. "Tolstoy's Attitude Toward the Woman
     Problem, " Dial, 49 (1 Dec. 1910), 449-451.

767 "Count Tolstoi's New Tale, " RRs, 1 (April 1890), 330-347.

768 Dillon, E. J. "The Kreutzer Sonata, " Universal R, 6 (March
     1890), 293.

769 Ellis, K. "Ambiguity and Point of View in Some Novelistic
     Representations of Jealousy, " Mod Lang Notes, 86 (Dec.
     1971), 891-909. A discussion of sexual jealousy as a

complex emotional state with reference to The Kreutzer
Sonata.

770 Gay, S. E. "The Kreutzer Sonata, " Modern R, 2 (May 1893),
99.

771 Green, Dorothy. "The Kreutzer Sonata: Tolstoy and Beethov-
en, " MSS, 1 (1967).

772 Hapgood, Isabel F. "Tolstoi's The Kreutzer Sonata, " Nation,
50 (7 April 1890), 313-315.

773 Hardwick, Elizabeth. "Seduction and Betrayal, Part II, " NY
R Books, 20, no. 10 (14 June 1973), 6-10. Contains a
discussion of The Kreutzer Sonata and Resurrection with
reference to seduction and betrayal.

774 Ingersoll, Robert G. "Tolstoi and The Kreutzer Sonata, "
Truth Seekers, 17: 580-581. A partial reprint of his
article in the N Amer R of the same title.

775 Ingersoll, Robert G. "Tolstoi's Kreutzer Sonata, " N Amer R,
151 (Sept. 1890), 289-290. Also in Love the Redeemer.
London: Progressive Publishing Co. , 1890; 15pp.

776 Ilyin, Eugene K. "Notes on the Kreutzer Sonata and an Account of a Meeting with Tolstoy, " World R, 14 (April
1950), 57-60.

777 Karpman, Benjamin. "The Kreutzer Sonata; A Problem in
Latent Homosexuality and Castration, " Psychoanalytic R,
24 (1938), 20-48.

778 "The Kreutzer Sonata, " Atheneaum, 96 (12 July 1890), 60.

779 "The Kreutzer Sonata, " Catholic W, 51 (August 1890), 688-689.

780 "The Kreutzer Sonata, " Critic, n. s. 13 (24 May 1890), 255.

781 "The Kreutzer Sonata, " Lit W, 21, no. 12 (7 June 1890), 183.

782 Lynch, Hannah. "Fécondité Versus The Kreutzer Sonata, "
Fortn R, n. s. 73 (Jan. 1900), 69-78. Also in Balzac L,
2 (1900).

783 Petrov, Basil B. "About Women, " Rus Stud, 5, no. 1 (Sept.
1928), 23-26. Concerning Tolstoy's views of women.

784 Pritchett, V. S. "Tolstoy's Marriage Novels, " New St and
Na, 28 (28 Oct. 1944), 287-288.

785 Rosegger, P. G. "The Kreutzer Sonata, " Open Court, 5
(1891), 2795-2796.

786 "Tolstoy the Woman-Hater as Revealed by His Private Journal, " Cur Op, 63 (19 Oct. 1917), 268-269.

787 Wanamaker, M. , and A. Comstock. "Tolstoi and The Kreutzer Sonata, " Forum, 10 (Nov. 1890), 264-265.

788 Whipple, C. K. "The Kreutzer Sonata, " Open Court, 5 (7 May 1891), 2796-2798.

789 Yarmolinsky, A. "Two Letters by L. Tolstoy, " SEER, 8, no. 23 (Dec. 1929), 242-248. An introduction to two letters on The Kreutzer Sonata and non-resistance to evil.

See also: 4, 39, 42, 450, 459, 467, 470, 516, 623, 709, 1050, 1166, 1240, 1258, 1559, 1593

FICTION--RESURRECTION

BOOKS

790 Goldenweiser, Alexander S. Crime a Punishment and Punish-
     ment a Crime: Leading Thoughts of Tolstoi's "Resurrec-
     tion." Washington, D. C. , 1909; 59p. Tolstoy's purpose
     in Resurrection is identified as being the exposure of the
     unreasonableness of the modern system of justice. In
     particular, his view of crime as a punishment inflicted
     on society for its own baseness is defended against con-
     temporary criticism, and Resurrection is praised for the
     type of feelings that it evokes in the reader. It is ad-
     mitted that some of Tolstoy's views are extreme and con-
     tradictory, but this is not seen as "detracting one whit
     off the moral significance" of the novel. Moreover, al-
     though the novel is rooted in Russian conditions it is con-
     sidered to have universal applicability because "crime is
     a punishment and punishment a crime the world over."

791 Maude, Aylmer. A Report and Account of the "Resurrection"
     Fund. Chelmsford, England, 1901; 26p. A report on the
     status of and justification for the drive to raise sufficient
     funds for the translation of Resurrection by the author's
     wife.

ESSAYS AND CHAPTERS from general works

792 Hearn, Lafcadio. "A Note upon Tolstoy's Resurrection" in
     Life and Literature. Freeport, N. Y. : Books for Li-
     braries Press, 1969 (reprint of 1917 publication); 300-307.
     Resurrection is discussed as a religious novel, in the
     moral use of the word, in which Tolstoy presents a de-
     vastating attack on the immorality of the machinery of
     state which crushes the weak and innocent. The highly
     negative reaction of the Russian state and Orthodox
     Church to the novel is seen as a testimony to its effec-
     tiveness and an illustration that "trying to improve a re-
     ligious conception may be quite as dangerous as to attack
     it." Resurrection is criticized, however, for containing
     overstatements and half-truths, especially in regard to the
     possibility of a world without laws, courts, and prisons.

793 Maude, Aylmer.   "How Tolstoy Wrote Resurrection" in TF,
       128-148.   A discussion of Tolstoy's intent in writing
       Resurrection as being the exposure of the "defects in so-
       cial, political, national, and religious conventions" against
       the background of his difficulties in writing and publishing
       the novel.

INTRODUCTIONS TO EDITIONS of Resurrection

794 Edmonds, R.   Resurrection.   Trans. by R. Edmonds.   Balti-
       more: Penguin, 1966; 567p.

795 Hodge, Alan.   Resurrection.   Trans. by Vera Traill.   New
       York: New American Library, 1961; 430p.

796 Maude, Aylmer.   Resurrection.   Trans. by Louise Maude and
       Aylmer Maude.   London: Oxford, 1933; 461p.

797 Maude, Aylmer.   Resurrection.   Trans. by Louise Maude and
       Aylmer Maude.   London: Simpkin, 1901.

798 Maude, Aylmer.   Resurrection.   Trans. by Louise Maude and
       Aylmer Maude, with a preface by George Gibian.   New
       York: Norton, 1966; 499p.

799 McMillin, Arnold B.   Resurrection.   Trans. by Vera Traill.
       London: Heron Books, 1968; 560p.

800 Scammell, Michael.   Resurrection.   Trans. by Louise Maude
       and Aylmer Maude.   New York: Washington Square
       Press, 1963; 507p.

801 Simmons, Ernest J.   Resurrection.   Trans. by Leo Weiner.
       New York: Heritage, 1963; 403p.

802 Wells, H. G.   Resurrection.   Trans. by Louise Maude and
       Aylmer Maude.   London: Oxford, 1928 (Centenary Edi-
       tion); vol. 19, 461p.

PERIODICAL ARTICLES

803 Bienstock, J. W.   "Tolstoy," Independent, 54 (4 Dec. 1902),
       2891-2892.   A survey of Tolstoy's recent literary activity
       with emphasis on Resurrection.

804 Bjerragaard, C. H.   "On Tolstoy's Resurrection," Ideal R,
       12 (May 1900), 127.

805 Deschamps, G.   "Tolstoy's Resurrection: A Review," Balzac
       L, no. 3 (1900), 1-14.

806 Dircks, W. "On Tolstoy's Resurrection, " Dome, 5 (Jan.
     1900), 217-220.

807 Doumic, Rene. "Count Tolstoi's New Romance, " Eclectic M,
     135 (1900), 86-94. Translated from Revue des Deux
     Mondes.

808 Fodor, Alexander. "L. Tolstoj and G. Kennan, " HAB, 21
     (1970), 49-53. A case for Kennan's influence on Resur-
     rection.

809 Garnett, Constance, and Edward Garnett. "Tolstoy and Re-
     surrection, " N Amer R, 173 (April 1901), 504-519.

810 Gibson, A. E. "The Message of Tolstoy's Resurrection, "
     Metaphysical M, 14 (May 1901), 317-338.

811 Goldenweiser Alexander S. "Tolstoy's Resurrection: Crime
     a Punishment and Punishment a Crime, " Survey, 25 (3
     Dec. 1910), 392-404. Also in Med Women's J, 27 (1920),
     195-204.

812 Krauskopf, Joseph. "The Reign of Right--Based on Resur-
     rection by Count Leo Tolstoy, " Our Pulpit, 15, no. 4
     (Dec. 1901), 49-56.

813 Maude, Aylmer. "The Later Works of Tolstoy, " Bookman,
     11 (June 1900), 359-365. A survey of Tolstoy's works
     in his later years including Resurrection and What Is Art?

814 "On Resurrection, " RRs, (L), 21 (Feb. 1900), 167-175.

815 Payne, W. "Resurrection, " Dial, 28 (16 May 1900), 401-402.

816 Peck, Harry T. "Resurrection, " Bookman, 11, no. 2 (April
     1900), 176-179.

817 "Resurrection, " Academy, 64 (1903), 82-83.

818 "Resurrection, " Athenaeum, 1 (7 April 1900), 431.

819 "Resurrection, " Athenaeum, 1 (21 Feb. 1903), 251.

820 "Resurrection, " Chaut, 31 (May 1900), 111-112.

821 "Resurrection, " Critic, 36 (1900), 355-356.

822 "Resurrection, " Harper's W, 47 (1907), 418.

823 "Resurrection, " Independent, 52 (1900), 779-781.

824 "Resurrection, " Independent, 55 (26 March 1903), 744-746.

825   "Resurrection, " Literature, 6 (7 April 1900).

826   "Resurrection, " Nation, 70 (3 May 1900), 345.

827   "Resurrection, " Nation, 71, (1900), 287.

828   "Resurrection, " Sewanee R, 8 (April 1900), 244-246.

829   "Resurrection: Criticism, " Outlook, 147 (12 Oct. 1927), 165-
         166. A discussion of the motion picture based on Tol-
         stoy's Resurrection.

830   Soissons, Count de.   "On Tolstoy's Resurrection, " Humani-
         tarian, 17 (Dec. 1900), 403.

831   Soloviev, Vladimir S.   "A Letter to Count Tolstoy on Resur-
         rection, " Contemp R, 96 (1909), 217-221.

832   Symons, Arthur.   "Tolstoi and the Others, " Sat R, 95 (21
         Feb. 1903), 227-228.   A discussion of the art of Tolstoy
         with special reference given to Resurrection.

833   "Tolstoi's New Book, " Academy, 56 (11 March 1899), 306.
         An introduction to Resurrection prior to its appearance
         as a serial in Russia and other European cities.

834   "Tolstoi's New Novel, " Academy, 57 (9 Sept. 1899), 255-256.
         A discussion of Tolstoy's motives for writing Resurrec-
         tion, suggesting he no longer had the thoughts and urges
         of youth and therefore wrote with a different philosophy.

835   "Tolstoi's New Novel, " Pub Op, 26, no. 13 (30 March 1899),
         406.

836   Tolstoy, Ilya.   "How My Father Wrote Resurrection, " Theater,
         45 (May 1927), 40, 68.

837   Van Westrum, A. S.   "Resurrection, " Bookbuyer, 20 (April
         1900), 230-231.   Also in Independent, (29 March 1900),
         779-781.

838   Walker, John B.   "Discontinuance of Count Tolstoy's Novel
         Made Necessary by the Violation of Every Important De-
         tail of the Contract with Count Tolstoy's Agents, " Cos-
         mopolitan, 27 (1899), 447-449.

839   West, Rebecca.   "A Commentary on Books and Things, "
         Time and Tide, 9, no. 50 (14 Dec. 1928), 1229-1231.

      See also: 4, 40, 45, 450, 451, 459, 709, 773, 1050, 1264,
         1829.

Section III continued

FICTION--WAR AND PEACE

BOOKS

840 Christian, R. F. Tolstoy's War and Peace, A Study. Oxford,
England: Clarendon, 1962; 184p. A detailed examination
of the process followed by Tolstoy in writing War and
Peace by analyzing "draft versions of the novel, Tolstoy's
diaries, notebooks and letters, the historical and biographical sources he used, and secondary critical literature about the novel. " The evolution of the novel is traced
through its various drafts with Tolstoy's concern identified
as being "to render characters more consistent" and "to
improve the account of their mutual relationships. " The
historical sources consulted by him are illustrated as are
the sources from his own life which shaped the novel's
non-historical characters. The virtue of selflessness and
the evil of selfishness are regarded as the novel's central
theme. Additionally, the language, structure, and characterizations of War and Peace are analyzed, and it is
maintained that, more important than whether it is an epic
or a historical novel, is the fact that it represents a new
stage in the European novel because of its concern for
historical, ethical, and religious problems on a scale
never before attempted. Excerpts in WPMT, 1456-1480;
and TCCE, 102-110. Reviewed in:
   Listener, (13 Dec. 1962), 1020, by Michael Futrell.
   New Sta, (30 Nov. 1962), 794, by Robert Taubman.
   Slav R, 22, no. 3 (1963), 599, by Rene Wellek.
   SEER, 42, no. 97 (1963), 211, by Richard Hare.
   Times Lit Sup, (28 Dec. 1962), 1003.

841 Fowler, Austin. Leo Tolstoy's War and Peace. New York:
Simon & Schuster, 1965; 112p. A study guide providing
chapter summaries, character sketches, and critical notes
along with analysis of plot, structure and technique.

842 Freedman, Elaine H. War and Peace: Chapter Notes and
Criticism. New York: American R. D. M. A study guide
containing a brief biography of Tolstoy, a chapter-by-
chapter summary of War and Peace, and a sketch of each
character.

843 Gibian, George, ed. War and Peace, the Maude Translation:
     Backgrounds and Sources; Essays in Criticism. New
     York: W. W. Norton, 1966; xix, 1484p. , bib. 1484.
     The Maude translation of the novel precedes a short his-
     tory of its publication. Its conception and writing are
     presented by way of extracts from Tolstoy's letters and
     diaries in which he discusses various aspects of his work.
     Also presented are three draft versions of Tolstoy's intro-
     duction to War and Peace, and an article written by him
     (Russky Arkhiv, 1868) in which he discusses the novel as
     a chronicle of the times, his use of the French language
     in the novel, his characters' names, and, particularly,
     his philosophy of history. There follows a collection of
     essays and excerpts (individually annotated below) which
     critically analyze various aspects of War and Peace.

844 Juhasz, Leslie A. Tolstoy's War and Peace. New York:
     Barrister, 1966.

845 Lacey, R. , ed. War and Peace: A Full Guide to the Serial.
     London: British Broadcasting Corp. , 1972.

846 Sturman, Marianne. War and Peace. Notes. Lincoln, Neb. :
     Cliff's Notes, 1967; 114p. , bib. 113-114. A brief biog-
     raphy of Tolstoy precedes a study guide presenting a
     synopsis of the novel along with character analysis, and
     an examination of structure, themes and technical devices.

847 Tolstoy's War and Peace: An Introduction to the Series of
     Broadcasts of the B. B. C. London: British Broadcasting
     Corp. , 1943.

ESSAYS AND CHAPTERS from general works

848 Boyer, Paul. "Chez Tolstoi" in LTCA, 112-113. Boyer quotes
     Tolstoy as acknowledging a major debt to Stendhal for his
     insight into warfare. Tolstoy is quoted as having said:
     "for all I know about war, my first master is Stendhal. "
     Translated from Chez Tolstoi (Paris, 1901).

849 Brown, E. K. "Interweaving Themes" in Rhythm in the Novel.
     Toronto: University of Toronto Press, 1963; 78-85. A
     study of thematic structure in War and Peace, with unity
     seen as resting in its continual movement from "separate-
     ness to union. " The worlds of War and Peace, it is ar-
     gued, gradually, forcibly and dramatically come together,
     personally and intellectually. The characters Kutuzov and
     Karatayev are discussed as examples of this movement as
     is the rise of the Rostov family. The novel is regarded
     as being so complexly cohesive that "not a page may be
     skimmed without loss to one's total impression. " Also in
     WPMT, 1411-1415.

850   Cairns, Huntington, et al.   "Leo Tolstoy, War and Peace" in
      Invitation to Learning.   New York: New Home Library,
      1942; 154-166.   The greatness of the novel is judged to
      be a consequence of its epic-heroic nature.   Several of
      its lead characters are discussed, as is the question of
      its central theme which is isolated as being, quoting Lub-
      bock, "the ebb and flow of life. " Contrary to Lubbock's
      interpretation, however, is the assertion that War and
      Peace is a cohesive work of art because of the integration
      between scenes of war and peace provided so skillfully by
      Tolstoy.

851   Christian, R. F.   "Style in War and Peace" in TCCE, 102-
      110.   Repetition is isolated as the most characteristic
      feature of Tolstoy's style.   Tolstoy uses repetition, it is
      contended, to characterize individuals by presenting a col-
      lection of their mannerisms, gestures, and physical fea-
      tures.   Repetition is also seen in his phrasing as a means
      of stressing points, especially in introductory sentences.
      Excerpt from his Tolstoy's War and Peace: A Study.

852   Christian, R. F.   "The Theme and Art of War and Peace" in
      WPMT, 1456-80.   The central theme of War and Peace
      is interpreted as being the contrast between two opposite
      states: selfishness and selflessness.   Characters are dis-
      cussed as they illustrate these two states, with special at-
      tention given to Kutuzov.   Structurally, it is maintained
      that the novel is best analyzed as a dynamic, as opposed
      to static, creation since it grew with Tolstoy as he wrote
      it.   A uniform flow is nonetheless seen because of Tolstoy
      continuously presenting people and phenomena in terms of
      their opposites, as symbolized by the novel's title.   Ex-
      cerpt from his Tolstoy's War and Peace: A Study, 104-
      08, 124-150.

853   Cook, Albert.   "The Moral Vision: Tolstoi" in The Meaning
      of Fiction.   Detroit: Wayne State University Press, 1960;
      179-201.   An analysis of the moral meaning of War and
      Peace with lesser attention given to Anna Karenina.   It is
      argued that Tolstoy presents his moral message by way of
      sequences of observed and analyzed "moral gestures" made
      by his characters which are then "perfectly fused into the
      theme of the novel. " Examples are given from both novels
      to substantiate this claim, and those who criticize the
      works, especially War and Peace, for lack of unity are
      themselves criticized.   Also in TCCE, 111-126.

854   Cook, Albert.   "The Unity of War and Peace" in WPMT, 1398-
      1411.   A discussion of the unity of the novel being based
      on the cohesiveness of its moral vision.   See the previous
      annotation for a discussion of this interpretation.   Also in
      Western R, 22, no. 4 (Summer 1958), 243-255.

855 Crawford, Virginia M. "War and Peace" in Studies in Foreign
     Literature. Port Washington, N. Y. : Kennikat, 1970 (re-
     print of 1899 publication); 276-308. War and Peace is
     labeled a true epic in that it is "an imaginative work
     based on a great national upheaval, permeated by an in-
     tense patriotism" and is seen as being "little short of
     Homeric. " The artistry of the novel is viewed as being
     the source of its worldwide fame--as opposed to its phi-
     losophy, which adds little to the work. Additionally, it
     is claimed that Tolstoy's spiritual conversion and conse-
     quent activities as a preacher represent a terrible blow
     to world literature which will always be in debt to him
     for his literary creations, especially War and Peace.

856 Dataller, Roger. "The Historical Novel" in The Plain Man
     and the Novel. London: Nelson, 1940; 47-62. War and
     Peace is positively assessed for its authenticity, stem-
     ming from Tolstoy's research of and experience with war,
     and for its epic sweep. The internal structure of the
     novel, however, is criticized for "Russian verbosity, and
     characters leaping from one extreme to another in the ap-
     proved Russian fashion. "

857 Dragomirov, M. I. "Count Tolstoy's War and Peace from a
     Military Standpoint" in LTCA, 42-44. A positive assess-
     ment, by a Russian general and military writer, of Tol-
     stoy's descriptions of battle scenes. Tolstoy's portrayals
     are seen as being superior to traditional historical ac-
     counts of warfare because he presents a living picture, as
     opposed to a narrow and sterile one, by way of characters
     who appear as real men with moral and intellectual qual-
     ities that determine their functioning in battle. Translated
     from Oruzheyny Sbornik, no. 4, 1968.

858 Eikhenbaum, Boris M. "The Genre of War and Peace in the
     Context of Russian Literary History" in WPMT, 1442-45.
     War and Peace is discussed as a novel that reflects
     changes that took place in Russian life and in Tolstoy dur-
     ing the years 1863 to 1873. It is claimed that Tolstoy
     moved, in response to the intellectual climate of the dec-
     ade, from writing a "war-and-family" chronicle to writing
     an epic to express his historical-philosophical views, and
     that the resulting literary genre represented somewhat of
     a cross-section of earlier genres. Excerpts translated
     from Lev Tolstoy: Kniga Vtoraya 60ye Gody (Leningrad-
     Moscow, 1931), 401-03.

859 Eikhenbaum, Boris M. "Tolstoy's Essays as an Element of
     Structure" in WPMT, 1444-45. Tolstoy's philosophical
     digressions in War and Peace are discussed as stylistic
     and structural "boundary marks" separating stages of the
     novel. The increasing frequency and solemnity of the
     digressions, culminating in the epilogue, are interpreted

as intended by Tolstoy to be elements of the epic genre
analogous to the digressions of the Iliad. Excerpts translated from Lev Tolstoy: Kniga Vtoraya, 60ye Gody, 375-
78.

860   Elliott, George P. "A Piece of Lettuce" in A Piece of Lettuce
      and Other Essays. New York: Random House, 1957; 246-
      270. The necessity of and difficulties associated with in-
      corporating mundane or "bourgeois" events in a truly real-
      istic piece of literature is examined, with War and Peace
      presented as an example of how Tolstoy successfully dealt
      with this problem. It is maintained that, in spite of the
      mass of small and frequently petty details in the novel,
      Tolstoy is able to command the reader's attention by pre-
      senting a picture that so closely resembles life that the
      events that occur are accepted without question.

861   Fadiman, Clifton. "War and Peace" in Party of One: The
      Selected Writings of Clifton Fadiman. New York: World
      Publishing Co., 1955; 176-202. The qualities responsible
      for labeling War and Peace "a great novel" are isolated
      and discussed. Examined is the tremendous scope of the
      novel (war and peace, good and evil, life and death, love
      and hate); Tolstoy's harmonizing of various themes; the
      novel's naturalness ("as if nature herself were guiding his
      pen"); and its timelessness due to its characters being
      eternally valuable as symbols of men and women. Addi-
      tionally, Tolstoy's views on war and history and the inclu-
      siveness of his knowledge are also applauded. The novel's
      principal defect is seen as its lack of technical perfection.
      Also in his introduction to War and Peace (New York:
      Simon & Schuster, 1942), 1370.

862   Fadiman, Clifton. "War and Peace Fifteen Years After" in
      Any Number Can Play. New York: World Publishing Co.,
      1957; 361-370. Fifteen years after the author's initial
      reading and analysis of War and Peace (see item 861), a
      second, and more critical, judgment is made of the novel.
      The contention that War and Peace is a "historical novel"
      is questioned, and Tolstoy is criticized for his lack of
      subtlety and for the predictability of his characters. The
      novel is, however, still seen as a great one in that it
      forces a certain amount of introspection on the reader in
      response to Tolstoy's treating so effectively the question
      of the meaning and value of life.

863   Farrell, James T. "History and War in Tolstoy's War and
      Peace" in Literature and Morality. New York: Vanguard,
      1946; 214-230. A summary of Tolstoy's theory of history
      and an analysis of its role and significance in War and
      Peace. Emphasized in the discussion are Tolstoy's fatal-
      istic views on warfare and his de-emphasis of the role
      played by individuals in history. Also in UKCR, 13, no.
      1 (1946), 24-33.

864   Farrell, James T.   "Leo Tolstoy and Napoleon Bonaparte" in
      Literature and Morality, 246-266.   Tolstoy's assault on
      Napoleon is seen as being symbolic of Tolstoy's rejection
      of individualism and elevation of the role played in history
      by the selfless man.   Separate from his philosophy of his-
      tory, the historical accuracy of his assault on Napoleon is
      questioned.

865   Farrell, James T.   "Tolstoy's Portrait of Napoleon" in Liter-
      ature and Morality, 231-245.   Examined is the difference
      between Tolstoy's characterization of Napoleon and all
      other characterizations in the novel.   It is considered ob-
      vious that "Tolstoy's moral indignation rises and he ex-
      presses his own positive moral views" whenever dealing
      with Napoleon.

866   Farrell, James T.   "Tolstoy's War and Peace as a Moral
      Panorama of the Tsarist Feudal Nobility" in Literature and
      Morality, 185-213.   A discussion of six characters in War
      and Peace in terms of the insights that they, and the novel
      in general, provide into the nature of the Russian aristoc-
      racy and "the moral consequences" of their life pattern.

867   Forster, Edward M.   "The Story" in Aspects of the Novel.
      New York: Harcourt, Brace, 1927; 63-4.   War and Peace
      is discussed as a masterpiece not because of its characters
      or episodes, but for the "immense area of Russia over
      which episodes and characters are scattered. "   In spite
      of the tremendous scope of the novel and Tolstoy's shifts
      in point of view, it is maintained that the novel has cohe-
      sion because the reader, in the long run, "accepts it all. "

868   Freeborn, Richard.   "War and Peace" in The Rise of the Nov-
      el.   Cambridge, England: Cambridge University Press,
      1973; 208-266.   A study of the origins of War and Peace,
      with parallels made to Tolstoy's intent in writing other
      pieces of fiction, precedes an analysis of the novel's lead-
      ing characters, especially Pierre and Andrei.   Also dis-
      cussed is Tolstoy's sense of history, his fatalism, and
      the process of "birth, renewal, and self-discovery" that
      rests beneath the novel.   The study concludes with an
      examination of Tolstoy's depiction of the "inconstancy of
      the physical man and the imperishability of the spiritual. "
      In all, the novel is praised for its scope, depth, and
      power.

869   Galsworthy, John.   "Six Novelists in Profile: An Address,
      1924" in Castles in Spain and Other Essays.   London:
      Heinemann, 1927; 145-171.   War and Peace is praised as
      the "greatest novel ever written, " an accolade due largely
      to "the creative energy" of Tolstoy and to his sincere be-
      lief in that which he was attempting to convey.   This pro-
      found sincerity that was Tolstoy's leading characteristic

as an author is seen as enabling him to follow his impulses in writing rather than be bound by "literary self-
consciousness" as lesser artists are. Also in his Can-
delabra: Selected Essays (New York: Scribner's, 1933),
133-156.

870 Golding, William G. "Tolstoy's Mountain" in The Hot Gates
and Other Occasional Papers. New York: Harcourt,
Brace & World, 1965; 121-25. The maze of sub-plots
and characters in War and Peace, along with Tolstoy's
complex philosophy, and the rapid shifts in the novel from
battle to domestic scenes are collectively regarded as being responsible for the heaviness of the novel and the difficulty in reading it: "War and Peace is more than a
mountain ... it is a world" and is "definitely not for summer reading ... on the orchard wall. " Additionally, Tolstoy is criticized for his view of history as being part of
a huge movement indiscernible to man, although his contention that Napoleon had little control over the historical
outcome of his battles is supported.

871 Hackett, Francis. "War and Peace" in Horizons: A Book of
Criticism. New York: Huebsch, 1918; 171-77. Standard
assessments of War and Peace as a historical panorama
of Russia's "Napoleonic experience" are criticized before
a discussion is presented on the novel's most distinctive
feature--seen by Hackett as Tolstoy's ability to depict life
vividly. Plot as well as philosophy are considered secondary to the spirit with which Tolstoy writes: "By what
sensitive and mysterious process the spirit of the creator
steals into a narrative, gives it his livingness, no one has
yet defined. But it is this subtle presence ... which
makes the novel an artistic form. " Originally in New Republic, 8 (1916), 215-17.

872 Hamburger, Kate. "The Technique of Decentralization" in
WPMT, 1480-81. War and Peace is judged to be a
remarkable novel for its use of open form or decentralization. The lack of any central figure who reacts to
events and communicates to the reader is discussed, and
Tolstoy's making his points in the novel by way of material distributed over spheres of life through a group of
characters in each sphere is seen as representing Tolstoy
at the height of his mastery of narrative art. Excerpt
translated from Leo Tolstoi: Gestalt und Problem (Göt-
tingen and Zurich, n. d), 159-161.

873 Hardy, Barbara. "Forms and Themes" in Tellers and Listen-
ers: The Narrative Imagination. London: Athlone Press,
1975; 150-54. An analysis of the scene in War and Peace
where Natasha relates to Pierre her feelings about Andrei's
death, and Pierre describes to her his terrible experiences associated with the French invasion. The dynamic

interaction of feeling between the two characters, this
listening and telling experience, is interpreted as having
led their relationship to a new and higher level, and is
deemed a testimony to Tolstoy's artistic ability.

874 James, Henry. "The Tragic Muse" (preface) in The Art of
the Novel. New York: Scribner's, 1962; 70-97. Tolstoy
is mentioned on page 84. It is maintained that "a picture
without composition" is unpremeditated art, and that War
and Peace, as a "loose baggy monster," lacks such composition and therefore is artistically deficient. Tolstoy's
realism is praised in spite of the novel's mixture of
"queer elements of the accidental and arbitrary" which
are seen as defying artistic meaning. Also in LTCA, 104;
and WPMT, 1395-96.

875 Leontiev, Konstantin. "The Greatness and Universality of
War and Peace" in WPMT, 1389-91. See under entry
481 for annotation. Excerpt translated from O Romanakh
Gr. L. N. Tolstogo (Moscow, 1911). Additional excerpt
in LTCA, 80-96.

876 Lubbock, Percy. The Craft of Fiction (1921). New York:
Viking, 1957; pp. 26-58 (no separate part specifically on
Tolstoy). It is argued that War and Peace is a novel
without a center and that Tolstoy never realized this. The
epic proportions of the novel are considered as making
effective composition impossible even though it appears
that Tolstoy knows where he is at all times. An analysis
of the novel's structure follows, with its central strand
at first appearing to be the "flow and ebb of the recur-
rent tide of life"; later, it is claimed, the Napoleonic
clash seems to dwarf this initial strand. It is concluded
that Tolstoy was perhaps unwittingly writing two novels,
therefore confusing the reader. Excerpt in WPMT, 1396-
98.

877 Lukacs, Georg. The Historical Novel. London: Merlin, 1962
(no separate part on Tolstoy). War and Peace is not
judged to be a broad historical novel but rather a collection of episodes from the Napoleonic wars serving as background for the human development of the novel's main
characters. Tolstoy's lengthy discussions on warfare and
Napoleon are not seen as historical but rather philosophical in nature. War and Peace is interpreted as an historical novel only in the sense that it is a realistic novel
presenting popular life as foundation of historical happen-
ings. In conclusion, the magnificence of the novel is accepted, but the validity of Tolstoy's view of history is
questioned in light of the movement of radical democracy
contemporary with Tolstoy. Excerpt in WPMT, 1423-29.

878 Matlaw, Ralph E. "Mechanical Structure and Inner Form:
A Note on War and Peace and Dr. Zhivago" in WPMT,

1416-1423.   The structural differences between the first
and second editions of War and Peace, especially the
placing of the epilogue, are examined with reference to
Tolstoy's motives for the alterations.   It is maintained
that Tolstoy changed the sequence of the volumes so that
the novel would not end with a family scene but with the
philosophical statement that appears in the epilogue because "he wanted the final impression to be didactic
rather than novelistic. "   Parallels are then made to Pasternak's Dr. Zhivago, especially the placement of Pasternak's poems in comparison to Tolstoy's placement of his
anti-historical epilogue.   Also in Symposium, 16, no. 4
(Winter 1962), 288-295.

879 Maugham, William Somerset.   "Tolstoy and War and Peace"
in An Introduction to Ten Novels and Their Authors.   New
York: Greenwood, 1968; 273-299.   War and Peace is
considered to be "the greatest of all novels" because of
its grand sweep and vast array of characters against the
background of a momentous period in history.   Tolstoy's
intent in writing the novel is discussed as are the sources
he used to construct his characters and episodes.   In addition, several of the novel's main characters are favorably assessed along with the epilogue.   Also in Great Novelists and Their Novels.   Phila. : (Winston, 1948), 17-39.

880 Morgan, Charles.   "Tolstoy: The Second Epilogue" in Reflections in a Mirror.   New York: Macmillan, 1945; 201-216.
Tolstoy's message in the second epilogue to War and
Peace is judged to be that "the more men become group
conscious, the more they surrender their free will. "
This contention, along with his considering the formation
of groups as a prime cause for war, is criticized on the
grounds that he failed to distinguish good groups from
evil ones, and consequently is guilty of gross oversimpli-
fication.

881 Morgan, Charles.   "Tolstoy: War and Peace" in Reflections
in a Mirror, 192-200.   Tolstoy is regarded as having had
a dual purpose in War and Peace: "to express himself
in relation to individual men and women" and to "present
his values in a society considered historically. "   It is
agreed that he improvised considerably as he wrote the
novel--not out of poor planning but because his philosophy
was still developing and, moreover, he wished to express
his views "not in the conventional form of the novel but
only in an 'unpremeditated' social and historical improvi-
sation. "

882 Muir, Edwin.   "The Chronicle" in The Structure of the Novel,
99-100.   War and Peace is discussed as a "comprehensive
picture of life both in time and space, " but with the element of time considered to be the most important factor.

The unifying factor in the novel is regarded as the process of continuous change itself, which provides "the universal behind the particular, " and that those critics who
fail to see unity have overlooked the fact that a novel can
revolve around fate as an organizing principle.

883 Pisarev, Dmitri. "The Old Gentry" in WPMT, 1377-1380. It
is claimed that Tolstoy created the characters of War and
Peace so well that they assume an identity in the reader's
eyes independent of that intended by Tolstoy. An analysis
of the character Nicholas Rostov is presented as an example of how, separate from the central purpose of Tolstoy in creating him, Rostov inspires thoughts in the
reader on the meaningless nature of the life led by the
Russian gentry of the 19th century. Excerpt translated
from Sochineniya (Moscow, 1956), vol. 4, 370-371, 393-
397 passim.

884 Rexroth, Kenneth. "Tolstoy, War and Peace" in Classics Revisited. Chicago: Quadrangle, 1968; 263-67. War and
Peace is praised for the fullness of its characters, dramatic intensity, and unflinching integrity of its author as
well as for its philosophic message. Many of the ideas
behind the novel, which Tolstoy preached later in his
life, such as that men must learn to live simple and peaceful
lives, are seen as being very relevant to today's world.

885 Sampson, R. V. "Leo Tolstoy" in The Discovery of Peace.
London: Heinemann, 1973; 108-167. An analysis of the
nature of power, ambition, and warfare as exemplified by
the characters of War and Peace. The sources of Tolstoy's views on warfare are traced, with much reference
to the influence of Proudhon as contended by Eikhenbaum,
and are then discussed largely in terms of the contradictions present in them. The leading contradictions in Tolstoy's views are seen as being that war is evil and irra-
tional yet essential and part of God's plan; that leaders have
no power in directing warfare yet are responsible for the
suffering caused by warfare; and that history is predestined
yet man has free will. In spite of these contradictions,
Tolstoy is applauded for "pricking the bubble of power as no
one before him had ever come near to doing, " and for the
clarity of his moral understanding of the will to power.

886 Shklovsky, Victor. "Details in War and Peace" in WPMT,
1429-1442. The details of War and Peace, which are defined as "fine points not relating to the plot, which chiefly
characterize the epoch or the people, " are discussed as
a subject that has divided scholars in their assessment
of the novel. Examples of Tolstoy's use of detail are
presented, as are the opinions of Turgenev, Merezhkovsky,
and Pokrovsky on this subject. Excerpt translated from

Material i stil v romane L. Tolstogo 'Voyna i mir' (Moscow, 1928), 86-108.

887   Simmons, Ernest J.   "The Writing of War and Peace" in
      Slavic Studies.   Freeport, N. Y. :   Books for Libraries
      Press, 1972 (reprint of 1943 publication); 180-198.   A
      discussion of how many aspects and characters of War
      and Peace developed out of the acquaintances and events
      of Tolstoy's life.   Also examined is the style of the
      novel, with the point being made that it differs signifi-
      cantly from that of his post-conversion years, when his
      life and attitude toward his work had changed.   In partic-
      ular, it is claimed that since he wrote War and Peace in
      an atmosphere of love and family happiness, the novel
      projects a love of life and a glorification of the family
      idea.   Other influences on the novel are considered, es-
      pecially the intellectual circles of the 1860's.

888   Strakhov, Nicholas.   "The Russian Idea in War and Peace" in
      WPMT, 1382-87.   The basic meaning of War and Peace
      is interpreted as resting in Tolstoy's presentation of
      simplicity, goodness, and truth as being at the heart of
      true greatness.   Kutuzov and Napoleon, it is maintained,
      are portrayed by Tolstoy as examples of true and false
      greatness respectively.   More generally, the novel is
      viewed as depicting the superiority of meek heroism (Rus-
      sian) over active heroism (French).   Excerpt translated
      from Kriticheskie Stati ob I. S. Turgeneve i L. N. Tol-
      stom (St. Petersburg, 1895).

889   Strakhov, Nicholas.   "The Significance of the Last Part of
      War and Peace" in WPMT, 1380-81.   A brief analysis is
      presented of the end of Volume VI as the denouement of
      War and Peace.   The regeneration of Pierre and Natasha
      is seen as being symbolic of the revival of Russia after
      the years of struggle and suffering associated with the
      wars with the French.   Excerpt translated from his re-
      view of War and Peace in Zarya, January 1870.

890   Strakhov, Nicholas.   "Tolstoy's War and Peace" in Literature
      and National Identity, 119-167.

891   Strakhov, Nicholas.   "War and Peace, Volumes I, II, III, IV"
      in LTCA, 45-7.   War and Peace is compared to Pushkin's
      The Captain's Daughter on the grounds that it bears more
      resemblance to this work than to any other in Russian
      literature.   The two are said to be similar in tone and
      subject, in "inward spirit, " and, most importantly, both
      are family chronicles--a genre of literature started by
      Pushkin and developed to its fullest by Tolstoy in War and
      Peace.   Translated from Zarya, February 1869.

892   Turgenev, Ivan.   "Comments on War and Peace" in WPMT,
      1387-1389.   Presented are comments made by Turgenev

in 1868, 1870 and 1880 about Tolstoy and War and Peace. The early assessments note serious deficiencies in the novel, especially Tolstoy's "childish philosophy" which often makes it a "boring and unsuccessful reading." The 1880 statement, however, praises Tolstoy for his realism in depicting Russian life and calls the novel "a great work by a great writer." Excerpt translated from Russkie Pisateli o Literature, ed. by S. Balukhaty (Leningrad, 1939). For similar negative comments by Turgenev, see his "Letters to I. P. Borisov" in LTCA.

893   Turgenev, Ivan. "Letter to P. V. Annenkov" in LTCA, 40-41. In an 1868 letter, Turgenev criticizes Tolstoy and War and Peace for historical charlatanism, excessive inclusion of petty detail, and lengthy observations on his own feelings. Translated from Polnoe Sobranie Sochineniy i Pisem.

894   Wilson, Edmund. "The Original of Tolstoy's Natasha" in Classics and Commercials: A Literary Chronicle of the Forties. New York: Farrar, Straus, 1950; 442-452. A discussion of the life of Tolstoy's sister-in-law Tatiana Behrs (Kuzminskaya), who served as the model for Natasha of War and Peace, with emphasis on the important episode in her life that did not work its way into the novel--her frustrated engagement to Tolstoy's older brother Sergei.

INTRODUCTIONS TO EDITIONS of War and Peace

895   Bayley, John. War and Peace. Trans. by Ann Dunnigan. New York: New American Library, 1968; 1456p.

896   Edmonds, Rosemary. War and Peace. Trans. by Rosemary Edmonds. Harmondsworth: Penguin, 1969; 2 vols., 1444p.

897   Fadiman, Clifton. War and Peace. Trans. by Louise Maude and Aylmer Maude. New York: Simon & Schuster, 1942; 1370p.

898   Gibian, George, ed. War and Peace, the Maude Translation: Backgrounds and Sources; Essays in Criticism. New York: W. W. Norton, 1966; 1484p.

899   Maude, Aylmer. War and Peace. Trans. by Louise Maude and Aylmer Maude. London: Oxford, 1933; 3 vols., 1744p.

900   Maude, Aylmer. War and Peace. Trans. by Louise Maude and Aylmer Maude. New York: Heritage, 1943; 2 vols., 1711p.

901   Maude, Aylmer. War and Peace. Trans. by Louise Maude
        and Aylmer Maude. New York: Heritage, 1962; 2 vols.,
        1632p. Including repros. of paintings of Verestchagen.

902   Vogue, Maurice de. War and Peace. London: Everyman's
        Library, 1911; 3 vols.

903   Walpole, Hugh. War and Peace. Trans. by Louise Maude
        and Aylmer Maude. London: Oxford, 1930-32 (Centenary
        Edition).

PERIODICAL ARTICLES

904   Banta, Lucille. "Interview with a Soviet Film Director and a
        Star: War and Peace," Am Dialogue, 5 (1970), 34-36.

905   Bayley, John, and Timothy Binyon. "War and Peace: An
        Exchange," Es in Criticism, 18 (1968), 100-104.

906   Bier, Jesse. "A Century of War and Peace--Gone, Gone with
        the Wind," Genre, 4 (1971), 107-141.

907   Brash, W. B. "Tolstoy's War and Peace," Lon Q R, 169
        (April 1943), 122-130.

908   Chapple, Richard L. "The Role and Function of Nature in
        L. N. Tolstoy's War and Peace," NZSJ, 11 (1973), 86-
        101.

909   Clifford, E. "War and Peace and the Dynasts," Mod Philol,
        54 (August 1956), 33-44.

910   Cook, Albert. "The Unity of War and Peace," Western R,
        22 (Summer 1958), 243-255. Also in TCCE, 111-126;
        "The Moral Vision: Tolstoy," in The Meaning of Fiction,
        179-201; and WPMT, 1398-1411.

911   Cowley, M. "This War and Peace," New Republic, 106 (11
        May 1942), 642-643.

912   Curtis, James M. "The Function of Imagery in War and
        Peace," Slav R, 29, no. 3 (1970), 460-480.

913   Debreczeny, Paul. "Freedom and Necessity: A Reconsidera-
        tion of War and Peace," Papers on Lang Lit, 7 (1971),
        185-198.

914   Duffy, Christopher. "Borodino," Listener, 88, no. 2269 (21
        Sept. 1972), 369-371. A description of how the Battle of
        Borodino was restaged for BBC's War and Peace.

915   Dukas, Vytas, and Glenn A. Sandstorm. "Taoistic Patterns in
        War and Peace," SEEJ, 14, no. 2 (1970), 182-193.

916 Eikhenbaum, Boris. "Tolstoi's War and Peace: A New The-
     ory, " Criterion, 2, no. 42 (Oct. 1931), 50-57. The in-
     fluence of Proudhon on Tolstoy's War and Peace is dis-
     cussed.

917 Elliot, George P. "Piece of Lettuce, " Kenyon R, 25 (Spring
     1963), 295-313. Also in Elliot, George P. , A Piece of
     Lettuce, 246-270.

918 Fadiman, Clifton. "Ghost of Napoleon; Thoughts After Read-
     ing War and Peace, " Atlantic M, 169 (May 1942), 538-
     547.

919 Fadiman, Clifton. "Party of One: War and Peace, " Holiday,
     20 (August 1956), 6.

920 Fadiman, Clifton. "War and Peace, " New Yorker, 17 (31
     Jan. 1942), 57-60.

921 Farrell, James T. "History of War in Tolstoy's War and
     Peace, " UKC R, 13, no. 1 (1946), 24-33.

922 Farrell, James T. "Tolstoy's War and Peace, " UKC R, 11,
     no. 4 (1945), 265-282.

923 Feuer, Katherine B. "Alexis de Tocqueville and the Genesis
     of War and Peace, " Calif Slavic S, 4 (1967), 92-118.

924 Feuer, Katherine B. "Book That Became War and Peace, "
     Reporter, 20 (1959), 33-36.

925 Findlater, J. H. "Tolstoy as Novelist, " Living Age, 230 (24
     (24 August 1901), 488-496. Also "Great War Novels, "
     National R, 37 (1901), 776-786.

926 Garrison, W. P. "War and Peace, " Nation, 79 (27 Oct.
     1904), 338-339. A discussion of the Garnett and Dole
     translations.

927 Golding, William G. "Tolstoy's Mountain, " Spectator, 207 (8
     Sept. 1961), 325-326. Also in Golding, William G. Hot
     Gates and Other Occasional Papers, 121-125.

928 Gordon, M. "Tolstoy's Encyclopedia of Ideas and Human Con-
     duct: War and Peace, " Sat R Lit, 25 (17 Oct. 1942), 8-9.

929 Greenspan, E. "Tolstoy: Colossus in the Classroom, " Eng
     J, 57, no. 7 (Oct. 1968), 965-971. On War and Peace
     as an excellent novel for the secondary school population.

930 Greenwood, E. B. "Tolstoy's Poetic Realism in War and
     Peace, " Critical Q, 11 (Autumn 1969), 219-233.

931 Hackett, Francis. "The Greatest Novel," New Republic, 8
     (1916), 215-217. Also in Hackett, Francis, Horizons, A
     Book of Criticism, 171-177.

932 Hagan, John. "On the Craftsmanship of War and Peace," Es
     in Criticism, 13 (Jan. 1963), 17-49.

933 Hagan, John. "A Pattern of Character Development in Tol-
     stoj's War and Peace: P'er Bezuxov," TSLL, 11 (1969),
     985-1011.

934 Hagan, John. "A Pattern of Character Development in Tol-
     stoj's War and Peace: Prince Anrej," SEEJ, 13, no. 2
     (1969), 164-190.

935 Hagan, John. "Patterns of Character Development in Tolstoj's
     War and Peace; Nicholas, Natasha and Mary," PMLA, 84
     (March 1969), 235-244.

936 Hare, R. "Tolstoy's Motives for Writing War and Peace,"
     Rus R, 15, no. 2 (April 1956), 110-121.

937 Harkins, William E. "A Note on the Use of Narrative and
     Dialogue in War and Peace," Slav R, 29, no. 1 (1970),
     86-92.

938 Howard, Sidney. "My Favorite Fiction Character. Natasha
     Rostova in Tolstoy's War and Peace," Bookman, 62 (Feb.
     1926), 670-671.

939 Jepsen, Laura. "Prince Andrey as Epic Hero in Tolstoy's
     War and Peace," So Atlantic B, 34, no. 4 (1969), 5-7.

940 Kirkland, Joseph. "Tolstoi and the Russian Invasion of the
     Realm of Fiction," Dial, 7 (1886), 79-81. A discussion
     of War and Peace and Childhood, Boyhood, Youth.

941 Laugel, Auguste. "Tolstoi's 'Peace and War'," Nation, 40
     (1885), 70-71.

942 Lee, C. Nicholas. "Philosophy and Artistic Devices in the
     Historical Fiction of L. N. Tolstoy and M. A. Alsanov,"
     Am Contribs, 2 (1968), 239-259.

943 Lengyel, József. "Marginal Notes on Tolstoy's War and
     Peace," Mosaic, 6, no. 2 (Winter 1973), 85-102. Trans.
     by Zita McRobbie.

944 Leon, Philip. "Who Makes History? A Study of Tolstoy's
     Answer in War and Peace," Hibbert J, 42 (1944), 254-258.

945 Lyngstad, Alexander H. "Tolstoj's Use of Parentheses in
     War and Peace," SEEJ, 16, no. 4 (1972), 403-413.

946 Lytle, Andrew N. "The Image as a Guide to Meaning on the Historical Novel, " Sewanee R, 61 (Summer 1953), 408-426.

947 "Man Who Wrote the Book, " Life 41 (20 August 1956), 69-76, illus. On War and Peace with illustrations of Yasnaya Polyana.

948 Manning, C. A. "Significance of Tolstoy's War Stories, " in PMLA, 52 (Dec. 1937), 1161-1169.

949 Matlaw, Ralph. "Mechanical Structure and Inner Form: A Note on War and Peace and Dr. Zhivago, " Symposium, 16, no. 4 (Winter 1962), 288-295.

950 Maude, Aylmer. "Tolstoy's Final Revision of War and Peace, " Times Lit Sup, 29 (18 Dec. 1930), 1087.

951 Maude, Aylmer. "War and Peace. A Correction, " Times Lit Sup, 21 (9 March 1922), 157. A letter to the editor correcting a misprint in War and Peace, possibly made by Sofia Tolstoy during one of her recopyings of the manuscript. States that the river crossed on 13 June 1812 was the Viliya not the Vistula.

952 McCourt, E. A. "Tolstoy's War and Peace, " Queen's Q, 49, no. 2 (May 1942), 147-156.

953 O'Faolain, S. "Greatest of War Books: Tolstoy's War and Peace, " Yale R, n. s. 30, no. 1 (Sept. 1940), 141-149.

954 Overton, G. "War and Peace: Do You Remember It?" Mentor, 17 (Jan. 1930), 47.

955 Payne, William. "War and Peace, " Dial, 6 (1886), 299.

956 Pomorska, K. and M. Drazen. "Tolstoj's Rotary System, " Ricerche Slav, 17-19 (1970-1972), 453-465. On symbolism in War and Peace.

957 Rexroth, K. "War and Peace, " Sat R, 50 (11 Nov. 1967), 10, 67.

958 Rzhevsky, N. "Shape of Chaos: Herzen and War and Peace, " Rus R, 34 (Oct. 1975), 367-381.

959 Schakhowskoi, Zinaida. "War and Peace, Literary Appreciation, " Message, (May 1945), 53-55.

960 Silbarjoris, F. R. "War and Peace on the Screen, " Col Engl, 18 (Oct. 1956), 41-45.

961 Siminov, K. "On Reading Tolstoy: An Essay on the Centenary of the First Edition of War and Peace, " Partisan R, 38, no. 2 (1971), 208-216.

962   Sorokin, B.   "Moral Regeneration: N. N. Strakhov's Organic
      Critiques of War and Peace, " SEEJ, 20 (Summer 1976),
      130-147.

963   States, Bert O.   "The Hero and the World: Our Sense of
      Space in War and Peace, " Mod Fict St, 11, no. 2 (Sum-
      mer 1965), 153-164.

964   Stilman.   "War and Peace, " Am Contribs, (1963).

965   Thale, J.   "War and Peace: The Art of Incoherence, " Es in
      Criticism, 16 (Oct. 1966), 398-415.

966   "Tolstoi, " Bookbuyer, 3, no. 8 (Sept. 1886), 296.   On a new
      translation of War and Peace and how this publication to-
      gether with the deaths of Hugo and Turgenev clearly makes
      Tolstoy number one in European literature.

967   "Tolstoi's Excisions in War and Peace, " Living Age, 316 (17
      Feb. 1923), 429-432.   A discussion of deletions in War
      and Peace based upon Birjukov's revised edition.

968   "Tolstoi's War and Peace, " Lit W, 17, no. 21 (16 Oct. 1886),
      348-349.   Also in Spectator, 60 (5 Feb. 1887), 202-203.

969   "War and Peace, " Lit W, 21, no. 3 (1 Feb. 1890), 39.   A
      review of the Dole translation of War and Peace.

970   "War and Peace, " Nation, 50 (27 March 1890), 259-260.

971   "War and Peace: A Reading of Destiny, " Times Lit Sup, 14
      (7 Oct. 1915), 337-338.   An examination of the impact of
      War and Peace after the "Great War. "

972   Wasiolek, Edward.   "The Theory of History in War and Peace, "
      Midway, 9 (1968), 117-135.

973   Wedgewood, C. C.   "Count Leo Tolstoi, " Contemp R, 52
      (August 1887), 249-263.   A comparison of Tolstoy's War
      and Peace and Thackeray's Vanity Fair with a discussion
      of Tolstoy's views on Christianity.   Also in Eclectic M,
      109 (1887), 634-643.

974   Williams, O.   "War and Peace, " National R, 117 (August
      1941), 232-238.

975   Wilson, E.   "Original of Tolstoy's Natasha, " New Yorker, 24
      (28 August 1948), 63-66.

976   "Writings of Tolstoy, " Harper's M, 114 (Feb. 1907), 479-482.
      A survey of Tolstoy's War and Peace.

DISSERTATIONS

977 Bradshaw, David G. "The Aesthetic Treatment of Historical,
     Moral and Philosophical Themes in L. N. Tolstoy's Vojna
     i Mir, and Victor Hugo's Les Miserables, " University of
     North Carolina, 1974.

978 Feuer, Kathryn. "The Genesis of War and Peace, " Columbia
     University, 1965.

979 Key, William C. "The Use of the Future Tense in Leo Tol-
     stoy's War and Peace, " University of Pennsylvania, 1965.

980 Lewis, Robert P. "Deception and Revelation: A Study of
     Three Systems of Characterization in Tolstoy's War and
     Peace, " Columbia University, 1972.

See also: 10, 39, 67, 74, 147, 220, 314, 448, 450, 451, 458,
     459, 460, 464, 466, 468, 474, 481, 489, 493, 495, 496,
     497, 498, 500, 506, 507, 514, 515, 524, 532, 586, 592,
     602, 614, 615, 666, 709, 717, 726, 727, 732, 741, 994,
     1236, 1263, 1264, 1280, 1285, 1335, 1361, 1666, 1681,
     1755, 1767, 1772, 1778, 1784, 1786, 1787, 1814, 1815,
     1824, 1831, 1837, 1839, 1861, 1867, 1868, 1895, 1942,
     1948, 1954, 1955, 1971, 1988, 2047.

FICTION--OTHER WORKS

BOOKS

981 Zweers, A. F. Grown-up Narrator and Childlike Hero: An
     Analysis of the Literary Devices Employed in Tolstoy's
     Trilogy: Childhood, Boyhood, Youth. The Hague: Mou-
     ton, 1971. An analysis of the "literary devices by which
     a child's world is evoked" in Tolstoy's trilogy. Isolated
     and discussed is his technique of writing about a child,
     who is Tolstoy, from the adult perspective yet employing
     two first person singulars. Also examined are the in-
     sights which Tolstoy's characterizations provide into his
     beliefs and life, followed by a survey of the critical liter-
     ature on Childhood, Boyhood, Youth, and how the trilogy
     compares to other accounts, in Russian literature, of
     childhood.

ESSAYS AND CHAPTERS from general works

982 Babel, Isaac. "Babel Answers Questions about His Work: An
     Interview of 28 September, 1937" in LTCA, 203-04. The
     Soviet writer praises Tolstoy for his truthfulness in his
     life and literature, and isolates Hadji Murat as the work
     of Tolstoy that best demonstrates his "stripping off all
     outer layers with a sense of truth. " Also in You Must
     Know Everything, ed. Nathalie Babel, 1970.

983 Baring, Maurice. "Tolstoy's Last Play" in Punch and Judy
     and Other Essays. Garden City, N. Y. : Doubleday, Page,
     1924; 327-332. An examination of the sources for Tol-
     stoy's play The Living Corpse, and a summary of its plot
     precedes a discussion of the play as a "miracle of detail
     and realism, a triumph of artistic interpretation. " Two
     scenes are then presented as examples of Tolstoy's art-
     istry.

984 Barrett, William. "Existentialism as a Symptom of Man's
     Contemporary Crisis" in Spiritual Problems in Contempo-
     rary Literature, ed. Stanley Hopper. New York: Harper,
     1952; 139-152. Tolstoy is isolated as an example to prove

124

the contention that modern existentialism has its "roots in the profound upheavals of civilization during the past two centuries. " Tolstoy's The Death of Ivan Ilych is then discussed as a "basic scripture for existential thought, " its existential message being interpreted as that "modern life has alienated the individual from himself, " and that, therefore, "modern man has lost the meaning of life. " Tolstoy is seen as arguing that nothing less than the awful presence of death can shock man into seeing sense to life--hence the fate of Ivan Ilych.

985 Chandler, Frank W. "Exponents of Russian Realism: Tolstoy and Gorky" in Modern Continental Playwrights. New York: Harper & Row, 1931; 64-78. Tolstoy's late-in-life turn to writing plays is interpreted as being part of his search for a better vehicle to propound his ethical doctrines. The theme of each of his plays is then isolated, and his link to "naturalism" discussed. Special attention is given to his The Power of Darkness as a highly effective peasant tragedy elucidating the means by which "the ignorant and weak succumb to evil and how wickedness may be replaced by repentance. "

986 Chernyshevsky, N. G. "Childhood and Boyhood, and Army Tales by Count L. N. Tolstoy" in LTCA, 30-34. An analysis, by the Russian revolutionary writer and critic, of Tolstoy's insight into "the psychological process, its forms, its laws" as exhibited in three of his works. Tolstoy's Army Tales receives particular praise for its use of "inner monologue" revealing that he, more so than any other writer, has the ability to analyze the very soul of man. Translated from Sovremennik (Dec. 1856).

987 Donskov, Andrew. "Tolstoy's Peasant Plays--The Peasant as the Natural Educator" in The Changing Image of the Peasant in Nineteenth Century Russian Drama. Helsinki: Finnish Academy of Sciences, 1972; 117-158. Tolstoy is seen as not just an artist who studied the "language and sayings" of the peasant, but as "the first Russian dramatist who was intensely associated with this class. " His dramatic contribution to the portrayal of the peasant is interpreted as meager if analyzed for "theme, character, and language, " but unique because of the intenseness of his belief in the "peasant interpretation of life, " and the artistic sophistication that he employed in propagating this belief.

988 Dukes, Ashley. "Tolstoy and Gorky" in Modern Dramatists. Freeport, N. Y. : Books for Libraries Press, 1967 (reprint of 1912 publication); 181-89. It is argued that a unique characteristic of Russian playwrights, Tolstoy and Gorky in particular, is their incessant questioning of life's meaning and its place in their philosophy. This char-

acteristic is judged to be responsible for "the appearance
of incompleteness and incoherence" in Russian plays.
Tolstoy's The Power of Darkness is discussed as an example of confused and poor drama for the sake of presenting his ideals on the Russian peasant: "Tolstoy's
dramas have a certain grand barbaric simplicity and that
is all. "

989   Forster, E. M.   "Three Stories by Tolstoy" in Two Cheers
      for Democracy.   New York: Harcourt, 1951; 208-212.
      A discussion of The Cossacks, The Death of Ivan Ilych,
      and Three Hermits as three works which, though very
      different from each other, represent the central theme of
      Tolstoy's later works: that simple people and the simple
      way of life are best.   This theme is seen as being pre-
      sented in The Cossacks by way of praise for the free,
      open and simple life; in Death of Ivan Ilych through
      the simple and compassionate character Gerasim; and
      in Three Hermits by way of the simple saint who
      is the tale's hero but an imbecile in the world's
      eyes.

990   Glicksberg, Charles I.   "Tolstoy and The Death of Ivan Il-
      yitch" in The Ironic Vision in Modern Literature.   The
      Hague: Nijhoff, 1969; 81-86.   Death is discussed as the
      supreme paradox of existence whose irony can only be
      countered by faith which provides meaning to life.   Tol-
      stoy's The Death of Ivan Ilych is analyzed as a source
      of dramatic insight into the "conspiracy the mind en-
      gages in to deny the reality of death. "   Tolstoy is also
      seen as using this writing as a means to deliver his
      message on redemption as the source of life's mean-
      ing.

991   Hamilton, Clayton M.   "Two Plays by Count Leo Tolstoy:
      The Living Corpse and The Power of Darkness" in Seen
      on the Stage.   New York: Holt, 1920; 144-153.   Tol-
      stoy's late conversion into playwriting is discussed, and
      the plays The Living Corpse and The Power of Darkness
      are presented as examples of his extraordinary realism
      and poignant dialogue in his dramatic works.   The
      former play is viewed as being unconventional in
      structure, technique, and subject matter, whereas
      The Power of Darkness is interpreted as more of a
      Western piece of drama.

992   Howe, Irving.   "Leo Tolstoy: The Death of Ivan Ilyich" in
      Classics of Modern Fiction.   New York: Harcourt Brace
      Jovanovich, 1972; 113-178.   Tolstoy's aim in The Death
      of Ivan Ilych is seen as being to describe the universal
      experience of death by way of a common man so as to
      have concrete means of conveying the abstract.   Ivan is
      presented as the typical American "organization man"

with a gray, thoughtless life until death's approach
leads him "to discover the truth about his humanity."
In this sense, it is claimed, each of us, including
Tolstoy himself, has something to learn from Ivan
Ilych.

993 Lamm, Martin. "Leo Tolstoy" in Modern Drama. New York:
Philosophical Library, 1953; 182-193. The Power of
Darkness is commended as an inspiration to the modern
drama of the people, with Tolstoy's realism, particularly
his use of peasant dialect, seen as masterful: "there is
a genuine flavour of the mujik's hovel in this play." His
other dramatic works are examined, and Tolstoy is applauded for providing insight into "a cross-section of the
soul of the Russian people." Also discussed are the
autobiographical elements in his plays as well as the
didactic nature of these works.

994 Parry, Albert. "Tolstoy at Sevastopol" in Russian Cavalcade,
A Military Record. New York: Washburn, 1944; 75-90.
An account of how Tolstoy came to serve in the Russian
army and the role he played at Sevastopol precedes a
summation of his record of events that occurred at Sevastopol. Parallels are drawn to War and Peace in that at
Sevastopol Tolstoy believed the Russian troops, not the
commanders, were the heroes and the movers of battles.
Only occasionally, however, is he seen as having criticized warfare; rather, his major focus is on man's actions and reactions in face of death.

995 Poggioli, Renato. "Tolstoy's Domestic Happiness: Beyond
Pastoral Love" in The Oaten Flute: Essays on Pastoral
Poetry and the Pastoral Ideal. Cambridge, Mass.: Harvard University Press, 1975; 265-282. Domestic Happiness is presented as a classic example of the theme of
pastoral love, in that youthful, feminine beauty captivates
the senses of an older man. It is argued, however, that
the pastoral romance fails in this instance because Tolstoy has Masha mature morally to the point where she
sees through the fantasy world of sentimental love. It is
suggested that Tolstoy wrote Domestic Happiness to prove
that he was correct in his decision to terminate his own
relationship with a young girl that he once tutored.

996 Shestov, Lev. "The Last Judgment: Tolstoy's Last Works"
in In Job's Balances: On the Sources of the Eternal
Truths. Athens: Ohio University Press, 1975; 83-138.
Tolstoy's last works, especially, The Death of Ivan Ilych,
Father Sergius, and Master and Man, are discussed as a
means of gaining insight into his attitude towards death
and dying. His concern for such a philosophical subject
as death is viewed as marking a return to his early role
of philosopher, and a step away from his role as a

preacher. His writings on death are commended for their insight into the phenomenon of death, an insight seen as originating in his own fear of dying. Also in TCCE, 157-172.

997   Stenbock-Fermor, Elisabeth. 'Elements of Folklore in an Early Work of Tolstoy" in For Roman Jakobson: Essays on the Occasion of His 60th Birthday, 11 October 1956. The Hague: Mouton, 1956; 531-537.

998   "Tolstoy's 'Childhood and Youth'" in RLMEF, 17-22. An anonymous and highly critical review of Childhood and Youth in which Tolstoy's philosophy is regarded as being non-existent, the incidents discussed "trivial, " and the whole production "insipid. " Originally in Sat R, (29 March 1862).

999   Turgenev, Ivan. "A Letter to A. V. Druzhinin" in LTCA, 35. A short note (1857) on Tolstoy's Landlord's Morning commending the work for its "language, sincerity and characterization" but criticizing his contention that it is essential to improve the condition of the peasants. Translated from Polnoe Sobranie Sochineniy i Pisem, 1960-1968.

1000 Turgenev, Ivan. "A Letter to A. A. Fet" in LTCA, 47. A brief (1874) comment on Tolstoy's The Cossacks as not only his greatest work but also the supreme work of Russian fiction.

1001 Turgenev, Ivan. "A Letter to A. A. Fet" in LTCA, 35. In a short note (1864), Tolstoy's Polikushka is mentioned as a masterful piece of fiction though somewhat wasteful in material. Translated from Polnoe Sobranie Sochineniy i Pisem.

1002 West, Ray B. , Jr. , and Robert W. Stallman. "Leo Tolstoi's Three Arshins of Land, or How Much Land Does a Man Need?" in The Art of Modern Fiction. New York: Rinehart, 1949; 122-134. Tolstoy's chief device in this short story is judged to be that of irony, and his basic theme that "flesh and bones are the only materialistic things a man can take to his grave. " His ideas on the uselessness and harmfulness of material possessions are discussed as a moral lesson for the peasantry.

INTRODUCTIONS TO EDITIONS of the other works

1003 Aitken, Eleanor. Master and Man. London: Cambridge University Press, 1970; 101p.

1004 Andreyev, Nikolay. Master and Man, and Other Parables and Tales. London: Dent, 1959; 320p.

1005 Bain, R. N. More Tales from Tolstoi. Trans. by R. N.
      Bain. London: Jarrold, 1902.

1006 Bain, R. N. Tales from Tolstoi. Trans. by R. N. Bain.
      London: Jarrold, 1901.

1007 Bayley, John. Childhood, Boyhood. Youth. Trans. by Leo
      Weiner. Mount Vernon: Colish, 1972; 379p.

1008 Beresford, Michael. The Death of Ivan Ilych. Chicago:
      Russian Language Specialties, 1966; 172p. (Text in Rus-
      sian; introduction in English.)

1009 Carr, Arthur C. The Death of Ivan Ilych. New York:
      Health Sciences Pub. Corp. , 1973; 68p.

1010 Edmonds, Rosemary. Childhood, Boyhood, Youth. Trans. by
      Rosemary Edmonds. Harmondsworth, England: Pen-
      guin, 1964; 319p.

1011 Edmonds, Rosemary. The Cossacks, The Death of Ivan Ilych,
      and Happy Ever After. Trans. by Rosemary Edmonds.
      Baltimore: Penguin, 1960; 334p.

1012 Fisher, Dorothy C. Stories and Legends. Trans. by Louise
      Maude and Aylmer Maude. Harmondsworth, England:
      Penguin, 1946; 223p.

1013 Foote, Paul. Master and Man, and Other Stories. Trans.
      by Paul Foote. Harmondsworth, England: Penguin,
      1977; 271p.

1014 Gosse, Edmund. Work While Ye Have the Light. London,
      1890.

1015 Graham, Stephan. The Death of Ivan Ilych. Trans. by Louise
      Maude and Aylmer Maude. London: Oxford, 1934 (Cen-
      tenary Edition); vol. 15, 411p.

1016 Granville-Barker, H. Plays. Trans. by Louise Maude and
      Aylmer Maude. London: Oxford, 1928 (Centenary Edi-
      tion); vol. 17, 398p.

1017 Hichens, Robert. Two Hussars. Trans. by Louise Maude
      and Aylmer Maude. London: Oxford, 1933 (Centenary
      Edition); vol. 5, 439p.

1018 Hogarth, C. Childhood, Boyhood, Youth. London: Dent,
      n. d. , 314p.

1019 Hopkins, Arthur. Redemption and Two Other Plays. New
      York: Boni & Liveright, 1919; 245p.

1020 Howells, William Dean. Master and Man. New York: Appleton, 1895; 165p.

1021 Howells, William Dean. Sevastopol. Trans. by Millet. New York, 1887.

1022 Joy, Charles R. Lyof Tolstoy; An Anthology. Boston: Beacon, 1958; 254p.

1023 Korotky, V. Fables, Tales and Stories: A Captive in the Caucasus. Moscow: Foreign Language Press, 1960; 83p. (Text in Russian; introduction in English.)

1024 Leslie, Shane. Sevastopol and Tales of Army Life. Trans. by Louise Maude and Aylmer Maude. London: Oxford, 1932 (Centenary Edition), vol. 4, 472p.

1025 Magarshack, David. The Death of Ivan Ilych. New York: New American Library, 1960; 304p.

1026 Mason-Manheim, Madeline. Twenty-three Tales. Trans. by Louise Maude and Aylmer Maude. London: Oxford, 1928 (Centenary Edition), vol. 13, 298p.

1027 Maude, Aylmer. Childhood, Boyhood, Youth. Trans. by Louise Maude and Aylmer Maude. London: Oxford, 1930; 413p.

1028 Maude, Aylmer. Esarhaddon and Other Tales and Letters from Tolstoy. Trans. by Louise Maude and Aylmer Maude. London: Richards, 1904; 426p.

1029 Maude, Aylmer. Father Sergius and Other Stories and Plays. Trans. by Aylmer Maude. Freeport, N.Y.: Books for Libraries Press, 1970; 426p.

1030 Maude, Aylmer. Ivan Ilych and Hadji Murat and Other Stories. Trans. by Louise Maude and Aylmer Maude. London: Oxford, 1935; 411p.

1031 Maude, Aylmer. Sevastopol and Other Stories. Trans. by Louise Maude and Aylmer Maude. London: Richards, 1903.

1032 McMillin, A. B. The Cossacks; The Raid. Trans. by A. R. MacAndrew. London: Heron, 1969; 279p.

1033 Mirsky, Dmitri S. Hadji Murat. Trans. by Louise Maude and Aylmer Maude. London: Oxford, 1934 (Centenary Edition), vol. 15, 411p.

1034 Morton, Miriam. Twenty-two Russian Tales for Young Children. Trans. by Miriam Morton. New York: Simon & Schuster, 1969; 57p.

1035   Neider, Charles. Tales of Courage and Conflict. Garden
       City, N. Y. : Doubleday, 1958; 574p.

1036   Phelps, William. Childhood, Boyhood, Youth. Trans. by
       Louise Maude and Aylmer Maude. London: Oxford,
       1928 (Centenary Edition); vol. 3, 404p.

1037   Pinero, Arthur W. Fruits of Enlightenment. Trans. by E.
       J. Dillon. London: Heinemann, 1900; 284p.

1038   Rahv, Philip. The Cossacks and The Raid. Trans. by A.
       R. MacAndrew. Chicago: Dial, 1961; 224p.

1039   Rahv, Philip. Sevastopol. Trans. by F. Millet. Ann Arbor:
       University of Michigan Press, 1961; 222p.

1040   Reeve, F. D. Short Masterpieces. Trans. by Margaret
       Weltin. New York: Dell, 1963; 380p.

1041   Rosenthal, Raymond. Fables and Fairy Tales. Trans. by
       Ann Dunnigan. New York: New American Library,
       1962; 141p.

1042   Simmons, Ernest J. Childhood, Boyhood, Youth. Trans. by
       Isabel F. Hapgood. New York: Lear, 1949; 379p.

1043   Simmons, Ernest J. Nikolenka's Childhood. New York:
       Random House, 1963; 173p.

1044   Simmons, Ernest J. Short Novels, Stories of Love, Seduc-
       tion and Peasant Life. Trans. by Louise Maude and
       Aylmer Maude. New York: Random House, 1965-1966;
       2 vols. (455p. , 576p.).

1045   Tolstoy, Alexandra. Short Stories. Trans. by Arthur Men-
       del and Barbara Makanowitsky. New York: Bantam
       Books, 1960; 554p.

1046   Underwood, E. G. , and Nevill Forbes. A Prisoner in the
       Caucasus. London: Oxford, 1917.

1047   Walsh, Walter. The Great Parables. London: C. W. Dan-
       iels, 1906; 156p.

1048   West, Rebecca. Polikushka. Trans. by Louise Maude and
       Aylmer Maude. London: Oxford, 1933 (Centenary Edi-
       tion); vol. 5, 439p.

PERIODICAL ARTICLES

1049   Bailey, L. "Tolstoy as a Playwright, " Drama, 110 (Autumn
       1973), 50-55.

1050   Battersby, H. F. P. "Leo N. Tolstoy," Edinbg R, 194, no.
        397 (July 1901), 49-72. A survey of 15 of Tolstoy's
        writings, 1895-1900, includes Confession, Resurrection,
        Master and Man, What Must We Do Then, and Kreutzer
        Sonata.

1051   Beerbohm, Max. "Dramatic Translation," Sat R, 99 (21 Jan.
        1905), 76-77. Beerbohm's response to Shaw's attack on
        his critique of Maude's translation of Power of Darkness.

1052   Beerbohm, Max. "The Stage Society," Sat R, 98 (1904),
        823-824. A review of Power of Darkness.

1053   Bertensson, Sergei. "The History of Tolstoy's Posthumous
        Plays," ASEER, 14, no. 2 (1955), 265-268.

1054   Birbell, Francis. "The Drama: Tolstoy as Dramatist,"
        Nation, 44, no. 61 (1928), 208. On the performance,
        on stage, of Power of Darkness and Fruits of the En-
        lightenment.

1055   Burton, R. "The Living Corpse and The Cause of It All,"
        Dial, 52 (16 June 1912), 470.

1056   Cahan, A. "Posthumous Works of Tolstoy," Bookman, 35
        (April 1912), 209-212. A review of Father Sergius,
        Hadji Murat, The Living Corpse and The Forged Coupon.

1057   Cate, Hollis L. "On Death and Dying in Tolstoy's The Death
        of Ivan Ilych," Hartford St Lit, 7 (1975), 195-205.

1058   Chertkova, Anna. "The Question of Tolstoy's Posthumous
        Works," Rus R, 3, no. 2 (1914), 165-170.

1059   "Childhood, Boyhood, Youth," Dial, 7 (1886), 79.

1060   "Childhood, Boyhood, Youth," Sat R, (29 March 1862).

1061   "Count Tolstoi: Interesting Reminiscences of His Youth,"
        RRs, 2 (1890), 698-699.

1062   "Count Tolstoi's Early Reminiscences," Spectator, 62 (1 June
        1889), 762-764.

1063   "Count Tolstoy's Literary Remains," Outlook, 97 (25 March
        1911), 615-616. On Tolstoy's posthumous works.

1064   Dayananda, Y. J. "The Death of Ivan Ilych: A Psychological
        Study on Death and Dying," Lit and Psych, 22 (1969),
        191-198.

1065   "The Death of Ivan Ilych," Athenaeum, 2 (Nov. 1902), 680.

1066   "The Death of Ivan Ilych and Other Stories, " Nation, 102 (6
         Jan. 1916), 23-24.   Trans. by C. Garnett.

1067   "The Devil, " Bookman, 64 (Sept. 1926), 105.

1068   "The Devil, " Bos Trans, (24 April 1926), 2.

1069   "The Devil, " Lit R, (26 June 1926), 6.

1070   "The Devil, " New Republic, 46 (19 May 1926), 415.

1071   "The Devil, " New Statesman, 27 (1 May 1926), 83.

1072   "The Devil, " NY Times, (18 April 1926), 8.

1073   "The Devil, " Sat R Lit, 2 (19 June 1926), 875.

1074   "The Devil, " Spectator, 136 (17 April 1926), 722.

1075   Donskov, Andrew.   "L. N. Tolstoj's Sources for His Play
         The First Distiller, " Can S P, 15 (1973), 375-381.

1076   Donskov, Andrew.   "Tolstoj's Use of Proverbs in Power of
         Darkness, " Rus Lit, 9 (1974-1975), 67-80.

1077   Douglas, A.   "Dramatic Works, " N Y Herald Trib Bk R,
         (22 July 1923), 19.

1078   Dworsky, Nancy.   "Hadji Murat: A Summary and a Vision, "
         Novel, 8 (1975), 138-146.

1079   Eaton, W. P.   "Tolstoy's Drama, " Freeman, 7 (27 June
         1923), 377-378.

1080   Fanger, D.   "Nazarov's Mother: Notes toward an Interpreta-
         tion of Hadji Murat, " Iberomania, (1974), 99-104.

1081   "Father Sergius and Other Stories, " Athenaeum, 1 (13 Jan.
         1912), 38.

1082   "Father Sergius and Other Stories, " Nation, 94 (20 June
         1912), 614.

1083   "Father Sergius and Other Stories, " RRs, 46 (August 1912),
         253.

1084   Firkins, O. W.   "Power of Darkness: Criticism, " Rev, 2
         (7 Feb. 1920), 137-138.

1085   Flower, B. O.   "A Review of Tolstoi's Plays, " Arena, 32
         (Dec. 1904), 671-673.   Includes Fruits of Culture, Power
         of Darkness, and First Distiller.

1086   Flower, B. O.   "Sevastopol and Other Military Tales," Arena
         32 (July 1904), 105-106.

1087   "Forged Coupon and Other Stories," Athenaeum, 2 (18 Nov.
         1911), 621.

1088   "Forged Coupon and Other Stories," Catholic W, 95 (April
         1912), 112.

1089   "Forged Coupon and Other Stories," Nation, 94 (20 June
         1912), 614.

1090   "Forged Coupon and Other Stories," N Y Times, 17 (25 Feb.
         1912), 97.

1091   "Forged Coupon and Other Stories," Spectator, 107 (25 Nov.
         1911), 904.

1092   "Fruits of Culture," Academy, 64 (1903), 407-408.

1093   "Fruits of Culture," Academy, 69 (1905), 761-762.

1094   "Fruits of Culture," Catholic W, 52 (Feb. 1891), 758.

1095   "Fruits of Culture," Harper's M, 82 (April 1891), 806.

1096   "Fruits of Culture," Nation, 52 (12 March 1891), 227.

1097   Hackett, Francis.   "Power of Darkness: Criticism," New
         Republic, 21 (4 Feb. 1920), 296.

1098   Hackett, Francis.   "Tolstoy's Redemption," New Republic,
         16 (19 Oct. 1918), 349.

1099   "Hadji Murat," Athenaeum, 1 (27 Jan. 1912), 95.

1100   "Hadji Murat," Catholic W, 95 (April 1912), 111.

1101   "Hadji Murat," Cur Lit, 52 (1912), 478-479.

1102   "Hadji Murat," Nation, 94 (20 June 1912), 613.

1103   "Hadji Murat," N Y Times, 17 (25 Feb. 1912), 97.

1104   "Hadji Murat," N Amer R, 195 (June 1912), 863-864.

1105   "Hadji Murat," Outlook, 101 (29 June 1912), 500.

1106   "Hadji Murat," RRs, 45 (June 1912), 761; 46 (August 1912),
         253.

1107   Hagan, John.   "Ambivalence in Tolstoy's The Cossacks,"
         Novel, 3 (1969), 28-47.

1108   Hagan, John. "Detail and Meaning in Tolstoy's Master and Man, " Criticism, 11 (Winter 1969), 31-58.

1109   Halperin, Irving. "The Structural Integrity of The Death of Ivan Ilyich, " SEEJ, 5, no. 4 (Winter 1961), 334-340.

1110   Hartley, L. P. "Stories and Dramas, " Sat R, 142 (18 Dec. 1926), 778.

1111   Heard, John. "The Power of Darkness by Count Tolstoy, " Lit W, 18 (1887), 297-298.

1112   Henley, William E. "New Novels, " Academy, 14 (24 August 1887), 187. A review of The Cossacks.

1113   Hirschberg, W. R. "Tolstoy's The Death of Ivan Ilyich, " Explicator, 28, no. 3 (1969), item 26.

1114   Irwin, K. W. "Toward a Phenomenology of Death, " Dial, 11 (Summer 1972), 177-182.

1115   Jellife, S. E. , and L. Brink. "Alcoholism and the Phantasy Life in Tolstoi's Redemption, " N Y Med J, 109 (1919), 92-97.

1116   Jennings, R. "Tolstoy as a Dramatist, " Spectator, 141 (10 Nov. 1928), 687-688.

1117   Kallaur, Constantine H. "The Writing History of Tolstoy's The Devil with particular Emphasis on the Ending, " Nassau R, 2 (1971), 30-33.

1118   Krutch, J. W. "The Living Corpse, Revival at Civic Repertory Theater, N. Y. C. , " Nation, 129 (25 Dec. 1929), 785-786.

1119   Krutch, J. W. "Redemption; Criticism, " Nation, 127 (5 Dec. 1928), 640-641. On The Living Corpse as a drama.

1120   Laugel, A. "Tolstoi's Souvenirs, " Nation, 42 (18 March 1886), 234. A discussion of Tolstoy's youth as providing examples of his later genius.

1121   Lee, C. Nicholas. "Dreams and Daydreams in the Early Fiction of L. N. Tolstoj, " Am Contribs, 2 (1973), 373-392.

1122   Lewishon, L. "The Power of Darkness; Criticism, " Nation, 110 (7 Feb. 1920), 178.

1123   "The Light That Shines in the Darkness, " Athenaeum, 1 (13 Jan. 1912), 38.

1124 "The Light That Shines in the Darkness," N Amer R, 195 (June 1912), 863.

1125 Lindstrom, T. S. "From Chapbooks to Classics: The Story of The Intermediary," ASEER, 16, no. 2 (April 1957), 190-201. A discussion of The Intermediary as a disseminator of Tolstoy's stories among the people.

1126 "Living Corpse," Bellman, 12 (11 May 1912), 595.

1127 "Living Corpse," Nation, 94 (20 June 1912), 614.

1128 "Living Corpse," N Y Times, 17 (25 Feb. 1912), 97.

1129 "Living Corpse," RRs, 46 (August 1912), 253.

1130 "A Long Exile (God Sees the Truth but Bides His Time)," Lippincott's M, 90 (Dec. 1912), 747-754.

1131 Lykiardopoulos, M. "Redemption," New Sta, 14 (1919), 11-12.

1132 MacGowan, K. "New Plays for Old: Tolstoy's Living Corpse," New Republic, 17 (9 Nov. 1918), 46.

1133 "Master and Man," Bookman, 1 (July 1895), 409-410.

1134 "Master and Man," Bookman (L), 8 (May 1895), 47-48.

1135 "Master and Man," Critic, 23 n. s. , (15 June 1895), 435.

1136 "Master and Man," Lit W, 26, no. 13 (29 June 1895), 201.

1137 Mirsky, Dmitri S. "Stories and Dramas," Nat and Ath, 40 (4 Dec. 1926), 340.

1138 "More Tales from Tolstoi," Lit W, 19, no. 1 (7 Jan. 1888), 10. A review of A Russian Proprietor, Albert, Three Deaths, Two Hussars, Prisoner in the Caucasus, and Cossacks.

1139 Moses, M. J. "Tolstoy Drama in America: Redemption," Bellman, 25 (7 Dec. 1918), 628-631.

1140 Nabokoff, C. "Tolstoy's Power of Darkness and Alexander III," Spectator, 138 (14 May 1927), 841-842.

1141 Nolan, P. T. "Tolstoy's Power of Darkness: Genre as a Meaning," Ecl Theatre J, 17 (March 1965), 1-9.

1142 Noyes, George R. "Tolstoy's Literary Technique in The Cossacks," Proc Am Philol Asso, 39 (Nov. 1908), 52-58.

1143 Ober, Warren. "The Three Bears from Southey to Tolstoy,"
      BNYPL, 73 (Dec. 1968), 659-666. A discussion of Tol-
      stoy's version of the tale of the three bears.

1144 Olney, James. 'Experience, Metaphor and Meaning: The
      Death of Ivan Ilyich," J Aesth Art and Crit, 31 (Fall
      1972), 101-114.

1145 Pachmuss, Temira. "The Theme of Love and Death in Tol-
      stoy's The Death of Ivan Ilyich," ASEER, 20, no. 1
      (Feb. 1961), 72-83.

1146 Paulding, J. K. "At the Berlin Theater: Tolstoy's Power of
      Darkness," Nation, 72 (17 Jan. 1901), 47-48.

1147 Pavlov, P. "Tolstoy's Novel Family Happiness," Slavonic R,
      7 (Jan. 1929), 492-510.

1148 Pawley, R. "Tolstoy's Posthumous Works," Nation, 92 (1911),
      600-602.

1149 Payne, A. S. "Tolstoy's Dramas," Bookman, 45 (Dec. 1913),
      312-314.

1150 Pisarev, D. "Three Deaths: A Story by L. N. Tolstoy," 11
      (1969), 186-195.

1151 "Plays of Tolstoy," Bookman (L), 46 (May 1914), 88.

1152 "Posthumous Works of Tolstoy," Grinnell R, 16 (June 1921),
      454.

1153 "Posthumous Works of Tolstoy," Lit R, (12 March 1921), 8.

1154 "Posthumous Works of Tolstoy," Nation, 94 (20 June 1912),
      613-615.

1155 "The Power of Darkness," Academy, 64 (1903), 407-408.

1156 "The Power of Darkness," Academy 69 (1905), 761-762.

1157 "The Power of Darkness," Nation, 72 (17 Jan. 1901), 47-48.

1158 "The Power of Darkness by Count Tolstoi," Lit W, 18, no.
      19, (17 Sept. 1887), 702.

1159 Preston, Harriet W. "Leo Tolstoy's The Cossacks," Atlantic
      M, 42 (Dec. 1878), 702.

1160 "Redemption," Lit D, 43 (1911), 978-979.

1161 "The Russian Proprietor and Other Stories," Pub Op, 35, (31
      Dec. 1887), 286.

1162   "Sevastopol and Other Military Tales," Athenaeum, 2 (28 Dec. 1901), 871.

1163   "Sevastopol and Other Military Tales," Lit W, 18 (1887), 234-235.

1164   "Sevastopol and Other Military Tales," Nation, 78 (24 March 1903), 238.

1165   "Sevastopol and Other Military Tales," Reader, 4 (June 1903), 115.

1166   Sharp, W.   "Work While Ye Have the Light," Academy, 39 (31 Jan. 1891), 109-110.   Also discusses The Kreutzer Sonata.

1167   Shestov, Lev.   "Tolstoy's Memoirs of a Madman," Slavonic R, 7 (1929), 465-472.

1168   Smith, J. H.   "Tolstoy's Childhood, Boyhood, Youth," J of Ed, 17 (April-May 1895), 220-262.

1169   Sorokin, Boris.   "Ivan Il'ich as Jonah: A Cruel Joke," Can Slavic S, 5 (1971), 487-507.   Discusses the inconsistencies in Tolstoy's moral philosophy.

1170   Stakhovich, M.   "The Question of Tolstoy's Posthumous Works," Rus R, 2, no. 2 (1913), 143-153.

1171   "Stories and Dramas," Bos Trans, (4 Dec. 1926), 8.

1172   "Stories and Dramas," Lit R, (18 Dec. 1926), 3.

1173   "Stories and Dramas," Nation, 124 (12 Jan. 1927), 45.

1174   "Stories and Dramas," New Republic, 49 (26 Jan. 1927), 283.

1175   "Stories and Dramas," New Sta, 28 (12 Feb. 1927), 540.

1176   "Stories and Dramas," N Y Times, (14 Nov. 1926), 7.

1177   "Stories and Dramas," Sat R Lit, 3 (27 Nov. 1926), 343.

1178   "Stories and Dramas," Spectator, 137 (30 Oct. 1926), Sup. 752.

1179   "Stories and Dramas," Sprg Rep, (16 Feb. 1927), 10.

1180   "Stories and Dramas," Theater Arts M, 11 (Jan. 1927), 76.

1181   "Stories and Dramas," Times Lit Sup, (4 Nov. 1926), 765.

1182   "Tales from Tolstoi," Atheneaum, 2 (28 Dec. 1901), 871. Trans. R. N. Bain.

1183   "Three of Tolstoi's Stories, " Lit W, 18, no. 4 (19 Feb.
       1887), 54. On Death of Ivan Ilych, The Romance of a
       Horse and A Poor Devil.

1184   "Tolstoi as a Dramatist, " Academy, 64 (25 April 1903), 407-
       408.

1185   "A Tolstoian Dispute, " Living Age, 336 (March 1929), 40.
       On the source of Tolstoy's Where Love Is, There Is God
       Also, averring it was taken from an unsigned tale in an
       English magazine.

1186   "Tolstoi Drama a Broadway Sensation, " Theater, 28 (Dec.
       1918), 358-359. A review of The Living Corpse under
       the title of Redemption.

1187   "Tolstoi's Childhood, Boyhood, Youth, " Lit W, 17, no. 15
       (24 July 1886), 243-244.

1188   "Tolstoi's Ivan Ilyich and Other Stories, " Lit W, 18, no. 15
       (23 July 1887), 229-230. Also on Where Love Is, There
       Is God Also, The Three Mendicants, Two Old Men and
       Ivan the Fool.

1189   "Tolstoi's Sebastopol, " Lit W, 18, no. 15 (23 July 1887), 234-
       235.

1190   "Tolstoi's The Cossacks, " Lit W, 18, no. 2 (22 Jan. 1887),
       30.

1191   "Tolstoy's Childhood and Youth, " Sat R, (29 March 1862).
       Also in RMLEF, 17-22.

1192   "Tolstoy's Last Words to the World, " Cur Lit, 40 (Feb. 1906),
       172-173. Translated from Mercure de France.

1193   "Tolstoy's Literary Technique in The Cossacks, " Proc Am
       Philol Asso, 39 (1909), 52-58.

1194   "Tolstoy's Plays, " Academy, 69 (22 July 1905), 761-762. A
       discussion of Power of Darkness and Fruits of the En-
       lightenment.

1195   "Tolstoy's Plays, " Times Lit Sup, 28 (10 Jan. 1929), 25.
       Review of Power of Darkness, The Living Corpse and
       The Light Shines in the Darkness.

1196   "Tolstoy's Voice from the Grave Heard in a Gruesome Play, "
       Cur Lit, 52 (Jan. 1912), 91-93. Review of The Living
       Corpse.

1197   Trahan, Elizabeth. "L. N. Tolstoj's Master and Man: A
       Symbolic Narrative, " SEEJ, 7, no. 3 (Fall 1963), 259-
       268.

1198   Turner, C. J.   "The Language of Fiction: Word Clusters in
       Tolstoy's The Death of Ivan Ilyich, " Mod Lang R, 65
       (1970), 116-121.

1199   "Two Notable Books: The Invaders and Confession, " Pub Op,
       4, no. 27 (15 Oct. 1887), 47.

1200   Van Doren, M.   "First Glance: The Devil, " Nation, 122 (23
       June 1926), 699.

1201   "What Men Live By and Other Tales, " New Republic, 15 (13
       June 1918), 355.

1202   "What Men Live By and Other Tales, " RRs, 58 (August 1918),
       219.

1203   Woodward, James B.   "Tolstoy's Hadji Murat: The Evolution
       of Its Theme and Structure, " Mod Lang R, 68 (Oct.
       1973), 870-882.

1204   Woolf, L.   "Power of Darkness, " Nation, 34 (1924), 766.

1205   "Work While Ye Have the Light, " Athenaeum, 96 (20 Dec.
       1890), 850.

1206   "Work While Ye Have the Light, " RRs, 2 (Nov. 1890), 462.

1207   Yarmolinsky, Avraham.   "Stories and Dramas, " N Y Trib
       Bk R, (9 Jan. 1927), 2.

DISSERTATIONS

1208   Cohen, Elliot F.   "The Genre of the Autobiographical Account
       of Childhood--Three Test Cases: The Trilogies of Tol-
       stoy, Aksakov and Gorky, " Yale University, 1973.

1209   Eros, Carol C.   "Tolstoj's Tales of The Caucasus and Liter-
       ary Tradition, " University of Wisconsin, 1973.

1210   Freling, Roger N.   "A Critical Study of Leo Tolstoy's Plays:
       The Power of Darkness and The Living Corpse, " Univer-
       sity of Washington, 1971.

1211   Jahn, Gary R.   "L. N. Tolstoj's Stories for the People on
       the Theme of Brotherly Love, " University of Wisconsin,
       1972.

1212   Kornman, William R.   "Tolstoj and the Drama, " Stanford
       University, 1973.

1213   Matual, David M.   "Tolstoj's Vlast' T'my: History and An-
       alysis, " University of Wisconsin, 1971.

Section IV

PHILOSOPHY (GENERAL)

BOOKS

1214 Crosby, Ernest H. Tolstoy and His Message. London: Fi-
field, 1911; 96p. A spiritual biography of Tolstoy, by a
personal friend, concentrating on his moral, religious,
and philosophical views rather than his fiction. The
sources of his spiritual crisis are identified and his ethical beliefs summarized by way of analysis of On Life,
the work considered to be the foundation of his ethical
works. In all, his philosophy is positively assessed,
and Tolstoy is commended for his tireless and sincere
pursuit of the "true path." Reviewed in:
  Arena, 30 (Dec. 1903), 660-662.
  Open Court, 17 (Dec. 1903), 708-712.

1215 Daniel, C. W. Tolstoy's Teaching. London: C. W. Daniel,
1919.

1216 Dillon, Emile J. Count Leo Tolstoy. A New Portrait. London: Hutchinson, 1934; 286p., illus. A critical account
of Tolstoy's philosophic, religious, and ethical views,
with emphasis on their shortcomings. In particular, the
contradictory nature of his beliefs is stressed; they are
seen as stemming from the acute opposition of the physical and spiritual sides of his personality. Respect is
nonetheless maintained for his intellect, humanitarianism,
and literary talent.

1217 Greenwood, E. B. Tolstoy: The Comprehensive Vision. New
York: St. Martin's Press, 1975; 184p., bib. 172-176.
A philosophical analysis of Tolstoy based on the contention that since he "was constantly searching in his life
for a comprehensive vision--a vision equal to the confusion of a life," his character, work, and life can be
best understood from a philosophic perspective. His
creations and activities are thus discussed as a means
of discerning his contribution to answering such questions
as, What is the nature of happiness? Does history
have a meaning? and Can men find truth in matters of
religion? Over a score of his works are analyzed, with

142

insight provided into his asceticism, ethics and religious
beliefs, as well as his views on warfare, death, history
and modern civilization. The study concludes with a
discussion of the relevancy to today of Tolstoy's philosophy, with his beliefs judged to have "much to offer us
as individuals who have to face the perennial facts of
time, bereavement and death. " Reviewed in:
Mod Fic St, 21 (Winter 1975-1976), 621-625, by J.
M. Curtis.
Rus R, 35 (Oct. 1976), 490-491, by N. Rzhevsky.
SEER, 54 (April 1976), 277-278, by Richard Freeborn.
TLS, (7 Nov. 1975), 1329.

1218 Harrison, I. H. Tolstoy as Preacher. London, 1895.

1219 Kamakhya-Natha, Mitra. The New Pilgrim's Progress; or,
Tolstoy, the Man and the Meaning of Life. Bankipur,
1909; 51p.

1220 Knowlson, T. Sharper. Leo Tolstoy. A Biographical and
Critical Study. London: Warne, n. d. , 190p. , bib. 178-
190. Tolstoy's life and writings before his conversion
are discussed generally; then, an analysis is given of
his moral, social, and religious philosophy, his views
on art, and his influence on Russia and the world. The
analysis is consistently critical, with his views on marriage and sex seen as warped, his peasant idealism misfounded, his social-political philosophy destructively
anarchistic, and his interpretation of art excessively
narrow-minded and extreme. Tolstoy's influence, nonetheless, is viewed as major, especially in politics and
social affairs, and he is praised for sincerity and courage
throughout his life. Excerpt in TCLA, 78-82.

1221 Kvitko, David. A Philosophic Study of Tolstoy. New York:
Columbia University Press, 1927; 119p. A discussion
of Tolstoy's views on religion, morality, history, science, education, and art, and his relationship to meta-
physics. The consistency of his beliefs is stressed, and
it is denied that he underwent a spiritual crisis that
significantly altered his philosophy of life. The same
"religio-moral principles" are seen in his early writings
as in his later works, the only distinction being that
they are not as completely developed.

1222 Lavrin, Janko. Tolstoy: An Approach. New York: Russell
and Russell, 1968 (reprint of 1946 publication); 166p. ,
portrait. It is maintained that only by clarifying the relationship between Tolstoy the prophet and Tolstoy the
artist can insight be gained into "the essential Tolstoy. "
His works are discussed for the insight they provide into
the complex nature of his personality, and it is contended

they demonstrate that no division took place in his life
with his conversion but rather "a kind of shifting of the
center of gravity" from one side of his personality to
the other, which, "far from eliminating his inner conflict, actually increased it. " The duality of his personality between the energetic lover of life and the coldly
rational moralist is examined for its sources and influence on his philosophy. It is concluded that in spite of
the contradictions and extremism in his beliefs, stemming from his inner turmoil, Tolstoy's reputation as an
artist of supreme ability is unassailable. Reviewed in:
   Cur Hist, 10 (June 1946), 539.
   New Yorker, 22 (30 March 1946), 95.
   N Y Times, (17 March 1946), 3, by James T. Far-
      rell.
   Sat R Lit, 29 (13 April 1946), 56, by Ernest J.
      Simmons.
   Wkly Bk R, (1 Sept. 1946), 10, by Irwin Edman.

1223 Lloyd, J. A. T.   Two Russian Reformers: Ivan Turgenev,
      Leo Tolstoy. London: Paul, 1912; 335p. , illus. The
      inseparability of the artist and reformer-philosopher in
      Tolstoy is established, and seen as descriptive of his
      entire life. No division, therefore, took place in his
      life with his spiritual awakening, it is argued, because
      his intense search for a principle to make the contradic-
      tions of life explicable, his introspection, and his con-
      cern for moral perfection are characteristic of all his
      work. Tolstoy's Confession is quoted to substantiate
      this point: "this feeling of the glow of life was no new
      sensation, it was old ... I returned ... to the past. "
      Reviewed in:
         Dial, 50 (16 Feb. 1911), 129.
         Independent, 70 (16 March 1911), 572.
         Lit D, 42 (18 Feb. 1911), 316.
         Nation, 92 (16 March 1911), 272.
         N Y Times Bk R, 16 (19 Feb. 1911), 90.

1224 Maude, Aylmer.   The Teaching of Tolstoy.   Manchester, Eng-
      land, 1900.

1225 Perris, George H.   The Life and Teaching of Tolstoy.   Lon-
      don: Richards, 1904; v, 273p. A discussion of Tolstoy
      as "no arm-chair philosopher" but rather a prophet, in
      the tradition of Moses, Christ, and Sakya Muni, with
      close contact with the popular heart. " His life and work
      are briefly surveyed with the conclusion reached that he
      represents "the qualities of the best peasant type carried
      to the point of genius, " a genius irreverent, volcanic,
      and prone to overstatement, but consistent, sincere, and
      admirable.

1226 Redfern, P.   Tolstoy: A Study.   London, 1907. A survey
      of Tolstoy's life and philosophy emphasizing the contra-

dictions in his lifestyle and the fatal flaws in his teaching. Reviewed in:
Cur Lit, 43 (Dec. 1907), 644-5.

1227 Seltzer, Thomas. Tolstoi: A Critical Study of Him and His
Works. New York: Werner, 1901; 62p. An analysis
of Tolstoy's views on philosophy, government, property,
and art precedes a short sketch of each of his major
literary works. The continuity in his life is stressed,
and his intellectual development treated within the confines of the contention that from his youth he had a meditative, brooding disposition and was skeptical of authority. The study ends with a reproduction of 26 one-paragraph evaluations by critics of Tolstoy and his beliefs.

1228 Spence, Gordon William. Tolstoy the Ascetic. London: Oliver and Boyd, 1967; xiii, 154p., bib. 145-151. "A
moral and philosophical valuation of Tolstoy, looking at
him not so much in his historical context as in his role
as seeker of truth and a teacher of what he thought were
eternal truths. " Central to this analysis is the identification of "dualism" in Tolstoy's philosophy between inevitability and freedom, and the physical and the spiritual, a characteristic of his thought which is seen as
weakening its validity. Also presented is a critique of
G. Steiner's attempt to associate Tolstoy with the Grand
Inquisitor of Dostoevsky's The Brothers Karamazov. Reviewed in:
Rus R, 28 (April 1969), 222-24, by Kathryn Feuer.
SEEJ, 13 (Summer 1969), 244-5, by C. Nicholas
Lee.
TLS, (8 Feb. 1968), 126.

1229 Turner, Charles E. Count Tolstoi as Novelist and Thinker.
New York: Haskell, 1974 (reprint of 1888 publication);
191p. A discussion of the philosophy behind Tolstoy's
leading writings with, at Tolstoy's request, few biographical details provided. His eloquence, sincerity, and
courage in the face of the criticism his ideas encountered
in high Russian circles are praised, but the practicality
of that which he preached, especially in politics and
economics, is seen as highly questionable.

ESSAYS AND CHAPTERS from general works

1230 Arnold, Matthew. "Count Leo Tolstoi" in Essays in Criticism
(second series). London: Macmillan, 1896; 253-299.
Tolstoy is chastized for abandoning the work of poet and
artist for that of philosopher, prophet, and social reformer. Anna Karenina is discussed as an example of
his greatness as a writer, while his religious views are
analyzed as proof of his shortcomings as a philosopher.

Originally in Fortn R, (Dec. 1887); also in LCTA, 60-80.

1231 Baring, Maurice. "Tolstoy and Tourgeniev" in Landmarks in Russian Literature. New York: Barnes & Noble, 1960 (reprint of 1910 publication); 50-73. It is claimed that while Tolstoy venerated the "ideal of the simple peasant," he is an example of another ideal, that of stubborn, prideful spirit. His fiction is then discussed in light of his inability to project an answer to life's meaning; as a consequence is the loneliness or void associated with his heroes. Even in his Confession where he thought he had found truth, he failed to find a philosophy of life that was sound, leaving him unable to live a life consistent with his beliefs.

1232 Baudouin, Charles. "Tolstoy and the Realist Faith" in Contemporary Studies. Freeport, N.Y.: Books for Libraries Press, 1969 (reprint of 1924 publication); 24-7. The heart of the doctrine of "Tolstoyism" is isolated as being the "realist faith," defined as "a religion of action not prayer." His worship of physical labor is examined as is his practical nature as proof of this contention. It is concluded that although his realism may not fill the needs of the spirit, it certainly fills those "which are most urgent," and is therefore relevant to the modern world.

1233 Bellman, Harold. "Leo Tolstoy" in Architects of the New Age. London: Sampson Low, Marston, 1929; 141-161. Tolstoy is seen as an admirable example of that type of man who "in the blinding light of new revelation" discovers life's meaning and then redesigns his existence accordingly. The sacrifices made by him and the suffering through which he went are considered the true measure of his greatness rather than his work as moralist and author. His search for and discovery of life's meaning, and consequent activities, are then discussed, and it is concluded that Tolstoy the seeker "touches the universal heart of the world."

1234 Berdayev, Nicolas. The Russian Idea. New York: Macmillan, 1948 (no separate chapter on Tolstoy). Tolstoy is regarded as a representative of Russian religious populism, asceticism, and genius, and as a thinker without parallel in the West where no examples exist of genius repudiating itself and its social milieu for the desire "to mingle with the earth and the people." A separate Russian characteristic, "the consciousness of guilt," is seen as making Tolstoy quite different from Rousseau whose belief in a "social contract" was also at odds with Tolstoy's philosophy of Christian anarchism. Criticized is the practicality of his religious views, and it is stated

that he failed to see that good must act in a world pervaded by evil: "there is a force which enslaves and a
force which liberates. " Excerpt in LTCA, 236-8.

1235 Berlin, Isaiah. "Tolstoy and Enlightenment" in TCCE, 28-51.
Following support for Mikhailovsky's contention that Tolstoy is as penetrating and enlightening a philosopher as
author, the sources of his philosophy are traced to a
blend of influences from the 18th-century Enlightenment
and 19th-century Russian and European societies. Like
Rousseau, it is claimed, he believed in the natural good-
ness of man and the corrupting influence of modern society. In his own time, he was influenced by the radicals'
condemnation of political oppression and economic ex-
ploitation, but affected also by the reactionaries' rejection of science, reform, and material progress. His
views on education are presented as an example of his
philosophic orientation. Originally in Mightier than the
Sword (London: Macmillan, 1964); also in Encounter,
16 (Feb. 1961), 29-40.

1236 Buck, Philo M. "The Perplexed in Spirit--Tolstoi" in The
World's Great Age: The Story of a Century's Search for
a Philosophy of Life. New York: Macmillan, 1936; 166-
196. Tolstoy is presented as the symbol of the restless
and searching 19th century, the epitome of its triumph
and bewilderment. His protest against industrialization,
materialism, and the moral emptiness of the new age is
sympathetically treated. His melancholy if not tragic life
is judged to be a response to his longing to return to the
age of man's innocence amidst a century that could only
criticize and ridicule his views.

1237 Chesterton, Gilbert K. "Tales from Tolstoy" in The Common
Man. London: Sheed and Ward, 1950; 160-64. Tol-
stoy's belief in the desirability of re-establishing "communication with the elemental" or "returning to nature"
is viewed as being impossible and unnatural. Also criticized is the means employed to propagate this belief
claiming that didactic art is stilted art. A lesser version of the argument developed by Chesterton in his "Tolstoy and the Cult of Simplicity" (see item 1239).

1238 Chesterton, Gilbert K. "Tolstoy" in Leo Tolstoy, G. K.
Chesterton, G. Perris and E. Garnett, eds. New York:
Pott, 1903; 40. Tolstoy's philosophy is criticized for
extremism and absurd conclusions, and it is argued that
the best example of his rigidly doctrinaire beliefs in
practice is the case of the religious sect the Doukhobors,
whose fanatical and impractical ideas attracted international attention when the group was persecuted by the
tsarist government and assisted by Tolstoy in emigrating
from Russia.

1239 Chesterton, Gilbert K.   "Tolstoy and the Cult of Simplicity"
      in Varied Types.   Freeport, N. Y. :   Books for Libraries
      Press, 1968 (reprint of 1903 publication); 125-146.   Tol-
      stoy's work is viewed as a genuine and noble appeal to
      simplicity in life, but his didactic method of presentation
      is criticized.   An artist, it is argued, teaches more by
      his works' character than by his "pompous moral dicta:
      The bad fable has a moral, while the good fable is a
      moral. "   Chesterton laments that "we do not know what
      to do with this small and noisy moralist who is inhabit-
      ing one corner of a great and good man. "   Also in Nine-
      teen Modern Essays, Archbold and Jakson, eds.   (New
      York: Longmans, 1926), 222-231; Twelve Types (London,
      1902); and Simplicity and Tolstoy (and Other Essays).
      London: Humphreys, 1912; 1-28.

1240 Clive, Geoffrey.   "Tolstoy and the Varieties of the Inauthen-
      tic" in The Broken Icon: Intuitive Existentialism in Clas-
      sical Russian Fiction.   New York: Macmillan, 1970;
      86-127.   After various examples and usages of the "in-
      authentic" are presented, Tolstoy's critique of inauthen-
      ticity (hypocrisy) in religion, history, and life in general
      is discussed.   Tolstoy is labeled a master at "unmask-
      ing the inauthentic"; examined as proof of this statement
      is his exposure of the inauthentic life as led by Ivan
      Ilych, and his assault on society's hypocritical views of
      sex and love as portrayed in The Kreutzer Sonata.

1241 Craigie, P. M.   The Science of Life.   New York: Scott-
      Thaw, 1904 (no separate chapter on Tolstoy but discussed
      on 34-49).   Tolstoy's philosophy of life is described as
      a highly negative one based on "paralyzing ideas" which,
      if followed, would stifle human development.   It is
      claimed that if Tolstoy had felt in his youth as he thinks
      in his old age, he would have accomplished very little.
      He is seen as being admirable for attempting to re-order
      his life in line with his convictions, but is criticized for
      trying to apply universally his own unique philosophy of
      life.

1242 Darrow, Clarence.   "Leo Tolstoy" in Verdicts Out of Court.
      Chicago: Quadrangle Books, 1963; 186-200.   Tolstoy is
      praised as a man who left his "favored class" and took
      his place beside the humble and the weak to work and
      live with them.   How Tolstoy came to make such a de-
      cision is discussed, with the key seen as being his belief
      that the meaning of life should be sought not among phi-
      losophers but among laborers "who create their lives and
      ours. "   The same logic which brought him to identify
      with the peasants is also viewed as the source of his
      criticism of modern capitalist civilization.

1243 De Selincourt, Basil.   "Tolstoy" in Towards Peace and Other
      Essays Critical and Constructive.   Freeport, N. Y. :

Books for Libraries Press, 1967 (reprint of 1932 publication); 45-54. A critical assessment of Tolstoy's religious, artistic, and political views as being the unhealthy product of a spiritual division within him as well as of "his failure to make peace with himself" at any time in his life. In this sense, he is judged to be "typically Russian" since Russia is a paradoxical society divided against itself. Although his views on life and its meaning are not accepted, his works of fiction are nonetheless seen as being classics.

1244   Dixon, W. Macneile. "Tolstoy" in An Apology for the Arts. A discussion of the restless spiritual development of Tolstoy, which brought him to "reject the whole structure of modern civilization"--its art, culture, states, laws, property and military system--yet still find no happiness within himself. His philosophy is seen as a response to the many wretched conditions in the world, but Tolstoy is criticized for over-emphasizing the extent of these conditions and for overlooking the happiness in the world. Additionally, those who chastize Tolstoy for failing to practice what he preached are judged to have a narrow-minded and overly practical perspective.

1245   Dupuy, Ernest. "Lyof Tolstoi" in Great Masters of Russian Literature. New York, 1886; 215-338. An analysis of Tolstoy's spiritual awakening as presented in his Confession as a means of establishing a framework within which to discuss his life, work, and philosophy. Two stages to his development are identified, an early one characterized by "exclusive development of the ego" and a later one characterized by the "absolute sacrifice of the ego." Between these two extremes, the mental states through which he passed are examined as a means of gaining insight into the nature of his beliefs. No attempt is made to advance or refute his philosophy.

1246   Edie, James M., et al. "Critics of Religion and Culture: Tolstoy" in Russian Philosophy. Chicago: Quadrangle Books, 1969; vol. II, 201-212. Tolstoy is placed within the broad development of anti-Western thought in 19th-century Russia, with parallels being drawn between his thought and that of the early Slavophiles. The impact of Rousseau and Schopenhauer on the philosophy is discussed, especially in reference to his anarchism. Excerpts from The Law of Violence and the Law of Love follow this brief assessment of his beliefs.

1247   Ellis, Havelock. "Tolstoy" in My Confessional. Questions of Our Day. Boston: Houghton Mifflin, 1934; 122-125. A discussion of the author's earlier assessment of Tolstoy as being overly favorable and overlooking the weaknesses in Tolstoy's thought. It is stated that, although

his artistic ability is beyond question, "he was not an
artist in life" where no match was to be found for the
intellectual force and sincerity of his novels. His philosophy is then examined and criticized for "prejudiced,
unbalanced, and narrow" intellectual judgments.

1248 Ellis, Havelock. "Tolstoy" in The New Spirit. Washington,
D. C. : National Home Library, 1935; 167-218. A survey of Tolstoy's major writings giving special attention
to their autobiographical elements and to the basic principles of his philosophy. His thought, especially as expressed in his didactic works, is viewed as being characterized by a tendency to oversimplify problems and
adopt extreme solutions, but nonetheless he is praised
for the sincerity and tenacity of his beliefs. Also discussed is the spread of his philosophy throughout Russia,
particularly among the common people.

1249 Faussett, Hugh I'Anson. "The Testimony of Tolstoy" in Po-
ets and Pundits. Port Washington, N. Y. : Kennikat,
1967 (reprint of 1947 publication); 13-30. A positive
assessment of Tolstoy's ideals and morality. His struggle to determine truth and live accordingly is illustrated
by episodes from his life. His exceptional concern for
the well-being of his fellow man is noted, and he is seen
as a leading example of that which all men should do:
counter in life, by deeds and philosophy, all that dehu-
manizes.

1250 Garnett, Edward. "Tolstoy's Place in European Literature"
in Leo Tolstoy. New York: Pott, 1903; 40. Tolstoy is
presented as the leading symbol of the spiritual unrest,
in response to the questionable condition of the modern
European world, which developed within Europe's intellectual community at the turn of the century. For this
reason he is judged to be of as much importance to
Europe as to Russia. It is concluded that he will stand
in European literature as "the conscience of the modern
world" and for "the triumph of the European soul against
civilization's routine and dogma. "

1251 Grierson, Francis. "The Prophet without Honour" in The
Invincible Alliance and Other Essays Political, Social and
Literary. Freeport, N. Y. : Books for Libraries Press,
1969 (reprint of 1913 publication); 31-40. A satirical
account of how Tolstoy would be viewed stripped of his
title, independence, and prestige, and transferred to
London. Humorous and fanciful reactions of aristocrats,
critics, and reporters are presented about his beliefs
and personality.

1252 Grierson, Francis. "Tolstoy" in Modern Mysticism and Other
Essays. Port Washington, N. Y. : Kennikat, 1970 (re-

print of 1899 publication), 57-70. A highly critical discussion of Tolstoy's philosophy as "the story of conflict-
ing emotions and intellectual paradox ending in mental
disorder. " In particular, he is assailed for mistaking
"mere humility for religion, and poverty for progress"
and is labeled a malicious literary nihilist whose unbalanced mind is "strongly tinged with Oriental mysticism
and Russian superstitions. "

1253   Griggs, Edward H. "Tolstoy" in Moral Leaders: A Hand-
book of Twelve Lectures. New York: Heubsch, 1905;
47-50. An outline of Tolstoy's moral philosophy within
the context of a Russia depicted as a mysterious mingling
of Occident and Orient covered by a "film of French culture. " The combination in his philosophy of aristocratic
and peasant qualities is considered to be a consequence
of the heterogenous nature of Russian culture. Although
commended for recognizing that effective social reform
"is always a question of the regeneration of the individual, " Tolstoy is criticized for the dogmatic nature of his
beliefs.

1254   Hake, Alfred E. "The Light of Russia" in Regeneration: A
Reply to Max Nordau. New York: Putnam, 1896; 108-
131. An attack on Max Nordau's contention, advanced
in his book Degeneration, that Tolstoy's works and philosophy represent a type of insanity and are popular
chiefly because his readers suffer from the same general
affliction. In defense of Tolstoy, his fiction is judged to
be a realistic picture of Russia presented with great
artistic skill, and his life and work are seen to be devoted to the "regeneration of the race. " Nordau's negative assessment of Tolstoy is further assaulted by reference to particular points of Tolstoy's beliefs that Nordau
misinterpreted. For Nordau's argument see "Tolstoism"
in Degeneration (New York: Appleton, 1895), 144-171,
entry 1268.

1255   Halperin, George. "Count Leo Tolstoy" in Tolstoy, Dostoevsky, Tourgenev: The Three Great Men of Russia's
World of Literature. Chicago: Chicago Literary Club,
1946; 3-30. It is argued that the vast difference in the
quality of Tolstoy's work as an artist and as a moralizer
makes it difficult to evaluate him, as does the fact that
it is impossible to separate these two facets of his life.
The source of this duality in Tolstoy is identified as his
living amidst the end of the agrarian feudal Russia and
the rise of capitalist Russia: "the penitent noble at-
temps to appease his conscience and to oppose the advent
of capitalism by creating a social idyll. " This attempt
is considered to be symbolized in his fiction by the shift
in his attention from the nobles of War and Peace to the
peasants of Anna Karenina.

1256   Hearn, Lafcadio.   "Tolstoi's Vanity of Wisdom" in Essays in
       European and Oriental Literature, ed. by Albert Mordell.
       New York: Dodd, Mead, 1968; 195-199.   An analysis
       of Tolstoy's philosophy with much reference to Anna
       Karenina. His insight into the process of studying the
       meaning of life is applauded as is his conclusion that a
       simple existence is the best type of life for man.   Tol-
       stoy's contention that common, ignorant peasants have
       better insight into life's meaning is supported by way of
       reference to the tale of Buddha and the common man.

1257   Heller, Otto.   "Leo Tolstoy: A Study in Revivalism" in
       Prophets of Dissent: Essay on Maeterlinck, Strindberg,
       Nietzsche, and Tolstoy.   New York: Knopf, 1918; 161-
       216.   Tolstoy's spiritual evolution is traced from his
       early hedonistic life to his religious conversion as a
       response to currents in both Russian and European soci-
       ety.   To prove this contention, the spiritual content of
       War and Peace, Anna Karenina, Resurrection, and What
       Is Art? is examined as a reaction to the environment in
       which he lived, and, consequently, Tolstoy is regarded
       as being more of a reflector than an innovator.   Even
       though he did not serve the world as a creator of phi-
       losophy, it is concluded that he was a most admirable
       individual and can be considered "the greatest humani-
       tarian of the century. "

1258   Howells, William Dean.   "The Philosophy of Tolstoy" in
       Criticism and Fiction and Other Essays, ed. by William
       Gibson.   New York: New York University Press, 1965;
       167-179.   It is maintained that Tolstoy's "real life"
       dates from his efforts to make his life harmonious with
       that of the Russian peasant.   How he came to this deci-
       sion, its effect on his personal life, and how he con-
       verted it into a philosophy touching religion, art, soci-
       ety, and life in general are all discussed.   Tolstoy's
       concern for finding life's meaning is also seen as being
       at the heart of his artistic creations, making them com-
       mendable works, except for The Kreutzer Sonata, "his
       one great mistake, and a discord in the harmony of his
       philosophy. "   Also titled "Lyof Tolstoy" in Library of
       the World's Best Literature, ed. Charles Warner (New
       York: International Society, 1897); vol. 14, 985-994;
       excerpts in LTCA, 101-103.

1259   Howells, William Dean.   "Tolstoy" in My Literary Passions.
       New York: Harper and Brothers, 1895; 250-258.   Tol-
       stoy's views on art, religion, and life are positively as-
       sessed, and his great influence on Howells' ethics and
       aesthetics is discussed.   Particularly upheld is Tolstoy's
       support of a simple, Christian life.   It is admitted that
       he did not fully follow his own teachings, yet his life is
       seen as "no less instructive because in certain things it

seems a failure. " Also in Essays from Five Centuries,
eds. W. T. Hastings and K. O. Mason (Boston: Houghton, 1929), 292-296; American Literary Criticism, ed.
by B. Matthews (New York: Longmans, 1904), 265-270;
and Harper Essays, ed. by H. S. Canby (New York:
Harper and Brothers, 1927), 282-287.

1260 Kaufmann, Walter. "Tolstoy versus Dostoevsky" in Existentialism, Religion and Death: Thirteen Essays. New
York: Meridan, 1976; 15-27. It is argued that many
critics misinterpret Tolstoy and his works because they
see his characters as "bathed in his love" instead of as
individuals whom he presents negatively--full of failings
and self-deceptions. Tolstoy's greatness is identified
as resting in his penetrating honesty and introspection
which is infectious: "in inviting us to sit in judgment,
Tolstoy calls on us to judge ourselves. " This quality
is seen as being consistent throughout all of his works,
but only Anna Karenina is discussed as an example.
Reprinted from Religion from Tolstoy to Camus (New
York: Harper and Brothers, 1961); 2-12.

1261 Larkin, Maurice. "Experience versus the Intellect: Tolstoy"
in Man and Society in Nineteenth Century Realism: Determinism and Literature. Totowa, N. J.: Rowman &
Littlefield, 1977; 111-120. It is contended that much as
Tolstoy despised the mainstream of Western intellectual
thought, he nonetheless lived in and was influenced by a
milieu heavily touched by Western determinism. In particular, his internal conflicts are portrayed as "an individual reflection of the great debate between Westerners
and Slavophiles, " a debate which he partially resolved
in his fiction but never in real life. His assertion, in
Anna Karenina, of the value of experience over intellect
is viewed as an attempt to establish the supremacy of
traditional Russia over Western rationalism.

1262 Lee, Vernon. "Tolstoi as a Prophet: Notes on the Psychology of Asceticism" in Gospels of Anarchy. New York:
Brentano's, 1909; 103-132. Tolstoy's views on art,
religion, and society are summarized and then criticized
for being overly harsh and, in fact, absurd. It is maintained, however, that his philosophy is not totally useless because the disruptive effect that his prophecies
have on us is "one of the necessary purifiers of our
souls. " Thus Tolstoy's continually asking us "to what
purpose?" is viewed as valuable introspection even if
our answers to his questions differ from his own.

1263 Leslie, Shane. "Leo Tolstoy" in Salutation to Five: Mrs.
Fitzherbert, Edmund Warre, Sir William Butler, Leo
Tolstoy, and Sir Mark Sykes. Freeport, N. Y.: Books
for Libraries Press, 1970 (reprint of 1951 publication);

99-132. Tolstoy's life and works are discussed in light of two of his essential goals: a world without war, and a world where all people love each other. Also presented are his moral and religious views in general, and how they affected his personal life, particularly his family. The essay concludes with a brief survey of the contradictions that plagued his life.

1264 Macy, John. "Tolstoy" in The Critical Game. New York: Boni and Liveright, 1922; 65-92. Tolstoy's spiritual struggle is discussed, and it is stated that "in ceaseless pursuit of truth, Tolstoy went through the most stirring intellectual and moral experience which modern man has undergone. " His conflict with modern civilization is noted before turning to an analysis of War and Peace, Anna Karenina, and Resurrection as examples of his relentless passion for truth. The essay concludes with an examination of Tolstoy's assault on church and state, his work here being seen as valuable for focusing attention on evils rather than for suggesting viable, positive alternatives.

1265 Masaryk, Thomas. The Spirit of Russia: Studies in History, Literature and Philosophy. New York: Macmillan, 1961; vol. II (no separate section on Tolstoy). Tolstoy's views on a wide range of subjects are discussed as is his relationship with leading Russians of the time. His nihilism, anarchism, and mysticism as well as his attitude toward art and science are briefly surveyed, and his beliefs are compared and contrasted to those of Leontiev, Soloviev, and Pobedonostsev.

1266 Maude, Aylmer. "Right and Wrong" in TP, 185-218. An examination of the nature of morality with little direct reference to Tolstoy but with obvious agreement in principle with his views on the subject. In essence, it is maintained that there is a "divine spark" or "soul" innate to man which is the "basis of morality, " and that many philosophers, especially the materialists, err in their analysis of morality by overlooking this fact. Also in New Order, (Sept. 1898).

1267 Miliukov, Paul. "The Classical Period" in Outlines of Russian Culture: Part II, Literature. Philadelphia: University of Pennsylvania Press, 1942; 25-49. Tolstoy is placed in the context of the development of the Russian intelligentsia in that he is somewhat close to the image of the "repentant nobleman" who seeks "to imitate the plain people in order to attain spiritual self-perfection. " His links to populism are pointed out as is his isolation from radical elements in Russia.

1268 Nordau, Max. "Tolstoism" in Degeneration. New York: Appleton, 1895; 144-171. Tolstoyism is presented as a

conception of life rather than an aesthetic theory, and is
used as an example of the degeneration which is seen as
characteristic of late 19th-century European civilization.
Tolstoy's beliefs are deemed to be a type of "mental
aberration" based on arbitrary and mystical thought, and
degenerate due to their skepticism, negativism, and
brooding introspection. His influence and popularity in
the world are regarded as being not the result of the excellence of his writings, but due to the "mental condition
of his readers" who "are ripe for degenerate mysticism. "
See Alfred Hake, "The Light of Russia" in Regeneration:
A Reply to Max Nordau, 108-131, for a refutation of
Nordau's criticism of Tolstoy, entry 1254.

1269 Noyes, George R. "The Essential Elements in Tolstoy's
      Ethical System" in Anniversary Papers by Colleagues and
      Pupils of George Lyman Kitredge. Boston, 1913; 295-
      303.

1270 Perris, George H. "Tolstoy as a Writer" in Leo Tolstoy.
      New York: Pott, 1903; 40. It is claimed that much of
      the misunderstanding surrounding Tolstoy's literature and
      philosophy is due to failure to remember that "Tolstoy
      is a Russian in the first place. " This Russian environ-
      ment, filled with "morbid introspection and the spirit of
      revolt, " is identified as the source of his assault on the
      established conventions of Western civilization, and is
      also regarded as the root of his intense desire to dis-
      cover life's meaning.

1271 Phelps, William L. "Tolstoi" in Essays on Russian Novelists.
      New York: Macmillan, 1917; 170-214. A survey of
      Tolstoy's life precedes comments on the loss suffered
      by the literary world because of his spiritual conversion.
      His basic philosophy is not seen as being clearly divided
      at the point of his conversion since "his mental view-
      point is the same in 1855 and 1905, " but rather the
      change was in his conduct: "In his views on art, morals
      and religion Tolstoy developed, but he did not change.
      He simply followed his ideas to their farthest possible
      extremes. " His fiction is then discussed, with War and
      Peace and Anna Karenina receiving most attention.

1272 Plekhanov, George. "Tolstoy and Nature" in LTCA, 137-140.
      Tolstoy is viewed, by the Russian Marxist writer and
      critic, as a master at depicting that which awakens in
      the reader, and Tolstoy, a sense of unity with nature.
      It is suggested that at the very moments when he felt
      this unity, Tolstoy most strongly sensed the horror of
      death because he realized that some day he would lose
      his identity to this nature. The Christian concept of the
      immortality of the soul is considered to have provided
      only small consolation for him in those instances in which

he dwelled on death, hence his life long spiritual crisis.
Translated from Zvezda, no. 4 (1924).

1273 Poggioli, Renato.   "A Portrait of Tolstoy as Alceste" in The
      Phoenix and the Spider: A Book of Essays about Some
      Russian Writers and Their Views of the Self.   Cam-
      bridge, Mass. :   Harvard University Press, 1957; 49-
      108. Discussed is Tolstoy's lifelong struggle to "recon-
      cile the lower and higher demands of the self, " and his
      subsequent failure to do so because of an irresolvable
      "conflict between his mind and his heart. " To facilitate
      analysis of this complex struggle, Tolstoy is cast in the
      role of Molière's character Alceste, the rationale being
      that both individuals were obsessed with pursuit of truth
      and sincerity, were misanthropes, and were influenced
      by two inner and opposing voices: reason and sentiment.

1274 Rahv, Philip.   "Tolstoy: The Green Twig and the Black
      Trunk" in Image and Idea: Twenty Essays on Literary
      Themes. Norfolk, Conn. : New Directions Books, 1957;
      87-104. It is argued that there is no division in Tol-
      stoy's life or philosophy due to his spiritual crisis, and
      no discontinuity in his career: "His personality and
      artistic talent retain their unity and vitality" before and
      after the crisis.   The title of the essay is symbolic of
      its basic contention in that the green twig is associated,
      by way of a tale told to him in his youth by his brother,
      with the key to happiness in his early life; whereas the
      black trunk, filled with his religious and ethical writings
      of his post-crisis career, is representative of the same
      quest for happiness in his later life.   Also in Literature
      and the Sixth Sense, 134-149; and New Partisan Reader,
      208-220, under the title "Concerning Tolstoy. "

1275 Robertson, John M.   "Tolstoy" in Explorations.   London:
      Watts, 1923; 69-111.   An examination of Tolstoy in the
      roles of moral philosopher, art critic, and fiction writ-
      er.   The ideas which he developed as he functioned in
      each of these capacities are summarized, with those as-
      sociated with "Tolstoy the moral prophet" considered to
      be most responsible for his world-wide following.

1276 Roosevelt, Theodore R.   "Tolstoy" in Literary Essays, vol.
      14 of The Works of Theodore Roosevelt.   New York:
      Scribner's, 1924; 411-417.   Tolstoy's literary genius is
      acknowledged, but his philosophy is condemned for being
      impractical and of meaning only to feeble and fantastic
      folk.   Tolstoyism in America is depicted as absurdly
      comic and as the antithesis of the creative and practical
      spirit responsible for America's greatness.   His philos-
      ophy is also seen as being harmful in Russia where it
      has had a paralyzing effect on the Russian Duma.   Also
      in Outlook, 92 (15 May 1909), 103-105; and Cur Lit, 47
      (1909), 64-66.

1277 Roubiczek, Paul. "Tolstoy: The Struggle for Virtue, " in
      The Misinterpretation of Man: Studies in European
      Thought of the Nineteenth Century.   Port Washington,
      N. Y. : Kennikat, 1968 (reprint of 1947 publication); 199-
      226.   Tolstoy is portrayed as "one of the first Russians
      to reach a leading place in the cultural life of Europe
      without giving up his specifically national character. "
      In spite of his world stature, his philosophy is criticized
      for its excessive passivity and opposition to progress.
      Additionally, his religious views are attacked for failure
      to understand the significant role played by "religious
      symbols" which he so detested.   The ultimate refutation
      of his beliefs is seen as his own life, which was poi-
      soned by his philosophy.

1278 Royce, Josiah.   "Tolstoy and the Unseen Moral Order, " in
      Liber Scriptorium.   New York: Author's Club, 1893 (1st
      (in series); 488-497.   Tolstoy is deemed to be "out of
      sympathy with the whole prevailing tendency of recent
      ethics toward realism" in that his ethics, like those of
      Kant and Schopenhauer, are those of idealism.   His in-
      tense introspection is acknowledged to be "unmistakenly
      morbid, " but it is argued that from this stage of suffer-
      ing Tolstoy passed to one of calm and enlightenment
      which led him to his philosophy of love and non-resist-
      ance.   He is praised for reminding the world in its age
      of realism that life's true meaning rests in the unseen
      moral order of God's universe.

1279 Sarolea, Charles.   "Tolstoy the Byzantine, " in Great Russia:
      Her Achievements and Promise.   New York: Knopf,
      1916; 107-117.   The only way to understand Tolstoy, it
      is argued, is by placing him within "the mental and
      spiritual climate in which his genius developed"--that is,
      one laden with contradictions due to the transplanting of
      European philosophy to primitive social, political, and
      economic conditions.   By viewing him as a product of
      such an environment, his complex and paradoxical nature
      is easier to comprehend though no more acceptable.   A
      lengthy list of contradictions in his life and philosophy
      is then presented.

1280 Shestov, Lev.   "Dostoevsky and Nietzsche: The Philosophy
      of Tragedy" in Essays in Russian Literature, ed. Spencer
      Roberts.   Athens: Ohio University Press, 1968; 3-183.
      The pessimistic philosophy of Dostoevsky is contrasted
      with the idealistic views of Tolstoy.   In particular, Tol-
      stoy's concern for countering skepticism and pessimism
      is interpreted as being antithetical to the philosophy ex-
      pressed by Dostoevsky in his works: "the philosophy of
      tragedy is in principle hostile to the philosophy of the
      commonplace. "   Dostoevsky's reaction to Tolstoy's views
      and works is discussed with most reference to War and
      Peace and Anna Karenina.   Excerpt in LTCA, 123-26.

1281 Shestov, Lev. "The Good in the Teaching of Tolstoy and
        Nietzsche: Philosophy and Preaching, " in Dostoevsky,
        Tolstoy and Nietzsche. Athens: Ohio University Press,
        1969; 1-140. Tolstoy's conversion from the role of
        philosopher, as in War and Peace, to that of preacher
        in his later years is interpreted as being a response to
        his inability to face the realities of life and, particularly,
        the horror of death. His lack of faith is isolated as the
        crucial source of his need to expound on faith. He is
        seen as similar to Nietzsche in that both suffered in
        search of a higher truth to bring spiritual comfort to
        their tortured lives.

1282 Strakhov, Nicolas. "Critical Essays on I. S. Turgenev and
        L. N. Tolstoy, " in LTCA, 56-7. Tolstoy's philosophy
        of life is viewed as resting on his aspiration to present
        the simple and good life, not in abstract form, but in
        "all its plenitude and wholeness, " and to assert that
        simplicity, meekness and self-humiliation are at the heart
        of Russian national uniqueness. Excerpt translated from
        Kriticheskie Stat'i ob I. S. Turgeneve i L. N. Tolstom
        (1885).

1283 Untermeyer, Louis. "Leo Tolstoy, " in Makers of the Modern
        World. New York: Simon & Schuster, 1955; 121-131.
        A short sketch of Tolstoy's life and philosophy emphasiz-
        ing the "contradictions woven into his fibers" precedes a
        discussion of the inconsistencies that are most outstand-
        ing, the leading one being that he preached austerity yet
        lived amidst luxury. His yielding to compromise only
        ended, it is claimed, with his 1910 flight from the com-
        forts of Yasnaya Polyana. In conclusion, he is labeled
        not the "most flawless artist nor the loftiest soul" ever
        produced by Russia, but rather as the greatest moral
        force in Russian literary history.

1284 Vogue, E. M. de. "Nihilism and Mysticism--Tolstoy, " in
        The Russian Novel. New York: Doran, 1914; 271-332.
        Tolstoy is depicted as a representative of the "new Rus-
        sia, restive of European control, " and the protagonist
        of "the state of the Russian soul known under the name
        of nihilism. " As his life progressed, however, he is
        seen as having tempered his nihilism and eventually
        abandoning it for a brand of religious mysticism. There
        follows a discussion of the leading points of his religious
        and philosophical beliefs. Also in The Russian Novelists.
        Boston: Lothrop, 1887; 209-269; excerpt in LTCA, 57-60.

1285 Wedgwood, Julia. "Count Leo Tolstoi" in Nineteenth Century
        Teachers and Other Essays. London: Hodder and
        Stoughton, 1909; 274-291. A summary of Tolstoy's phi-
        losophical views precedes a critical analysis in which
        his doctrine of non-resistance is rejected for being im-

practical, and his religious beliefs, though praiseworthy, are deemed to be realizable only by saints. Also assailed is his negative opinions on the "principle of civil and family life. " Tolstoy's works of fiction, especially War and Peace, are positively assessed, and his realism is labeled "masterful" though sometimes overly detailed and undramatic. Originally in the Contemp R, 52 (August 1887), 249-263; and Eclectic M, 109, (1887), 634-643.

1286 Willcocks, M. P. "Tolstoi" in Between the Old World and the New. Studies in Literary Personality. London: Allen and Unwin, 1925; 216-232. The fine qualities of Tolstoy's fiction are discussed before turning to a critical survey of his philosophy. His thought is seen as representing "the Eastern ideal" of "a yielding of the soul to the divine current" directly opposed to the Western ideal of material progress. His ideas on science, moral law, art and religion are all regarded as being representative of "the Slav idea" and alien to Europe.

1287 Zenkovskii, V. V. "L. N. Tolstoy" in A History of Russian Philosophy. New York: Columbia University Press, 1953; vol. II, 386-399. Tolstoy is discussed as a superlative artist and a great thinker who influenced not only Russia but the rest of the world. The individuals who influenced his thinking are examined, most notably Rousseau, Lavrov, Mikhailovsky, and Schopenhauer. His moral and religious beliefs are then analyzed, with the contention being that he always remained a disciple of Christian principles even though he rejected Christ's divinity. His attempt to found a new way of life on a religious basis is judged to be his most original contribution to the world.

1288 Zenkovskii, V. V. "N. N. Strakhov, L. N. Tolstoy, and N. K. Mikhailovsky" in Russian Thinkers and Europe. Ann Arbor, Mich.: American Council of Learned Societies, 1953; 114-135. Tolstoy's philosophy is interpreted as being a response to two broad trends in Russian intellectual circles: the desire to move closer to the common people, and the rejection of the principles of modern European civilization. Rousseau's influence on Tolstoy's philosophy of the simple life is examined as are his visits to Europe which served to increase his spirit of nationalism and his love of simple, Russian life and values.

PERIODICAL ARTICLES

1289 Adams, Maurice. "Ethics of Tolstoy and Nietzsche, " Int J Ethics, 11 (1900), 82-105. Also "Tolstoy and Nietzsche, " RRs, 22 (Nov. 1900), 614-615.

1290   Arnold, Matthew. "Count Leo Tolstoi," Fortn R, 48 (Dec.
       1887), 783-799.

1291   Bachelli, Richaro. "The Sincere Penitent," Adam, nos. 284-
       286 (1960), 147-152.

1292   Bauman, A. A. "The Elements and Character of Tolstoy's
       Weltanschauung," Int J Ethics, 23 (Oct. 1912), 59-76.

1293   Buck, P. M., Jr. "Great False Prophets," Unpop R, 8
       (Oct. 1917), 262-281. The inconsistencies between Tol-
       stoy's philosophy and life style are discussed. He is
       seen as highly egotistical and individualistic.

1294   Cark, Walter H. "Skepticism and Faith in the Creativity of
       Tolstoi," ANQ, 3 (Jan. 1963), 5-14. Tolstoy's genius
       is seen as being due to the combination of faith and
       skepticism in his life. A brief résumé of his life is
       given from this perspective.

1295   Casseres, Benjamin de. "Idealism of Tolstoy," International,
       8 (April 1914), 129-130.

1296   Casseres, Benjamin de. "The Two Tolstoys," Putnam M, 1,
       no. 6 (March 1907), 728-730. A comparison of Tolstoy
       before and after his conversion.

1297   Colum, M. M. "Tolstoy and the End of an Epoch," Forum,
       97 (March 1937), 160-161. A review of Tolstoy's philos-
       ophy.

1298   "Count Leo Tolstoi," Literature, 3 (30 July 1898), 73-74.
       Tolstoy is criticized for abandoning his fiction; his phi-
       losophical views are seen as rash.

1299   "Count Tolstoy's Theories," Chaut, 9 (1888), 149-152. Also
       in Critic, 33 (Sept. 1898), 184.

1300   Crosby, Ernest H. "Count Tolstoy as Philosopher, Prophet
       and Man," Arena, 25 (April 1901), 429-439.

1301   Crosby, Ernest H. "Count Tolstoy, His Philosophy," Fact
       and Fiction, (Jan.-June 1897). A series of six articles
       later included in his book Tolstoy and His Message, 1911.

1302   Crosby, Ernest H. "Count Tolstoy, the Peasant Nobleman,"
       The Pilgrim, 2-3 (June 1901), 5.

1303   Crosby, Ernest H. "Count Tolstoy's Philosophy of Life,"
       Arena, 15 (Jan. 1896), 279-285.

1304   Crosby, Ernest H. "Snap-shots at Tolstoy," Whim, 1, no. 6
       (July 1901), 158-162.

1305   Curtis, J. M.   "Shestov's Use of Nietzsche in His Interpretation of Tolstoy and Doestoevsky," TSLL, 17 (1975), 289-302.

1306   Davis, Charles J.   "Tolstoi! Teacher!," Personalist, 9 (1928), 88-99, 194-202.

1307   Downes, R. P.   "Leo Tolstoy," Great Thoughts, 8 (May 1901), 104-106. A discussion of Tolstoy's philosophy and religious ideas, and the harmony between his life and views.

1308   Drake, D.   "Light from Tolstoy on Russia," Int J Ethics, 30 (Jan. 1920), 190-195.

1309   Edgerton, William B.   "The Artist Turned Prophet: Leo Tolstoj after 1880," Am Contribs, 2 (1968), 61-85.

1310   "The Ethics of Leo Tolstoy," Overland M, n. s. 13 (1899), 651-656.

1311   Flew, A. G.   "Tolstoy and the Meaning of Life," Ethics, 73, no. 2 (Jan. 1963), 110-118.

1312   Flower, B. O.   "Prophets of the Nineteenth Century," Arena, 24 (Nov. 1900), 552-558. Ward's book, Prophets of the Nineteenth Century, 1900, serves as a springboard for analysis of Tolstoy's philosophy and religious ideas.

1313   Gorodetzky, Nadejda.   "Literature of Questions," Can Slavic S, 2, no. 1 (Spring 1968), 100-110. A discussion of the questions asked by Tolstoy on the nature of man, morality, religion, society, government and philosophy.

1314   "Great Russian Moralists," Dial, 49 (1 Dec. 1910), 445-446.

1315   Gribble, Francis.   "Tolstoy," Fortn R, 95 (Jan. 1911), 153-163. An examination of Tolstoyism with parallels to Rousseau.

1316   Hapgood, N.   "Ethics of Realism," Harvard M, 8, no. 3 (May 1889), 102-106.

1317   Hartley, L. P.   "The Unwilling Master," Adam, nos. 284-286 (1960), 170-171. On Tolstoy's fiction being responsible for his greatness whether he likes his works as art or not.

1318   Hazlitt, H.   "Marxism or Tolstoyism?," Nation, 136 (18 Jan. 1933), 68-70.

1319   Henderson, Archibald.   "The Message of Tolstoy," Forum, 45 (Feb. 1911), 142-150. Analysis of Tolstoy's philosophy of life, religion and art.

1320   Hyman, Laurence W.   "Moral Values and Literary Experi-
          ence, " J Aesth Art and Crit, 24 (Summer 1966), 545-
          547.

1321   "Is Tolstoi a 'Crank'?, " Lit W, 18, no. 17 (20 August 1887),
          264.   A critical analysis of Maurice Thompson's assault
          on Tolstoy's character and sincerity.

1322   "An Italian View of Tolstoy, " RRs, 4 (Oct. 1891), 335.   A
          survey of the article "Damnation of Tolstoy, " (Italian) by
          G. Boglietti.

1323   Kumar, Jainendra.   "The Vocation of Love, " Adam, nos.
          284-286 (1960), 164.

1324   Lampert, Evgenii.   "On Tolstoi, Prophet and Teacher, "
          Slav R, 25 (4 Dec. 1966), 604-614.

1325   Lee, Vernon.   "Tolstoy as Prophet: Notes on the Psychology
          of Asceticism, " N Amer R, 182 (April 1906), 524-541.

1326   Lohr, Frederick.   "Tolstoy, " Now, n. s. 2, no. 2 (1944),
          51-57.   A survey of Tolstoy as a novelist and a social
          thinker as well as of his philosophy, social views and
          theoretical works.

1327   Long, R. E.   "Count Tolstoy in Thought and Action, " RRs
          (L), 24 (July 1901), 33-41.   Tolstoy's ideas on philos-
          ophy, war, and religion are examined.

1328   Madariaga, Salvador de.   "The Message of Tolstoy, " Adam,
          nos. 284-286 (1960), 153-160.   On Tolstoy's philosophy,
          religious views, and ideas on anarchy.

1329   Malia, M. E.   "Adulthood Refracted: Russia and Leo Tol-
          stoy, " Daedalus, 105 (Spring 1976), 169-183.

1330   Mann, Thomas.   "Tolstoy, " Dial, 85 (1928), 453-457.
          Praises Tolstoy's quest for truth but his philosophy is
          not fully accepted.

1331   Massingham, Henry W.   "Philosophy of a Saint, " Contemp R,
          78 (Dec. 1900), 809-820.

1332   Maude, Aylmer.   "Right and Wrong, " New Order, (Sept. 1898).
          Also in Maude, Aylmer, Tolstoy and His Problems (1904),
          185-218.

1333   Mayer, F.   "Tolstoy as World Citizen, " Personalist, 28 (Oct.
          1947), 357-369.   A positive assessment of Tolstoy as the
          best representative of the "Russian mind" and a survey
          of his fiction and philosophic and aesthetic views.

1334   Miliukov, Paul.   "Leo Tolstoy and the Russian People, " New
       Russia, 3, no. 45 (1920), 457-461.   A discussion of
       Tolstoy as the embodiment of the Russian people.   Tol-
       stoy's views are seen as being consistent throughout his
       life, no conversion but a continuum.

1335   Mirsky, D. S.   "Tolstoy, " Slavonic R, 7 (June 1928), 77-80.
       A discussion of the conflicts within Tolstoy which are
       evident in his works.

1336   "Mr. Maurice Thompson on Mr. Howells, " Lit W, 18, no. 18
       (3 Sept. 1887), 281-282.   A defense of Howells' views
       on Tolstoy, his philosophy, and art against Thompson's
       attack in an article in the Chicago Sunday Times.

1337   Oyen, Hendrik.   "The Belief of Tolstoy, " Universitas, 2
       (1964), 30-38.

1338   Rod, Edward.   "Tolstoi, " Living Age, 222 (2 Sept. 1899),
       629-633.   A positive examination of his philosophy with
       Tolstoy seen as being consistent philosophically through-
       out his entire life.

1339   Roosevelt, Theodore R.   "Tolstoy: An Estimate, " Outlook,
       92 (15 May 1909), 103-108.   See Van Ness, Thomas,
       "Tolstoy, Another View, " Outlook, 92 (5 June 1909),
       336-337, for a response to Roosevelt.   Also in Roose-
       velt, Theodore R, Literary Essays (1924), 411-417.
       Partly reprinted in Cur Lit, 47 (1909), 64-66.

1340   Shahani, R. G.   "Hinduism in Tolstoy, " Asiatic R, 28 (Oct.
       1932), 664-669.

1341   Sheldon, Walter L.   "Tolstoy from an Ethical Standpoint, "
       Ethical R, 2 (1889), 65-82.

1342   "Some of the Words of a Free Man, " Cur Lit, 31 (1902), 402.

1343   Spence, G. W.   "Suicide and Sacrifice in Tolstoy's Ethics, "
       Rus R, 22 (April 1963), 157-167.

1344   Steiner, Edward A.   "Tolstoy: The Heart of Russia, " Outlook,
       75 (7 Nov. 1903), 537-544.   A survey of Tolstoy's life
       in Moscow and his views on the simple life and religion.

1345   Suhrawardy, A. A.   "An Indian on Tolstoi, " Calcutta R, 60
       (1936).

1346   "Tolstoi on Life, " Lit W, 19, no. 12 (9 June 1888), 179.

1347   "Tolstoi, Sage, Economist and Novelist, " J of Ed, 68 (15
       Oct. 1908), 395-396.

1348 "Tolstoi's Forthcoming Book," Cur Lit, 30 (June 1901), 651-
      652. A review of Tolstoy's What Is Right?

1349 "Tolstoi's Miscellanies," Lit W, 31, no. 13 (1 Nov. 1901),
      216-217. A survey of Tolstoy's political and social
      views and his work with the Dukhobors based on his
      correspondences.

1350 "Tolstoy and His Theories. Apropos of the Jubilee of His
      Life Work," Critic, 33 (1898), 184-189. A discussion
      of Tolstoy's philosophy with reference to Perris, G. H.,
      The Life and Teachings of Leo Tolstoy (1901).

1351 "Tolstoy the Great Russian Moralist," Dial, 49 (1 Dec. 1910),
      445-446. An article, ten days after the death of Tol-
      stoy, examining his philosophy and contributions to lit-
      erature.

1352 "Tolstoy, the Man, Artist and Guide," Chaut, 61 (Jan. 1911),
      152-154.

1353 "The Twentieth Century's Greatest Rebel," Cur Lit, 50 (Jan.
      1911), 62-64. A general discussion of Tolstoy's views
      with reference to Maude, Aylmer, The Life of Tolstoy
      (1910).

1354 Van Ness, Thomas. "Tolstoy, Another View," Outlook, 92
      (5 June 1909), 336-337. A critique of Roosevelt's attack
      on Tolstoy in Outlook, 92 (15 May 1909), 103-108.

1355 Ward, M. A. "Count Tolstoi," Cur Lit, 29 (August 1900),
      154-155. Excerpts from Ward, M. A., Prophets of the
      Nineteenth Century (1900).

1356 Warner, Charles D. "A Locoed Reformer," Harper's M, 81
      (Oct. 1890), 806-807. An assault on Tolstoy's philos-
      ophy. Also in Pub Op, 9, no. 26 (4 Oct. 1890), 601.

1357 Wedgewood, Julia. "Count Leo Tolstoi," Contemp R, 52
      (August 1887), 249-263. Also in Wedgewood, Julia,
      Nineteenth Century Teachers and Other Essays (1909),
      274-291; and in Eclectic M, 109 (1887), 634-643.

1358 Wendland, Johannes. "Tolstoy's Philosophy," Open Court,
      25 (Jan. 1911), 8-15.

1359 Weston, Bruce. "Leo Tolstoy and the Ascetic Tradition,"
      RLT, 3 (Spring 1972), 297-309.

1360 "What Do We Think of Tolstoy?," Lit D, 98 (29 Sept. 1928),
      26-28. Written in response to the centenary of his birth.
      Tolstoy's philosophy and writings are evaluated.

165 Philosophy

1361 Wilkinson, William C. "Tolstoi, " Homiletic R, 17, no. 1
(Jan. 1889), 16-27; 17, no. 2 (Feb. 1889), 107-116. A
discussion of Tolstoy's greatness, moral sincerity and
intellectual qualities with much reference to War and
Peace.

1362 Willett, Maurita. "Tolstoy's Trinity: Truth, Simplicity,
Love. " BSUF, 11 (1970), 53-59.

1363 Williamson, C. "The Ethics of Three Russian Novelists, "
Int J Ethics, 35 (1925), 217-237.

1364 Yarros, Victor S. "The Decline of Tolstoy's Philosophy, "
Chaut, 18 (March 1894), 703-707.

DISSERTATIONS

1365 Buchan, Scott A. "Russia and the East: A Study of Writers
Who Considered Russian Civilization to Be Fundamentally
Different from That of Western Europe, " University of
Pittsburg, 1974.

1366 Kvitko, David. "A Philosophic Study of Tolstoy, " Columbia
University, 1927. See his book of the same title (item
1221).

See also 1, 2, 3, 5, 6, 7, 8, 9, 12, 13, 14, 15, 16, 17,
18, 19, 20, 22, 23, 24, 25, 26, 27, 28, 29, 30, 31,
32, 34, 42, 51, 52, 54, 64, 69, 70, 77, 85, 86, 89,
99, 103, 106, 112, 113, 118, 120, 126, 127, 135, 147,
148, 154, 155, 172, 173, 175, 177, 178, 179, 180, 181,
182, 183, 184, 185, 186, 187, 188, 189, 191, 193, 194,
196, 197, 198, 199, 200, 201, 203, 204, 205, 206, 208,
210, 211, 213, 215, 216, 218, 220, 222, 226, 228, 229,
234, 243, 246, 251, 254, 271, 277, 291, 312, 315, 323,
328, 330, 332, 333, 347, 354, 358, 361, 370, 371, 380,
384, 388, 389, 407, 449, 452, 454, 455, 456, 457, 463,
464, 465, 470, 472, 474, 475, 483, 484, 486, 488, 491,
492, 499, 503, 509, 510, 512, 513, 515, 516, 519, 521,
525, 526, 533, 539, 552, 559, 560, 561, 567, 568, 578,
583, 589, 604, 607, 628, 641, 643, 654, 659, 663, 666,
693, 755, 757, 775, 793, 810, 853, 885, 1169, 1375,
1442, 1487, 1503, 1510, 1512, 1513, 1516, 1518, 1521,
1522, 1532, 1535, 1538, 1573, 1616, 1666, 1671, 1675,
1677, 1679, 1681, 1704, 1711, 1712, 1713, 1716, 1722,
1748, 1801, 1802, 1803, 1804, 1805, 1806, 1812, 1813,
1817, 1822, 1826, 1835, 1836, 1838, 1840, 1877, 1896,
1901, 1910, 1931, 1951, 1961.

Section V

ART AND AESTHETICS

BOOKS

1367 Eiloart, Arnold. Shakespeare and Tolstoy. London, 1909.

1368 Garrod, H. W. Tolstoy's Theory of Art. Oxford, England:
      Clarendon, 1935; 25p. Tolstoy's views on art are sum-
      marized and then critically assessed for the contention
      that good art consists of an individual consciously pass-
      ing his feelings on to others or provoking in them "a
      spiritual union with the artist and other readers." Such
      a definition of art is regarded as dangerous because, by
      its concern for form and not substance, it "opens the
      flood gates to art" for ethics and politics thereby reduc-
      ing art to "a disguised socialism." What Is Art? is,
      nonetheless, applauded for exposing perverted art and
      for having the "heroic quality which characterizes all of
      Tolstoy's best works." Also in The Study of Good Let-
      ters. Oxford: Clarendon, 1963; 37-54.

1369 Gibian, George. Tolstoj and Shakespeare. The Hague: Mou-
      ton, 1957; 47p. Similarities between Tolstoy and Shake-
      speare, such as vividness of characterization and devo-
      tion to the truth, are identified before Tolstoy's intense
      dislike of Shakespeare is analyzed. It is maintained that
      Tolstoy's antipathy was lifelong and based on objection
      to Shakespeare's language, ideas, plots, characteriza-
      tions, and lack of a religious tendency. Tolstoy conse-
      quently condemned him as an aristocratic writer, with
      no sympathy for the common man, and blind to the de-
      mands of moral justice. He is also considered to have
      reacted negatively to the excessive admiration given
      Shakespeare during the second half of the 19th century.

1370 Knight, George W. Shakespeare and Tolstoy. London: Eng-
      lish Association, 1934; 27p. Tolstoy's attack on Shake-
      speare is regarded as justifiable in some ways but,
      overall, based on a "fundamental misunderstanding of
      Shakespeare's art." Tolstoy is thought to be blind to
      Shakespeare's use of image and symbol, and therefore
      failed to comprehend the essence of his artistry: "To

166

understand Shakespeare one must make this original ac-
ceptance: to believe in people who speak poetry, thence
in human action which serves a poetic purpose, and fin-
ally in strange effects in nature which harmonize with
persons and their acts. "

1371 Maude, Aylmer. Tolstoy on Art and Its Critics. London:
     Oxford, 1925; 30p. A critical survey of a variety of
     reviews of What Is Art? from such sources as the Daily
     Chronicle, Sunday Times, Manchester Guardian, Inde-
     pendent, Times Literary Supplement, and the Boston
     Transcript. Most attention is devoted to George Bernard
     Shaw's review, which is criticized particularly for mis-
     interpreting Tolstoy's views on the peasant as the best
     judge of art. See Shaw, "Tolstoy on Art" in Selected
     Non-Dramatic Writings, 427-432 for a reproduction of his
     review of What Is Art?

ESSAYS AND CHAPTERS from general works

1372 Beardsley, Monroe C. "The Artist and Society" in Aesthetics
     from Classical Greece to the Present; A Short History.
     University: University of Alabama Press, 1975; 308-313.
     Tolstoy is thought to be the individual who most thorough-
     ly and uncompromisingly formulated and expressed the
     concept of the social responsibility of art. His theory
     of art is then summarized and its leading contention
     identified as being that art is a medium for the commun-
     ication of feelings. The most astonishing aspect of What
     Is Art? is considered to be its broad and furious assault
     on what are usually regarded as the greatest artistic
     creations of Western culture.

1373 Crane, Walter. "Note on Tolstoi's 'What Is Art?'" in Ideals
     in Art. London: Bell, 1905; 69-75. An attack on Tol-
     stoy's artistic philosophy on the grounds that he erred
     in trying to limit art "to those forms which are capable
     of appealing to everybody" because this would limit art
     to far too few and simple forms. His interest in a
     primitive, communal life is identified as the source of
     his call for a simple, universal art, yet his denial of
     beauty as an acceptable artistic criterion is also an at-
     tack on simple, peasant handicraft art, which is beautiful,
     and therefore is seen to be contradictory to his idealiza-
     tion of peasant life.

1374 Ducasse, C. J. "What Has Beauty to Do with Art?" in
     TCLA, 120-125. No essential connection is regarded
     as existing between beauty and art since there is both
     ugly and beautiful art, a contention which is supported
     by reference to Tolstoy's What Is Art? His artistic
     views are then linked to those of Vern (Esthetique, 1878),

and his definition of art as the communicator of feeling,
as opposed to the language of expression, is critically
assessed. Also in J Philos, 25 (1928), 181-186.

1375 Flaccus, Louis William. "Tolstoi" in Artists and Thinkers.
      Freeport, N. Y.: Books for Libraries Press, 1967 (re-
      print of 1916 publication); 140-160. Tolstoy's theory of
      art is discussed as a means of providing insight into the
      interplay of art and philosophy as well as into his outlook
      on life. The vitality of his artistic philosophy is con-
      sidered to be admirable, but the theory itself is criti-
      cized: "Tolstoy's one-sided, narrow interpretation of
      modern culture ... spoils his theory of art." Excerpt
      in TCLA, 87-94.

1376 Garrod, H. W. "Tolstoy's Theory of Art" in The Study of
      Good Letters. Oxford, England: Clarendon, 1963; 37-
      54. Also in Garrod's Tolstoy's Theory of Art (see item
      1368).

1377 Hall, Vernon, Jr. "Tolstoi" in A Short History of Literary
      Criticism. New York: New York University Press,
      1963; 133-140. A summation of Tolstoy's philosophy of
      art stressing his emphasis on an art which is popular,
      realistic, and message ladden. Tolstoy's contention
      that modern society lacked true art is also repeated.
      No attempt is made to interpret or pass judgment on
      his views.

1378 Harris, Julia, ed. Joel Chandler Harris, Editor and Essay-
      ist: Miscellaneous Literary, Political and Social Writ-
      ings. Chapel Hill: University of North Carolina, 1931.
      Not available for annotation. Listed as containing an
      essay on Tolstoy's criticism of Shakespeare.

1379 Hearn, Lafacdio. "Tolstoy's Theory of Art" in Life and Lit-
      erature. Freeport, N. Y.: Books for Libraries Press,
      1969 (reprint of 1917 publication); 288-299. Tolstoy is
      criticized for the extremity of some of his judgments in
      What Is Art?, but a number of his points are supported,
      specifically that the best art is that which communicates
      to the largest number of people, and that common people
      are certainly capable of appreciating good art. In all,
      What Is Art? is called "a very great and noble book ...
      fundamentally true from beginning to end." Excerpts in
      TCLA, 95-98.

1380 Huneker, James. "Dostoievsky and Tolstoy, and the Younger
      Choir of Russian Writers" in Ivory Apes and Peacocks.
      New York: Scribner's, 1915; 52-88. A highly critical
      assessment of Tolstoy's artistic views claiming that "if
      the peasant ... is to be the criterion of art," art would
      be "a cross between fireworks and the sign writing of

the Aztecs. " In spite of his "crack-pot" philosophy of art, Tolstoy is still considered to be a superior literary talent. A favorable review of Merezhkovski's biography of Tolstoy is also included.

1381   Knowlson, T. Sharper. "Art Criticism" in TCLA, 78-82. Tolstoy's definition of art as "the expression of human feelings with a view to affect others with like feelings" is commended for being refreshingly simple. He is criticized, however, for failing to establish specific norms for measuring good art, and for insisting that art is not good unless it can be appreciated by the greatest number of people. It is contended that if the common people are the best critics, "where is there one among their numbers who can write an analysis like Tolstoy's Guy de Maupassant?" Excerpt from Leo Tolstoy: A Biographical and Critical Study, 129-142. A more general annotation of this work appears under entry 1220.

1382   Knox, Israel. "Notes on the Moralistic Theory of Art: Plato and Tolstoy" in TCLA, 102-04. The essence of art is seen as being viewed differently by Plato and Tolstoy: "To Plato, art was an irresponsible creation...; to Tolstoy, it was a real and necessary human activity. " The similarities in their philosophies of art are, however, thought to outweigh this distinction in that both demanded that art serve a moral purpose, and, more importantly, both had delicate artistic sensibilities yet failed to recognize that art is most imaginative and effective in conveying a moral message when it is "the free and spontaneous criticism of life. " Excerpt from Int J Ethics, 41 (July 1931), 501-510.

1383   Knox, Israel. "Tolstoy's Esthetic Definition of Art" in TCLA, 98-102. Critics of What Is Art? are questioned for having concentrated on Tolstoy's views on morality and art to the neglect of his esthetic message. Tolstoy's contention that good art consists of "the infectious communication of emotions, " rather than mere expression, is discussed as "the other half" of What Is Art? His intent in using the words "infectious, " "communication, " and "emotions" is analyzed as a means of understanding his esthetic definition of art. Also in J Philos, 27 (1930), 65-70.

1384   Lawrence, D. H. "The Novel, " in Reflections on the Death of a Porcupine and Other Essays. Bloomington: Indiana University Press, 1969; 103-123. A critical account of Tolstoy's moral philosophy and artistic beliefs on the grounds that his preoccupation with man as a sinner, and with devising a literary form to preach his own brand of "the good life, " has led his art to become didactic and "a bore. " Pierre of War and Peace is put forth as an

example of a "dead" character, as opposed to "quick,"
who cannot hold the reader's interest because of his
sterility. Tolstoy is also attacked for not being true to
his own character but creating a false version of himself with whom he could never live harmoniously.

1385 Lee, Vernon. "Tolstoi on Art" in Gospels of Anarchy. New
      York: Brentano's, 1909; 133-158. Tolstoy's assault on
      art is interpreted to be the logical extension of his pre-
      vious attacks on all other aspects of modern civilization.
      His philosophy is thought to be correct in that modern
      art often is artificial and difficult to appreciate, and
      sometimes is unwholesome. However, the extreme con-
      clusions that he draws from his observations are labeled
      "unwarranted," especially his reducing art "to an adjunct
      of ethical education." Also criticized is his failure to
      see man's need for beauty as being an innate one, and
      his overall static, as opposed to evolutionary, view of
      art. Excerpt in TCLA, 57-66.

1386 Macy, John. "Tolstoi's Moral Theory of Art" in TCLA,
      66-78. The extremism and sweeping condemnations in
      What Is Art? must be put aside, it is argued, so that
      a balanced judgment of the work can be reached. Seen
      as valid are Tolstoy's claims that much money and time
      is wasted on perverted art, and that many accept as a
      work of art that which is technically skillful but devoid
      of substance. Tolstoy is criticized for discarding
      beauty, because there can be no universal definition of
      the word, as the measure of art in that he overlooks the
      fact that all of man's judgments (Tolstoy's included) are
      subjective and thus cannot possibly be universally ac-
      cepted. He is also criticized for insisting that art serve
      morality and that the common man be the judge of true
      art. Also in Cent M, 62 (June 1901), 298-307.

1387 Maude, Aylmer. Tolstoy on Art and Its Critics. London:
      Milford, 1925; 30. A reproduction of George Bernard
      Shaw's critical review of What Is Art? precedes a sur-
      vey of a series of reviews of Tolstoy's artistic beliefs.
      See under entry 1371 for annotation.

1388 Maude, Aylmer. "What Is Art?" in TP, 66-127. A repro-
      duction of Maude's 1899 introduction to Tolstoy's What
      Is Art? in which Tolstoy's views are summarized and
      support given to his plea for truthfulness, morality, and
      purpose in art. Also included is an article published
      by Maude in defense of Tolstoy against various critics
      of What Is Art? on the grounds most critics have misin-
      terpreted his intent and message. The translations of
      the work are also seen as a source of confusion about
      his philosophy of art. Specific errors by translators
      and critics are pointed out, and Tolstoy's true intent re-

stated. Also in Essays on Art (London: Richards, 1902), 46; article in Contemp R, 78 (August 1900), 241-254.

1389 Moore, George. Avowals. London: Riverside Press, 1919; 137-164 (no separate chapter title on Tolstoy). Tolstoy's views expressed in What Is Art? are criticized, especially his contention that art must be harnessed to the service of morality. His major works of fiction are then discussed, with special attention given to the harm done to his writings by his attempt to make them serve morality. Anna Karenina is singled out for containing excessive moralizing, but The Kreutzer Sonata receives most criticism: "every jot of Tolstoy's ugly temperament went into the composition of this book." Also in Lippincott's M, 72 (Nov. 1903), 608-616 (Dec. 1903), 697-703.

1390 More, Paul Elmer. "Tolstoy; or, The Ancient Feud between Philosophy and Art" in Shelburne Essays (first series). New York: Putnam, 1906; vol. I, 139-224. The feud between philosophy and art is traced back to Plato, with Tolstoy's views placed within this context. Tolstoy's leading contentions are re-stated, and he is criticized for denying that beauty can serve as the standard for art yet offering no acceptable positive alternative. His religious beliefs are also attacked for being negative and dreary, which, in turn, is the source of his failing to see the spiritual joy and warmth of Christianity. Also in The Modern Reader; Essays on Present Day Life and Culture, W. Lippmann and A. Nevins, eds. (Boston: Heath, 1936), 618-628; and Atlantic M, 86 (Sept. 1900), 337-347.

1391 Murry, John M. "Keats and Tolstoy" in John Middleton Murry: Selected Criticism, ed. Richard Rees. London: Oxford University Press, 1960; 195-206. Tolstoy's philosophy of art is summarized and two essentially unsound contentions identified: that art must be judged in light of "feelings inculcated by Christianity," and that art should communicate feelings that all men are affected by. His artistic views are then briefly and unfavorably contrasted with those of Keats.

1392 Orwell, George. "Lear, Tolstoy and the Fool," in Shooting an Elephant and Other Essays. New York: Harcourt, Brace, 1950; 32-52. An attack on Tolstoy's critique of Shakespeare's King Lear and on his philosophy of art in general. It is maintained that Tolstoy, in the case of Shakespeare, misinterpreted his use of the fool in Lear and therefore missed much of his intent in the play. His intolerant attitude toward Shakespeare and those who praised his art is seen as being unbalanced as is his

artistic philosophy for demanding that art serve a moral
and religious purpose. Also in Polemic, 7 (March
1947); and Listener, 25 (1941).

1393 Saha, Narayan Chandra. "Tolstoy and Shakespeare" in Shakespeare Commemoration Volume, ed. by T. Sen. Calcutta: Dhur, 1966; 159-169. Shakespeare scholars are
criticized for too often dismissing Tolstoy's attack on
Shakespeare as the product of the fanatically moralistic
Tolstoy of his later years instead of analyzing the specific sources of his assault. His criticism of Shakespeare's moral neutrality and his annoyed impatience
with the blind worshippers of Shakespeare are considered
to be prime sources of his antipathy as is his partially
justifiable dislike of Shakespeare's characterizations and
plot constructions.

1394 Shaw, George Bernard. "Tolstoy on Art" in Selected Non-
Dramatic Writings of George Bernard Shaw, ed. by Dan
Laurence. Boston: Houghton Mifflin, 1965; 427-432.
What Is Art? is criticized for directing art toward the
peasant and for claiming that the peasant is the best
judge of art on the grounds that Tolstoy wholly idealized
the common man ignoring the fact that he has the same
vices as the bourgeoisie and aristocracy except that he
is poorer. His definition of art as that which transmits
one man's feelings to another is, however, accepted, as
is his contention that art must be a vital force in the
education of man. Originally in The Daily Chronicle,
(10 Sept. 1898). Also in Pen Portraits and Reviews,
256-260; A. Maude's Tolstoy on Art and Its Critics, 3-
10; and LTCA, 105-111.

1395 Stacy, Robert H. "Tolstoy or Dostoevsky" in Russian Literary Criticism, A Short History. Syracuse, N. Y. :
Syracuse University Press, 1974; 80-86. Tolstoy's views
on art are briefly summarized before being rejected as
"absurd and repugnant. " The non-sensical nature of his
philosophy of art, however, is not considered as having
had a negative influence on his own artistic creations,
which are judged to be great works of fiction.

1396 Symons, Arthur. "Tolstoi on Art, " in Studies in Prose and
Verse. New York: Dutton, 1922; 173-182. Tolstoy's
theory of art is applied to the leading works in world
literature to determine their place in his theory, a place
regarded as uniformly low on the artistic scale. Also
questioned is his establishing the simple-minded, common man as the judge of art on the basis that "the un-
educated judgment can have only very slight value in
determining what is true and false in art. " Excerpt in
TCLA, 82-87.

1397 Wasiolek, Edmund. "Tolstoy's The Death of Ivan Ilytch and
      Jamesian Fictional Imperatives" in TCCE, 146-156. A
      study of the disparity between Tolstoy's later technique
      and contemporary literary predispositions as repre-
      sented by the artistic beliefs of Henry James. James'
      contention that a successful piece of fiction should never
      "interpret experience and even less prescribe what it
      should be" is sharply contrasted with Tolstoy's belief
      that good art must be message ladden. James is criti-
      cized for questioning fiction which presents an "arbi-
      trary" view of reality on the grounds that his critique
      itself is based upon an arbitrary conception of what con-
      stitutes good fiction. It is concluded that each work of
      art is best judged on its own assumptions. The Death
      of Ivan Ilych is then favorably assessed for its fidelity
      to Tolstoy's assumptions on the nature of life and art.
      Also in Mod Fict St, 6, no. 4 (Winter 1960-1961), 314-
      324.

1398 Wellek, Rene. "Russian Conservative Critics: Leo Tolstoy"
      in A History of Modern Criticism, Vol. IV, The Late
      Nineteenth Century. New Haven, Conn. : University
      Press, 1965; 280-291. What Is Art? is not seen as the
      fanatical product of the elderly, post-conversion Tolstoy
      but rather as "a logical consequence of his constant,
      basic preoccupations. " The leading ideas of the work
      are then re-stated and placed within the context of the
      philosophy he followed during his entire adult life. It
      is argued that no matter how much one disagrees with
      his artistic views, they cannot be simply dismissed
      since they raise important questions still unsolved,
      namely the divorce between the artist and the masses,
      and the entire issue of the value of a popular, universal
      literature.

1399 Wimsatt, William K. , Jr. , and Cleanth Brooks. "The Real
      and the Social: Art as Propaganda" in Literary Criti-
      cism: A Short History. New York: Knopf, 1957; 454-
      474. Tolstoy's theory of art is commended for giving
      pointed expression to the aesthetic problem of whether
      non-didactic art is bound to be hedonistic. His negative
      commentary on modern art, however, is labeled "hor-
      rifying" in its sweep, and his arguing for art as a
      "monitor and propagandist for social progress" is con-
      sidered to have a direct link to contemporary Marxist
      literary criticism.

INTRODUCTIONS TO EDITIONS of What Is Art? and another work

1400 Greene, Militsa. What Is Art? London: Bradda, 1964, 251.

1401 Maude, Aylmer. What Is Art? Trans. by A. Maude. Lon-
      don: Constable, 1905, 278.

1402   Maude, Aylmer. What Is Art? Trans. by A. Maude. Lon-
        don: Oxford, 1929 (Centenary Edition).

1403   Tomas, Vincent. What Is Art? Trans. by A. Maude. New
        York: Library of Liberal Arts, 1960.

1404   Maude, Aylmer. Tolstoy on Art. Trans. by A. Maude.
        New York: Haskell, 1972 (reprint of 1924 publication).

PERIODICAL ARTICLES

1405   Adamovitch, George. "Tolstoy as an Artist," Rus R, 19
        (April 1960), 140-149.

1406   Austin, L. F. "Leo Tolstoy as a Critic of Maupassant,"
        Academy, 53 (1898), 180-181. Also in Cur Lit, 23
        (May 1898), 397-398.

1407   Bell, Clive. "Tolstoy on Art," Nat and Ath, 36 (7 March
        1925), 779.

1408   Bennett, J. "Tolstoy's What Is Art?," Musical T, 41
        (March 1900), 159-161; (April 1900), 231-233; (July
        1900), 446-448.

1409   Boyd, Ernest. "What Is Art?," Independent, 114 (25 April
        1925), 476.

1410   Bryusov, Valery. "On Art," RLT, 11 (Winter 1974), 201-
        210.

1411   Craig, E. G. "Tolstoy and Shakespeare," Drama, 10 (1934).

1412   Daniels, C. B. "Tolstoy and Corrupt Art," J Aesth Ed, 8,
        no. 4, (Oct. 1974), 41-49.

1413   Diller, G. P. "The Bolshevist Theory of Art," Poet Lore,
        31 (Sept. 1920), 454-459.

1414   Dole, Nathan A. "Tolstoy on Art," Bos Trans, (14 March
        1925), 4.

1415   Doumic, Rene. "Count Tolstoy's Theory of Art," Living
        Age, 218 (1898), 607-614.

1416   Dowd, J. "Tolstoy's Criticism of Modern Art," Pub Op,
        25 (2 Feb. 1899), 149. Also in Art Exchange, (Jan.
        1898).

1417   Ducasse, C. J. "What Has Beauty to Do with Art?," J
        Philos, 25 (1928), 181-186. Also in TCLA, 120-125.

1418   Geiger, Don. "Tolstoy as a Defender of a 'Pure Art' That Unwraps Something, " J Aesth Art Crit, 20 (Fall 1961), 81-89.

1419   Green, M. "Morality of Lolita, " Kenyon R, 28 (June 1966), 352-377. An application of Tolstoy's philosophy of art to Nabokov's Lolita.

1420   Halperine-Kaminsky, E. "Tolstoy on the Music of Wagner, " Music, 14 (August 1898), 345-356.

1421   Hare, Richard. "Did Tolstoy Correctly Diagnose the Disease of Modern Art?, " SEER, 36, no. 86 (Dec. 1957), 181-188.

1422   Headings, Philip R. "The Question of Exclusive Art: Tolstoy and T. S. Eliot's Wasteland, " R Langues V, 32 (1966), 82-95.

1423   Hornblow, Arthur. "Tolstoy's Denunciation of Contemporary Art, " Bookman, 12 (Dec. 1900), 383-387.

1424   Humboldt, C. "Tolstoy and Art, " Masses and Mainstream, 3 (August 1950), 69-84.

1425   Huybers, E. A. "Tolstoi, " Literature, 3 (6 August 1898), 116. A discussion of the futility of any attempt to evaluate art on a rigid basis such as in What Is Art?

1426   Hyde, George M. "Tolstoy's Gospel of Art, " Bookman, 8 (1898), 148-150.

1427   Jahn, G. R. "The Aesthetic Theory of Leo Tolstoy's What Is Art?, " J Aesth, 34, no. 1 (Fall 1975), 59-65.

1428   Kane, Robert J. "Tolstoy, Goethe and King Lear, " Shksp Asso B, 21, no. 4 (1946), 159-160.

1429   Kenworthy, John C. "On Tolstoy's What Is Art?, " St George, 1 (April 1898), 67-71.

1430   Knox, Israel. "Notes on the Moralistic Theory of Art: Plato and Tolstoy, " Int J Aesth, 41 (July 1931), 507-510. Also in TCLA, 102-104.

1431   Knox, Israel. "Tolstoy's Esthetic Definition of Art, " J Philos, 27 (1930), 65-70.

1432   Laugel, Auguste. "Tolstoy on Art, " Nation, 67 (1898), 275-276, 308-309.

1433   Lee, Vernon. "Tolstoy on Art, " Quarterly R, 191 (April 1900), 359-372. Also in Gospels of Anarchy, 133-158; and TCLA, 57-66.

1434 Levin, Y. D. "Tolstoy, Shakespeare and the Russian Writers
      of the 1860's, " Oxford S P, 1 n. s. (1968), 85-104. A
      discussion of Tolstoy's opinion on Shakespeare based on
      psychological, social, and ethical as well as aesthetic
      considerations.

1435 Lowe, C. "Arts and the Average Man, " Can Mus J, 3
      (Winter 1959), 21-24.

1436 Macy, John A. "Tolstoy's Moral Theory of Art, " Century,
      62 (June 1901), 298-307. Also in TCLA, 66-78.

1437 Marvin, F. S. "Tolstoi on Art, " Positivist R, 7 (June 1899),
      110-113.

1438 Maude, Aylmer. "Tolstoy's Relation to Art, " Sackbut, 7,
      no. 7 (Feb. 1927), 183-186.

1439 Maude, Aylmer. "Tolstoy's Theory of Art, " Contemp R, 78
      (August 1900), 241-254. Also in TP, 102-127.

1440 Mayor, Joseph B. "Tolstoy as a Shakespeare Critic, " Royal
      Soc Lit Trans, 2, no. 28 (1908), 23-55.

1441 Mirsky, Dmitri S. "Tolstoy on Art, " SEER, 3 (March 1925),
      739-740.

1442 Moore, George. "Avowals, " Lippincott's M, 72 (Nov. 1903),
      608-616; 72 (Dec. 1903), 697-703. Also in Avowals
      (item 1389), 137-164.

1443 More, Paul Elmer. "The Ancient Feud between Philosophy
      and Art, " Atlantic M, 86 (Sept. 1900), 337-347. Also
      in Shelburne Essays, 1 (1906), 193-224; and The Modern
      Reader: Essays on Present Day Life and Culture, 618-
      628.

1444 Murry, John M. "The Essence of Art, " Forum, 74 (1925),
      562-573.

1445 Orwell, George. "Lear, Tolstoy and the Fool, " Polemic, 7
      (March 1947). Also in Shooting an Elephant and Other
      Essays, 32-52; Listener, 25 (1941).

1446 Parkin, C. F. "Tolstoy's What Is Art?, " NZSJ, 4 (1969),
      54-67.

1447 Perris, C. H. "Tolstoy's What Is Art?, " Architectural R,
      4 (Oct. 1898), 213.

1448 Phythian, Ernest J. "Tolstoy's What Is Art?, " Manchester
      Q, 20 (April 1901), 184-203.

1449   Porter, Alan. "Tolstoy on Art, " Spectator, 134 (21 March
        1925), 451.

1450   "The Quarterly on Tolstoi, " RRs, 22 (1900), 91-92. A synop-
        sis and brief discussion of the Quarterly Reviews, April,
        1900 article on What Is Art?

1451   Read, Herbert. "Tolstoy's Theory of Art, " Adam, nos. 284-
        286 (1960), 18-23.

1452   Rudy, Peter. "Tolstoy on Shakespeare, " SEEJ, 14 (1970), 92.

1453   Shorter, Kingsley. "Writers and Writing: Tolstoy's Com-
        plaint, " New Leader, 54 (17 May 1971), 21-23.

1454   Silbarjoris, Rimvydas. "Lev Tolstoy: Aesthetics and Art, "
        RLT, 1 (1971), 58-72.

1455   Silbarjoris, Rimvydas. "Tolstoy's Aesthetics in Soviet Per-
        spective, " Bucknell M, 18 (1971), 103-116.

1456   Spielman, M. H. "What Is Art?, " Literature, 3, no. 4 (30
        July 1898), 77-79.

1457   Thurber, A. "Tolstoy's Art, " Sewanee R, 22, no. 3 (July
        1914), 329-340.

1458   "Tolstoy, " Living Age, 268 (Jan. 1911), 46-50. A study of
        the relationship between Tolstoy's views on art and his
        fiction.

1459   "Tolstoy and Corrupt Art, " J Aesth Ed, 8, no. 4 (Oct. 1974),
        41-49.

1460   "Tolstoy on Art, " Pop Science M, 53 (Oct. 1898), 553-556.

1461   "Tolstoy on Art, " Times Lit Sup, (14 May 1925), 328.

1462   "Tolstoy on Shakespeare, " Catholic W, 84 (March 1907), 836.

1463   "Tolstoy on Shakespeare, " Cur Lit, 42 (Jan. 1907), 46.

1464   "Tolstoy on Shakespeare, " Independent, 62 (21 Feb. 1907),
        441.

1465   "Tolstoy on Shakespeare, " Lit D, 34 (9 Feb. 1907), 218.

1466   "Tolstoy on Shakespeare, " Living Age, 323 (4 Oct. 1924), 64-
        65.

1467   "Tolstoy on Shakespeare, " N Y Times, 11 (8 Dec. 1906), 850.

1468   "Tolstoy on Shakespeare, " RRs, 35 (Feb. 1907), 253.

1469   "Tolstoy, Shakespeare and the Drama," Nation, 124 (12 Jan.
       1927), 45.

1470   "Tolstoy's Theory of Art," Quarterly R, 191 (April 1900),
       359-372.

1471   Tomas, Vincent. "Kandinsky's Theory of Painting," Br J
       Aesth, 9, no. 1 (1969), 19-38. A discussion of Kandin-
       sky's theory of art and its similarities to that of Tolstoy.

1472   "The Verdict of the World on Tolstoy's Assault on Shake-
       speare," Cur Lit, 43 (1907), 200-203.

1473   Wasiolek, Edmund. "Tolstoy's The Death of Ivan Ilytch and
       Jamesian Fictional Imperatives," Mod Fict St, 6, no. 4
       (Winter 1960-1961), 314-324.

1474   "What Good Is Art?," Etude, 63 (August 1945), 423-424.

1475   "What Is Art?," Bib Sacra, 55 (1898), 772-773.

1476   "What Is Art?," Book News, 17, no. 193 (Sept. 1898), 23.

1477   "What Is Art?," Critic, 33 (Sept. 1898), 184-189.

1478   "What Is Art?," Lit W, 29, no. 18 (3 Sept. 1898), 277.

1479   Wheal, Elizabeth. "What Is Art?," Hum Asso B, 21 (1970),
       14-16.

1480   Wolkonsky, S. "Tolstoi's Negations," Living Age, 213 (12
       June 1897), 771-774. A criticism of Tolstoy's views on
       art and negative ideas on progress.

1481   Yarros, Victor S. "Tolstoy on Art and Beauty," Dial, 24
       (April 1898), 249-251.

DISSERTATIONS

1482   Ater, Leroy E. "An Examination of Three Major Novels in
       World Literature in Light of Critical Precepts Derived
       from Tolstoy's What Is Art?," Univ. of So. Cal., 1964.

1483   Moore, Arthur U. "Art, Community and Theatre. A Study
       of the Theories of Five Nineteenth Century Artists:
       Tolstoy, Wagner, Nietzsche, Appia, Rolland," Cornell
       University, 1936.

       See also: 39, 50, 59, 80, 133, 161, 323, 333, 341, 465,
       507, 523, 524, 539, 549, 560, 569, 576, 603, 635, 636,
       641, 665, 707, 813, 1220, 1243, 1259, 1275, 1319, 1320,
       1333, 1336, 1800, 1807, 1809, 1841, 1870, 1871, 2031,
       2034, 2035, 2044.

Section VI

EDUCATION

BOOKS

1484 Baudouin, Charles. Tolstoi: The Teacher. Trans. by Fred
Rothwell. New York: Dutton, 1923; 218p. A discussion of the origin and development of Tolstoy's educational philosophy precedes a favorable analysis of its
basic principles. Although Tolstoy never coordinated
his educational views into one complete work, a funda-
mental unity is seen in his pedagogical thought centered
about the desire to eliminate in education all "that hind-
ers the free development of life. " This prime contention
is linked to various aspects of his work in education,
and it is concluded that his thought and efforts make him
the ideological father of the experimental science of
teaching. Also included are a number of documents
supplied by Paul Biriukov, friend and disciple of Tolstoy,
concerning Tolstoy's educational views and work. Reviewed in:
    Lit D, (July 1924), p. 593, by Alexander Nazaroff.
    Lit R, (14 July 1924), p. 820, by Arthur Ruhl.
    New Sta, 22 (Jan. 1924), p. 404.
    N Y Times, (4 May 1924), p. 23.

1485 Crosby, Ernest H. Tolstoy as a Schoolmaster. Chicago:
Hammersmark, 1904; 94p. An account, by the friend
of Tolstoy, of the leading features of the school established at Yasnaya Polyana. No separate analysis of his
philosophy of education is provided, but his beliefs become apparent by way of descriptions of his views on
such subjects as discipline, methodology, and examination. Special support is given for his emphasis on
"teaching the child when it wishes to learn, " "making
the child its own chief teacher, " and "providing the wid-
est possible range of subjects" to select for study.
Over all, sympathy is shown for Tolstoy's non-structured
approach to learning. Originally published as a series
of articles in The Whim, (Nov. 1900); also in his Complete Education (Toledo, 1903).

ESSAYS AND CHAPTERS from general works

1486   Baudouin, Charles.   "Tolstoy as Educationalist, " in <u>Contem-</u>
          <u>porary Studies.</u>   Freeport, N. Y. :   Books for <u>Libraries</u>
          <u>Press, 1969</u> (reprint of 1924 publication); 19-23.   It is
          argued that the ideas that Tolstoy saw as essential in
          the regulation of life were but a generalization for adults
          "of the ideas he had always advocated where children
          were concerned, " namely the importance of love, free-
          dom, and the avoidance of the use of force.   Support
          for this contention is provided by examples from how
          his school at Yasnaya Polyana functioned.

1487   Mayer, Frederick.   "Tolstoy, " in <u>The Great Teachers.</u>   New
          York: Citadel Press, 1976; 273-286.   The ideas and
          methods associated with Tolstoy's teachings as a novel-
          ist, moralist, and educator are examined, with special
          concern for his work in education.   Presented in a fav-
          orable light are his beliefs that education must not be
          "indoctrination" if the dignity of the individual is to be
          maintained, that educators must accept "a sense of so-
          cial responsibility, " and that "man can progress only
          through self-examination. "   Tolstoy's philosophy and in-
          fluence outside of education are also discussed though
          in a more critical manner.

INTRODUCTIONS

1488   Archambault, Reginald.   <u>Tolstoy on Education.</u>   Trans. by
          Leo Weiner.   Chicago: University of Chicago Press,
          1967; 360p.

PERIODICAL ARTICLES

1489   Battersby, H.   "Tolstoy as a Schoolmaster, " <u>W Work</u>,   19
          (Feb. 1912), 244-250.

1490   Bunnell, W. S.   "Tolstoy and Freedom: An Examination of
          the Implications of His Educational Ideals, " <u>Resch St</u>, 11
          (Jan. 1955), 32-51.

1491   Calam, John.   "Tolstoy on Education, " <u>Sat R Lit</u>, 51 (March
          1968), 80.

1492   Crosby, Ernest H.   "A True Story, " <u>Whim,</u> (Nov. 1901).   A
          series of articles on Tolstoy's school at Yasnaya Poly-
          ana.   See Crosby's <u>Tolstoy as a Schoolmaster</u> (item
          1485).

1493   Davis, A. O.   "Tolstoy's Magic Rod: The Tolstoy School and
          Museum at Yasnaya Polyana, " <u>Survey</u>, 49 (March 1923),
          698, 740.

181   Education

1494 Duane, Michael. "Tolstoy at School," New Society, (7 March
      1968), 351-352.

1495 Farrar, F. W. "Count Tolstoi on Education," Forum, 1888.

1496 Goncharov, N. K. "Pedagogical Ideas and Practice of L. N.
      Tolstoi," Soviet Ed, 4 (Oct. 1962), 3-15.

1497 Mirguet, V. "Tolstoy as a School Superintendent," Pub Op,
      39, no. 13 (23 Sept. 1905), 403. Translated from Revue
      des Belgique.

1498 "The Montessori Method at Work. Tolstoy and Montessori,"
      Times Ed Sup, (4 Sept. -18 Dec. 1919).

1499 Mueller, R. J. "Enter and Leave Freely: A Description of
      Count L. Tolstoy's School at Yasnaya Polyana," Phi
      Delta Kappan, 44 (June 1963), 435-437.

1500 "Pass or Fail--1845," Alberta J Ed Res, 15, no. 2 (Jan.
      1969), 71-75.

1501 Pioli, Giovanni. "Leo Tolstoy; the Educationalist," Contemp
      R, 107 (1915), 263-266.

1502 Radosavljevich, Paul R. "The Spirit of Tolstoy's Experimen-
      tal School," Sch and Soc, 29, no. 737 (9 Feb. 1929),
      175-183; 29, no. 738 (16 Feb. 1929), 208-215.

1503 Roszack, Theodore. "Tolstoy: The School Was All My Life,"
      Times Ed Sup, 2966 (24 March 1972), 1681, illus. A
      discussion of a two-part BBC film on the life of Tolstoy.

1504 Sadler, Michael E. "Education According to Tolstoy," Ed R,
      41 (May 1911), 433-440.

1505 Shneidman, N. N. "Soviet Approaches to the Teaching of Lit-
      erature. A Case Study: L. Tolstoy in Soviet Educa-
      tion," Can S P, 15 (1973), 325-350.

1506 "Tolstoi's Ideas on Education," School J, (Oct. 1890). Also
      in Pub Op, 9, no. 26 (4 Oct. 1890), 606-607.

1507 "Tolstoy on Education," SEER, 47 (1969), 540-541.

1508 Vaikshan, B. A. "Educators of Other Lands on Leo N. Tol-
      stoy," J Sov Ed, 1 (Nov. 1958).

1509 Zweers, A. F. "Tolstoy on Education," Can Slavic S, 4
      (Summer 1970), 347-348.

See also: 66, 523, 733, 929, 1306, 1645, 1879.

Section VII

RELIGION

BOOKS

1510 Craufurd, Alexander H. The Religion and Ethics of Tolstoy.
London: Unwin, 1912. Tolstoy is labeled as "great an
ethical and spiritual guide" as he was an author. It is
denied that his religious conversion represented an ab-
negation of his artistic views or qualities, but rather his
novels "were only a prelude to his conversion," which,
like his fiction, was the outcome of personal experience
and intuition combined. His religious beliefs are then
summarized, and it is suggested that the mixture of
melancholy and hopefulness that characterizes them is due
to the fact that he was pessimistic over the current condition of the world but optimistic as to its eventual deli-
verance: "Real mysticism is both sorrowful and always
rejoicing." Other aspects of his thought are not as
favorably assessed; in particular he is criticized for trying to make art "too exclusively moral and social" and
his pacifist views are rejected on the grounds that "as
long as there are tyrants ... in the world, it is necessary that they should be actively resisted."

1511 Holmes, John Haynes. Leo Tolstoy: A Sermon. New York:
Church of the Messiah, 1911; 27p. A sermon given
three weeks after Tolstoy's death in which his literature,
philosophy, and life style are all commended. Tolstoy's
renouncing of literature at the time of his religious conversion, and his devotion to moral preaching thereafter
is discussed in a positive light. Those who fault his
"unorthodox" interpretation of the New Testament and
his renunciation of literature are criticized for overlooking the point that his love for humanity, peace, and justice all developed as a result of his conversion and far
outweigh the negative side of the later Tolstoy. In conclusion, his conversion is considered to be the natural
consequence of a thinking-feeling man living in the conditions of late 19th-century Russia.

ESSAYS AND CHAPTERS from general works

1512   Atkins, Gaius Glenn.   "Tolstoy's Confessions" in Pilgrims of
        the Lonely Road.   Freeport, N. Y.: Books for Libraries
        Press, 1967 (reprint of 1913 publication); 281-334.   Tol-
        stoy is considered to be admirable not for his beliefs,
        which may or may not be correct, but for his pursuit of
        faith, for readjusting his own life, and for trying to re-
        adjust that of the world in line with his convictions.
        His spiritual development is then traced up to and in-
        cluding his conversion as revealed in his Confession.
        No final judgment is passed on his convictions, though
        he is called "a better witness than a guide, " but he is
        upheld as a fine example to the world because of his
        "passionate humanity, persistent courage and kindling
        fidelity to his own ideals. "

1513   Burns, Cecil D.   "Tolstoy and Christianity" in The Principles
        of Revolution: A Study in Ideals.   London, 1920; 89-
        108.   Tolstoy's views on the evilness of property and
        violence are presented, and his alternative to modern
        society, Christianity as a practical guide to life, is dis-
        cussed.   Emphasized is that his support of non-resist-
        ance as the path to true Christianity must be studied in
        light of his belief that workers must organize production
        for themselves--that is, return to a simple existence
        based upon small production units.   This belief is seen
        as being the truly revolutionary aspect of his thought,
        but his failure to consider any organizational means to
        reach this simple, Christian existence is thought to
        represent a fatal obstacle to its realization.

1514   Cheslet, William.   "Tolstoy's Reassertion of Christianity" in
        Modern and Near Modern; Essays on Henry James,
        Stockton, Shaw and Others.   New York: Grafton Press,
        1928; 212-215.

1515   Clutton-Brock, Arthur.   "The Remedy: A Review of Tol-
        stoy's Christianity and Patriotism" in More Essays on
        Religion.   Freeport, N. Y.: Books for Libraries Press,
        1971 (reprint of 1928 publication); 169-175.   Tolstoy's
        attack on patriotism as an emotion that has outlived its
        usefulness is summarized, and he is criticized for fail-
        ing to suggest any means for dealing with the "evil" of
        patriotism.   The remedy is seen as not preaching against
        patriotism, as Tolstoy did, but in "discovering the un-
        conscious causes of it in the human mind. "   Christianity,
        it is argued, taught what Tolstoy preached for 2000 years
        yet war and patriotism remain; hence a scientific ap-
        proach to the problem is needed.

1516   Eddy, G. Sherwood.   "The Modern Discovery of God" in Man
        Discovers God.   Freeport, N. Y.: Books for Libraries

Press, 1969 (reprint of 1942 publication); 185-192. Tolstoy's religious philosophy is examined and judged to be
"characteristically Russian" in that it is extreme and
impractical as a guide to life. He is seen as being at
his best as a critic, a destroyer, but deficient as a
teacher or a positive reformer. It is concluded that his
philosophy, though humanistic, is not acceptable, and,
in fact, failed to bring peace of mind even to its author.

1517   Farrar, F. W. "Count Leo Tolstoi" in Social and Present
Day Questions. Boston, 1891; 343-54. A discussion of
Tolstoy's interpretation of Christianity, with much reference to his Confession. Also in Forum, 6 (Oct. 1888),
109-124.

1518   Florovsky, George. "Three Masters: The Quest for Religion in Nineteenth Century Russian Literature" in Man-
sions of the Spirit, ed. George Panichas. New York:
Hawthorn, 1967; 157-179. An account of Tolstoy's religious awakening precedes a critical analysis of his religious beliefs and overall philosophy of life. He is considered to be most impressive as an outspoken critic of
"human ills and contradictions, " but his positive program
is viewed as being "poor and somewhat superficial, "
never going beyond an "invitation to understand and with-
draw. " His aggressive invectives contrasted with the
poverty of his program is seen as paradoxical, and his
Christ appears to be just a "teacher of the happy life"
who Tolstoy spoke about "without any fervent spark. "
Also in CLS, 3 (1966), 119-137.

1519   Giddings, Franklin H. "The Gospel of Non-resistance" in
Democracy and Empire with Studies of Their Psychological, Economic and Moral Foundations. New York: Macmillan, 1900; 341-357. Tolstoy is considered as the
leader and spokesman for the Christian principle that the
good life consists of "the surrender of earthly possessions and perfect obedience to the command to resist
not evil. " However, since the world is engaged in an
arms race and examples of imperialism abound, Tolstoy's gospel of non-resistance is rejected as being un-
realistic. Also rejected are the opposite philosophies
of Darwin and Nietzsche dealing with survival of the fit-
test. A middle position between the extremism of Tolstoy and his opposites is suggested as the best path for
the world to follow.

1520   Hunter, Robert. "How Tolstoy Sought the Truth and Tried to
Live the Truth" in Why We Fail as Christians. New
York: Macmillan, 1919; 8-33. An account of the religious views of Tolstoy and how he attempted to live his
life in line with them precedes a comparison between
his teachings and those of Christ. Tolstoy's simple

habits, love of physical labor, and communion with the
peasants are seen as the principal ways he tried "to
live the truth, " but, in reality, his philosophy is viewed
as unrealizable because of its severity. It is regarded
as impossible to find a world of men willing to become
ascetics for the sake of Christianity, and that some material basis for Christianity is necessary.

1521 James, William. "The Divided Self" in The Varieties of Re-
      ligious Experience: A Study in Human Nature. New
      York: Random House, 1929; 180-185. Tolstoy's disen-
      chantment with his surroundings after his religious awak-
      ening is seen to have abated as he came to the realiza-
      tion that it was only the life of the educated classes that
      repulsed him, a realization based on his observation of
      the peace of mind had by the common, uneducated man.
      His subsequent pursuit of a simple, Christian existence
      is considered to be an extension of this realization. Ex-
      cerpt in LTCA, 123-24.

1522 James, William. "The Sick Soul" in The Varieties of Reli-
      gious Experience: A Study in Human Nature. 146-154.
      Tolstoy's Confession is presented as a classic case of
      "religious melancholy" leading to anhedonia or "passive
      loss of appetite for all life's values" which, in turn,
      led him to a painful and continuous search for philosophic
      relief from a world that came to appear remote and
      sinister.

1523 McAlpin, Edwin A. "Tolstoi's Conception of Christianity" in
      Old and New Books as Life Teachers. Garden City,
      N. Y. : Doubleday, Doran, 1928; 154-172. Tolstoy's in-
      terpretation of Christianity is summarized, and its heart
      isolated as being the removal of "religion out of the
      realm of dialectics and making it a practical science of
      daily life. " The rules he outlined as guidelines for life
      are simple and easy to understand, it is granted, but
      nearly impossible to practice. Separate from the ques-
      tion of the practicality of his concept of Christianity,
      Tolstoy is seen as deserving support for proposing that
      religion be "a vital element in life. "

1524 Muggeridge, Malcolm. "Leo Tolstoy: 1828-1910" in A Third
      Testament. Boston: Little, Brown, 1976; 146-179. A
      television script in which Tolstoy, along with five other
      individuals, is discussed in terms of his need "to be
      called back to God to rediscover humility and, with it,
      hope. " His religious conversion and general philosophy
      are examined as an extension of his search for a mean-
      ing for life.

1525 Niebuhrs, Richard. Christ and Culture. New York: 1951.
      Contains a section on Tolstoy's religious philosophy.
      Unavailable for annotation.

1526   Panin, Ivan.   "Tolstoy the Artist" in <u>Lectures on Russian</u>
       <u>Literature</u>.   New York: Putnam, 1889; 154-189.   In his
       fiction, Tolstoy is regarded as a spokesman for God be-
       cause he proclaims "what is permanent and everlasting:
       obedience to God and love to man. "   For this reason,
       he is seen as representing the greatest combination of
       lofty aspirations and artistic skill that is possible, a
       combination which has determined the essential character
       of his art: "it does not so much depict the event itself
       as its effect on the soul. "

1527   Panin, Ivan.   "Tolstoy the Preacher" in <u>Lectures on Russian</u>
       <u>Literature</u>, 190-220.   Tolstoy is discussed as a mes-
       senger of God "sent to gather together the erring flock
       ... to the folds of Christ. "   In addition to following the
       words of Christ as a practical guide to life, the philos-
       ophy of Tolstoy is deemed to rest on the principle of
       "the supremacy of the heart over the head as a meta-
       physical guide to life. "   Support is also given to his
       emphasis on the brotherhood of all men.

1528   Poteat, Edwin M.   "Tolstoy: Religion without Redemption"
       in <u>The Scandal of the Cross: Studies in the Death of</u>
       <u>Jesus</u>.   New York: Harper and Brothers, 1928; 142-182.
       Tolstoy's rejection of the Christian concept of redemption
       as embodied in Christ, his view of Christ as a great
       sage and not a divine being, and his general outlook on
       life are discussed with parallels drawn to Buddhism.
       Although Tolstoy is applauded for the sincerity of his
       convictions and for trying to live his life in accord with
       his beliefs, his religious philosophy is seen as suffering
       from a fatal flaw, "his missing the essential fact: the
       forgiveness of sins through our Lord Jesus Christ. "

1529   Smith, Bradford.   "Tolstoy: Christian Pacifism" in <u>Men of</u>
       <u>Peace</u>.   Philadelphia: Lippincott, 1964; 157-181.   A
       discussion of Tolstoy's quest for a meaning to life pre-
       cedes a commentary on his Christian pacifism and an-
       archism.   His religious and ethical writings are analyzed
       and positively assessed for their nobility, but the work-
       ability of his philosophy is questioned, particularly in
       light of his own failure to live in line with his beliefs.

1530   Sprague, Leslie W.   "Lyof N. Tolstoy and the Social Message
       of Christianity" in <u>Six Lectures on Social Messages of</u>
       <u>Some Nineteenth Century Prophets</u>.   Philadelphia, 1903;
       12-16.

1531   Tsanoff, Radoslav A.   "Count Leo Tolstoy" in <u>Autobiographies</u>
       <u>of Ten Religious Leaders</u>.   San Antonio, Texas: Trinity
       <u>University Press, 1968; 201-229</u>.   Tolstoy's religious
       philosophy is presented by way of events from his life
       which illustrate its basic principles, with supporting in-

formation being drawn from his writings, both fiction and essays. Additionally, comparisons are made between the leading points of his philosophy and the teachings of Christ.

1532   Tsanoff, Radoslav A. "The Gospel of Tolstoy the Apostle" in The Problem of Life in the Russian Novel. Houston: Rice Institute Pamphlet, 1917; 238-272. Tolstoy's spiritual awakening is regarded not as a sudden change but one that "must have been lurking in his inner nature during his whole life." The roots of this awakening are traced, and his religious-ethical beliefs summarized with frequent mention of his works. It is admitted that his ideal of life may not be realizable, but his quest for spiritual perfection is nonetheless considered admirable.

1533   Turgenev, Ivan. "Letter to D. V. Grigorvich" in LTCA, 55. An 1882 letter in which Tolstoy's Confession is praised for its "sincerity, truthfulness and power of conviction," but criticized for being based on a gloomy, false premise leading to nihilism. Translated from Polnoe Sobranie Sochineniy i Pisem.

1534   Wallace, Archer. "Leo Tolstoy" in The Religious Faith of Great Men. Freeport, N.Y.: Books for Libraries Press, 1967 (reprint of 1934 publication); 38-42. Tolstoy's abandonment of his faith during his youth is identified as the source of his early spiritual misery and fruitless quest for life's meaning. His conversion is positively portrayed and his unique brand of Christianity briefly summarized. His greatest contribution is judged to be his "honest attempt to apply to modern life the world renouncing ethics of Jesus."

1535   Ward, May Alden. "The Gospel of Count Tolstoi" in Prophets of the Nineteenth Century: Carlyle, Ruskin, Tolstoi. Boston: Little, Brown, 1900; 137-189. Tolstoy's life and works are discussed as a means of tracing the steps which led him to become a most striking example of an attempt to live the life of Christ. His military and university years, his work in education, and his family life, it is argued, all failed to bring meaning to his existence and brought him to a spiritual crisis for which modern philosophy and civilization could provide no relief. His observation that the simple masses had meaningful lives because of faith is viewed as that which led him to his interpretation of Christianity as a practical guide to life.

INTRODUCTIONS TO EDITIONS

1536   Garland, Hamlin. The Kingdom of God Is Within You, and Peace Essays. Trans. by A. Maude. London: Oxford, 1937 (Centenary Edition); 516p.

1537 Garnett, Edward. Christianity and Patriotism. Trans. by
      Constance Garnett. London: Cape, 1922; 112p.

1538 Hall, Bolton. What Tolstoy Taught. London: Chatto & Wind-
      us, 1913; 275p.

1539 Hopper, S. R. Lift Up Your Eyes: Religious Writings of
      L. Tolstoy. New York: Julian Press, 1960; 581p.

1540 Lyttleton, Edith. Confession, and What I Believe. London:
      Oxford, 1933; 539p., vol. 11.

1541 Martin, Mary. Kingdom of God Is Within You. Trans. by
      L. Wiener. 1951; 380p.

1542 Maude, Aylmer. Confession, The Gospel in Brief and What
      I Believe. Trans. by A. Maude. London: Oxford,
      1940; 539p.

1543 Maude, Aylmer. Kingdom of God and Peace Essay. Trans.
      by A. Maude. London: Oxford, 1936; 591p.

1544 Maude, Aylmer. On Life and Essays on Religion. Trans.
      A. Maude. London: Oxford, 1934; 412p.

1545 Rexroth, Kenneth. The Kingdom of God Is Within You.
      Trans. by L. Wiener. New York: Noonday, 1961; 380p.

1546 Smith, Sybil. On Life. Trans. by A. Maude. London: Ox-
      ford, vol. 12.

1547 Stanton, Theodore. The Higher Life. New York: 1910.

1548 Zweig, S. Living Thoughts of Tolstoy. Trans. by B. Mus-
      sey. New York: Longmans, 1939; 154p.

1549 Zweig, S. Living Thoughts of Tolstoy. Greenwich, Conn.:
      Faucett, 1963; 160p.

PERIODICAL ARTICLES

1550 Abraham, J. H. "Religious Ideas and Social Philosophy of
      Tolstoy, " Int J Ethics, 40 (Oct. 1929), 105-120.

1551 Bascom, J. "The Complexity of Religious Beliefs, " Dial,
      28 (Jan. 1900), 18-20. A review of Christian Teaching.

1552 Bixby, J. T. "Tolstoy and the New Quakerism, " Arena, 28
      (August 1902), 133-151.

1553 Blavatsky, H. P. "The Science of Life, " Theosoph Tract S,
      2 (1890). A review of Tolstoy's views on science and
      life.

1554   Blavatsky, H. P.   "A True Theosophist--Count Tolstoy, "
       Theosoph Tract S, nos. 1 or 2 (1890).

1555   Brinton, C.   "Tolstoy Under the Ban of the Church, " Critic,
       37 (Sept. 1900).

1556   Carpenter, Bishop B.   "Reply to The Kingdom of God Is With-
       in You, " New Review, 10, 186.

1557   Carpenter, Fredric I.   "A Letter from Tolstoy, " New Eng Q,
       4, no. 4 (Oct. 1931), 777-782.

1558   "The Christian Teaching, " Pub Op, 25 (3 Nov. 1898), 569.

1559   "Christianity and Woman's Love.   Colonel Ingersoll on Count
       Tolstoy, " RRs, 2 (Oct. 1890), 343.   A discussion of
       Ingersoll's attack on the Kreutzer Sonata in the North
       American Review.

1560   "Church and State, " Lit W, 22, no. 7 (28 March 1891), 113-
       114.   A review of Church and State and On Money.

1561   Clarallan, David.   "Tolstoy's Doctrine of Jesus, " Open Court,
       22 (Sept. 1908), 513-521.

1562   "Count Tolstoi on Essential Christianity, " Outlook, 52 (10
       August 1895), 210-211.

1563   "Count Tolstoi's Excommunication, " Outlook, 67 (13 April
       1901), 841-842.   Also in Independent, 52 (Oct. 1900),
       2401-2402.

1564   "Count Tolstoi's Gospel Stories, " Pub Op, 10, no. 2 (18 Oct.
       1890), 46.

1565   "Countess Tolstoi's Protest, " Pub Op, 30, no. 16 (18 April
       1901).   Concerning Countess Tolstoy's protest over her
       husband's excommunication.   Also in Outlook, (April
       1901).

1566   "Creative Peace: Tolstoy on Non-resistance, " Times Lit Sup,
       21, no. 1768 (Dec. 1935) 865-866.   A review of Kingdom
       of God Is Within You and four other essays in the Cen-
       tenary Edition of Tolstoy's works.

1567   Crosby, Ernest H.   "Tolstoy's Plan of Redemption, " Living
       Age, 219 (1898), 386-388.

1568   Cuffe, H. O.   "Tolstoy's Book The Kingdom of God Is Within
       You; Christianity According to Tolstoy, " Lucifer, 19
       (Dec. 1896), 330.

1569   "The Decree of Tolstoy's Excommunication, " Cur Lit, 31
       (1901), 232.

1570 Dicast. "Failure of Count Leo Tolstoy's Religion, " Independent, 53 (March 1901), 725-727.

1571 Dillon, E. J. "Count Tolstoy's Faith and Practice, " RRs, 5 (Jan. 1892), 35-37.

1572 Dirscherl, Denis. "The Crisis of Faith in Leo Tolstoy, " Am Ben R, 17 (1966), 229-237.

1573 Eggleston, F. O. "Count Tolstoi and the Problems of Life, " Unitr R, 34 (July 1890), 79-83.

1574 Evans, Henry R. "Lyof Tolstoi--the Thirteenth Apostle, " New Age, 26 (1918), 248-252.

1575 "The Excommunication of Tolstoi, " Pub Op, 28, no. 25 (21 June 1910), 788.

1576 "The Excommunication of Tolstoy, " Independent, 52 (4 Oct. 1900), 2401-2402. Also in Outlook, 67 (13 April 1901), 841-842.

1577 "The Excommunication of Tolstoy, " Pub Op, 29, no. 15 (11 Oct. 1900), 465-466.

1578 Farrar, F. W. "Count Leo Tolstoi, " Forum, 6 (Oct. 1888), 109-124. A discussion of Tolstoy's Christianity with much reference to his Confession. Also in Farrar, F. W. , Social and Present Day Questions (1891), 343-354.

1579 Farrar, F. W. "Count Tolstoy's Religious Views, " Forum, 6 (Dec. 1888), 337-349.

1580 Faville, John. "Count Lyoff N. Tolstoi on Immorality, " Andover R, 5 (12 May 1888), 120-121.

1581 Faville, John. "Tolstoy on Immortality, " Andover R, 9 (1888), 499-511.

1582 Florovsky, George. "Three Masters: The Quest for Religion in the Nineteenth Century, " CLS, 3 (1966), 119-137.

1583 Fülöp-Miller, Rene. "Tolstoy, the Apostolic Crusader, " Rus R, 19 (April 1960), 99-121.

1584 Gunning, W. D. "Tolstoy and Primitive Christianity, " Open Court, 1 (1887), 398-400.

1585 Hale, E. E. "Confessions of Leo Tolstoy, " Lend a Hand, 2, no. 9 (Sept. 1887), 531-537.

1586 Heier, Edmund. "A Note on the Pashkovites and Leo N. Tolstoy, " Can S P, 5 (1961), 114-121. A discussion of

Tolstoy's negative impression of the Pashkovites even
though their humanitarian ideals were similar to his own.

1587   Heier, Edmund.   "Tolstoj and the Evangelical Revival among
       Russian Aristocracy, " RLT, 9 (1971), 28-48.

1588   Horton, S.   "On Tolstoy, " Prim Meth Q R, 33 (Jan. 1891),
       37.

1589   Houghton, R. C.   "Count Lyof Tolstoi, " Methodist R, 71, no.
       3 (May-June 1889), 377-394.   A discussion of Tolstoy's
       religious views and his interpretation of Christ with
       reference to My Religion, Confession and Anna Karenina.

1590   "How Tolstoy Defined the Best Religion, " Cur Lit, 50 (Feb.
       1911), 182-183.

1591   Hubbard, Sara C.   "The Confession of Count Tolstoi, " Dial,
       8 (Oct. 1887), 125-127.   Concerning Tolstoy's religious
       views with reference to My Religion and My Confession.

1592   Hutton, John A.   "Pilgrims in the Region of Faith, " Edinbg
       R, (1913), 103-146.

1593   Ingersoll, Robert.   "Ingersoll on Tolstoi, " Freethought, 3
       (1885), 583.

1594   Jackson, S. T.   "The People's Prophet, " Methodist R, 68
       (Sept. 1908), 780-786.

1595   Jahn, G. R.   "Structural Analysis of Leo Tolstoy's God Sees
       the Truth but Waits, " St Short Fic, 12 (Summer 1975),
       261-269.

1596   Jutten, D. B.   "The Religion of Count Tolstoy, " Baptist Q R,
       10 (1888), 307-331.

1597   Keeble, Samuel.   "The Religious Teaching of Count Tolstoi, "
       W Meth M, 121 (1898), 745-751.

1598   Knowlson, Thomas S.   "Tolstoy's My Confession.   The Con-
       fession of an Inquiring Spirit, " Great Thoughts, 5 (Jan.
       1900), 263.

1599   Krauskopf, Joseph.   "The Apostle of Russia, " Our Pulpit, 9,
       no. 4 (1895-1896).

1600   Krauskopf, Joseph.   "Tolstoi Excommunicated, " Our Pulpit,
       14, no. 4 (11 Nov. 1900), 1-7.

1601   L., A. F.   "Remarkable Phenomena in Connection with the
       Portraits of Count Tolstoy, " Outlook, 69 (7 Dec. 1901),
       950-951.   A discussion of the charge by the Orthodox

Church that the facial expressions in Tolstoy's portraits have become more satanic since his excommunication.

1602   Large, E. C. "Towards Tolstoy," Adelphi, 13, no. 11 (August 1937), 428-431. On the religious views of Tolstoy.

1603   Laugel, A. "Tolstoi's My Religion," Nation, 41 (1885), 298-299.

1604   "Lift Up Your Eyes, the Religious Writings of Tolstoy. A review," Christ C, 77 (12 Oct. 1960), 1188.

1605   Mallet, E. M. "The Theosophy of Tolstoi," Theosoph R, 26 (March 1900), 48-53.

1606   Manning, Clarence A. "The Religion of Leo Tolstoy," Am Church M, 23 (1928), 278-289.

1607   Marston, H. J. "Count Tolstoi on Christ's Christianity," Churchman, n. s. 10 (1895), 360-366.

1608   Matual, D. "On the Poetics of Tolstoj's Confession," SEEJ, 19, no. 3 (Fall 1975), 276-287.

1609   Maude, Aylmer. "Root of Religion," Sackbut, 7, no. 11 (June 1927), 314-316. On Tolstoy's My Confession.

1610   Mayhew, William H. "Tolstoi's Latest Book," New Church R, 2 (1895), 255-265.

1611   Monahan, Michael. "Tolstoy," Papyrus, 1, nos. 5-6 (March 1911), 1-4. Concerning Tolstoy's views on religion and Christianity.

1612   "My Religion," Lit W, 16, no. 25 (12 Dec. 1885), 480. A discussion of the translation of this work from Russian to French to English.

1613   Nash, J. V. "The Religious Evolution of Tolstoy," Open Court, 43 (1929), 641-649.

1614   "On Tolstoy's Excommunication," Independent, 53 (1901), 1662-1666.

1615   P., C. S. "The Teachings of Tolstoi," Theosoph R, 27 (15 Oct. 1900), 155-158.

1616   Patterson, L. "Literary, Religious and Philosophical Ideas of Leo Tolstoy," Chris East, 10 (1929), 153-158.

1617   Patton, William. "Count Tolstoi and the Sermon on the Mount," New Eng M, 46 (Feb. 1887), 140-154.

1618 "Prophet of the Lord; Tolstoy's Christianity and Patriotism,"
      Nation (L), 30 (4 March 1922), 824-825.

1619 Read, R. H. "The Apostle of Russia," Good Words, 33
      (July 1892), 448-452.

1620 "Resolution of the Synod in the Matter of Leo N. Tolstoi,"
      Literature, 6 (30 June 1900), 489-490.

1621 Richardson, Robert K. "Resist not Evil: Opinions about
      War in Accord with Christian Doctrine," Int J Ethics,
      27 (Jan. 1917), 225-238.

1622 Rickaby, Joseph. "The Preachings of Christ and the Practice
      of His Churches. A Reply to Count Tolstoi," New Re-
      view, 10 (1894), 195-198.

1623 Ripon, W. B. "The Preachings of Christ and the Practice
      of His Churches. A Reply to Count Tolstoi," New Re-
      view, 10 (1894), 186-187.

1624 Robertson, John M. "Tolstoy and the Ethics of Jesus,"
      Free R, 4 (June 1895), 214-232.

1625 Rogers, J. Guinness. "The Preachings of Christ and the
      Practice of His Churches: A Reply to Count Tolstoi,"
      New Review, 10 (1894), 198-204.

1626 Sampson, G. "Saint and Prophet," Bookman, 41 (Nov. 1911),
      102.

1627 "The Sermon on the Mount: Or the Creed? Count Tolstoi's
      Condemnation of the Churches," RRs, 9 (Feb. 1894),
      207-208.

1628 Sinclair, William. "The Preachings of Christ and the Prac-
      tice of His Churches. A Reply to Count Tolstoi," New
      Review, 10 (1894), 188-195.

1629 Smith, Charles E. "Tolstoy's Religious and Social Teach-
      ings," C Lit M, (Oct. 1928), 300-311.

1630 Spinka, M. "The Soul of Tolstoy," Christ C, 45 (16 August
      1928), 998-999.

1631 Stead, William T. "Count Tolstoy the Prophet," Independent,
      59 (19 Oct. 1905), 915-917.

1632 Steiner, Jesse F. "Count Leo Tolstoy," Reformed Church R,
      20 (1916), 396-424.

1633 Stepun, F. "The Religious Tragedy of Tolstoy," Rus R, 19
      (April 1960), 157-170.

1634   Thompson, Lloyd. "Tolstoy's Christianity," Whim, 1, no. 6
        (July 1901), 163-168.

1635   Thurber, A. "Tolstoy's Religion," Open Court, 28 (Jan.
        1914), 1-12.

1636   "Tolstoi's Book The Kingdom of God Is Within Us--Christian
        Anarchism," RRs (L), 9 (1894), 306-307.

1637   "Tolstoi's Confession and Creed," Lit W, 18, no. 17 (20 Au-
        gust 1887), 266-267. A review of Tolstoy's My Confes-
        sion and The Spirit of Christ's Teaching.

1638   "Tolstoi's Excommunication," Cur Lit, 31 (1901), 232.

1639   "Tolstoi's Kingdom of God," Lit W, 25, no. 7 (7 April 1894),
        104-105.

1640   "Tolstoi's Religion," Lit W, 17 (6 March 1886), 78-79.

1641   "Tolstoy and the Church," Cur Lit, 30 (Jan. 1901), 5.

1642   "Tolstoy and His Religion," Pub Op, 6 (1888), 120.

1643   "Tolstoy and the Orthodox Religion of Russia," RRs, 29 (1904),
        344-345.

1644   "Tolstoy on the Office of a Priest," Open Court, 25 (1911),
        616.

1645   "Tolstoy on the Value of Old Testament Study by the Young,"
        J of Ed, 82 (1915), 288-289.

1646   "Tolstoy's Declaration of Faith," Pub Op, 31 (1901), 561-562.
        Translated in condensed form from the Revue Bleue,
        Paris.

1647   "Tolstoy's Defiance to the Russian Church," Independent, 53
        (18 July 1901), 1693-1694. An editorial supporting Tol-
        stoy's religious convictions but acknowledging the Russian
        Orthodox Church's excommunication of him as part of its
        nature and function.

1648   "Tolstoy's Formal Excommunication," Pub Op, 30, no. 12
        (21 March 1901), 371.

1649   "Tolstoy's My Confession and The Spirit of Christian Teach-
        ing," Lit W, 18 (1887), 266-267.

1650   "Tolstoy's Reply to the Tsar," Chaut, 50 (May 1908), 438-
        439. Concerning Tsar Nicholas II's request that Tolstoy
        reconcile with the Orthodox Church.

1651 "Tolstoy's The Four Gospels Harmonized and Translated, "
      Biblical W, 9 (1897), 231.

1652 "Tolstoy's The Four Gospels Harmonized and Translated, "
      RRs (L), 11 (1891), 371.

1653 "Tolstoy's The Four Gospels Harmonized and Translated, "
      Sat R, 83 (1897), 448-449.

1654 Tsakni, N. "Mystical Pessimism in Russia, " Contemp R,
      53 (March 1888), 406-417.

1655 Vittum, E. M. "Tolstoy and the Modern Church, " New Eng
      M, 48 (1888), 54-65.

1656 Von Koeber, R. "On Tolstoi, " Lucifer, 7 (Sept. 1890), 9.

1657 "What Is Religion, " Critic, 41, no. 4 (Oct. 1902), 379.

1658 "What Is Religion?, " Hartf Sem R, 13, no. 1 (Nov. 1902), 70.

1659 "What Is Religion?, " Lit W, 33, no. 7 (July 1902), 103.

1660 Wheeler, W. "The Social and Religious Teachings of Tol-
      stoi, " Prim Meth Q R, 21 (Oct. 1899), 601.

1661 Wilder, Charlotte F. "Tolstoy: Man, Reformer, Author, "
      Methodist R, 88 (1906), 941-953.

1662 Willcox, Louise C. "Tolstoy's Religion, " N Amer R, 193
      (Feb. 1911), 242-255.

1663 Worcester, John H. "Count Leo Tolstoy as a Reformer, "
      Pres Ref R, 2 (July 1891), 459-471.

1664 Zweig, Stefan. "The Artificial Christian, " Rus Stud, 5, no.
      1 (Sept. 1928), 12-18.

DISSERTATIONS

1665 Wilks, R. "The Literary Criticism of D. S. Merezhkovsky
      with Special Reference to Religiya L. Tolstogo i Dos-
      teevskogo, " London: University of London, 1973.

      See also: 19, 24, 28, 29, 30, 32, 42, 51, 69, 77, 78, 99,
      103, 106, 118, 120, 133, 147, 150, 154, 155, 172, 300,
      333, 446, 451, 533, 561, 583, 1214, 1218, 1219, 1228,
      1231, 1232, 1234, 1243, 1252, 1254, 1256, 1259, 1262,
      1263, 1265, 1268, 1272, 1277, 1278, 1284, 1285, 1287,
      1294, 1296, 1299, 1303, 1307, 1312, 1319, 1324, 1325,
      1327, 1331, 1332, 1337, 1344, 1350, 1352, 1355, 1366,
      1555, 1677, 1711, 1712, 1713, 1716, 1722, 1724, 1801,
      1827, 1893, 1930, 1944, 2030, 2054.

HISTORY, GOVERNMENT,
LAW, SOCIETY, AND ECONOMY

BOOKS

1666 Berlin, Isaiah. The Hedgehog and the Fox: An Essay on
Tolstoy's View of History. New York: Simon & Schuster, 1953; 86p. The title symbolizes two types of individuals, those who relate everything to a "single central
vision, " and those who pursue many ends related to no
central moral or aesthetic principle. Within this con-
ceptual scheme of monism-pluralism, Tolstoy is placed
and regarded as being somewhat contradictory in that
"by nature he was a fox, but believed in being a hedgehog. " The conflict between what he was and what he
believed in can best be seen, it is argued, in his view
of history. There follows an application of the hedgehog-
fox construct to the origins of Tolstoy's theory of history, especially his motives for holding the theory, with
much reference to War and Peace and his personal letters for supporting information and examples. Portions
in Oxford S P, 2 (1951), 17-54; and WPMT, 255-273.
Reviewed in:
    ASEER, 14, no. 1 (1955), 122, by Ernest J. Sim-
        mons.
    Atlantic M, 193 (April 1954), 87.
    Catholic W, 179 (Sept. 1954), 477, by N. Roodkow-
        sky.
    Ethics, 64 (July 1954), 313, by G. L. Kline.
    Manch G, (18 Dec. 1953), 4, by Max Beloff.
    Nation, 178 (13 March 1954), 233, by Leon Edel.
    New Sta and Na, 46 (12 Dec. 1953), 768, by A. J.
        P. Taylor.
    New Yorker, 30 (25 Sept. 1954), 131, by W. H.
        Auden.
    N Y Times, (14 Feb. 1954), 4, by William Barrett.
    Spectator, (1 Jan. 1954), 20, by Rex Warner.
    Yale R, 43 (Summer 1954), 607, by Rene Wellek.

1667 Chertkov, Vladimir G. Christian Martyrdom in Russia; The
Persecution of the Spirit-Wrestlers (or Doukhobors) in
the Caucasus. London: Brotherhood, 1897; 110p. An

account, by Tolstoy's friend and disciple, of the persecution of the Doukhobors by the tsarist government precedes a reproduction of the plea made on their behalf
by the author which led to his exile from Russia. Included is a discussion of Tolstoy's involvement with the
Doukhobors, especially his assistance in their emigration
to Canada, and his reaction to the government's banish-
ment of Chertkov.

1668 Darrow, Clarence S. , and Arthur Lewis. Marx versus Tolstoy, a Debate. Chicago: Kerr, 1911; 124p. A clash
between the philosophies of non-resistance and revolution
in a simulated debate with Darrow representing the former position and Lewis the latter. In attacking the universality of the non-resistance beliefs of Tolstoy, Lewis
claims that the theory has validity for Tolstoy and all of
Russia because active resistance to powerful absolute
monarchies has frequently meant death, but it is not
applicable to democratic societies where the workers'
struggle can benefit by use of violence. In all, the philosophy of non-resistance is thought to be one of despair.
Tolstoy is supported by Darrow who claims that violence
is futile in all societies because it is always the common man who loses. The only means of advancing the
interests of the masses is considered to be through a
brotherhood of all men which refuses to participate in
any undertaking which entails violence.

1669 Elkington, Joseph R. The Doukhobors. Philadelphia: Fer-
ris, 1903.

1670 Gottschling, A. Tsar and Tolstoi. London, 1899; 35p. A
condemnation of violence and absolutism, and an argument for international peace with much reference to
Tolstoy's philosophy for support.

1671 Lednicki, Waclaw. Tolstoy between War and Peace. The
Hague: Mouton, 1965; 167p. Tolstoy, in his early life,
is seen as part of a milieu which was highly patriotic
and anti-Polish and which affected him powerfully enough
that he too held unfavorable opinions of Poland. However, as he matured intellectually, he reversed his early
beliefs and became a champion of Polish rights and virtues. Excerpts are taken from his works to demonstrate
the evolution of his attitude toward Poland, and it is
suggested that understanding of this evolution is a significant means of gaining insight into that which brought
Tolstoy to his spiritual awakening. Reviewed in:
SEEJ, 9 (Winter 1965), 441-2, by Elizabeth Trahan.
Slav R, 25, no. 2 (1967), 359, by Louis Shein.
SEER, 44, no. 2 (1966), 493-94.
TLS, (9 Sept. 1965), 780.

1672 Mataram, Dande. Open Letter to Count Leo Tolstoy in Reply to His "Letter to a Hindoo. " New York: 1909; 47p. A response to Tolstoy's views on non-resistance and love in which Indian conditions are described and seen as representing a case where Tolstoy's pacifism would not work, but only lead to perpetual British domination of India.

1673 Maude, Aylmer. An Experiment in Communism: The Doukhobor Commentary on Tolstoyism. London, 1904.

1674 Maude, Aylmer. A Peculiar People: The Doukhobors. New York: AMS Press, 1970 (reprint of 1904 publication); 338p. An account of Tolstoy's initial contact with the Doukhobors, his appeals on their behalf, and his work in helping them to relocate is presented by the friend of Tolstoy who had an active role in the Doukhobors' relocating in Canada. In addition, a separate chapter ("A Criticism of Tolstoy") appears in which Tolstoy's principles of non-resistance and repudiation of property are rejected. It is argued that he over-simplified in his analysis of government and property in that there are numerous cases of good, moral and progressive government, just as there are many instances where property and selfishness do not go hand in hand.

1675 Mittal, Sarla. Tolstoy: Social and Political Ideas. Meerut, India: Meenakshi Prakashan, 1966; viii, 238p. , bib. 224-231. A discussion of the origin, meaning, and impact of Tolstoy's views on non-resistance, the state, and the social-economic system of tsarist Russia. His beliefs are consistently presented in a positive vein, and his influence on India, especially by way of his impact on Gandhi, is seen as an important one. It is maintained that Tolstoy is without parallel as a political and social reformer of the non-violent strain, and he is commended for being a "revolutionary" and a "humanist" at the same time.

1676 Stanoyevich, Milivoy S. Tolstoy's Theory of Social Reform; His Doctrine of Law, Money and Property. New York: Columbia University Press, 1926; 57p. A discussion of the relationship between Tolstoy's life and changing beliefs and the evolution of his social-economic views precedes an analysis of these views. The oppressive and conservative nature of the tsarist government is identified as the source for many of his negative views. Although his recognizing only divine, not human, law is thought to be admirable and his genuine concern for human welfare unquestionable, his social-economic beliefs are not accepted as a practical guide to reform but certainly served to focus attention on the need for reform. Also published as three separate pamphlets by the Liberty

Publishing Co. , Oakland (1916); also in Am Law R, 50 (Jan. 1916), 85-90; Am J Sociol, 31 (March 1926), 577-600, (May 1926), 744-762.

ESSAYS AND CHAPTERS from general works

1677 Birkhead, Alice. "The Reformer of the East" in Heroes of Modern Europe. Freeport, N. Y. : Books for Libraries Press, 1966 (reprint of 1913 publication); 216-227. A positive account of Tolstoy's attempt to merge with the common people and live a simple, pleasant existence. His work in education and with the Doukhobors, his renunciation of property, and his assault on war, government, organized religion, and modern civilization are linked to his quest for "ever new ways to reach the people. " His clashes with the tsarist government, and his eventual excommunication from the Russian Orthodox Church are discussed as is his attempt to flee from contact with official Russia and material civilization.

1678 Buchan, John. "Count Tolstoi and the Idealism of War" in Some Eighteenth Century Byways and Other Essays. London: Blackwood, 1908; 294-300. Tolstoy's view of warfare as "a sin against God's law and against the moral well-being of mankind, " and his consequent efforts to arouse individual conscience against war are criticized for overlooking the idealism associated with warfare. It is argued that when men have beliefs and loyalties which they hold firmly, and which differ sharply from those of other men, wars naturally follow, and that "only when ideals become faint" will warfare cease.

1679 Catlin, George. "Individuals and Anarchists: Count Leo Tolstoy" in The Story of Political Philosophers. New York: McGraw-Hill, 1939; 422-425. Tolstoy's Christian anarchism is discussed with parallels drawn to the beliefs of Thoreau and Rousseau. His ideas on property, science, art, and education are then analyzed as part of his general rebellion against modern civilization. Although his philosophy is deemed "reactionary, " it is nonetheless thought to be powerful and provocative.

1680 Cheney, Sheldon W. "The Value of Tolstoy's What Is to Be Done? to the Present Rebuilding of the Social Structure" in TBPE, 55-122. Tolstoy's philosophy is judged to be of value to the whole world, and not just Russia, because it attacks "the very foundations on which social justice and injustice are built. " His practical reforms, however, are considered inapplicable to America, where change has consistently come about through reform and education.

1681   Chiaromonte, Nicola.   "Tolstoy and the Paradox of History"
       in The Paradox of History: Stendhall, Tolstoy, Paster-
       nak and Others.   London: Weidenfeld and Nicolson,
       1971; 29-56.   Tolstoy's philosophy of history is sum-
       marized before a critique of Berlin's The Hedgehog and
       the Fox is presented.   The leading principles of Tol-
       stoy's philosophy of history are then discussed and com-
       mended, not because Tolstoy "solved the problem of
       history," but because he was the first modern writer
       "to rediscover the 'dependence not perceived by our
       senses' which lies at the core of our actions."

1682   Clutton-Brock, Arthur.   "Tolstoy and Russia" in More Essays
       on Books.   London: Methuen, 1921; 160-174.   Tolstoy
       is identified as the spiritual father of revolutionary dis-
       content in Russia, and, therefore, is regarded as indi-
       rectly responsible for the triumph of Bolshevism.   Even
       though he was opposed to violent change, it is argued
       that his undermining of authority and assault on the es-
       tablished social-economic system paved the way for ac-
       ceptance of revolution and communism, a fact which must
       lower world esteem for Tolstoy.

1683   Drury, Newton B.   "Tolstoy's What Shall We Do Then?--A
       Problem and an Attempt at a Solution" in TBPE, 177-
       218.   Tolstoy's isolation of the sources of poverty is
       discussed and his solution to the problem analyzed and
       labeled "sound as a general proposition but too rigidly
       applied."   The narrowness of his theory is thought to
       stem from an attempt to apply universally that which he
       devised to soothe his own conscience.   In spite of the
       theory's deficiencies, Tolstoy is applauded for isolating
       many truths associated with the problem of poverty.

1684   Fichter, Joseph H.   "Tolstoy and the Class Struggle" in
       Roots of Change.   New York: Appleton-Century, 1939;
       265-289.   Tolstoy is considered to be more responsible
       than anyone else in preparing Russia for the acceptance
       of communism because he was more widely read, known,
       and respected than all others associated with radical re-
       form in Russia.   His views on property, class distinc-
       tions, and on the abolition of the state are all seen as
       having promoted acceptance of the leveling principles of
       Marxism.   After the October Revolution, Tolstoy's phi-
       losophy of non-resistance is linked to the passive re-
       sponse by the peasants to the communist state.

1685   Hodgetts, E. A. Grayley.   In the Track of the Russian Fam-
       ine.   London: Unwin, 1892.   Unavailable for annotation
       but listed as having information on the famine and Tol-
       stoy's relief work among the Russian peasants.

1686   Ingersoll, Robert G.   "Tolstoy and Literature" in The Works
       of Robert G. Ingersoll.   New York: Farrell, 1900; vol.

8, 513-16. An interview with Ingersoll in which he attacks Tolstoy's views on non-resistance to violence as being "insane," and his opposition to progress as "the road back to barbarism." It is further stated that Tolstoy's popularity in America is in spite of his philosophy, not because of it.

1687 Jones, Bayard H. "Tolstoy and the Social Problems of Today" in TBPE, 7-54. Tolstoy's views in What Is to Be Done? are summarized and placed within the development of Russian thought, and are then criticized for being founded on too narrow a basis. His assault on money, property, and organized society in general is viewed as having value only in a semi-feudal system such as that which exists in Russia. Tolstoy's criticisms are considered to be relevant, however, because the questions on which he focuses are still problems today.

1688 Klenze, Camillo von. From Goethe to Hauptmann: Studies in a Changing Culture. New York: Biblo and Tannen, 1966 (reprint of 1926 publication); 258-275 (no separate section on Tolstoy). Tolstoy's belief that the Russian peasant was superior to the bourgeoisie and aristocracy, because of a moral depth stemming from "contact with the soil" is isolated as the principal source of his opposition to modern civilization, and the main impetus behind his mid-life conversion to the simple, Christian life. His treatment, in his fiction, of the common man is discussed, and it is maintained that he did not conceal the vices of the peasants but rather linked them to the evil environment in which they were forced to live. Examples from his fiction are presented to support this claim, and parallels are made to the ideas and treatment of the common man by Hauptmann and Zola.

1689 Krzyzrnowski, Jerzy R. "Thoreau in Russia" in Thoreau Abroad; Twelve Bibliographical Essays. Hamden, Conn.: Shoe String Press, 1971; 133-140. Tolstoy's positive reaction to the philosophy of Thoreau, especially to his On Civil Disobedience, is noted, and his words on his personal debt to Thoreau are repeated. His sincerity here is questioned, however, because his basic philosophic principles are judged to be more different than similar to those of Thoreau.

1690 Lawrence, D. H. Phoenix: The Posthumous Papers of D. H. Lawrence, ed. E. McDonald. New York: Viking, 1936; 246-47. In his introduction to Verga's Cavalleria Rusticana, Lawrence claims that Tolstoy's worship of the peasant and his way of life is perverted and based on a faulty assessment of peasant virtues: "the peasant mass is the ugliest of all human masses, most greedily selfish and brutal of all." Tolstoy's peasant views are con-

trasted with those of Verga, who admired the peasant
only as a "manifestation of pure, spontaneous, passion-
ate life. " Also in LTCA, 196-97.

1691   Lenin, V. I. "Heroes of 'Reservation'" in LLT, 42-49. A
       sharp critique of the V. Bazarov article, "Tolstoy and
       the Russian Intelligentsia" in Nasha Zarya, which had
       praised Tolstoy for having reached in his philosophy a
       synthesis that the whole of the Russian intelligentsia
       could accept. Also in Lenin's Collected Works (Moscow,
       1961), vol. 16, 368-73.

1692   Lenin, V. I. "Is This the Turning of the Tide?" in LLT, 36-
       40. A brief assault on those who tried to prevent a
       student demonstration against capital punishment on the
       grounds that it would show "a sincere lack of respect"
       for Tolstoy who had recently died. Also in Lenin's
       Collected Works, vol. 16, 320-22.

1693   Lenin, V. I. "Leo N. Tolstoy (1910)" in LLT, 27-33. Tol-
       stoy is praised for his protests against the state, church,
       capitalism, and private property, and is seen as a gifted
       spokesman for Russia in her post-feudal phase. Tolstoy
       is criticized, however, for his response to these evils
       in that he championed non-resistance, was highly religious,
       and remained aloof from the revolutionary movement.
       Also in Lenin's Collected Works, vol. 16, 323-27; and
       Ang-Sov J, (April 1941), 137-140.

1694   Lenin, V. I. "Leo N. Tolstoy and the Modern Labour Move-
       ment" in LLT, 36-40. Tolstoy's fiction and philosophy
       are discussed as a response to the "demolition of the
       pillars of old Russia" after 1861, with the source of his
       distinction from the representatives of the modern labor
       movement identified as being his patriarchal, naive
       peasant perspective: "Tolstoy mirrored the peasants'
       sentiments so closely that their naiveté ... and impotent
       reaction to the evils of capitalism" all became part of
       his doctrine. Also in Lenin's Collected Works, vol. 16,
       330-32.

1695   Lenin, V. I. "Leo Tolstoy as the Mirror of the Russian
       Revolution" in LLT, 20-27. Tolstoy is sharply criti-
       cized for his glaring contradictions and for failure to
       understand the Russian revolutionary movement, but is
       nonetheless seen as being "a mirror of the revolution"
       because his views represent rural-peasant protest against
       advancing capitalism: "Tolstoy expresses the specific
       features of our revolution as a peasant bourgeois revolu-
       tion. " Also in Lenin's Collected Works, vol. 16, 202-
       09; excerpts in WPMT, 1392-95; LTCA, 135-36.

1696   Lenin, V. I. "Tolstoy and His Epoch" in LLT, 49-54. Tol-
       stoy's epoch is isolated as that of 1861-1905, or the

transition from serfdom to capitalism in Russia. Tolstoy wrote and developed his philosophy, it is claimed,
at a time when many people were unsure as to the direction of "new Russia, " but by 1905, this direction
(bourgeois capitalism) was clear. The reactionary and
utopian features of his doctrine are seen as obscured
during this epoch, but clear by 1905--hence time has
passed him by. Also in Lenin's Collected Works, vol.
17, 49-53; Labour M, 10 (1928), 607-09; and LTCA, 140-
44.

1697 Lenin, V. I.   "Tolstoy and the Proletarian Struggle" in LLT,
      40-41. Tolstoy is discussed as the spokesman for those
      who detest the "masters of modern life" but who have
      not yet advanced to the point of "implacable struggle
      against them. " He is thus viewed as in the unenviable
      position of being half way between the defenders of the
      Old Regime and the class-conscious. Also in Lenin's
      Collected Works, vol. 16, pp. 353-54.

1698 Matthews, Lilian R.   "The Social Validity of Tolstoy's What
      Is to Be Done?" in TBPE, 219-259. Tolstoy's What Is
      to Be Done? is regarded as a powerful plea that moral
      truths be given due place in outward life, but the force
      of the plea is greatly lessened by its impracticality.
      Particularly criticized is his negativism and his failure
      to appreciate the enlightening role played by material
      progress.

1699 Maude, Aylmer.   "After the Tsar's Coronation" in TP, 161-
      184. An application to England of Tolstoy's views on
      the coronation of Nicholas II. Emphasized is the waste
      and extravagance of Western materialistic civilization.
      Also in the Epilogue to After the Tsar's Coronation (Lon-
      don: Brotherhood Publishing Co. , 1896).

1700 Maude, Aylmer.   "The Doukhobors: A Russian Exodus" in
      TP, 262-326. Historical background on the Doukhobors
      as a religious sect precedes a discussion of their plight
      as a consequence of their refusal to serve in the Rus-
      sian army. Tolstoy's involvement with the group, par-
      ticularly in assisting in their emigration to Canada, is
      also examined.

1701 Maude, Aylmer.   "Introduction to The Slavery of Our Times"
      in TP, 149-160. A summary of how Tolstoy relates non-
      resistance to various aspects of economic and political
      life. His main contention is identified as "that progress
      in human well-being can only be achieved by relying more
      on ... conscience and less and less on man-made laws. "

1702 Maude, Aylmer.   "War and Patriotism" in TP, 219-261. An
      application of Tolstoy's principle of non-resistance to the

war in South Africa as a means of attacking the position
of John Bellows, of the Society of Friends, a pacifist
who nonetheless supported England's actions in the war.
Also in New Age (August 1900).

1703 Sprading, Charles T. "Lyoff N. Tolstoy" in Liberty and
Great Libertarians. Los Angeles, 1913; 313-333.

1704 Stadling, Jonas, and Will Reason. In the Land of Tolstoi.
Experiences of Famine and Misrule in Russia. London:
Clarke, 1897; 1-74 (first five chapters of the work concern Tolstoy). Background information on Tolstoy's life
and a discussion of his work in education are presented
before a detailed account is given of his connection with
the famine of 1891-1892. Tolstoy's warnings to the government on the imminence of famine are noted, as is
the government's negative response to these "threats."
His criticism of the government's measures to cope with
the famine, and charges that the government had failed
to understand the true causes of the peasants' plight are
presented in a favorable light, as is his actual work
amidst the famine-stricken districts of rural Russia.

1705 Thompson, Stith. "The Value of the Ideal of Social Recon-
struction Set Forth in Tolstoy's What Is to Be Done?"
in TBPE, 123-176. Tolstoy's views on government are
said to be of some value in Russia, but of little use in
enlightened societies. His basic ideas on property and
the division of labor are regarded as contrary to human
nature and, therefore, cannot possibly meet human
needs. Tolstoy is praised only because his ideas highlight the need for all governments to be concerned with
the needs of the common people, and force healthy introspection of the reader.

1706 Trotsky, Leon. "Tolstoy: Poet and Rebel" in The Age of
Permanent Revolution: A Trotsky Anthology, ed. Isaac
Deutscher. New York: Dell, 1964; 326-330. Writing
just after Tolstoy's 80th birthday, Trotsky claims that
Tolstoy, despite all of his spiritual awakening, remains
an aristocrat "in the deepest and most secret recesses
of his creativeness." His vision of the world is seen as
consisting of only landlords and peasants, with himself
remaining in the role of patriarch. It is argued that
although Tolstoy was repelled by new, capitalistic order
in Russia, he reacted, because of his aristocratic heritage, by withdrawing into the past instead of aligning
himself with the progressive forces of the revolutionary
protest against capitalism. Also in Fourth Int, (May-
June 1951), 90-92.

1707 Woodcock, George. "The Prophet" in Anarchism: A History
of Libertarian Ideas and Movements. New York: World

Publishing Co., 1971; 222-235. Although Tolstoy did
not call himself an anarchist (because he believed the
word suggests violence), his basic doctrine is discussed
as being consistent with the "general anarchist pattern."
The sources of his anarchist beliefs are traced in line
with the contention that there was an anarchist strain in
him from his early manhood as demonstrated by the "naturalism, populism and dream of universal brotherhood"
in all his works. The influence on him of Proudhon and
Kropotkin is examined, and his impact on Gandhi briefly
surveyed.

1708   Woodcock, George, and Ivan Avakumovic. The Doukhobors.
       Toronto: Oxford University Press, 1968; 107-151 (no
       separate section on Tolstoy). Tolstoy's involvement with
       the Doukhobors is considered to be a consequence of his
       sympathy with them as peasants attempting to practice
       Christian anarchism. His marshaling of world opinion
       by way of articles that he wrote for the English press
       against the Doukhobors' persecution by the government
       is discussed, as is his role in collecting funds for the
       Doukhobors' relocation to Canada.

INTRODUCTION TO EDITIONS of political, social, and economic
writings

1709   Addams, Jane. What Then Must We Do? Trans. by A.
       Maude. London: Oxford, 1934 (Centenary Edition).

1710   Axon, W. E. The First Step; Essays on Morals of Diet.
       Trans. by Louise Maude and Aylmer Maude. London:
       Brotherhood, 1900; 82p.

1711   Berdayev, Nicholas. Essays from Tula. London: Sheppard,
       1949; 292p.

1712   Budberg, Baroness. The Law of Love and the Law of Vio-
       lence. Trans. by Mary Koutouzov. New York: Holt,
       1971; 101p.

1713   Garland, Hamlin. Recollections and Essays. Trans. by A.
       Maude. London: Oxford, 1937; 516p (Centenary Edi-
       tion).

1714   Maude, Aylmer. After The Tsar's Coronation. Trans. by
       A. Maude. London: Brotherhood, 1896.

1715   Maude, Aylmer. The Horror of War. Trans. by A. Maude.
       London, 1903.

1716   Maude, Aylmer. Recollections and Essays. Trans. by A.
       Maude. London: Oxford, 1937; 504p.

1717 Maude, Aylmer. Trans. by Louise Maude and Aylmer Maude.
      The Slavery of Our Times. London: Daniel, 1918.

1718 Maude, Aylmer. What Then Must We Do? Trans. by A.
      Maude. London: Oxford, 1925.

1719 Mayo, I. F. End of the Age and Crisis in Russia. Trans.
      by V. Chertkov. London: Heinemann, 1906; 94p.

1720 Nearing, Scott. War-Patriotism-Peace. New York: Van-
      guard, 1926.

1721 Nearing, Scott, and Ralph Templin. War-Patriotism-Peace.
      New York: Garland, 1975; 125p.

1722 Perris, George H. The Life and Teachings of Leo Tolstoy.
      London: Richards, 1901; 273p. (a book of extracts).

1723 Priluker, Yakov M. Count Tolstoy on Flogged and Floggers
      with Some Comment by Y. Priluker. London: Russian
      Reformation Society, 1899; 16p.

1724 Simmons, Ernest J. Selected Essays. Trans. by A. Maude.
      New York: Random House, 1964; 353p.

PERIODICAL ARTICLES

1725 Addams, Jane. "Tolstoy and the Russian Soldiers, " New Re-
      public, 12 (1917), 240-242.

1726 Addams, Jane. "What to Do Then?, " Rus Stud, 5, no. 1
      (Sept. 1928), 19-22.

1727 Berlin, Isaiah. "Lev Tolstoy's Historical Skepticism, " Oxford
      S P, 2 (1951), 17-54.

1728 Bernstein, J. "Tolstoy's Objections to Socialism, " Metaphysi-
      cal M, 16 (March 1902), 161-170.

1729 Bowen, C. M. "Peasant Life in Russian Novels, " Month, 130
      (July 1917), 23-30.

1730 "The Brave Old Man, " Independent, 65 (23 July 1908), 216-
      217. A discussion of Tolstoy's protest to the tsar over
      the hanging of 12 peasants convicted of robbery.

1731 Burgess, W. "Tolstoy and Social Impurity, " Statesman, 8
      (Oct. 1890), 5.

1732 Colbron, G. I. "Essays, Letters and Miscellanies, " Bookman,
      13 (1901), 182.

1733   Cooke, G. W.   "Revolutionary Tendencies in Modern Litera-
        ture: Leo Tolstoy, " UIS, 88 (30 June 1921), 279-281.

1734   "Count Leo Tolstoi's Philanthropy and the Government of the
        Czar, " Pub Op, 12 (5 March 1892), 550.   A survey of
        Tolstoy's work in the famine and the government's nega-
        tive reaction to it.   Translated from Neue Freie Presse,
        (14 Feb. 1892).

1735   "Count Tolstoi's Asceticism, " Book News, 7, no. 80 (April
        1889), 245.   An account of Tolstoy's self-imposed re-
        strictions in diet and life-style for the sake of his as-
        cetic beliefs.

1736   "Count Tolstoi's Reforms, " Spectator, 62 (16 Feb. 1889), 222-
        223.   A recounting of Tolstoy's call for absolute power
        to be given to the rural councils.

1737   "Count Tolstoy and the War, " Outlook, 77 (23 July 1904),
        679-681.   Tolstoy's views on the Russo-Japanese War
        are discussed.   Also in RRs, 30 (August 1904), 213-215.

1738   "Count Tolstoy on Non-resistance and the Negro Question, "
        RRs, 29 (1904), 731-732.

1739   Crosby, Ernest H.   "Count Tolstoi and Non-resistance, "
        Outlook, 54 (July 1896), 52-53.

1740   Dillon, Emile J.   "How Tolstoy Is Working in the Famine
        Districts, " RRs, 5 (1892), 39-42.

1741   Ecob, James H.   "The Russian Remedy, " Arena, 27 (June
        1902), 615-623.   An attack on Tolstoy's nihilism and
        socialism.

1742   Flower, B. O.   "Count Tolstoi on the Land Question, " Arena,
        34 (Dec. 1905), 631-636.

1743   Foner, P. S.   "Count Leo Tolstoy and the Violence in the
        Philippines, " Mass R, 12 (Spring 1971), 241-244.   Con-
        cerning a 1902 letter from Tolstoy to Herbert Walsh and
        Walsh's account of the circumstances.

1744   Gass, S. B.   "Tolstoy and the Doctrine of Peace, " Mid W Q,
        3 (1915), 1-16.

1745   "The Gospel of Disobedience, " RRs, 33 (Feb. 1906), 175.

1746   Gusev, Nikolai N.   "Tolstoy and Revolution, " Living Age, 308
        (15 Jan. 1921), 130-137.   Translated from Neue Freie
        Presse (27 Nov. 1920).

1747   Hapgood, Isabel F.   "Count Tolstoi and the Public Censor, "
        Atlantic M, 60 (July 1887), 57-67.

1748   Heier, E.   "Tolstoi and Nihilism," Can S P, 9, no. 4 (Winter
       1969), 454-465.

1749   Henderson, C. R.   "Attempts at Social Ethics," Dial, 30
       (June 1901), 400-402.   A discussion of Tolstoy's ethical
       views against the background of his The Slavery of Our
       Times.

1750   Johnston, C.   "Count Tolstoy and the War," Harper's W, 48
       (13 August 1904), 1244-45.   On Tolstoy's views on the
       Russo-Japanese War.

1751   Johnston, C.   "Tolstoy and the Russian Parliament," Harper's
       W, 49 (16 Sept. 1905), 1340-41.

1752   Kennan, George.   "Count Tolstoy and the Russian Govern-
       ment," Outlook, 34 (1887), 252-265.   Reprinted in Out-
       look, 96 (3 Dec. 1910), 769-781.

1753   Kennan, George.   "Student Disorders in Russia," Outlook, 97
       (29 April 1911), 968-974.   A sympathetic account of
       student demonstrations in response to the ban by church
       and state of any expression of public feeling over the
       death of Tolstoy.

1754   Kennan, George.   "Tolstoy and the First Russian Duma,"
       Outlook, 93 (18 Sept. 1909), 123-127.

1755   Kerner, R. J.   "Tolstoy's Philosophy of History," Calif U
       Chron, 31 (1929), 43-45.

1756   Ladoff, Isador R.   "Tolstoy Is Not a Socialist," Wilshire's
       M, (May 1903).   Also in Pub Op, 34 (May 1903), 655.

1757   Laugel, A.   "Tolstoi on Patriotism," Nation, 59 (1894), 171-
       172.

1758   Laughlin, J. L.   "A Criticism of Tolstoi's 'Money'," Open
       Court, 14 (April 1900), 193-228.

1759   Lenin, V. I.   "Tolstoy: An Appreciation," Ang-Sov J (April
       1941), 137-140.   Reprint of 1910 article; also in LLT,
       27-33; and Lenin's Collected Works (Moscow, 1961),
       vol. 16, 323-327.

1760   Lenin, V. I.   "Tolstoy and His Epoch," Labour M, 10 (1928),
       607-609.   Also in LLT, 49-54; Collected Works, vol.
       17, 49-53; and LTCA, 140-144.

1761   "Letter on Land Ownership in Russia," Craftsman, 10 (1907),
       88.

1762   Marcus, Joseph.   "A New Tolstoy Letter," Public, 21 (11

May 1918), 606-607.   Analysis of Tolstoy's letter to the
tsar on the nationalization of land for the peasants.

1763   Maude, Aylmer.   "Tolstoy and the War; Reply to the Prophet
of the Lord, " Nation (L), 30, no. 24 (11 March 1922),
858.

1764   Maude, Aylmer.   "Tolstoy's Mistake, " Bookman (L), 62 (August 1922), 208-209.   Maude's criticism of Tolstoy's
views on non-resistance as being oversimplifications, not
having universal applicability.

1765   Maude, Aylmer.   "War and Patriotism, " New Age, (August
1900), TP, 219-261.

1766   Mayo, I. F.   "The Philanthropist of the Russian Famine, "
Victorian M, 1 (March 1892), 307-316.

1767   Noyes, George R.   "Tolstoi's View of War, " Rus Stud, 5,
no. 1 (Sept. 1928), 8-17, illus.

1768   Noyes, George R.   "What Is to Be Done?, " Calif U Chron,
28 (July 1926), 343-345.

1769   Ogden, R.   "Tolstoy on the War, " Nation, 79 (1904), 26-27.

1770   "On Civil Disobedience and Non-violence, " TLS, (23 May
1968), 527.

1771   Oulianoff, Nicholas.   "Tolstoy's Nationalism, " R Nat Lit, 3
(1972), 101-124.

1772   "The Physiology of War; Napoleon and the Russian Cam-
paign, " Pub Op, 4, no. 49 (17 March 1888), 566-567.

1773   Pritchett, V. S.   "On Civil Disobedience and Nonviolence, "
New Sta, 75 (15 March 1968), 336.

1774   "The Russian Revolution, " RRs, 33, no. 193 (Jan. 1906), 52.
A discussion of Tolstoy's views about the revolution, including its origins and ideas on revolutions in general.

1775   Schevill, James.   "Tolstoy and the Peasants, " Prairie S, 36,
no. 1 (Spring 1962), 16.

1776   Shinkin, D. B.   "Culture and Word Analysis: A Method of
Analysis Applied to Rural Russia, " Am Sociol, 55 (1955),
329-348.

1777   "Socialism and Human Nature, " Nation, 89 (9 Dec. 1909),
560.   An attack on Tolstoy's socialist views.

1778   Spence, Gordon W.   "Tolstoy's Dualism, " Rus R, 20 (July
1961), 217-231.   An examination of Tolstoy's theory of

history, as presented in War and Peace, and its relationship to his later works.

1779 Stadling, Jonas. "With Tolstoi in the Russian Famine,"
Cent M, 24 (June 1893), 249-263. Also in In the Land
of Tolstoi (item 1704), 1-74.

1780 Stanoyevich, Milivoy S. "Tolstoy's Doctrine of Law," Am
Law R, 50 (Jan. 1916), 85-90.

1781 Stanoyevich, Milivoy S. "Tolstoy's Theory of Social Reform,"
Am J Sociol, 31 (March 1926), 577-600; (May 1926),
744-762. Both Stanoyevich articles are also in Tolstoy's
Theory of Social Reform (item 1676) 1-57.

1782 Steiner, Edward A. "Count Tolstoy's Sociological Views,"
Bib Sacra, 58, no. 229 (Jan. 1901), 179-186.

1783 "Tolstoi on Imperialism," Pub Op, 29, no. 24 (13 Dec. 1900),
749. A commentary on Tolstoy's views on American
imperialism.

1784 "Tolstoi on the Physiology of War," Lit W, 19, no. 5 (3
March 1888), 67.

1785 "Tolstoi, the Statesman," Independent, 53 (13 July 1901),
1390-1391. A recounting of Tolstoy's request made to
Nicholas II that he implement major land reforms.

1786 "Tolstoi's Physiology of War," Nation, 46 (26 April 1888),
335-346.

1787 "Tolstoi's Power and Liberty," Lit W, 19, no. 14 (7 July
1888), 221.

1788 "Tolstoi's Vain Cry for Martyrdom," W Work, 16 (Sept.
1908), 10, 638-10, 639. Tolstoy's protests against the
oppressive policies of the tsarist government are seen
as being so censored that they reach the outside world
but never the Russian audience for which they were intended.

1789 "Tolstoi's What to Do Then?," Lit W, 18, no. 20 (1 Oct.
1887), 315-317.

1790 Tolstoy, Alexandra. "Tolstoy and the Russian Peasant,"
Rus R, 19 (April 1960), 150-156.

1791 "Tolstoy and the Czar," Outlook, 61 (1899), 209-210.

1792 "Tolstoy Denounces Socialism," Pub Op, 33, no. 23 (4 Dec.
1902), 718.

1793 "Tolstoy's Device for Peace," Independent, 51 (13 April 1899),

1036-1037.   An editorial in response to an article by
Tolstoy concerning the upcoming peace conference in
which he called for the spirit of pacifism to prevail.

1794 "Tolstoy's Plan for Redemption," Living Age, 219 (5 Nov.
1898), 386-388.   A critical assessment of Tolstoy's
views on non-violence and his opposition to military con-
scription.

1795 Triggs, Oscar L.   "An Instance in Conversion," Open Court,
16 (Feb. 1902), 69-73.   An examination of Tolstoy's
views on the peasantry and the simple life.

1796 Trotsky, Leon.   "Tolstoy, Poet and Rebel," Fourth Int, 12
(May-June 1951), 90-95.   Also in The Age of Permanent
Revolution: A Trotsky Anthology, 326-330.

1797 Wilton, Robert.   "Tolstoy and Revolution," Times Lit Sup,
(14 March 1918), 126.   An attack on the claim that Tolstoy was the father of revolution in Russia.   Correspondences, Times Lit Sup, (21 March 1918), 141; (11
April), 173; (18 April), 185; (25 April), 197; (2 May),
209; (9 May), 221; and (23 May) 245.

1798 Wood, H.   "Count Tolstoy's Book: What to Do?," New Sci
R, 1 (Oct. 1894), 184.

DISSERTATIONS

1799 Hecht, Leo.   "Freedom for the Individual: Tolstoj's Struggle
Against Authority," Columbia University, 1974.

See also: 19, 24, 28, 29, 30, 32, 36, 42, 43, 48, 62, 69,
70, 71, 74, 76, 77, 78, 83, 84, 86, 89, 99, 103,
106, 109, 110, 120, 122, 124, 126, 127, 128, 137, 147,
154, 155, 172, 193, 222, 262, 294, 303, 333, 389, 391,
428, 504, 511, 537, 566, 583, 595, 624, 625, 789, 790,
811, 813, 857, 863, 864, 865, 866, 877, 882, 883, 885,
886, 909, 946, 985, 987, 993, 994, 1002, 1214, 1219,
1221, 1228, 1234, 1235, 1238, 1242, 1243, 1244, 1250,
1252, 1253, 1256, 1262, 1265, 1268, 1276, 1279, 1284,
1285, 1286, 1293, 1296, 1299, 1301, 1302, 1308,
1309, 1310, 1311, 1318, 1321, 1324, 1325, 1326, 1327,
1329, 1331, 1332, 1336, 1337, 1340, 1344, 1345, 1347,
1349, 1350, 1352, 1355, 1356, 1357, 1359, 1366, 1480,
1510, 1512, 1513, 1515, 1516, 1518, 1519, 1520, 1523,
1535, 1538, 1550, 1552, 1553, 1557, 1560, 1566, 1578,
1583, 1586, 1592, 1594, 1621, 1629, 1632, 1633, 1661,
1663, 1694, 1801, 1814, 1815, 1816, 1825, 1831, 1857,
1864, 1878, 1899, 1950, 1952, 1953, 1955, 1958, 1959,
1969, 1971, 1972, 1980, 1985, 1986, 1989, 1994, 1995,
2002, 2006, 2007, 2008, 2009, 2010, 2011, 2012, 2015,
2017, 2020, 2047.

Section IX

COMPARATIVE STUDIES

BOOKS

1800 Bakst, James. A Comparative Study of the Philosophies of
      Music in the Works of Schopenhauer, Nietzsche and Tol-
      stoy. 1942.

1801 Bodde, Derk. Tolstoy and China. Princeton, N. J. : Prince-
      ton University Press, 1950; 110p. Tolstoy's study of
      and views concerning China are presented along with ex-
      amples of the works which he read. The purpose of his
      Chinese studies is seen as being related to his quest for
      religious truth rather than his desire to gain any under-
      standing of China and its civilization. It is argued that
      his readings on China influenced his views on the state,
      non-resistance, religion, and music. However, since
      Tolstoy as a scholar and seeker of truth studied many
      cultures, it is considered to be a mistake to stress the
      influence of China on his beliefs.

1802 Borras, F. M. Maxim Gorky and Lev Tolstoy: An Inaugural
      Lecture. Leeds, England: Leeds University Press,
      1968; 19p. A short sketch of the literary development
      of Tolstoy and Gorky precedes a discussion of their re-
      lationship in 1901 when both were recovering, in Gas-
      para, from illnesses. Gorky is seen as having great
      respect for Tolstoy, though he was ideologically his op-
      posite. The awkward relations between Gorky and Tol-
      stoy are noted with the former quoted as feeling that
      "Tolstoy is the most astonishing man I have ever had the
      pleasure of seeing ... but for all my wonderment at
      him, I do not like him. " Also examined is his negative
      reaction to Tolstoy's 1910 flight from home which is
      seen as a plea for martyrdom. In conclusion, both men
      are praised for their love of truth and freedom, and for
      the courage to suffer for their ideals. See Gorky's Lit-
      erary Portraits, for a full account of his views on Tol-
      stoy.

1803 Davis, Helen E. Tolstoy and Nietzsche: A Problem in Bio-
      graphical Ethics. Intro. by John Dewey. New York:

New Republic, 1929; xiv, 271p. , bib, 269-271. Tolstoy
and Nietzsche are considered to be representative of two
opposing tendencies in mankind: renunciation/altruism/
pacifism versus self-assertion/egoism/militarism. Both
men, however, are regarded as having wrestled unsuc-
cessfully with the same problem: self-mastery. Discussed is their respective projections of their fundamen-
tal psychological needs into the cosmos seeing their own
problems as being universal and their resolution funda-
mental to human happiness. Therefore, it is argued
that when Tolstoy preached non-resistance, and Nietzsche
the warfare ideal, both were in quest of personal salva-
tion, but neither could find it.

1804   Speirs, Logan. Tolstoy and Chekhov. Cambridge, England:
       Cambridge University Press, 1951; 237p. Tolstoy and
       Chekhov are seen as having used art for different pur-
       poses and to have addressed different generations but,
       nonetheless, as having basically similar writings because
       they both founded their art on direct observations of life:
       "their works are not created but recreated. " Other sim-
       ilarities are isolated as their desire to "tell the truth, "
       concern with covering "the whole of life, " and their
       viewing art as a means of exploring life's purpose.
       Their fundamental distinction is identified as Tolstoy's
       religious perspective in his works, and Chekhov's lack
       of such a point of view. This study also contains a note
       (227-237) on D. H. Lawrence's debt to Tolstoy in The
       Rainbow.

1805   Steiner, George. Tolstoy or Dostoevsky: An Essay in the
       Old Criticism. New York: Random House, 1959; 354p. ,
       bib. 349-354. The general similarities of Tolstoy and
       Dostoevsky are discussed before an interpretive analysis
       is presented of their leading works. The two are seen
       as "the greatest of novelists" because they "excel in
       comprehensiveness of vision and force of execution. "
       They are placed in the context of the flowering of Rus-
       sian literature in the 19th century; individual works are
       discussed separately. Following an examination of their
       respective philosophies and religious views, a survey of
       Marxist criticism of Tolstoy and Dostoevsky is pre-
       sented.

1806   Steiner, Rudolf. Carnegie and Tolstoy. London: Collison,
       1930; 35p.

ESSAYS AND CHAPTERS from general works

1807   Abraham, Gerald E. "Tolstoy and Mussorsky" in Studies in
       Russian Music. New York: Scribner's, 1936; 87-101.
       Extraordinary complete agreement is illustrated between

the artistic views of Tolstoy and Mussorsky. Discussed
as points of similarity are: insistence on the unimpor-
tance of beauty in art; belief in art as a means of communication with fellow men; strong leaning toward realism and contempt of formal technique; and a tendency
to make the common masses more important than individual characters in their works. This last point is
seen as an extension of their mutual over-valuation of
the peasantry.

1808   Apostolov, Nikolay. "Tolstoy and Dickens" in FV, 71-86.
An account, by a disciple, of Tolstoy's highly favorable
impression of the works of Dickens. Dickens' literary
influence on Tolstoy is discussed with specific references to the words and works of Tolstoy. It is concluded that his impact on Tolstoy was second only to that
of Stendhal.

1809   Bakst, James. A History of Russian-Soviet Music. New
York: Dodd, Mead, 1962; 182-184 (no separate section
on Tolstoy). A brief comparison of Tolstoy, Dostoevsky, and Tchaikovsky stressing their mutual desire to
merge with the common people and favorably portray the
peasant way of life. Additionally, all three men are regarded as believing that the peasant has the best insight
into life's meaning.

1810   Baring, Maurice. "Tolstoy and Dostoevsky" in An Outline of
Russian Literature. New York: Holt, n. d.; 196-225.
Tolstoy's fiction is discussed, with emphasis placed upon
the intertwining of his personal life and his writings,
examples being provided from his works. Dostoevsky
is then presented as the antithesis of Tolstoy in religious beliefs, life habits, view of art, financial condition, and health.

1811   Beach, Joseph W. "Dramatic Present: Thackeray, Tolstoy"
in The Twentieth Century Novel: Studies in Technique.
New York: Century, 1932; 164-176. Tolstoy's Anna
Karenina and Thackeray's Vanity Fair are compared for
their sectioning, dispersal of material, and use of time.
Tolstoy is considered to have fewer sections by theme,
a "greater concentration of emphasis, " and a more intense use of time than Thackeray who gives only "one-
seventh as much space as Tolstoy to each day's occur-
rences. "

1812   Berdayev, Nicolas. The Russian Idea. New York: Macmil-
lan, 1948; 137-139 (no separate section on Tolstoy).
Although Tolstoy clearly had great love and respect for
Rousseau, many analysts are seen as over-emphasizing
Rousseau's impact on him, and ignoring the differences
between them. Tolstoy is considered to be more pro-

found and radical than Rousseau, and since he was pos-
sessed by the "Russian consciousness of guilt, " he could
never accept his own nature as being good. Rousseau
is not judged to have had as intense a search for the
meaning of life as Tolstoy, and his ideal state based on
a social contract is seen to be unacceptable to Tolstoy
who distrusted all forms of government.

1813   Beveridge, Albert J.   "Three Russians of World Fame" in
        The Russian Advance.   New York: Harper, 1904; 426-
        462.   A discussion of the similarities between Tolstoy
        and two well-known governmental personalities: S.
        Witte, statesman, and K. Pobedonostsev, Procurator of
        the Holy Synod and advisor to the tsar.   Although his
        philosophy is regarded as different from theirs, the three
        are considered alike because they are dogmatic, intoler-
        ant, and "unacquainted with the verb 'to fail'. "   Tolstoy's
        philosophy is then discussed on the basis of the author's
        conversations with him at Yasnaya Polyana, and it is
        concluded that fanatical and impractical views make him
        unpopular with Russian conservatives and liberals alike
        though respect is widespread for his artistic talents.

1814   Ehre, Milton.   "On August 1914" in ASCEDM, 365-371.   War
        and Peace and August 1914 are compared, with Solzhen-
        itsyn considered "no match for Tolstoy as an architect
        of epic narratives or as psychologist of the human mind. "
        His characters are regarded as less well developed than
        Tolstoy's: there are "no Natashas, Pierres or Andreis, "
        those unique Tolstoyan individuals.   Their novels are
        seen as differing also in that Solzhenitsyn's "peace" is
        underdeveloped in comparison to Tolstoy's.   However, the
        "war" aspect of August 1914 is considered to rate "with
        the best of Tolstoy. "   Solzhenitsyn's disagreement with
        Tolstoy's interpretation of the role of the individual in
        history is also discussed.   Also in Chicago R, 24, no. 3
        (1972), 153-157.

1815   Erlich, Victor.   "Solzhenitsyn's Quest" in ASCEDM, 351-355.
        Although the scope of August 1914 makes one think of
        Tolstoy, the novel is seen to be at odds with Tolstoy's
        view of military science and the role of leadership in
        directing war and history in general.   It is suggested
        that Solzhenitsyn is not so much concerned with counter-
        ing Tolstoy's fatalistic view of history as with attacking
        the "Marxist-Leninist brand of historical determinism. "
        Also titled "Solzhenitsyn's New Novel, " Dissent, (Fall
        1972), 639-641.

1816   Guthrie, Anna M. B.   "Wordsworth and Tolstoi" in Words-
        worth and Tolstoi and Other Papers.   London: Con-
        stable, 1922 (reprinted by Folcroft, 1974), 1-36.   Cer-
        tain similarities are seen as underlying the great differ-

ences between Tolstoy and Wordsworth, especially in regard to their favorable assessment of the value of the
simple life and belief in the necessity of religion in life.
The principal distinction between the two is judged to be
that "in Tolstoy, nature is always subordinated to man;
in Wordsworth, man is subordinate to nature." This
point is illustrated by references to their fiction, War
and Peace, Resurrection, Cossacks being cited in Tolstoy's case.

1817 Harden, Maximillian. "Tolstoi and Rockefeller" in Monarchs
and Men. London: Nash, 1912; 287-312. A clash of
the philosophies represented by Tolstoy and Rockefeller
is presented by means of a fictitious dialogue between
them. Tolstoy states his views on the meaning of life
resting in a simple, Christian, non-material existence,
and severely criticizes Rockefeller as a representative
of the evils of modern capitalist civilization. Rockefeller
challenges Tolstoy's beliefs with claims that they are
misfounded and useless, and charges Tolstoy with living
a life contradictory to his principles.

1818 Hare, Richard. "Tolstoy and Dostoevsky" in Russian Literature from Pushkin to Present Day. London: Methuen,
1947; 104-142. A comparison of Dostoevsky and Tolstoy
precedes a survey of the life and works of each. They
are regarded as differing in personality, subject matter
for their novels, life styles, and types of characters in
their fiction. Tolstoy's major works of fiction are
briefly discussed before his views on art, science, and
Christianity are summarized.

1819 James, Henry. "Turgenev and Tolstoy" in LTCA, 103-104.
The literary talents of Tolstoy and Turgenev are compared with the latter labeled "the novelist's novelist"
and more appealing to the Western world than Tolstoy.
It is also stated that Turgenev's fiction is superior to
Tolstoy's both in method and presentation. For other
critical comments by James on Tolstoy's art see entry
874.

1820 Karpovich, Michael. "Tolstoy and Dostoevsky: Two Spokes-
men for Russia" in World Literatures, ed. by Joseph
Remenyi. Pittsburgh: University of Pittsburgh Press,
1956; 241-252. The emergence of Dostoevsky and Tolstoy as novelists within the context of the rapid development of excellence in 19th-century Russian realism is
discussed before parallels are drawn between them. The
different life histories and temperaments of the two are
noted, and the distinctions in their views on religion and
art are examined. Similarities between Tolstoy and Dostoevsky are seen in their mutual concern for the "verities
of life" and their consequent intense introspection. In

conclusion, both men are praised for being "great prob-
ers of the human heart. "

1821 Lavrin, Janko. "Dostoevsky and Tolstoy" in Russian Writers
      Their Lives and Literature. New York: Van Nostrand,
      1954; 176-201. Dostoevsky and Tolstoy are regarded as
      different in that the former's art and thought are fully
      integrated whereas in Tolstoy there is a "gap between
      the great artist and the not so great moralist and think-
      er. " In addition, Dostoevsky's psychological insight is
      considered to be superior to Tolstoy's, and he is re-
      garded as having more success than Tolstoy in creating
      a new genre in literature: the modern philosophical
      novel. Although they are seen as sharing a mutual hos-
      tility to modern Western civilization, it is asserted that
      their alternatives differed in that Tolstoy looked back-
      ward, like Rousseau, to man's primitive communal ex-
      istence as his ideal, whereas Dostoevsky looked forward
      and hoped to alter man's consciousness through "creative
      Christianity. " For similar discussions by Lavrin, see
      his "Dostoevsky and Tolstoy" in A Panorama of Russian
      Literature (London: University of London Press, 1973),
      130-146; and "A Note on Tolstoy and Dostoevsky" in
      From Pushkin to Mayakovsky. A Study in the Evolution
      of a Literature (London: Sylvan, 1948), 146-156.

1822 Lavrin, Janko. "Tolstoy and Nietzsche" in Studies in Euro-
      pean Literature. Port Washington, N. Y. : Kennikat,
      1970 (reprint of 1929 publication); 131-155. Tolstoy and
      Nietzsche are discussed as the two extremes of an anta-
      gonism between two moral codes, and yet representative
      of an identical mentality: "Their work is an attempt to
      solve one and the same inner dilemma from opposing
      sides. " They thus came to champion opposing ideals,
      Nietzsche the aristocratic-aesthetic, and Tolstoy the
      democratic-ethical ideal, in an attempt not to found new
      theories, it is argued, but to bring peace of mind to
      their divided inner selves. Analyzed in light of these
      generalizations are their views of Christianity, morality,
      and altruism.

1823 Lawrence, D. H. "Cavalleria Rusticana by Verga" in Phoenix,
      240-250 (246-47 on Tolstoy). The worship of the peasant
      by Tolstoy is described as perverted and based on a
      faulty assessment of the virtue of this class which is de-
      scribed as "the ugliest of all human masses, most greed-
      ily selfish and brutal of all. " Contrasted with Tolstoy's
      view is that of Verga who admired the peasant in a
      "healthy" fashion as a "manifestation of pure, spontane-
      ous, passionate life. " For another publication of Law-
      rence's comparison of Tolstoy to both Verga and Hardy,
      see RLMEF, "Thomas Hardy, Verga and Tolstoy, " pp.
      139-147. Also see LTCA, 149-151, and 196-97 for a
      reproduction of both comparisons.

1824   Lawrence, D. H.   "Study of Thomas Hardy" in Phoenix: The
       Posthumous Papers of D. H. Lawrence. New York:
       Viking, 1936; 398-516 (479-81 on Tolstoy).
       Artistically, Hardy is seen as being similar to Tolstoy in that both
       authors set the small actions of their characters against
       the background of the immense power of a Nature which
       represents a morality incomprehensible to man. A meta-
       physical affinity is established between the two, and both
       are viewed as being far less impressive as philosophers
       than as artists.

1825   Leavis, F. R., and Q. D. Leavis.   "Dickens and Tolstoy:
       The Case for a Serious View of David Copperfield" in
       Dickens: The Novelist. New York: Random House,
       1970; 34-105. A discussion of the influence of Dickens
       on Tolstoy with prime attention given to the latter's in-
       terpretation and use of David Copperfield. Tolstoy's
       highly positive assessment of this novel is established
       and used to question the traditional interpretation of David
       Copperfield as merely "providing a kind of entertaining
       fiction." The best proof of the greatness of the novel in
       Tolstoy's eyes, however, is not seen by the Leavises as
       resting in his praise but rather use of it in War and
       Peace and Anna Karenina, the most important example
       being his modeling the relationship of Andrei and Natasha
       of War and Peace on that of David and Dora of David
       Copperfield.

1826   Mann, Thomas.   "Goethe and Tolstoy" in Essays of Three
       Decades. New York: Knopf, 1947; 93-175. A compari-
       son of Goethe and Tolstoy on a series of subjects begin-
       ning with a discussion of their religious views in terms
       of the former's "pagan-cultural idealism" and the latter's
       "Christian-social ethics." Points of similarity are seen
       in that both were influenced by the writings of Rousseau,
       and both attempted to suppress, willfully, their artistic
       talents for the sake of other concerns. Each, too, was
       driven by a powerful sense of ego. Also in Three Es-
       says, 3-140.

1827   Merezhkovski, Dmitri S.   "Dostoevsky and Tolstoi" in
       RLMEF, 75-98. The relationship of art and religion in
       Tolstoy and Dostoevsky is discussed before the various
       distinctions in their works of fiction are presented.
       Those differences emphasized are: their divergent meth-
       ods of communication, characterizations, especially in
       regard to protagonists, style, and, most importantly,
       their general philosophies. This comparison appears in
       part of the second section of Merezhkovski's Tolstoi as
       Man and Artist with an Essay on Dostoevski under the
       title "Tolstoi and Dostoevski as Artists."

1828   Moore, George.   "Turgenev and Tolstoy" in RLMEF, 31-46.
       An impressionistic discussion of Tolstoy's fiction in which

he is criticized for excessive moralizing precedes a
comparison, on a number of levels, of Tolstoy with Turgenev. Most attention is devoted to their respective
styles, philosophies, and principal themes, with Turgenev
treated more favorably than Tolstoy. Excerpt from
Avowals (annotated under entry 1389).

1829 Pritchett, Victor S. "Tolstoy" in Books in General. London:
     Chatto & Windus, 1953; 148-154. Tolstoy's English qual-
     ities are isolated and parallels drawn to the English real-
     ists Scott and Austen. His love of family life, farming,
     and sports are considered to be quite similar to the likes
     of an English countryman. In addition, his strict moral-
     ity is believed to have much in common with Puritan
     practical morality: "he has our particular Protestant
     madness. " Lastly, Resurrection is examined for its
     English qualities.

1830 Rahv, Philip. "The Death of Ivan Ilyich and Joseph K. " in
     Image and Idea: Twenty Essays on Literary Themes.
     Norfolk, England: New Directions, 1957; 121-140. Kaf-
     ka's The Trial is regarded as similar in theme and con-
     ception to The Death of Ivan Ilych. Essentially, both
     works are interpreted as protests against scientific ra-
     tionalism, modern civilization, and "the heresies of the
     man of the city whose penalty is spiritual death. " The
     works' characters, plots, and themes are discussed in
     support of this contention. Also in Literature and the
     Sixth Sense, 38-54; and So R, 1 (1939), 174-185.

1831 Rahv, Philip. "In Dubious Battle" in ASCEDM, 356-64. A
     variety of comparisons are made between August 1914
     and War and Peace with the conclusion reached that
     Solzhenitsyn is superior to Tolstoy in "his understanding
     of military strategy and tactics, quite as good as Tol-
     stoy in his scenes of battle, but altogether inferior to
     him in his representation of private life. " Tolstoy's
     characters in peace are regarded as lively and memor-
     able in relation to those of Solzhenitsyn. Overall, the
     two novels are thought to be similar in "manner and
     tone. "

1832 Russell, George W. "Tolstoi and George Sand" in The Living
     Torch. Plainview, N. Y. : Books for Libraries, 1970
     (reprint of the 1937 publication); 310-312. Tolstoy is
     considered to be similar to Sand in that both were frank
     revealers of themselves. However, it is maintained that,
     unlike Tolstoy, Sand did not allow the moralist within
     her to dictate her life or limit her artistic creations.

1833 Saintsbury, George. "Turgenev, Dostoevsky and Tolstoy" in
     RLMEF, 23-30. A positive assessment of the literary
     talents of Turgenev precedes a critique of those of Tol-

stoy and Dostoevsky whose works are judged to be crude, half-digested, and filled with irrelevancies when compared to the artistry of Turgenev. Also in Periods of European Literature, vol. XII, The Nineteenth Century (London: Blackwood, 1907).

1834 Schemann, Alexander. "A Lucid Love" in ASCEDM, 382-392. Solzhenitsyn is regarded as similar to Tolstoy in his concern for the contention that Russia has a unique destiny among the nations of the world and that Russians are endowed "with an unmatched ... spiritual perception." However, unlike his predecessors, he is seen as believing this contention to be a ruinous myth. Examples are taken from August 1914 to highlight his belief that this myth had a disastrous effect on the Russian army in World War I. Translated from Vestnik, no. 100 (1971), 141-152.

1835 Shestov, Lev. "Doestoevsky and Nietzsche. The Philosophy of Tragedy" in Dostoevsky, Tolstoy and Nietzsche. Athens: Ohio University Press, 141-332. The pessimistic philosophy of Dostoevsky is contrasted with the idealistic beliefs of Tolstoy. Tolstoy's concern for countering skepticism and pessimism is considered antithetical to the beliefs of Dostoevsky: "the philosophy of tragedy is in principle hostile to the philosophy of the commonplace." Dostoevsky's reaction to Tolstoy's views and works is discussed with most reference to War and Peace and Anna Karenina. Also in Essays in Russian History; The Conservative View: Leontiev, Rozanov, Shestov, 3-183. Excerpt in LTCA, 123-126.

1836 Shestov, Lev. "The Good in the Teaching of Tolstoy and Nietzsche" in Dostoevsky, Tolstoy and Nietzsche, 1-140. Tolstoy and Nietzsche are thought to be similar because both suffered in their lives while in search of higher truth to bring spiritual comfort, and because both felt a need to expound on faith and philosophy because of their mutual lack of faith. Additionally, Tolstoy's conversion from the role of philosopher, as in War and Peace, to that of preacher, in his later years, is interpreted as a response to his weak faith and consequent inability to face the realities of life and, especially, death.

1837 Street, A. E. "The Realities of War: Count Tolstoi and M. Verestchagin" in Critical Sketches. London: Kegan Paul, Trench, Trubner, 1894; 179-202. On the subject of warfare, the paintings of Verestchagin and the writings of Tolstoy are compared with similarities seen in their realism, pursuit of truth, and emphasis on art as a means of communication. Examples of their depiction of courage, battle, and death are given with much reference to War and Peace.

221   Comparative Studies

1838 Symons, Arthur. "The Russian Soul: Gorki and Tolstoy" in
      Studies in Prose and Verse. New York: Dutton, 1922.
      Gorky and Tolstoy are believed to be typically Russian
      because they "fanatically search for the meaning of life
      as if no one had ever thought of the matter before. "
      This characteristic, along with their mutual condemna-
      tion of modern Western civilization, is interpreted as a
      result of their living in a nation only recently civilized,
      thus enabling easy rejection of laws and conventions.

1839 Williams, Raymond. "Social and Personal Tragedy: Tolstoy
      and Lawrence" in Modern Tragedy. Stanford, Calif. :
      University of Stanford Press, 1966; 121-138. Tolstoy's
      Anna Karenina and Lawrence's Women in Love are studies
      as tales of relationships that end in tragedy. The nature
      of tragedy in Anna Karenina is discussed with the conten-
      tion that the novel had a deep effect on Lawrence, par-
      ticularly his Women in Love. However, in spite of the
      existence of several points of similarity between the two
      works, an overall distinction is maintained between the
      two types of tragedy, one social, the other personal.

1840 Zborilek, Vladimir. "Young Tolstoy and Rousseau: The
      Birth of the Rousseauan Hero in Tolstoy's Fiction" in
      Medieval Epic to the Epic Theater of Brecht, ed. by R.
      Armato and J. Spalek. Los Angeles: University of
      Southern California Press, 1968; 147-158. Tolstoy's dis-
      covery of and early interest in Rousseau is examined
      with special concern for his acceptance of the Rousseauan
      belief in the value of a "retreat from the world" as an
      answer to the "man versus society" problem. Their
      conception of "natural man" is then discussed, and Tol-
      stoy's trilogy Boyhood, Childhood, Youth is analyzed in
      terms of the character Nikolenka's being of the Rous-
      seauan mold.

PERIODICAL ARTICLES

1841 Abraham, Gerald E. "Tolstoy and Moussorgsky: A Parallel-
      ism of Minds, " Music and Letters, (Jan. 1931), 54-59.

1842 Arthos, J. "Ruskin and Tolstoy: The Dignity of Man, " Dal-
      housie R, 43 (Spring 1963), 5-15.

1843 Bernstein, E. "Turgenev and the Tolstoys, " New St and Na,
      7 (10 March 1934), 349-350.

1844 Bialik, H. N. "Their Coat of Arms Was Truth, " Sat R, 42
      (4 April 1959), 18-20. A discussion of the relationship
      between Tolstoy and the painter Leonid Pasternak.

1845 Blumberg, Edwina J. "Tolstoy and the English Novel: A
      Note on Middlemarch and Anna Karenina, " Slav R, 30,

no. 3 (Sept. 1971), 561-569. An analysis of the points
of similarity between Tolstoy and Eliot claiming that
Tolstoy borrowed from her.

1846   Bolkin. "Turgeniff and Count L. Tolstoi," RRs, 2 (1890),
369.

1847   Bondanella, Peter F. "Rousseau, the Pastoral Genre, and
Tolstoy's The Cossacks," So Hum R, 3 (1969), 288-292.

1848   "Books That Shaped Tolstoy," RRs, 33, no. 198 (June 1906),
582.

1849   Bordinat, Philip. "Anatomy of Fear in Tolstoy and Heming-
way," Lost Gen J, 3 (1975), 15-17.

1850   Borras, F. M. "A Common Theme in Tolstoy, Andreyev and
Bunin," SEER, 32, no. 78 (Dec. 1953), 230-235.

1851   Buyniak, Victor O. "Leo Tolstoy and Charles Dickens,"
SEES, 9, nos. 3-4 (Autumn-Winter 1964), 100-131.
Considers the influence of Dickens on the early Tolstoy
and Tolstoy's continued admiration for Dickens' humor,
ethics and social and moral views.

1852   Buyniak, Victor Q. "Leo Tolstoy and Matthew Arnold,"
Wascana R, 3, no. 2 (1968), 63-71.

1853   Buyniak, Victor S. "Stendhal as Young Tolstoy's Literary
Model," SEES, 5 (Spring 1960), 16-27.

1854   Cain, T. "Tolstoy's Use of David Copperfield," Critical Q,
15 (Autumn 1973), 238-246.

1855   Carr, E. H. "Two Russians: Tolstoy and Turgenev," Fortn
R, 132 (Dec. 1929), 823-826.

1856   Chanda, A. K. "Post Conversion Tolstoy and Kafka," JJCL,
2 (1973), 21-44.

1857   Colin, V. "Tolstoy and Galdos' Santiuste: Their Ideology on
War and Their Spiritual Conversion," Hispania, 53 (Dec.
1970), 836-841.

1858   "Count Leo Tolstoi and Montaigne," Nation, 42 (22 April
1886), 335-336.

1859   "Count Leo Tolstoi and Turgeneff," Nation, 42 (6 May 1886),
388-389.

1860   "Count Tolstoy and the Doctrine of Henry George," RRs, 17
(Jan 1898), 73-74.

1861   Curtis, J. M.   "Solzhenitsyn and Dostoevsky, " Mod Fic St,
       23 (Spring 1977), 133-151.   The relationship of Tolstoy
       to both men is discussed.

1862   "Dostoevsky and Tolstoy, " Times Lit Sup, 20 (Dec. 1928),
       997-998.

1863   Dvoichenko-Markov, E.   "Benjamin Franklin and Tolstoy, "
       Proc Am Philos Soc, 6, no. 2 (April 1952), 119-128.

1864   Dyck, J. W.   "Aspects of Nihilism in German and Russian
       Literature: Nietzsche-Tolstoy, " Hum Asso R, 25 (Sum-
       mer 1974), 187-196.

1865   Edgerton, W. B.   "Leskov and Tolstoy: Two Literary Here-
       tics, " ASEER, 12, no. 4 (Dec. 1953), 524-534.

1866   Edgerton, W. B.   "Tolstoy and Magalhaes Lima, " Comp Lit,
       28 (Winter 1976), 51-64.

1867   Ehre, Milton.   "On August 1914, " Chicago R, 24, no. 3
       (1972), 153-157.   A comparison of War and Peace and
       August 1914.   Also in ASCEDM, 365-371.

1868   Erlich, Victor.   "Solzhenitsyn's New Novel, " Dissent, (Fall
       1972), 63-641.

1869   Friedell, E.   "Tolstoy and Dostoevsky, " Living Age, 341
       (Sept. 1931), 57-61.

1870   Garden, E.   "Tchaikovsky and Tolstoy, " Music and Letters,
       55 (July 1974), 307-316.

1871   Geduld, Harry M.   "Bernard Shaw and Leo Tolstoy, " Calif
       Shavian, 4, no. 2 (1962), 1-9.

1872   Gilenson, Boris.   "Whitman in Russia, " Sov Lit, 5 (1969),
       176-181.   A discussion of the Russian reaction to Whit-
       man and his influence in Russia and on Tolstoy.

1873   Greenwood, E. B.   "Tolstoy, Wittengenstein, Schopenhauer,
       Some Connections, " Encounter, 30 (April 1971), 60-72.

1874   Grote, Prof.   "The Moral Systems of Tolstoi and Nietzsche, "
       Pub Op, 12, no. 25 (1 April 1893), 62.   Translation
       from an article by Grote in the Paris Revue des Revues.

1875   Hapgood, Isabel F.   "Count Tolstoy and Gabriele D'Annunzio, "
       Bookman, 3 (May 1896), 227-228.

1876   Hapgood, Isabel F.   "Tolstoy and Turgenieff, " Nation, 42
       (1886), 388-389.

1877   Harden, Maximilian. "Tolstoi and Rockefeller," Bookman,
       36 (1912), 410-419. Also in Monarchs and Men, 287-
       312.

1878   Harvey, Leon A. "Tolstoy and Lenin; a Study in Contrast,"
       Pan Am M, 31 (May 1920), 23-28 and 31 (June 1920),
       66-74.

1879   Hendrick, George. "Tolstoy's Quotations from Emerson in
       the Cycle of Reading," ESQ, 8 (1957), 29-31.

1880   Henriot, Emile. "Tolstoy on Dostoevsky," Adam, nos. 284-
       286 (1960), 16.

1881   Herrick, Robert. "Tolstoi and Henry James," Yale R, n. s.
       12 (Oct. 1922), 181-186.

1882   Howells, William D. "Scott and Tolstoi," Harper's M, 78
       (May 1889), 982-984. Also in Pub Op, 7, no. 3 (27
       April 1889), 64-65.

1883   Huneker, James G. "Dostoievsky and Tolstoy," Forum, 54
       (August 1915), 201-216.

1884   Hyde, G. M. "Ibsen and Tolstoy: Alike Yet Unalike," RRs,
       43 (April 1911), 476-477.

1885   Ireland, Denis. "Tolstoy and a Russian General," Dublin M,
       n. s. 19, no. 2 (April-June 1944), 32-38.

1886   Izioumov, A. "Leon N. Tolstoi et A. I. Herzen," Int R Soc
       Hist, 1 (1936), 257-272. The text is in French, but an
       English summary is provided.

1887   Jackson, Favid. "C. F. Meyer's Die Richterin: A Tussle
       with Tolstoy," Trivium, 9 (1974), 39-49.

1888   Johnston, Charles. "The Quarrel between Tolstoy and Ivan
       Turgenev," Academy, 38 (1 Nov. 1890), 292-293.

1889   Jones, Malcolm V. "Dostoevsky, Tolstoy, Leskov and red-
       stokiszm," J Rus S, 23 (1972), 3-30.

1890   Kaun, Alexander. "Tolstoy and Andreyev," Calif U Chron,
       26 (1924), 176-181.

1891   Kaun, Alexander. "Tolstoy and Gorky," Calif U Chron, 32
       (1930), 351-375.

1892   Kestner, Joseph A. "Tolstoy and Joyce: 'Yes'," JJQ, 9
       (1973), 484-486.

1893   Knight, George W. "Shakespeare's Spiritual Experience Com-

pared to that of Tolstoy," Occult R, (Feb.-March 1930),
103-107, 177-180.

1894   Kovalevski, Maksim M.   "Rousseau, Tolstoy and the Present
Age," RRs, 48 (1913), 486-488.   Excerpt translated from
Vestnik Yevropy, (1913), 343-352.

1895   Laber, J.   "Muted Echo of a Masterpiece," New Republic,
167 (7 Oct. 1972), 27-30.   A comparison of Solzhenitsyn's
August 1914 and Tolstoy's War and Peace.

1896   Lavrin, Janko.   "Tolstoy and Nietzsche," Slavonic R, 4 (June
1925), 67-82.

1897   "Leo Tolstoy and Feodor Dostoevsky," London Q, 1 (April
1888), 55-73.

1898   Mann, Thomas.   "Thoughts upon Goethe and Tolstoy," Living
Age, 312 (18 Feb. 1922), 409-412.   Translated from
Berliner Tageblatt, (25 Dec. 1921).

1899   Manning, C. A.   "Thoreau and Tolstoy," Contemp R, 137
(June 1943), 234-243.

1900   Maximoff, N.   "The Future of Russia: Marx, Tolstoy or
Dostoevsky," Rel in Life, 24 (1954-1955), 44-55.

1901   McLaughlin, Sigrid.   "Some Aspects of Tolstoy's Intellectual
and Social Development: Tolstoy and Schopenhauer,"
Calif Slavic S, 5 (1970), 187-248.   A detailed discussion
of Schopenhauer's influence on Tolstoy, especially on his
ethics.

1902   McLean, Hugh.   "Leskov, Ivann of Kronstadt: On the Origins
of Polunoshchniki," Slav R, 1 (1955), 93.

1903   Muchnic, Helen.   "Sholokhov and Tolstoy," Rus R, 16, no. 2
(April 1957), 25-34.

1904   Newmarch, R.   "Tchaikovsky and Tolstoy," Contemp R, 83
(Jan. 1903), 112-118.   Also in Living Age, 237 (4 April
1903), 58-63.

1905   Norton, G.   "Tolstoy and Montaigne," Nation, 42 (1886), 335-
336.

1906   Pickford, R. W.   "Déjà Vu in Proust and Tolstoy," Inter J
Psychoanal, 25 (1944), 155-165.

1907   Poltoratzky, Nikolai P.   "Lev Tolstoy and 'Vekhi'," SEER,
42, no. 99 (June 1964), 332-352.

1908   Poltoratzky, Nikolai P.   "Soviet Literary Criticism on Lev
Tolstoy and 'Vekhi'," SEEJ, 8, no. 2 (Summer 1964) 141-148.

1909   Portnoff, G.   "The Beginning of the New Idealism in the
          Works of Tolstoy and Galdos," Romainic R, 23 (Jan.
          1932), 33-37.

1910   "Rockefeller Versus Tolstoy: A Problem in Ethics," Cur Lit,
          46 (May 1909), 525-527.   A discussion of Harden's study.

1911   Rosen, N.   "Chaos and Dostoevsky's Women," Kenyon R, 20,
          no. 2 (1958), 257-277.   A commentary on Dostoevsky's
          portrayal of women in his fiction with some parallels
          drawn to Tolstoy.

1912   "Rousseau, Tolstoy and the Present Age," RRs, 48 (Oct.
          1913), 486-488.

1913   Rudy, Peter.   "Lev Tolstoj's Apprenticeship to Laurence
          Sterne," SEEJ, 15, no. 1 (1971), 1-21.   A positive in-
          fluence is seen on Tolstoy with Sterne regarded as his
          favorite writer.

1914   Rudy, Peter.   "Young Lev Tolstoj's Acquaintance with
          Sterne's Sermons and Griffith's The Koran," SEEJ, 4
          (1960), 119-126.

1915   Shanas, Mildred.   "Tolstoy and Dostoevsky in the Normal and
          Abnormal," Manitoba Arts R, 3 (1942), 48-58.

1916   Siefken, Hinrich.   "Man's Inhumanity to Man--Crime and
          Punishment: Kafka's Novel Der Progress and Novels by
          Tolstoy, Dostoevsky and Solzhenitsyn," Trivium, 7 (1972),
          28-40.

1917   Simmons, Ernest J.   "Tolstoj and Chekhov," Midway, 8, no.
          4 (1969), 91-103.

1918   Sokolow, J. A.   "Arriving at Moral Perfection: Benjamin
          Franklin and Leo Tolstoy," Am Lit, 47 (Nov. 1975),
          427-432.   An account of the impact on Tolstoy of Frank-
          lin's idea that happiness can only be based upon virtue.

1919   Stanislavsky, Konstantin S.   "Rubenstein and Tolstoy," Forum,
          71 (April 1924), 437-447.

1920   Stoddard, F. H.   "Leo Tolstoy and Matthew Arnold," Andover
          R, 10 (1888), 359-369.   Also in Congreg R, 3 (1888),
          20-30.

1921   Thurston, G. J.   "Alexis de Tocqueville in Russia," J Hist
          Ideas, 37 (April 1976), 289-306.

1922   "Tolstoi and Gorki," Living Age, 308 (5 March 1921), 574-
          576.   Translated from Neue Züriche Zeitung, (23 Jan.
          1921).

1923   "Tolstoi Compared with Ibsen, " Chaut, 31 (July 1900), 329-
       330.

1924   Tolstoy, Ilya L.   "Tolstoy and Henry George, " Land and
       Freedom, 28 (1928), 132-133.

1925   Tolstoy, Sofia.   "Tolstoy versus Turgenev, " Golden Bks M,
       20 (July 1934), 91-92.

1926   "Tolstoy and Ibsen, " New Sta, 32 (17 Nov. 1928), 188-189.

1927   "Tolstoy and Turgenev, " Living Age, 329 (24 April 1926),
       197-200.

1928   "Two Russian Realists, " London Q R, 70 (April 1888), 57.
       A comparison of Tolstoy and Dostoevsky.

1929   Wasiolek, Edmund.   "Ecclecticisms and Pluralisms: Trying
       to Find Dostoevsky and Tolstoy, " SNNTS, 4, 86-92.

1930   Watt, Lewis.   "Nietzsche, Tolstoy and the Sermon on the
       Mount, " Catholic W, 3 (1920), 577-587.

1931   Weiner, Leo.   "The Genetics of Tolstoy's Philosophy, " Rus
       Stud, 5, no. 1 (Sept. 1928), 27-29. A discussion of
       those who influenced Tolstoy other than Rousseau.

1932   Zborilek, Vladimir.   "Young Tolstoy and Rousseau, " USC
       Stud Comp Lit, 1 (1968), 147-158.

1933   Zimmerman, Eugenia N.   "Death and Transfiguration in
       Proust and Tolstoy, " Mosaic, 6 (1973), 161-172.

DISSERTATIONS

1934   Abcarian, Gilbert.   "Political Romanticism: Coleridge and
       Tolstoy, " University of California, 1957.

1935   Adams, Eleanora K.   "Franz Werfel and Leo N. Tolstoy:
       Affinities and Contrasts, " University of Pennsylvania,
       1973.

1936   Armstrong, Judith M.   "The Novel of Adultery in the Second
       Half of the Nineteenth Century in French, Russian, Eng-
       lish and American Literature, " University of Melbourne,
       1974.

1937   Buyniak, Victor.   "Leo Nikolayevich Tolstoy and the Early
       English Victorian Novelists: William Thackeray, Charles
       Dickens, Anthony Trollope and George Eliot, " University
       of Ottawa, 1970.

1938 Futtrell, M. H.   "Dickens and Three Russian Novelists: Gogol, Dostoevsky and Tolstoy, " University of London, 1955.

1939 Gasster, Susan C.   "Point of View in the Novels of Zola, Galdós, Dostoevsky and Tolstoy: A Study in the Development of the Novel, " George Washington University, 1968.

1940 Gubler, Donworth V.   "A Study of Illness and Death in the Lives and Representative Works of Leo Tolstoy and Thomas Mann, " Brigham Young University, 1971.

1941 Krzyzanowski, Jerzy R.   "Turgenev, Tolstoy and William Dean Howells: Transitions in the Development of a Realist, " University of Michigan, 1965.

1942 Kuk, Zenon M.   "Tolstoj's War and Peace and Zeromski's Ashes: A Comparative Study, " Ohio State University, 1973.

1943 Maurer, Sigrid H.   "Schopenhauer in Russia: His Influence on Turgenev, Fet and Tolstoy, " University of California at Berkeley, 1966.

1944 Murphy, Terry W.   "Dostoevsky and Tolstoy on Dickens' Christianity, " Kent State University, 1973.

1945 Reifsnyder, I. P.   "A Comparative Study of the Problems of Adolescent Heroes and Heroines in Russian and Soviet Literature, " New York University, 1963.

1946 Rempel, Margareta.   "Leo Tolstoy, Gerhart Hauptmann and Maxim Gorky: A Comparative Study, " University of Iowa, 1959.

1947 Rudy, Peter.   "Young Leo Tolstoy and Laurence Sterne, " Columbia University, 1957.

1948 Tumas, Elena V.   "The Literary Kinship of Leo N. Tolstoy and Romain Rolland: A Comparative Study of the Epic Dimensions of War and Peace and Jean-Christophe, " University of Southern California, 1964.

1949 Zborilek, Vladimir.   "Tolstoy and Rousseau: A Study of Literary Relationship, " University of California at Berkeley, 1969.

See also: 13, 14, 25, 35, 48, 49, 64, 65, 87, 134, 135, 177, 179, 448, 454, 455, 467, 480, 482, 487, 502, 507, 510, 517, 526, 533, 609, 621, 630, 631, 635, 636, 639, 643, 658, 665, 684, 706, 707, 715, 716, 724, 727, 737, 745, 750, 782, 808, 848, 891, 916, 923, 949, 958, 973, 976, 977, 1208, 1222, 1223, 1234, 1235, 1259, 1260,

1265, 1278, 1280, 1281, 1287, 1288, 1289, 1305, 1315,
1367, 1369, 1370, 1382, 1392, 1393, 1395, 1397, 1406,
1412, 1413, 1419, 1420, 1422, 1428, 1430, 1434, 1440,
1445, 1452, 1462, 1463, 1464, 1465, 1466, 1467, 1468,
1469, 1471, 1472, 1473, 1482, 1483, 1498, 1508, 1582,
1665, 1679, 1688, 1689, 1707, 1911, 1952, 1953, 1956,
1958, 1959, 1960, 1967, 1969, 1971, 1972, 1973, 1980,
1985, 1986, 1989, 1994, 1995, 2004, 2006, 2007, 2008,
2009, 2010, 2011, 2012, 2015, 2016, 2017, 2020, 2033,
2039, 2041, 2049, 2951, 2052, 2053.

BOOKS

1950 Das, Taraknath. Tolstoi and India. New York: American-
      Indian Press, 1950; 32p.

1951 Kenworthy, John C. Tolstoy: His Teaching and Influence in
      England. London: Brotherhood, n. d. ; 16p. Included in
      his Tolstoy: His Life and Works (New York: Haskell,
      1971) [annotated under entry 9.]

1952 Nag, Kalidas. Tolstoy and Gandhi. Intro. by K. N. Katju.
      Patna, India: Saran, 1950; xx, 136p. A survey of the
      similarities between Tolstoy and Gandhi precedes an ex-
      amination of the positive influence that he had on Gand-
      hi. Gandhi's early contact with Tolstoy is traced with
      special reference to Tolstoy's ideas on non-resistance
      and fasting. Also discussed are their correspondences,
      Tolstoy's "Letter to a Hindu, " and Gandhi's association
      with the "Tolstoy Farm. "

1953 Pyarelal, Nair. Thoreau, Tolstoy and Gandhi. New Delhi:
      Oxford, 1958; 20p. A brief discussion of the similarities
      in the beliefs of the three men is followed by a study of
      the contribution made by Tolstoy and Thoreau to the
      technique and philosophy of Gandhi.

ESSAYS AND CHAPTERS from general works

1954 Ahnebrink, Lars. "Tolstoy and Stephan Crane" in The Begin-
      nings of Naturalism in American Fiction, 1891-1903.
      New York: Russell and Russell, 1950; 343-360. Tol-
      stoy's influence on American fiction prior to 1900 is re-
      garded as being greater than that of any other writer,
      especially in the case of Stephan Crane who believed him
      to be the "supreme living author" of his time. War and
      Peace and Sevastopol are discussed as the two writings
      that most influenced Crane, with Tolstoy's views on war,
      heroism, the common soldier, and free will all influ-
      encing his Red Badge of Courage in particular.

1955 Davies, Ruth. "Tolstoy: Not Peace, but War" in The Great
      Books of Russia. Norman: University of Oklahoma
      Press, 1968; 234-275. Tolstoy's preaching of the gospel
      of peace is deemed to be "supreme irony" because it in-
      spired not peace but the spirit of revolution in Russia:
      "He who preached peace was answered ... by the sword. "
      In particular, his glorification of the peasants because
      he thought "them capable of bringing about a spiritual
      revolution ... unwittingly accelerated the momentum of
      social revolution. " Separately, War and Peace, is as-
      sessed as one of the greatest epics of all time.

1956 Feuer, Kathryn B. "August 1914: Solzhenitsyn and Tolstoy"
      in ASCEDM, 372-381. The influences of War and Peace
      and Tolstoy on August 1914 and Solzhenitsyn are believed
      to be many and complex. The actual discussion of Tol-
      stoy in August 1914 and its inclusion of Tolstoyans is
      examined before Solzhenitsyn's challenge to Tolstoy's
      assessment of history is analyzed. In spite of presenting
      differing theories of history, the novels are thought to
      have the same general purpose: "to comment on the
      present in terms of the past. "

1957 Hemmings, F. W. J. "Tolstoyism" in The Russian Novel in
      France, 1884-1914. London: Oxford, 1950; 177-194.
      A study of the influence of Tolstoy in France based on
      the contention that his philosophy and life style com-
      manded more attention than his fiction. His views on
      modern civilization, especially on society and religion,
      are considered to have been of special importance in his
      being accepted in France as the greatest critic of mod-
      ernism since Rousseau. Samples of thought of leading
      Frenchmen of the era are presented to substantiate this
      contention.

1958 McCarthy, Mary. "The Tolstoy Connection" in ASCEDM, 332-
      350. An analysis of the relationship between War and
      Peace and August 1914 claiming that in the novel Sol-
      zhenitsyn engaged in a polemic with Tolstoy over the role
      of the individual in history, countering Tolstoy's theory
      with his assertion that leadership is the essential and
      determining factor in warfare. Solzhenitsyn's disagree-
      ment with Tolstoy's doctrine of non-resistance is con-
      sidered odd in light of his characterization of Samsonov
      as almost "Tolstoyan" in his capacity for suffering and
      passive acceptance of his fate--which makes him appear
      as anything but the "great man" whom Solzhenitsyn sees
      as moving history. Originally in Sat R (16 Sept. 1972),
      79-96.

1959 Mikoyan, S. A. "Leo Tolstoy and Mahatma Gandhi" in
      Movements of People and Ideas from Times Prehistoric
      to Modern, ed. A. Guha. New Delhi: Indian Council
      for Cultural Relations, 1970; 235-241.

1960   Nag, Kalidas.   "Tolstoy and Gandhi" in Greater India.   Calcutta: Institute for Asian and African Relations, 1960; 1-70.

1961   Phelps, Gilbert.   "The Rousseau of His Time: The Impact of Tolstoy on English Thought and Fiction" in The Russian Novel in English Fiction.   London: Hutchinson, 1956; 138-155.   The impact of Tolstoy as both a novelist and preacher is analyzed with reference to numerous English writers and critics, including Arnold, Ellis, Shaw, Chesterton, Carlyle, Ruskin, Forster, Lawrence, and Lubbock.   The most noteworthy aspect of his appeal is thought to rest in his representing "a powerful counterweight to the challenge of science and rationalism that the age had produced," a counterweight strongly reminiscent of Rousseau.   His influence is regarded as greatest on the philosophical basis of English fiction rather than on its style or technique.

1962   Rilke, Rainer Maria.   "Letter to Herman Pongs" in LTCA. A brief note on how the author's visit to Tolstoy did not influence his works but rather made him aware of the weaknesses of Tolstoy's philosophy and the negative effects it was having on Tolstoy's own life.

PERIODICAL ARTICLES

1963   Addams, G. E.   "Tolstoy and Gandhi," Christ C, 48 (Nov. 1931), 1485-1488.

1964   Anderson, P. B.   "The Tolstoy Foundation," Rus R, 17 (Jan. 1958), 60-68.

1965   Battersby, H. F. B.   "Concord of the Steppes; Vlest, Rus, a Tolstoyan Colony, 1891," Living Age, 194 (30 July 1892), 300-308.

1966   Bourgeois, L. C.   "Tolstoy Colony, a Chilean Utopian Artistic Experience," Hispanic, 46 (Sept. 1963), 514-518.

1967   Budd, Louis.   "William Dean Howells' Debt to Tolstoy," ASEER, 9, no. 4 (Dec. 1950), 292-301.

1968   Cahan, A.   "Mantle of Tolstoy," Bookman, 16 (Dec. 1902), 328-333.   A survey of those Russian novelists regarded as following Tolstoy's realism and sympathy with the common man, with Korolenko, Gorky, and Chekhov regarded as the leading examples.   Also in Bookman, 32 (Jan. 1911), 541-545 as a review of Tolstoy's importance following his death.

1969   Daskupta, R. K.   "Tolstoy and Gandhi," Ed Misc, 5, nos. 1-2 (June-Sept. 1968).

1970 Dillon, E. J. "Count Tolstoy: His Disciples and Traducers, "
      RRs (L), 5 (1892), 414-416.

1971 Feuer, Kathryn B. "Solzhenitsyn and the Legacy of Tolstoy, "
      Calif Slavic S, 6 (1971), 113-128.

1972 Fischer, Louis B. "Count Leo Tolstoy and Mahatma Gandhi, "
      Search Light, (4 July 1949). A discussion of their cor-
      respondence with special attention given to Tolstoy's in-
      fluence on Gandhi.

1973 Fodor, Alexander. "Leo Tolstoy and Arvid Jarnefelt, " SEES,
      18 (1973), 112-116.

1974 Goldfarb, Clare R. "From Complicity to Altruism: The
      Use of Tolstoy in Howells, " Univ R, 32 (Summer 1966),
      311-317.

1975 Goldfarb, Clare R. "William Dean Howells: An American
      Reaction to Tolstoy, " CLS, 8 (1971), 317-337.

1976 Gribble, Francis. "Tolstoy and the Tolstoyans, " Fortn R,
      90 (Sept. 1908), 383-393. Also in Living Age, 259
      (Oct. 1908), 89-97.

1977 Harvey, John R. "Tolstoy in England, " Cambr Q, 5 (Fall
      1970), 115-133. A discussion of Tolstoy's influence in
      England with much reference to the works of Bayley
      and Christian.

1978 Herndon, Margaret N. "Hjalmar Hjorth Boyesen, " Am Scand
      R, 54 (1966), 268-274. Boyesen, a follower of William
      Dean Howells, is regarded as being more influenced by
      Tolstoy than by Howells.

1979 "Influence of Count Tolstoy, " Spectator, 105 (19 Nov. 1910),
      846-847. Tolstoy is commended as a novelist but not as
      a teacher.

1980 Jayaprakash, Narayan. "Tolstoy and India, " Gandhi M, 5
      (Jan. 1961), 61-64.

1981 Kazin, Alfred. "Tolstoy and His Quaker, " NY R Bks, 21 (28
      Nov. 1974), 33-34. Tolstoy's impact on Aylmer Maude
      is discussed.

1982 Kolehmainen, John. "When Finland's Tolstoy Met His Rus-
      sian Master, " ASEER, 16, no. 4 (1957), 534-541. A
      commentary on Arvid Jarnefelt's visit to Tolstoy.

1983 Koriakov, Mikhail. "Tolstoy in Soviet Hands, " Atlantic M,
      182 (Oct. 1948), 53-57.

1984 Kropotkin, P. A. "Tolstoy's Influence in Russia," Independent, 69 (1 Dec. 1910), 1183-1188.

1985 Lavrin, Janko. "Tolstoy and Gandhi," Adam, nos. 284-286 (1960), 165-166.

1986 Lavrin, Janko. "Tolstoy and Gandhi," Rus R, 19 (April 1960), 32-39.

1987 Leonov, Leonid. "The Impact of Tolstoy," Soviet R, 2 (1961), 34-50.

1988 Mathewson, Rufus W. "The Soviet Hero and the Literary Heritage," ASEER, 12 (Dec. 1953), 506-523. A study of the origins of the Soviet hero in literature with reference to the influence of Tolstoy's War and Peace.

1989 Maude, Aylmer. "Gandhi and Tolstoy," Contemp R, 137 (June 1930), 701-705.

1990 Maude, Aylmer. "Tolstoy's Place in Literature," Fortn R, 124, n. s. (Sept. 1928), 325-333.

1991 McCarthy, Mary. "The Tolstoy Connection," Sat R, (16 Sept. 1972), 79-96. Also in ASCDEM, 332-350.

1992 Merezhkovski, Dmitri S. "Tolstoi and Bolshevism," Living Age, 309 (7 May 1921), 333-337. Translated from Deutsche allgemeine Zeitung, (15 March 1921).

1993 Mikoyan, S. A. "Ideas Know No Boundaries," Soviet R, (30 Sept. 1969), 45-52. A survey of Tolstoy's influence on Gandhi.

1994 Mikoyan, S. A. "Leo Tolstoy and Mahatma Gandhi," Contemp, 13, no. 3 (March 1969), 24-26. Also in Mainstream, (1 March 1969), 19-21.

1995 Mikoyan, S. A. "Leo Tolstoy and Mahatma Gandhi," IAC, 18, no. 4 (Oct. 1969), 44-48.

1996 Montgomery, G. C. "The Influence of Lev Nikolayevich Tolstoi on American Literature," VP, 14 (1960), 6-7.

1997 Newcombe, J. M. "Was Chekhov a Tolstoyan?" SEERJ, 18, no. 2 (Summer 1974), 143-152.

1998 O'Nan, Martha. "The Influence of Tolstoy upon Roger Martin du Gard," KFLQ, 4, no. 1 (1957), 7-14.

1999 Parry, Albert. "Tolstoy Looks at America," Asia, 30 (Nov. 1930), 772-777.

2000   Rahv, Philip.   "The Death of Ivan Ilych and Joseph K, " So R,
       1 (1939), 174-185.

2001   Rao, Raja.   "Reflections on Tolstoy, " Adam, nos. 284-286
       (1960), 160-163.   Tolstoy is thought to be the most in-
       fluential of European authors in Asia, mostly because of
       his philosophical beliefs.

2002   Rose, A. G.   "Some Influences on English Penal Reform, "
       Sociol R, 3 (July 1955), 25-46.

2003   Rzhevsky, Nicolas.   "Idea and Heritage in Soviet Literature, "
       CLS, 6 (Dec. 1969), 419-434.   An analysis of Tolstoy's
       influence on Soviet novelist Alexander Fadeyev, especially
       his work The Rout.

2004   Sarolea, Charles.   "Was Tolstoy the Spiritual Father of Bol-
       shevism?, " Eng R, 40 (1925), 155-162.

2005   Schinz, Albert.   "Count Tolstoy and Edouard Rod, " Bookman,
       17 (August 1903), 645-647.   An examination of the effect
       of Tolstoy's Resurrection on the French writer Rod.

2006   Sen, Mohit.   "Tolstoy, Gandhi and the Peasant, " Mainstream,
       (4 Oct. 1969), 17-22.

2007   Shahani, Ranjee.   "Tolstoy and India, " Solidarity, 8 (1974),
       78-80.

2008   Shifman, Alexander.   "Gandhi-Tolstoy Correspondence, " Indian
       P B, 20, no. 4 (April 1970), 108-109.   Also in Soc Cong,
       (25 Oct. 1969), 30-31.

2009   Shifman, Alexander.   "Tolstoy and Gandhi, " Contemp, 13,
       no. 9, (Sept. 1969), 24-25.   Also in Soviet Land, 22,
       no. 19 (Oct. 1969), 30-31.

2010   Shifman, Alexander.   "Tolstoy and Gandhi, " Indian Lit, 12,
       no. 1 (March 1969), 5-20.

2011   Shifman, Alexander.   "Tolstoy and Gandhi, " Soc India, 15 (6
       Oct. 1973), 24.

2012   Shifman, Alexander.   "Tolstoy and Gandhi, " Soviet R, (3
       Sept. 1969), 34-44.

2013   Simmons, Ernest J.   "Tolstoy and the Kremlin, " Atlantic M,
       206 (Nov. 1960), 114-115.

2014   Slann, M.   "Tolstoy and the Beginnings of Kibbutz Ideology, "
       Judaism, 21, no. 3 (Summer 1972), 333-338.   A discus-
       sion of Tolstoy's influence on Aaron Gordon, who adapted
       Tolstoy's radical pacifism to his own philosophy.

2015 Smith, W. H. "The Pacifist Thought of William Jennings
      Bryan," Mennonite Q R, 45 (June 1971), 33-81. Tol-
      stoy's influence on Bryan's pacifism is considered.

2016 Spurdle, Sonia. "Tolstoy and Martin du Gard's Thibault,"
      CL, 23 (1971), 325-345.

2017 Tanvir, Habib. "India and Tolstoy," Soviet R, (29 Sept.
      1970), 53-58.

2018 "Tolstoy and the American Thinkers of the 19th Century,"
      CLS, 11 (1943), 29-31. A survey of Tolstoy's interest
      in and influence on American writers.

2019 "Tolstoy Colony in England," Pub Op, 30, no. 13 (26 Sept.
      1901), 398.

2020 "Tolstoy-Gandhi Correspondence," Modern R, (Feb. 1910),
      329-330.

2021 "Tolstoy Settlement in England," Pub Op, 27, no. 25 (21
      Dec. 1899), 782.

2022 "Tolstoyism," Pub Op, 22, no. 4 (28 Jan. 1897), 115.

2023 "What Tolstoy Means to America," Cur Lit, 45 (Oct. 1908),
      402-404.

2024 Wish, H. "Getting along with the Romanovs," S Atlan Q, 48
      (July 1949), 341-359. A study of Tolstoy's influence
      in America, especially on William Jennings Bryan, Wil-
      liam Dean Howells, Jane Addams, and Walt Whitman.

2025 Worland, F. E. , ed. The Tolstoyan (L), 1-2 (Nov. 1902-
      June 1903). A magazine based on Tolstoy's philosophy
      of life.

2026 Zucker, A. E. "The Genealogical Novel. A New Genre,"
      PMLA, 43 (June 1928), 551-560. Tolstoy's influence on
      Gorky's novel Decadence is discussed.

DISSERTATIONS

2027 Goldfarb, Clare R. "Journey to Altruria: William Dean
      Howells' Use of Tolstoy," University of Indiana, 1965.

2028 Hemmings, F. W. J. "The Influence of the Russian Novel on
      French Thinkers and Writers, with Particular Reference
      to Tolstoy and Dostoevsky," Cambridge University, 1951.

2029 Smith, Allan J. "Tolstoy's Fiction in England and America,"
      University of Illinois, 1939.

ADDITIONAL SOURCES

The following additions are necessary due to entries lo-
cated in reference works published after the bibliography
was compiled, and to errors and omissions in the or-
ganization of the bibliography.

2030   Andreev, German.   "The Christianity of L. N. Tolstoy and
       of the Contributors to From Under the Rubble, " in The
       Samizdat Register, ed. by Roy A. Medvedev.   New
       York: W. W. Norton, 1977; 267-314.   The basic prin-
       ciples of Tolstoy's Christianity are summarized before a
       highly critical analysis is given of the work From Under
       the Rubble.   Tolstoy is praised for his interpretation of
       Christianity as a set of teachings to guide mankind to-
       wards achieving its goal rather than as a supernatural
       philosophy embodied in a dogmatic institution such as the
       Russian Orthodox Church.   The view of Christianity held
       by the authors of From Under the Rubble, on the other
       hand, is judged to be narrow, doctrinaire, and a poor
       basis for a revived Christianity in Russia.   Their ver-
       sion of the history of the Russian Orthodox Church is
       labeled as "partisan" and highly inaccurate (numerous
       examples are given), and parallels are drawn to the type
       of biased history taught by the Marxist regime that the
       authors hope to discredit.   It is concluded that if Russia
       is to be rekindled spiritually, it is Tolstoy's teachings
       that must be "extracted from under the rubble. "

2031   Bakalar, Paul F.   "A Critique of Tolstoy's What Is Art, "
       Northwestern University, 1976.   (dissertation)

2032   Bayley, John.   Introduction to Great Short Works of Leo Tol-
       stoy.   Trans. by Louise Maude and Aylmer Maude.   New
       York: Harper, 1967; 685p.

2033   Biryukov, Paul.   "Tolstoy and the Orient, " Modern R, (Feb.
       1927), 199-202.

2034   Breitburg, S.   "The Bernard Shaw-Tolstoy Controversy about
       Shakespeare, " Lit H, 37 (1940), 617-632.

2035   Breitburg, S.   "Tolstoy Reading Hamlet and Assisting at Its
       Performance, " Int Lit (1939), 11-12, 233-250.

2036 Collis, John S. Leo Tolstoy. London: Burns and Oates,
        1969; 124p. , illus. (A Polestar Pictorial Biography.)
        A general survey of the major incidents in Tolstoy's
        life accompanies comments on his basic writings. Most
        notable are the sections on Tolstoy's family life.
        Stressed is the negative side of his marriage as evi-
        denced by disputes with his wife over family, property,
        and Tolstoy's followers. Numerous illustrations and
        photographs are included.

2037 Courtney, William L. "Tolstoi as Man and Artist" in The
        Development of Maurice Maeterlinck and Other Sketches
        of Foreign Writers. Port Washington, N. Y. : Kennikat
        Press, 1971 (reprint of 1904 publication); 119-128. An
        analysis of Merezhkovski's critical biography of Tolstoy,
        which is praised for its uniquely Russian perspective.
        Typical Western assessments of Tolstoy are summarized
        and labeled superficial for not understanding the contin-
        uity in his works and beliefs as presented so well by
        Merezhkovski. Merezhkovski is criticized, however, for
        being difficult to comprehend in some sections, especially
        in his comparison between Tolstoy and Dostoevsky, but
        in all a very favorable assessment.

2038 Day-Lewis, C. Introduction to Anna Karenina. Trans. by
        Rochelle S. Townsend. London: Book Society, 1943;
        714p.

2039 Feuer, Kathryn B. "Tolstoy and Stendhal: Human Freedom
        and Artistic Determinism, " Russia: Essays, no. 569,
        117-134.

2040 Fitzjohn, Bernard S. Introduction to A Captive in the Cau-
        casus. London: Bradda Books, 1962; 79p.

2041 Hahn, Beverly. "Chekhov and Tolstoy" in Chekhov: A Study
        of the Major Stories and Plays. New York: Cambridge,
        1977; 135-155.

2042 "How Tolstoy and Tolstoy's Wife Wrote Novels, " Cur Op, 57
        (July, 1914), 49.

2043 Lampert, Evgenii. "Tolstoy" in Nineteenth Century Russian
        Literature: Studies of Ten Russian Writers, ed. by John
        Fennell. Berkeley: University of California Press,
        1973; 261-292. It is asserted that "Tolstoy's own art
        provides exhaustive revelation of his character just as
        his character presents an extraordinary work of art. "
        This generalization provides the context within which
        Tolstoy's leading works of fiction are analyzed. There
        follows a discussion of his personality, religious and
        artistic views, literary style, and his vision of the world.

2044 Maude, Aylmer. Essays on Art. London: Richards, 1902;
      46p. An introduction to What Is Art? which summarizes
      and lends support to Tolstoy's views.   There follows the
      article "Tolstoy's Theory of Art," which defends Tolstoy
      against the many critics of his views on art on the
      grounds that the critics have misinterpreted the intent of
      his message. Also in TP, 66-127; and Contemp R, 78
      (Aug. 1900), 241-254.

2045 Meyers, Jeffrey. "Leo and Sofya Tolstoy: The Bondage of
      Love" in Married to Genius. New York: Harper and
      Row, 1977; 15-37. The love between Tolstoy and his
      wife in the early years of their marriage is discussed,
      but emphasis is placed on their later conflicts involving
      sex, love, property, art, and Tolstoy's fame. The roots
      of their marital problems are judged to have rested in
      Tolstoy's changing world views, especially his rejection
      of conventional social and sexual norms which he believed
      his wife represented.

2046 Mitchell, Paul M. "Lev Nikolaevitch Tolstoy in Pre-Soviet
      Russian Literary Criticism," Indiana University, 1977.
      (dissertation)

2047 Raleigh, John H. "Tolstoy and the Ways of History" in To-
      wards a Poetics of Fiction, ed. by Mark Spilka. Bloom-
      ington: Indiana University Press, 1977; 211-224. Tol-
      stoy's view of history, as presented in War and Peace,
      is discussed as a multi-dimensional one having three
      basic perspectives. Most attention is given to what is
      called the "vertical dimension" of history, or "the total
      chain of circumstances extending from the present back
      into the past and, inferentially, into the future." The
      actual working of history on this level is seen by Tolstoy
      as being unfathomable to and uncontrolable by man. Tol-
      stoy, it is argued, also had a horizontal perspective on
      history consisting of "impulses and forces ... cutting
      across and complicating the vertical chain." The verti-
      cal perspective of history is seen as being presented by
      Tolstoy in abstract discussions in War and Peace, where-
      as the horizontal perspective is interwoven into its
      dramatic parts. A third dimension to his presentation
      of history is referred to as "the dispensation from above"
      and consists of a Deity providing "some sense to the
      grand course of human affairs." It is concluded that
      Tolstoy believed history, in all of its multi-dimensional
      complexity, must remain a mystery to man because "the
      instrument, human reason, by which it is apprehended
      is equivocal in its operations ... it is limited in some
      areas and blind in others."

2048 Reeve, F. D. Afterword to The Cossacks and The Raid.
      Trans. by A. R. MacAndrew. New York: New Amer-
      ican Library, 1961; 224p.

2049   Senn, A.   "P. I. Biriukov: A Tolstoyan in War, Revolution,
       and Peace, " Rus R, 32 (July 1973), 278-285.

2050   "Sevastapol and Other Military Tales, " Independent, 56 (June
       1903), 1503.

2051   Simpson, Lucie.   "Tolstoy and Shakespeare" in The Secondary
       Heroes of Shakespeare and Other Essays.   London:
       Kingswood Press, 1951; 53-60.

2052   Speirs, Logan.   "Tolstoy and Chekhov: The Death of Ivan
       Ilych and A Dreary Story, " Oxford R, 8 (1968), 81-93.

2053   Walker, Roy.   "Swinburne, Tolstoy and King Lear, " English,
       7 (Spring 1949), 282-284.

2054   "What Is Religion?" Pub Op, 32, no. 23 (5 June 1902), 729.

243

SUBJECT INDEX

No attempt has been made to "index the indexes" of the 2,000+ sources that have been listed but rather to group all broad studies under various general subject headings, and to list the principal focus of all other sources.

The following works are sufficiently comprehensive to be considered as sources for virtually all major subjects listed in the index: 1-3, 7, 9, 12-15, 26, 129, 130, 179-182, 188, 191, 193, 196, 197, 199-201, 204, 205, 222.